RADIOACTIVE GOVERNANCE

Radioactive Governance

*The Politics of Revitalization
in Post-Fukushima Japan*

Maxime Polleri

NEW YORK UNIVERSITY PRESS
New York

NEW YORK UNIVERSITY PRESS
New York
www.nyupress.org

© 2026 by New York University
All rights reserved

Please contact the Library of Congress for Cataloging-in-Publication data.

ISBN: 9781479836826 (hardback)
ISBN: 9781479836833 (paperback)
ISBN: 9781479836871 (library ebook)
ISBN: 9781479836864 (consumer ebook)

This book is printed on acid-free paper, and its binding materials are chosen for strength and durability. We strive to use environmentally responsible suppliers and materials to the greatest extent possible in publishing our books.

The manufacturer's authorized representative in the EU for product safety is
Mare Nostrum Group B.V., Mauritskade 21D, 1091 GC Amsterdam, The Netherlands.
Email: gpsr@mare-nostrum.co.uk.

Manufactured in the United States of America

10 9 8 7 6 5 4 3 2 1

Also available as an ebook

À Norah

CONTENTS

List of Figures and Tables ix
List of Abbreviations xi
Fukushima: A Ten-Year Timeline xiii

Introduction: A Tale of Two Fukushimas 1

1. Nuclear Monsters and Nuclear Saviors 31

2. The Theater of Expertise 55

3. The Rise of Citizen Science 84

4. Everything Is Under Control 116

5. Commodifiable Phantasm 143

6. Postpolitical Uncertainties 172

7. Radioactive Performances 195

8. Conflictual Collaboration 221

Epilogue 255

Acknowledgments 263

Notes 265

Index 307

About the Author 323

FIGURES AND TABLES

FIGURES

Figure I.1. A map of Japan with its prefectures   6

Figure 1.1. Antinuclear demonstrations in Hiroshima   33

Figure 2.1. Initial evacuation zone   61

Figure 2.2. A map by the US Department of Energy showing the extent of radioactive contamination   64

Figure 3.1. Citizens testing radiation with a Geiger counter in Fukushima   96

Figure 3.2. Protest in Tokyo to evacuate the children from Fukushima   105

Figure 4.1. A monitoring post in Fukushima city   120

Figure 4.2. Rearrangement of evacuation zoning   125

Figure 4.3. The gates of Iitate   131

Figure 4.4. The result of decontamination   138

Figure 5.1. The garden of Mme. Yamaguchi   160

Figure 5.2. The game of *suikawari*   166

Figure 6.1. The Mizunami Underground Research Facility   174

Figure 6.2. The Antinuclear Tent in downtown Tokyo   191

Figure 7.1. Teaching devices at DIP   208

Figure 7.2. The decontamination box model   210

Figure 7.3. NIRS's Heavy Ion Medical Accelerator   214

Figure 8.1. Farmers creating their own radiological maps   238

Figure 8.2. Testing wild mushrooms for contamination   244

TABLES

Table 1.1. A timeline of Japan's embrace of nuclear power   39

Table 2.1 Evacuation procedures and restricted areas   60

Table 3.1. Causes of mistrust following 3.11   93

LIST OF ABBREVIATIONS

ABCC: Atomic Bomb Casualty Commission
ALARA: As low as reasonably achievable
BQ: Becquerel
CEC: Center for Environmental Creation
DIP: Decontamination Info Plaza
DIY: Do-it-yourself
DPJ: Democratic Party of Japan
FHMS: Fukushima Health Management Survey
HLW: High-level radioactive waste
IAEA: International Atomic Energy Agency
ICRP: International Commission on Radiological Protection
JAEA: Japan Atomic Energy Agency
LDP: Liberal Democratic Party
LNT: Linear nonthreshold
LSS: Life Span Study
METI: Ministry of Economy, Trade, and Industry
MEXT: Ministry of Education, Culture, Sports, Science, and Technology
MITI: Ministry of International Trade and Industry
MOE: Ministry of the Environment
MSV: Millisievert
NGO: Nongovernmental organization
NIRS: National Institute of Radiological Sciences
NISA: Nuclear and Industrial Safety Agency
NPO: Nonprofit organization
NSC: Nuclear Safety Commission
NUMO: Nuclear Waste Management Organization
PRPC: Practical radiological protection culture
STS: Science and technology studies
SV: Sievert

TEPCO: Tokyo Electric Power Company
UNSCEAR: United Nations Scientific Committee on the Effects of Atomic Radiation
μSv: Microsievert
WBC: Whole-body counter
WHO: World Health Organization

FUKUSHIMA

A Ten-Year Timeline

March 11, 2011: A powerful earthquake and tsunami damage the Fukushima Dai'ichi nuclear power plant situated in the prefecture of Fukushima, Japan.

March 12–15, 2011: A loss of reactor core cooling in units 1, 2, and 3 leads to three nuclear meltdowns, hydrogen explosions, and the release of radioactive contamination. On March 15, residents living within a twenty-kilometer radius of the plant are evacuated. Those living within a twenty- to thirty-kilometer radius are required to shelter inside their homes.

March 17, 2011: The government establishes provisional regulation values for radioactive contamination in food and water.

March 21, 2011: Food products exceeding regulation values are restricted from shipping.

April 12, 2011: The International Atomic Energy Agency categorizes Fukushima as a "Level 7" accident on the International Nuclear and Radiological Event Scale. This represents the highest level possible for a nuclear disaster.

April 19, 2011: The government raises the annual radiation exposure limit in Fukushima from 1 mSv/y to 20 mSv/y. This twentyfold increase, which exceeds the predisaster recommended public health limits, causes public outcry and national protests.

April 29, 2011: Toshiso Kosako, a radiation safety expert and a special advisor to the Cabinet, resigns from his position in protest of the increased allowable threshold in Fukushima.

June 16, 2011: The government launches "Specific Spots Recommended for Evacuation" after discovering areas with doses above 20 mSv/year falling outside of the official evacuation zone.

August 26, 2011: Naoto Kan, the prime minister of Japan and president of the Democratic Party of Japan, announces his resignation. He is replaced by Yoshihiko Noda.

August 2011: Enactment of the Act on Special Measures Concerning the Handling of Environment Pollution by Radioactive Materials Discharged by the NPS Accident Associated with the Tōhoku District. The Ministry of the Environment becomes responsible for implementing radioactive decontamination activities.

March 30, 2012: Evacuation zones are reorganized under three different areas according to the level of radiation expected to be received by residents. Area 1 (green) corresponds to areas in which evacuation orders are ready to be lifted (dose under 20 mSv/year). Area 2 (orange) encompasses locations where residents are not permitted to reside (20 to 50 mSv/year). Area 3 (red) represents areas where it is expected that residents will be unable to return in the near future (exceeding 50 mSv/year).

May 5, 2012: Japan's nuclear power plants are gradually shut off for safety inspection. Japan's last operating reactor is shut off on this date.

June 2012: More than 160,000 individuals have officially evacuated from Fukushima Prefecture.

July 5, 2012: Publication of the Fukushima Nuclear Accident Independent Investigation Commission report. Commissioned by the National Diet of Japan, the independent report argues that the nuclear disaster was man-made. The report blames the government, the regulatory authorities, and utility companies.

December 16, 2012: Yoshihiko Noda, prime minister of Japan and member of the Democratic Party of Japan, announces his resignation. He is replaced by Shinzo Abe.

September 7, 2013: During a successful pitch for Tokyo to host the 2020 Olympic Games, Shinzo Abe argues that the situation at Fukushima is "under control." His remarks provoke criticism and generate widespread discontent.

December 20, 2013: The government publishes a policy paper entitled "Accelerating the Fukushima Reconstruction from the Nuclear Disaster." The government's top priority becomes the revitalization of Fukushima.

March 11, 2014: The government gradually starts to lift evacuation orders in Fukushima and promotes a swift return of evacuees to their former homes.

March 11, 2016: Five years after the disaster occurred, more than one hundred thousand evacuees have not returned to their homes in Fukushima.

March 31, 2017: The government cuts off housing assistance for voluntary evacuees, forcing many to return to Fukushima.

April 1, 2017: Restricted areas have decreased, representing 2.7 percent of Fukushima Prefecture.

August 21, 2019: The Fukushima prefectural government announces the end of its health survey of expecting and nursing mothers, judging that radiation had had no negative effects on the health of mothers and their children.

September 16, 2020: Shinzo Abe, prime minister of Japan and leader of the Liberal Democratic Party, announces his resignation. He is replaced by Yoshihide Suga.

Introduction

A Tale of Two Fukushimas

It was spring in 2016 when I first visited Atsuo Tanizaki's farm on the outskirts of a small village in Japan's Fukushima Prefecture. The air was warm. The nearby mountains were thick with emerald forests of Japanese cedar, konara oak, and hinoki cypress. A troop of wild red-faced monkeys stopped foraging to watch us as we walked by. And woven through it all—air, water, land, plants, and living bodies—were unseen radioactive pollutants. Almost everything now carried invisible traces of the 2011 meltdowns at the Fukushima Dai'ichi nuclear power plant.

With his Geiger counter, a device used for detecting radiation, Tanizaki began taking measurements near his field. In some places, the radiation level dropped, becoming almost insignificant. But here and there, beside a ditch or near a pond, the level was dangerously high. Tanizaki called these areas "hot spots," and they were scattered across the landscape of his village. Today, more than a decade after the 2011 nuclear disaster, the region remains contaminated by radioactive pollution. Though attempts at removing radioactive pollutants continue, a new realization has taken hold among many of Fukushima's farmers: There is no going back to an uncontaminated way of life.

For an anthropologist interested in contamination, Fukushima throws into sharp relief the question of what it means to live in a permanently polluted world. That is why I began coming to Japan and spending time with farmers such as Tanizaki. I wanted to understand the social dynamics of this new world: to understand how radioactivity is governed after a nuclear disaster, and how different groups clash and collaborate as they attempt to navigate the road to recovery.

In Fukushima, I expected to find social bonds pushed to their breaking point. Stories of postdisaster collapse circulate in our collective consciousness—tales of mistrust, fear, and isolation, accompanied by images of abandoned towns reclaimed by wildlife. And I found plenty of that. A sense of unraveling has taken hold in rural Fukushima. Village life has been transformed by forced evacuations and ongoing relocations. Many communities remain fragmented, and some villages are still abandoned. Residents remain uncertain about the adverse health effects of living in the region. In Fukushima, I found a society collapsing under the weight of radioactive pollution.

But that is only part of the story. I also found plenty of solidarity being leveraged to revitalize the region. Rather than evacuating Fukushima for good, many people, like Tanizaki, have taken matters into their own hands, embracing novel practices for living alongside toxic pollution. These practices involve forging relationships with scientists, starting decontamination experiments, piloting projects to create food security, and developing ways to monitor a changing environment. Among rice fields, orchards, and flower beds, novel modes of social organization are emerging—new ways of living in a future we will one day all reckon with.

The story of this disaster began under the Pacific Ocean, at 2:46 p.m. on March 11, 2011. At that moment, a magnitude 9.0 earthquake off the coast of northeastern Japan caused a devastating tsunami that claimed the lives of nearly twenty thousand people.[1] It also triggered the events that led to the meltdown of three reactors at the Fukushima Dai'ichi nuclear power plant. As a result of these meltdowns, pressure increased dramatically within the power station's facilities, leading to explosions that released dangerous radionuclides like cesium-134, cesium-137, strontium-90, and iodine-131 into the air. These radionuclides, which have life spans ranging from days to centuries, blew across northeastern Japan. So much radioactive matter was discharged that the International Atomic Energy Agency (IAEA) classified Fukushima as a "major accident"—with the only other one being the 1986 Chernobyl nuclear disaster.[2] As radioactive pollutants accumulated, health risks like cancers and ailments affecting the immune system increased. To protect the population, the Japanese state forced more than 160,000 citizens living near the reactors to evacuate.[3] The name "Fukushima" soon joined the ranks of Three Mile Island and Chernobyl as symbolizing nuclear disaster and being emblematic of the Anthropocene—the period in which "human activity is the dominant influence on the environment."[4]

At first, Tanizaki believed he had escaped the worst of the radiation because his village was not in the mandatory evacuation area. But when the wind carried radionuclides—invisible, tasteless, odorless—far beyond computer models, his village became heavily contaminated, and the government ultimately forced him to leave. Like others, Tanizaki was relocated to temporary housing. As the months became years, Tanizaki longed to return to his life as a farmer. But what would he farm? His land had been irradiated, and no one wanted to eat food grown near a nuclear disaster. To help citizens recover their way of life, the government launched an official "politics of revitalization" for Fukushima, investing trillions of yen to clean up and decontaminate the region before repatriating evacuees, while promoting tourism and food consumption through a massive public relations campaign. Part of the cleanup involved storing tainted topsoil in large plastic bags known as "*furekonbaggu*" (literally "flexible container bags"), which were then stacked in piles throughout the countryside. Tanizaki's village was now covered in millions of bags of radioactive topsoil—black pyramids of the Anthropocene—while the government deliberated over a permanent disposal site.

The sight of these man-made mounds of radioactive waste did not deter people from coming back to Fukushima. Indeed, the first citizens to willingly return were primarily elderly farmers for whom Fukushima was their "native land," a concept that the Japanese call "*furusato*." This was the case for Jun'ichiro Nakagawa, a farmer in his late sixties who had returned to his village to grow beautiful Alstroemeria flowers in his greenhouses. As he explained to me in 2017, "It's the place where I was born. I always wanted to come back to this place. Seeing the sun rise, seeing the moon at night. Seeing the blueness of the sky . . ." For Nakagawa, the love for his native land trumped any concerns over potential adverse health effects. In fact, he was more than happy to talk about his flowers with a foreigner and eager to show his beautiful solarium: "At the beginning, it was really hard to try and grow flowers all alone, especially in these horrible conditions, but now I'm happy that I did." In a landscape of black bags filled to the brim with radioactive soil, the flowers of Nakagawa are an attempt to bring color back to the lives of those who wish to return to and live in Fukushima. They symbolically reshape the narrative of postdisaster village life, which has been overshadowed by tragedy. Flowers helped Nakagawa make his village beautiful again, enabling him to take pride in his decision to return to what many believed would be a nuclear wasteland.

* * *

Far from Fukushima, in a fully packed auditorium of Tokyo's House of Councillors, I listened to a very different narrative given by Akiko Uno, the founder of the National Refugee Association. Unlike some farmers, Akiko Uno has no intention of ever returning to Fukushima. When the disaster happened, Uno left Fukushima voluntarily, worried about adverse health effects associated with radiation exposure. With a group of concerned mothers, she formed an association that seeks government support in relocating from an environment that many consider harmful to themselves and their children. Uno's anxieties were triggered by a change in the radiation threshold for evacuating the public from contaminated areas in Fukushima. In 2011, Japanese officials adjusted the threshold of allowable radiation exposure to an amount twenty times higher than before the disaster.[5] Initially, state experts explained this change by contending that a massive relocation of citizens would prove more harmful than raising the threshold of permissible radiation exposure, especially since vulnerable people might die in the process. This decision caused considerable controversy and failed to convince mothers like Akiko Uno of Fukushima's safety.

In front of a packed audience hall, Uno invites other mothers to share their experiences of the disaster. A young mother slowly walks to the microphone and begins to share her story. She explains the initial difficulty in trying to rationalize an invisible danger, her incredulity at the change of radiation threshold, the lack of support that she received while evacuating on her own, and the constant worries that her children might develop ailments in the future. Her voice breaking, she softly says, "Now all I see on TV are revitalization projects for Fukushima, but that doesn't mean anything to me." After a short pause she bursts into tears, her sobs drowning out the electrical whine of the microphone.

Experiences like these were far from unique during my fieldwork in Japan. I heard mothers complain about strange ailments their children experienced after the disaster: chronic diarrhea, tiredness, and recurrent nosebleeds. Concerns were not only anecdotal. After the disaster, thyroid cancers among children increased in Fukushima.[6] Others refused to eat food produced in Fukushima, fearing that it might be dangerous. Statements like "What can I give to my children to eat? I don't know what to feed them anymore" were repeatedly heard, and mothers voiced their fears of even breastfeeding their infants. These fears were often at odds with claims made by the Japanese government, which repeatedly stated that the levels of radiation released during the disaster were too low to pose any major health risks. Nowadays, officials continue to assert that the more serious source of harm is the psychological fear linked with radiation.

Despite the government's reassurances, the many uncertainties stemming from the disaster were too much to handle for citizens like Uno. Tens of thousands like her relocated to other parts of Japan, driven by a desire to protect their children. For these "voluntary evacuees," permanent relocation was the only way to understand what "recovery" meant after a disaster that destroyed so many lives. In this context, love for one's native land was usually rendered meaningless.

Nevertheless, other factors were at play that forced many voluntary evacuees to return. As the Fukushima nuclear disaster slowly faded from memory, the government began to cut the financial assistance offered to evacuees like Akiko Uno. The rationale offered was that concerns about radioactive contamination were "scientifically" unwarranted. The withdrawal of subsidies that evacuees relied on to survive forced many mothers to return to an environment they considered dangerous—even deadly. "*Migoroshi*"—a word meaning "letting someone die"—was frequently uttered by the mothers I interviewed, who saw themselves as victims of state policies. Their voices brought to mind Michel Foucault's notion of biopower—a conceptual shorthand for the prerogative of a nation-state to "'make' live and 'let' die."[7]

Against a government arguing that the risk was minimal, voicing concerns about the safety of Fukushima became harder. Citizens like Uno were accused of being unpatriotic or of impeding the revitalization of Fukushima. "More and more, we are being depicted as 'annoying' people [*mendokusai*]," said one mother. She sighed resignedly before uttering, "I don't see any future [*mirai nai*]."

Figure 1.1. A map of Japan with its prefectures. Map by Tokyoship.

The Politics of Revitalization

Upon encountering these stories, one might imagine that they are describing the "recovery" from two distinct historical events, as the experiences they portray are so different. The same can be said about what constitutes a radiation hazard. From something that precludes farmers from returning to their beloved native land to a mother's feeling of having her womb transformed into a time bomb, radiation means quite different things to different people. During my research in Japan, I saw calls for immanent return competing against demands for permanent evacuation, as well as narratives of radiation danger pitted against accusations of "radiophobia," the supposedly groundless fear of radiation. While a gray zone exists between these two extremes, a particular narrative has gained momentum in defining the official scope, scale, and effects of this disaster. At a time when the sense of emergency is fading with each passing year, this book examines the evolution of the government's postdisaster narrative that is still under construction—and still contested.

This book's core argument is that dominant practices of governance have created a master narrative around the disaster, which is epitomized by what I call a "politics of revitalization." This politics of revitalization emphasizes a discourse of minimal or no radiation-related dangers, gradual repatriation of former evacuees, restarting of the country's nuclear power plants, and promotion of a resilient mindset in the face of adversity. This master narrative is performed against other understandings of recovery, like those of worried citizens fighting (so far unsuccessfully) for permanent evacuation. This book aims to illuminate how the biggest nuclear disaster since Chernobyl became framed within a narrative of revitalization.

When I talk about the "politics" of revitalization, I am not merely referring to activities associated with the ruling parties of Japan. Rather, I am referring to what French philosopher Jacques Rancière calls the "distribution of the sensible" (*le partage du sensible*).[8] The term refers to a system that defines modes of seeing, being, communicating, and doing within society.[9] It refers to a consensus around what is considered to be visible, audible, or sayable in particular political regimes.[10] The distribution of the sensible acts at the level of perception to imbue things with specific meanings.¹¹ It is a form of experience that naturalizes and reinforces boundaries for what institutions and citizens consider to be normal, factual, or self-evident.¹² At its core, the distribution of the sensible explores forms of social domination, that is, how the "thoughts, voices and actions of the dominated are made invisible and inaudible in the hierarchy of activities underpinning social orders."¹³ In the context of Fukushima, employing this concept highlights how citizens, state institutions, and scientific bodies mobilized specific ways of engaging with the nuclear disaster, thereby shaping the official narrative and practices of recovery.

The politics of revitalization that I describe in this book represents one distribution of the sensible around the nuclear disaster. It can be understood as a system of consensus and boundary making that presents specific discourses and activities as "official" narratives, while concerns from other individuals are depicted as the babblings of annoying (*mendokusai*) people.¹⁴ It creates a story in which the worst of the disaster is already over and in which it appears doubtful that radiation will have serious adverse health effects (unless psychological in nature). Those who "understand" this scenario are labeled as good citizens, while those questioning the governing discourse face harsh backlash.¹⁵ It is possible that a new distribution of the sensible will come to be associated with the name "Fukushima." Scholars working on nuclear tragedies have demonstrated that narratives around radioactive hazards are far from set in stone, and have shown how they have evolved in tandem with historical contingencies.¹⁶ But for now—in contrast to Chernobyl¹⁷—a politics of victimization has failed to gather strong political momentum and has no place in this distribution of the sensible.

Radioactive Governance

This book investigates how a politics of revitalization gained predominance over tropes of harm, trauma, and victimization, which is especially intriguing in a country like Japan, whose history is inseparable from the nuclear tragedy of atomic bombings. By analyzing how the social aspects of radiation hazards are managed after Fukushima, I map the diverse strategies, historical factors, and cultural logics that cement this politics, through a process I refer to as "radioactive governance."

In the natural sciences, radioactivity is a process in which unstable atomic elements gradually transform themselves into something more stable and immutable. In their quest for stability, unstable atoms get rid of their excess energy, emitting in the process radiation rays or particles. At the end of this process, known as transmutation, a new element emerges. In like fashion, my anthropological interest lies in understanding the governance process that transforms the story of Fukushima from an unstable situation of crisis to one of recovery. Amid scientific controversies, contradictory narratives of risk, and different hopes for the future, I examine the discourses discarded from Fukushima's nucleus, much like radioactive rays or particles, resulting in a new distribution of the sensible.

In discussions of governance, it is easy to associate the term with mere state power. But this is a reductionist way of looking at a complex concept. When I speak of governance, I refer to what Mark Bevir calls "all processes of governing, whether undertaken by a government, market, or network, whether over a family, tribe, formal or informal organization, or territory, and whether through laws, norms, power, or language."[18] While the study of the Japanese government remains a crucial part of this book, I draw heavily from scholars who refer to the importance of theorizing governance beyond the nation-state.[19] As Erik Swyngedouw explains, "Governance-beyond-the-state refers in this context to the emergence, proliferation and active encouragement . . . of institutional arrangements of 'governing' which give a much greater role in policy-making, administration and implementation to private economic actors on the one hand and to parts of civil society on the other in self-managing what until recently was provided or organised by the national or local state."[20] Social scientists have furthered our understanding of these processes. For instance, Tania Li highlights the importance of conceptualizing citizens' daily practices within the overall process of governance rather than depicting them as "targets of governmental strategies."[21] Timothy Mitchell has called attention to the role of expert bodies in governance interventions.[22] James Ferguson and Akhil Gupta stress the implication of market ideologies and the role of non-state actors in global governance.[23] This approach to governance thus "leaves behind conventional distinctions between state, civil society and the economy, between public and private and does not privilege one organization or institution, like the state, as the 'natural' or 'right' centre of governance."[24]

Accordingly, I do not employ a stereotypical understanding of governance, which is too often viewed as "fairly consistent, unified, and applied towards an over-arching goal."[25] Instead, I agree with Michael Hathaway, who explains that "unlike some portrayals of environmental governance that largely assume a unified system working towards similar goals, governance comes from a number of sources and exhibits a range of forms, which at times overlap and contradict each other."[26]

In the context of Fukushima, this conceptualization of governance allows me to account for a plurality of people, social practices, activities, and institutions that participate in managing a particular distribution of the sensible. It enables me to escape accounts of disaster governance that usually tell the same story: a corrupt government trampling over the rights of defenseless citizens. In resorting to this definition, my aim is not to take accountability away from the state. Rather, I simply wish to emphasize the fact that cementing a politics of revitalization after Fukushima is a process far too complex to merely focus on the role of state governance.

The Era of Emergency

Beyond creating a sense of urgency, in which state officials, scientists, and members of the population had to navigate the uncertainties brought about by the triple disaster of an earthquake, tsunami, and nuclear power plant failure, Fukushima stimulated tremendous attention from academics. In the chaos following 2011, scholars of Japan have pointed out the initial challenges of responding to a nuclear crisis, as well as the potential consequences for Japanese society.

For instance, in light of a lack of grounded data, anthropologists David Slater, Brigitte Steger, and Tom Gill rapidly disseminated field materials.[27] Their approach is epitomized by the notion of "urgent ethnography," a nonjudgmental process of collecting, archiving, and recording the impact of the triple disaster, produced in a timely manner through the voices of victims themselves.[28] Similarly, in her book *Precarious Japan*, Anne Allison examines how the nuclear disaster enhanced a sense of "social precarity" for the population.[29] She demonstrates that citizens have rationalized the nuclear disaster through processes of structural injustice and feelings of precariousness that existed well before 2011. Richard J. Samuels has also provided one of the first portraits of post-3.11 politics by underscoring how political elites mobilized disaster uncertainties to their own advantage.[30] As he ultimately argues, "Nearly two years later it was still too early to tell and too soon to conclude otherwise: a 3.11 master narrative was still under construction."[31]

As a first contribution, my book engages with the work of these authors to precisely outline the construction of a master narrative around disaster recovery. I thus focus not on analyzing a sense of urgency but on the process of governance that transformed a politics of uncertainty into a politics of revitalization. Furthermore, the fieldwork that I conducted happened in a different temporality. By August 2015—when I went to Japan to begin this research—the sense of urgency had dissipated. By this time the Japanese state had installed monitoring boards displaying radiation levels all over Fukushima, with people passing them by as if they were mere lampposts. Children possessed small Geiger counters, devices formerly associated with nuclear experts. And massive radioactive decontamination programs had gradually enabled evacuees to return to their former homes. My research happened in a context where it was no longer a sense of chaos that needed to be governed, but something else. This postdisaster period was epitomized by what one of my informants, a retired nuclear engineer, called the "era of emergency" (*kinkyū jidai*). As this nuclear engineer explained to me in 2016, "After 2011, we have been in a state of emergency [due to the increase of radiation exposure threshold]. More than five years have passed, and we are still in an official state of emergency. How many years will we be staying in this state! Japan has entered a continual era of emergency." It is precisely the attempt to establish a politics of revitalization within this so-called era of emergency that this book examines and that differentiates it from other works focusing on crisis management.

The volume's second contribution is to trace the historical evolution of governance practices surrounding nuclear disasters and, to a broader extent, radioactive contamination. Historically speaking, one element that characterizes the management of nuclear hazards is secrecy. Chernobyl, the only other major disaster comparable to Fukushima, was initially inseparable from state secrecy, in which all efforts were made to conceal the catastrophe. As opposed to Fukushima, Chernobyl happened near the twilight of the Cold War and was embedded in a strong Soviet culture of secrecy around nuclear infrastructure. What stands out in academic accounts of nuclear governance is usually a pattern of state secrets, orchestrated ignorance, media censorship, classified documentation, fact suppression, and tight control over nuclear-related information—in both communist and democratic countries.[32] In a nutshell, the governance of nuclear secrecy was concealed within the geopolitical tensions of Cold War policies, where military and security needs usually trumped medical or democratic concerns.

Unfortunately, this is a legacy that bears heavily on the science of radiation, the governance of nuclear disasters, and the understanding of Fukushima. At the same time, secrecy—understood as a grand-scale cover-up—is no longer a form of management that has its place in a post–Cold War democratic society like Japan. If we compare Fukushima with the aftermath of Chernobyl, when Ukraine was still part of the Soviet Union, we see two different pictures. One is embedded in opacity and secrecy. The other appears on the global screens of our world within hours. This is not to say that propaganda, ignorance, and the exercise of power do not exist after Fukushima—they do—but the stereotypical trope of the cover-up has no place in this story. What characterizes post–Cold War democratic societies is a governance that increasingly relies on international organizations and its own citizens to manage the aftermath of nuclear disasters. Thus, Fukushima embodies a shift toward the transnational governance of radiation risk and its population's comanagement of nuclear catastrophes. This is a sharp contrast with former historical events, when states often carefully guarded incidents surrounding nuclear exposure and when many citizens remained unaware of the scale of contamination.

As an anthropologist whose business is cultural difference, I aim to highlight the role of sociocultural factors in the governance of nuclear disasters. My account of Fukushima drastically differs from Adriana Petryna's *Life Exposed*, which examines post-Chernobyl Ukraine in the aftermath of the Cold War. Petryna argues that exposed populations of Ukraine have employed a politics of victimization to transform themselves into a class recognized by the state, thereby negotiating compensations and medical care.[33] As she observes, "Recognizing the deep vulnerabilities left behind by state interventions and failures to intervene, these citizens attempted to remake themselves into recognized sufferers of the state; sickness and citizenship fused together as damaged biologies became the basis for making citizenship claims under changing state and market structures, increasing poverty, and losses of security."[34] Petryna explains that it is only through nonrecovery that survivors of Chernobyl were able to access advantages in a struggling and changing economic market characterized by the shift from communism to capitalism.[35] In this state of affairs, debates surrounding the impacts of Chernobyl were linked with the collapse of the Soviet Union and the independence of Ukraine, political tumults that influenced disaster governance by pinpointing the former Soviet regime as the perpetrator of the tragedy. What becomes apparent after nuclear catastrophes is that issues of risk and recovery are inseparable from a set of ideas brought about by a change of politics, culture, or economic markets. However, Fukushima happened in a different context, which helped shape a politics of revitalization rather than one of victimization. By demonstrating that hazardous contaminants do not exist in isolation from historical contexts and by recording the cultural complexities of state and civilian responses, this book also analyzes the structural factors that led to different forms of governance for similar pollutants and similar disasters.

The third contribution of this book is to provide a richer theorization of governance in disaster studies. A major trend within ethnographies of disasters is the tendency to fall within a binary of "domination versus resistance."[36] In other words, disaster studies have historically contrasted the struggles of citizens (often depicted as victims) against the normative viewpoints of a larger dominating force. Countless accounts describe citizens' resistance against industrial polluters, government policies, institutionalized experts, media groups, or multinational corporations.[37] Popular words and phrases in these stories are "disparities," "disempowerment," "disjunctures," "conflicts," "victimization," "struggles," or "cultural dislocations." In a nutshell, disaster studies predominantly focus on a "regime of disconnection,"[38] with researchers focusing on the "we-they dichotomy."[39] It is precisely in this opposition that many compelling ethnographies of disasters find their force—through the association between (as Michel Foucault would put it) the "buried knowledges of erudition and those disqualified from the hierarchy of knowledges and sciences."[40] Indeed, anthropological inquiries into disasters have entertained what Foucault calls the "claims to attention of local, discontinuous, disqualified, illegitimate knowledges against the claims of a unitary body of theory which would filter, hierarchise and order them in the name of some true knowledge and some arbitrary idea of what constitutes a science and its objects."[41]

Focusing on these disparities is an important part of this book. At the same time, I remain wary of weaving another "David vs. Goliath" scenario, as this would impede understanding of nuanced aspects of governance that escape this binary. As George Marcus argues, "Ethnography has shown the effects of major events and large systems on the everyday life of those usually portrayed as victims . . . , but it has rarely been directed to answering macrosociological questions about the causes of events or the constitution of major systems and processes, usually represented more formally and abstractly in other conceptual languages."[42] Drawing from George Marcus's concerns, I see three problems in the binary of domination versus resistance.

First, depicting Fukushima as a "David vs. Goliath" story prohibits us from discerning the complexities of the state by producing a caricatured picture in which a homogeneous entity seamlessly manages radioactive hazards. As Mark Bevir points out, "The notion of the central state being in control of itself and civil society is a myth. The myth obscures the reality of diverse state practices that escape the control of the center because they arise from the contingent actions of diverse actors at the boundary of state and civil society."[43] Inspired by the work of Andrew Mathews, I believe that the state must be conceptualized as "a shifting group of loosely connected institutions that are unstable and often in conflict with one another."[44] State governance after Fukushima echoes this looseness as three different prime ministers were at the head of the government of Japan from 2011 to 2012. Furthermore, the nuances of state governance are complicated by the specificity of Japanese bureaucracy, notably by the vertically segmented administrative system (*tatewari gyōsei*), which is a form of sectionalism that leads to interministerial rivalries. During my fieldwork, I noticed that different ministries mobilized unique forms of expertise as well as specific materialities with respect to radiation hazards. Each state agency attempted to manage public risk perception in ways that sometimes appeared contradictory. For instance, while one ministry barely discussed radioactive contamination, another ministry was implicated in creating decontamination processes. While one ministry claimed that nuclear power ought to be restarted, another agency promoted renewable energy. While carbon monoxide was described by one ministry as a harm more serious than radiation hazards, tons of radioactive waste were burned by another in giant incinerators. While the irony seemed to be piled as high as the mountains of plastic bags in Fukushima, these contradictions should not be viewed as an impediment to state governance. Elizabeth Povinelli argues that "dissonance itself may be a means of conserving power as much as a source of interference to power."[45] Similarly, I found out that while managing different forms of nature, resources, or irradiated localities created governance problems, they also provided greater governmental maneuverability to reassert a politics of revitalization in Fukushima.

Second, focusing solely on the disconnect between states and civil society inhibits researchers from critically examining how citizens are invariably agents of governance. Scholars interested in power have historically theorized citizen movements through the lens of victims, protestors, or challengers, which echoes the "romance of resistance."[46] In this scenario, governance usually *happens* to people, and citizens are rarely viewed as complex political actors capable of participating in its process.[47] Furthermore, much as with the vision of a monolithic state, studying power via the sole focus of resistance paints citizens as "monochrome heroes dedicated to a struggle against power."[48] This view conceals how civil society can create its own sources of violence and reproduce categories of harm shared by the state.[49] Thus, part of this book analyzes how citizens' tactics—while unique in their way of expressing political discontent—also have their shortcomings (such as promoting social inequalities) while supporting normative systems of power. Ironically, a politics of revitalization is made possible by multiple actors who can very well have opposite end goals.[50]

Third, a focus that opposes states and civil society fails to examine the impacts of social actors who do not fall neatly within these two groups but who nonetheless impact the governance of disasters. In their study of neoliberal governmentality, James Ferguson and Akhil Gupta demonstrate that state functions are increasingly being outsourced to nongovernmental organizations (NGOs), intergovernmental organizations, grassroot movements, or economic markets.[51] They define this shift as a move toward an "emerging system of transnational governmentality."[52] Fukushima is inseparable from this system of transnational governmentality, being embedded in broader discourses of market ideologies and the monopoly of international experts. Consequently, part of this book highlights how these actors contribute to a worrisome neoliberal shift in the management of contamination, as tropes of self-resilience are conveniently delegated to disaster victims.

The final contribution made by this book lies at the meta-level, as it aims to uncover whether major shocks lead to radical and unprecedented changes within our societies. Debates surrounding this question have received considerable attention in the social sciences.[53] For instance, scholars point out that crises are regularly depicted as exceptional "moment[s] that marked a transition between epochs,"[54] as "non-routine" times as opposed to normal order,[55] or as events that contain the "seeds for structural and institutional change."[56] Narratives surrounding Japanese society are prone to analyze crises via this lens of radical change, pointing to events like the arrival of Commodore Perry in feudal Japan, Japan's defeat in World War II, and the implosion of Japan's bubble economy. Fukushima is no exception to such discourses, as Richard J. Samuels points out: "A profusion of extravagant claims dominated the 3.11 discourse. . . . The nation would undergo paradigmatic change and civilizational transformation. It was at an inflection point, a historic moment, a turning point that would lead to a new generation that would overhaul the nation and change everything."[57]

Within this book I argue that scholars working on crises should be careful about the optics of fundamental change. This realization is inspired by the seminal work of Anthony Oliver-Smith and Susanna Hoffman, who theorize disasters as "processual phenomena rather than events that are isolated and temporally demarcated in exact time frames."[58] There are many reasons for embracing this view while studying Fukushima. Indeed, describing Fukushima as an unprecedented event risks embracing an "almost functionalist assumption of general societal equilibrium prior to disaster onset."[59] Yet, even before 2011, Japan was far from resting in a state of equilibrium, affected as it was by an aging population, economic torpor, geopolitical tensions, and social precarity.⁶⁰ Focusing on catastrophes as a process highlights the importance of past historical factors in disaster governance while enabling researchers to empirically trace the patterns of sociocultural continuity that emerge after a crisis. Employing my analogy, when an unstable element transmutes itself into another element, it does not become a random new element. Rather, it follows a chain of natural decay. Similarly, I argue that crises do not create a tabula rasa, which leads to free-for-all sociocultural changes. They follow anthropological findings that have notably confirmed that disasters are prone to "accelerate processes of change already underway."⁶¹ To answer the initial question, changes do happen in the aftermath of crises, but they transpire in dialogue with prior social elements, which affect the realm of possibilities for the transformation of cultural and social institutions. As I will demonstrate through this book, the way toward a politics of revitalization was paved long before the advent of Fukushima. Paradoxically, to better understand sociocultural change, it is necessary to look back at patterns of sociocultural continuity.

Doing Fieldwork on Radioactive Grounds

The hallmark of anthropological research is ethnographic fieldwork, a form of qualitative study wherein the researcher focuses on a single community for an extended period.⁶² While fieldwork within a single group has its advantages, it proved too restrictive to enable me to theorize the plurality of governance around disaster recovery. My focus on governance required a "multi-site ethnography," which follows different connections across space.⁶³ This kind of ethnography, as Kim Fortun argues, aims to piece "together a picture of an 'object' with material from many (sometimes unexpected) places."⁶⁴ In that spirit, I analyze the governance of radioactive hazards within a priori unsuspected places, like tropes of nostalgia for one's native land, the 2020 Olympic games, narratives of global warming, and the future of energy sources. My research took place between 2015 and 2017 and was not restricted to a given location. Rather, it took me to urban and rural areas of Japan, predominantly in the prefectures of Fukushima, but also Tokyo, Chiba, Kanagawa, Saitama,

Nagano, Okayama, Kyoto, Osaka, Hiroshima, Gifu, Fukui, and Hyogo (among other places).

I began by collecting information and archival materials about Japan's nuclear history in various places, such as the Hiroshima Peace Memorial Museum and the Citizens' Nuclear Information Center based in Tokyo. There I was able to get a sense of Japan's nuclear history, especially by analyzing narratives around nuclear power. I also examined nuclear discourses in popular representations, history documents, school textbooks, public relations movies, comic books (*manga*), and cartoons (*anime*). Furthermore, I gathered official information about the nuclear disaster by focusing on state ministries' and nuclear agencies' documents.

To complement my understanding of historical materials, I interviewed a range of people directly affected by the disaster. These included residents of Fukushima, farmers living on contaminated landscapes, worried mothers, voluntary evacuees, nuclear engineers, decontamination laborers, members of antinuclear organizations, political activists, citizen scientists, medical doctors, epidemiologists, radiation biology scientists, radiation physicists, university professors, state bureaucrats, and town and city officials. This book employs a mixture of real names and pseudonyms to strike a balance between maximizing historical evidence and protecting the anonymity of participants. I use real names when the information surrounding an individual was gathered through public records or public conferences. I resort to pseudonyms when my information was acquired during formal interviews or informal conversations. In Japanese, surnames precede given names. This order was reversed so as not to confuse the English reader. All interviews conducted in Japanese have been translated by the author. In cases where the valence of a certain Japanese word does not have a clear equivalent for the English translation, I insert the word in question within brackets. The range of people whom I interviewed made me realize that simple questions such as "What is a radiation hazard?" or "What is recovery?" had no simple answer. Speaking to different groups equally highlighted how categories superposed on individuals are far from homogeneous. A nuclear engineer could well be a fervent antinuclear activist, and a voluntary evacuee could be a citizen scientist. Categories like "mothers," "activist," or "citizen" were porous and evolved drastically as the disaster kept unfolding.

While interviews were useful to impart a sense of the voices of affected individuals, they also had their limits. Initially, I faced difficulties in trying to get interviews with state officials. My inquiries ended up lost amid the electronic labyrinth of optic fibers or the automatic reply of a governmental inbox. Later, when I finally managed to interview state officials, the data that I gathered was fatuous at best. Often, information that I recorded was publicly available, and I rarely learned anything new. Consequently, I stopped focusing on what state officials *said* and began to examine what they *did* through a focus on everyday practices of post-disaster recovery. Luckily, when I went to Japan, Fukushima was on the verge of commemorating the fifth anniversary of the disaster, which enabled me to attend more than forty symposia, conferences, and speeches related to the disaster. Additionally, I engaged in direct observation of revitalization activities done by the state, participated in citizen-science meetings, attended a trial at the Fukushima District Court, explored risk-communication centers, stopped by public-relations events, visited nuclear research laboratories, examined decontamination activities, journeyed to evacuated zones, and traveled to abandoned towns.

Beyond these activities, I prioritized participant observation, which allows for the presence of the anthropologist within the lives of people they encounter. I participated in public demonstrations with mothers who advocated for evacuation; I helped citizens measure residual radiation; I tested food for contamination in civic laboratories; I made my own Geiger counter with an NGO; I volunteered to prepare food for evacuees of temporary housing; and I helped farmers to decontaminate their rice fields. Being with people—looking at how they live and participating in their activities, routines, events, joys, frustrations, hopes, and sorrows—was essential to gaining a better-grounded understanding of what "recovery" meant. Participant observation also highlighted sharp contrasts between narratives and actions. Gaps emerged between what people said they were doing and what they actually did. For instance, a clear difference existed between state policies, which appeared highly promising on paper, and the concrete actions taken by the government, which resulted in a limited conceptualization of what recovery meant.

The Politics of Fieldwork

While this book assembles different viewpoints through a multisite ethnography, I do not claim to have produced the definitive study of Fukushima. Rather, I would like the reader to see this ethnographic account through the metaphor of a Japanese woodblock print. Like a print of the floating world (*ukiyo-e*) made unique by the assemblage of specific woodblock plaques, a focus on different narratives produces a painting of its own by presenting a series of vantage points on radioactive hazards and postdisaster recovery. Within this portrait, I acknowledge my own partiality resulting from my investment in an anthropological practice of studying other epistemological practices. There are limitations when an ethnographer attempts to produce an "authoritative" narrative about a disaster. On that subject, Timothy Mitchell claims that expertise does not merely report knowledge forms; instead, it also works to format them.[65] As an anthropologist, I consequently play a specific role in generating "firsthand" accounts. Philosopher Isabelle Stenger criticizes this position, claiming that "the anthropologist produces, whether he wants it or not, a set relationship that is more often inherently asymmetrical: he reports to 'us' a knowledge about other groups without putting to the foreground the relationship upon which his knowledge comes, or by simply being at the service of a science to produce."[66]

While I have tried to foreground the relationship upon which my knowledge is derived, it still is undeniable that this book comes with its own cultural paradigm, influencing how data is presented, perceived, and rationalized. Following a rich tradition of anthropological autocritique, I do not present the information in this book as an innocent act of description.[67] I, too, generated an epistemic orientation in conceptualizing radiation hazards, fragmenting human experiences in the process of transforming the knowledge practice of my informants for the broader purpose of intellectual generalizations or anthropological explanations.[68] Beyond disciplinary lenses, an important part of this research was molded through my own experience in Fukushima.

I remember a precise event that made me more reflective of the researcher's positionality in studying disaster. In the spring of 2016, I was invited to witness the work of an organization in Fukushima composed mostly of farmers attempting to revitalize their region. At 5:30 in the morning, I was shaken out of bed by an old man named Masayuki Dobashi, who needed my help with some renovations at his center. We began moving old planks, which resulted in propelling a mist of wood particles into the air. The sight of the mist worried me: "What if I breathe those particles? Are they radioactive? Why didn't I bring a mask? What's the radiation level? Where are my gloves . . ." As I looked at the dust that covered my clothes, I felt edgy and disturbed, becoming a captive of the world of radiation. At night, I had nightmares of invisible radioactive particles locked in my lungs. A similar incident happened when Dobashi filled his gourd with water from a natural source. "If you're thirsty you can go and drink some water. It's clean [*kirei*]," he told me. I was taken aback by this offer. Many things were jostling in my mind: Was it really safe? How should I interpret the Japanese word "*kirei*"? Did he use it to mean "fresh" or "uncontaminated"? In the end, I took a small sip of water and began to feel anxious, wondering "what if?" For his part, Dobashi was gulping down large quantities of water without apparent concern.

These experiences made me realize that one cannot constantly live in a state of chronic anxiety about the potential adverse health effects of an invisible harm. It was precisely these kinds of "what if" moments—the impossibility of solidifying the risks involved in a particular activity—that were some of the most energy-draining aspects of living with radiation hazards. I noticed that many citizens in the village rarely talked about radiation risks. Dobashi and I never discussed the issue, but instead talked about the nature of the village, the name of its plants, the different shades of green, or the shacks that needed fixing. Dobashi taught me to enjoy the beauty of the "*satoyama*," a term that refers to bucolic visions of an ancestral way of life, where human beings lived in harmony with their surrounding nature.

After a few days in Dobashi's village, I stopped thinking about radiation. It physically exhausted me. I quickly became tired of wearing a mask to protect myself from radioactive particles and understood why many people found them uncomfortable. Rubber boots and long-sleeved shirts and pants, which served as tentative protection from contaminated mud and soil, equally became an impediment to everyday life in the hot summer months. The noise of the radiation monitoring also grates the nerves. I could still hear its annoying beeping in the corner of my mind when I lay in bed at night. Who said that radiation was noiseless?

After sharing the everyday life of these farmers, I naively thought that I had understood what Fukushima was all about, until one member of their organization criticized the current state of governance. "You know, Maxime-*san*, for us, state experts are people who have 90 percent of the knowledge, but no wisdom!" In Japanese, two words, "*shiru*" and "*wakaru*," can be used for the verb "knowing." "*Shiru*" means "to find out" or "to learn." It implies a process of acquisition of knowledge and information. "*Wakaru*," on the other hand, is closer to "understanding this knowledge." In a way, one can know something but not necessarily understand it. *Wakaru* shows a greater and more personal level of comprehension often based on a given context. For this citizen, state experts did not possess understanding in the latter sense, but only abstract knowledge in the former sense. Having been affected by radioactive contamination, this man strongly believed that the inhabitants of a place, the *jūmin* (literally: the people who reside there), were best suited to govern their own life in a post-Fukushima Japan.

Throughout this ethnography, I attempt to derive findings on the basis of whatever authority is derived from "having been there" in the field. This is the stereotypical anthropologist's justification of their own expertise. However, I must acknowledge at the outset that I can only endeavor to do so with humility. My ethnographic presence was partial. There is a huge difference between *being there* and *living there*. Generously funded by scholarships but not living every day in Fukushima, I could afford to throw out my rain boots after having walked on radioactive mud, take a critical stance on food safety, and even quickly move elsewhere anytime I might want. Many of my informants could not do the same. Thinking about radiation hazards as a nonlocal academic interloper is not the same as experiencing radiation hazards as a local resident farmer, one for whom the land is a precious heritage handed down from generation to generation.

It became clear to me that I was not a *jūmin* and that I would never truly understand Fukushima in the *wakaru* sense of the word. When I came back from fieldwork, colleagues asked me if I had been scared for my health. While it is true that I had experienced some anxieties, I also realized that fear was a luxury that many could not afford. While I had been anxious about unnecessary radiation exposure, I wrote this book in the comfort of my house, far from the dangers of the contaminated zone. In this context, it could have been tempting to criticize the views and actions of the people during fieldwork as they were seeking to revitalize their damaged locales. But what does it mean to see the world as an anthropologist, safely hidden from danger, while the informants upon whose hospitality and good graces I depended throughout my fieldwork literally have their feet in radioactive mud? Reckoning with the moral responsibilities of an anthropologist in a disaster area forced me to think seriously about the ethics of ethnographic writing in ways that no graduate seminar could. In this book, I have sought to do justice to the lives of those others upon whom my project and I depended, even though at times in the pages ahead I offer my own critical perspective about the politics of revitalization.

More importantly, reckoning with the responsibilities of ethnographic writing helped me to understand that not every citizen wants their life to be depicted via what Michelle Murphy calls "body-centric damage narratives."[69] For some, there are forms of harm greater than radiation exposure. In that line of thought, ethnographies of life in contaminated areas are increasingly producing scholarship that precisely moves beyond tropes of victimization associated with damaged biologies or nuclear hazards.[70] This "postvictimization" approach is gaining a lot of momentum in anthropology. For instance, anthropologist Ryo Morimoto has examined "how the radiation damage–centered discourse was and is still damaging residents, undermining their hopes to return to their lands and reestablish their personal, social, and spiritual ties."[71] Drawing from Eve Tuck's notion of "suspending damage," which goes against "research that intends to document peoples' pain and brokenness to hold those in power accountable for their oppression,"[72] Morimoto calls for "suspending radiological damage to explore a different 'Fukushima' than how it has been imagined and entertained."[73] Morimoto's call refuses to create further representations of damaged biologies, going against the "much-told stories of 'nuclear victimhood.'"[74]

The postvictimization turn in ethnography counters myopia around usual discourses of nuclear victimhood by humanizing individual responses. It highlights the internal logic of affected individuals, explaining why some people decide to remain in Fukushima despite contamination. This brings a deeper sense of place, much needed in nuclear studies. At the same time, I believe that this form of ethnography has important limits that make it too restrictive for studying the governance of toxic disasters.

First, it is important to acknowledge that tropes of nuclear victimhood have historically been the only tools by which exposed citizens have obtained nonnegligible political gains. For instance, Adryana Petrina demonstrates how crucial tropes of damaged biology were in post-Chernobyl Ukraine, as victimhood was one of the only means of survival by which disenfranchised citizens could navigate a post-Soviet economy.[75] Thus, victimhood is not merely a *passive* state. It is also a *productive* force that generates demands for political changes, equality, and reparations, especially when one considers the rich history of nuclear accountability in Japanese history.

Second, a form of relativism is present within this turn, which results in treating all viewpoints as equal. For instance, in wanting to go beyond tropes of damaged biology, anthropologist Yoko Ikeda argues that "people's sense of risk is relative" and that individuals in Fukushima "decided for themselves where danger ended and safety began."[76] Refraining from passing judgments on citizens' choices, Ikeda sets the discourse of both victimization and nonvictimization on a symmetrical plane: risk is relative, and so is the sense of victimhood. A potential consequence of this relativism is that anthropologists will remain analytically blind toward the forms of structural harms that bring disasters in the first place, while making capitalistic-induced catastrophes forgivable, so as to ethnographically respect the different experience of affected individuals.[77] Yet, narratives of nuclear risks are shaped by larger global systems that influence parts of citizens' practices and discourses. For example, knowledge about nuclear issues was deeply influenced by military secrecy, government propaganda, collusion with the energy lobby, and scientific controversies (to name but a few factors). These drastically impede a politics of victimization after nuclear accidents while shaping the understanding of recovery in specific ways. What affected individuals say and do is not the mere result of free will (e.g., risk is relative) but something molded by displays of power that frame and limit individual choices.

Third, due to the burden of compensation costs and potential changes to the status quo, a postvictimization turn is already encouraged by states, corporate lobbies, and regulatory agencies that do not want a politics of victimization to happen after nuclear disasters. As this book shows, Japan's politics of revitalization resulted in disregarding narratives about adverse health effects, pressure to silence critical voices, the cherry picking of experts in risk communication, and the termination of financial support for many evacuees. To be clear, the academic approach to this turn is different. For instance, Morimoto warns scholars not to unquestioningly "glorify and justify" lives within residual radiation,[78] and Murphy reminds us that "chemical relations are racist, harmful, even deadly."[79] Nonetheless, I agree with David Bond's critique that part of the call for suspending damage-based research "overlap[s] with the deep investments of [the nuclear,] petrochemical and fossil fuel industry in rendering the real injuries of their operations invisible."[80] While the postvictimization turn allows for a nuanced perspective of the experiences of people getting on with their lives in the aftermath of disasters, there is also the risk that abandoning the nuclear-victimhood concept entirely in our analyses could play into the PR strategies of major polluters who would downplay the harms they have caused. This could be a further blow to the independence of the academic community, which is already compromised in the nuclear domain.[81] Following Paul Rabinow, I believe that a necessary anthropological distance requires one to be "separate enough to prevent an easy identification [with one's informants], yet close enough to afford a charitable, if critical, understanding."[82] Though the postvictimization perspective contributes significantly to our understanding of disaster-impacted communities, I do not think this theoretical orientation affords me sufficient distance to study the phenomenon of radioactive governance, as it closely aligns with certain positions of the nuclear lobby. It is understandable that people in disaster-impacted areas may not want their experiences reductively assigned to one category, but it can also be true that a structural analysis of the social position of such communities is rendered incomplete if descriptions of nuclear victimhood and damaged biologies are abandoned.

Outline

In terms of structure, each chapter of this book examines a subaspect of "radioactive governance," or the strategies that transform an initial situation of crisis into a state of postdisaster recovery. Broadly, these strategies are the creation of a radiation-protection culture that makes long-term evacuation undesirable (chapter 1), the nitpicking of experts (chapter 2), the disregard of marginal voices (chapter 3), the use of technological fixes to "clean" disaster areas (chapter 4), the promotion of specific understandings of recovery (chapter 5), the strategic foreclosure of political deliberation (chapter 6), selective teaching practices (chapter 7), and neoliberal delegations of risks (chapter 8). While each chapter primarily centers on a key concept, I have also made an effort to preserve a chronological order that spans the initial ten years of the disaster.

Chapter 1 provides the historical background that led to the Fukushima nuclear disaster. In this chapter, I first offer a primer on the phenomenon of radioactivity. Then, I historicize the practices through which nuclear matters, such as issues of energy and radiation dangers, were defined before 2011. For instance, I consider the visceral effects of nuclear harms after Hiroshima, while analyzing how nuclear power was cemented in contradictory imaginaries, oscillating between Astro Boy, the childlike android powered by a nuclear heart, and Godzilla, the dinosaur-like monster born from nuclear tests. By drawing on interviews with nuclear engineers and materials gathered in museums, comic books (*manga*), and Japanese educational textbooks, I ask how historical factors created a myth of safety around nuclear power. I also bring an international perspective to bear on radiation hazards by outlining the ideologies that shaped radiation-protection culture in the management of nuclear disasters. The chapter argues that former historical contexts have drastically shaped the governance of radioactive contamination, thereby facilitating a politics of revitalization in Fukushima.

Chapter 2 examines the initial governance of the disaster in the first years. These include evacuation orders, initial comments on the health effects of the catastrophe, and changes in political leadership. In addition, I consider how the governance of radiation hazards primarily revolved around the management of expertise after Fukushima. Through a focus on state-sponsored conferences, I scrutinize what counted as expertise, what disciplines were prioritized, and who was invited to official risk-communication symposia. I analyze whether, in these conferences, the characteristics of radiation are portrayed as harmful or not, while exploring how recovery is conceptualized. I document how a politics of revitalization pinpoints the fear of radiation, posttraumatic stress disorders, reputational damages, and discriminatory practices as the "major" culprit of this disaster. I then focus on the work of medical doctors who criticized this politics by arguing for acknowledging the risks involved in radiation's adverse health effects. On the basis of interviews, I reveal the pressures, criticisms, and ostracization that these experts faced by highlighting contradictory narratives about radioactive contamination. This chapter argues that a successful politics of revitalization was inseparable from managing who could come to speak as an expert. Being a "proper" expert was a political issue mediated through sociocultural pressures.

Chapter 3 explores the rise of "citizen science" in the six years after the disaster (2011–2017), when affected individuals began dealing with radiation risks by mobilizing their own expert practices. I first consider how social bonds were pushed to their breaking point after this disaster, resulting in tales of mistrust, fear, and isolation in response to state experts' communication. I then focus on a group of mothers who used citizen science to promote a politics of victimization, ultimately trying to evacuate children from Fukushima. By following their activities in radiation workshops, food monitoring, and contamination tracking, I reveal the social pressures they faced in trying to talk about radioactive contamination. I also demonstrate how citizen science enabled mothers to express political dissatisfaction toward their government. While the mothers failed to bring about governance changes, they nonetheless promoted alternative understandings of recovery from those of the state. In this process, citizen science forged new communities, often participating in disaster governance by reimagining shared identities amid toxic legacies.

Chapter 4 studies state-sponsored programs of radioactive monitoring and decontamination, which began to gain a lot of ground after 2012 and continued for the rest of the decade. These practices drastically changed the initial restricted zones discussed in chapter 2. Through observations in laboratories that monitored radiation and attempts at decontaminating Fukushima, I question the consequences of rendering contamination technical. I then contrast remedial measures with the experiences of citizens who came back to Fukushima, most notably rice farmers. Their experiences included living in landscapes covered in millions of bags of radioactive topsoil while the government deliberated over a permanent disposal site. I documented farmers' disregard for the state's maps of radioactive contamination. Color-coded zoning restrictions made sense for government workers, but rice farmers did not experience their environment through shades of red, orange, and green. Their experiences demonstrate that remedial measures are technical fixes that are often ineffective. Notwithstanding the dissatisfaction of farmers, this chapter argues that monitoring and decontamination are governance techniques that have powerful symbolic functions. They demonstrate that even the most contaminated areas are not nuclear wasteland and "enable" the state to lift restrictions on other evacuation areas.

Chapters 5, 6, and 7 focus on broad strategies the Japanese state has employed to manage the disaster. Chapter 5 explains how the state has overseen radioactive hazards by going beyond scientific discourses or technical fixes. I focus on how state performances mobilized tropes of resilience and nostalgia around the concept of the "native land" (*furusato*) to promote a politics of revitalization. The concept of the "native land" is associated with traditional images of rural idylls and agricultural activities. Through observing public relations campaigns, I first examine how the state mobilized this imaginary by promoting Fukushima as an ideal "native land" that is strong, resilient, and open to tourism. Subsequently, I investigate the story of citizens from Fukushima, whose "native land" was transformed by forced evacuations, ongoing relocations, and residual radioactivity. For them, the "native land" is not a physical space but a set of social relationships that cannot coexist with the effects engendered by contamination. By investigating how different understandings of the *furusato* influenced the interpretation of radiation hazards, this chapter argues that engaging with the rural imaginary became a political touchstone for speaking about recovery. The phantasm of a place that was pure in the past confronted the state's phantasm of a place that could become pure again in the near future and thus open for prompt repatriation and economic commodification.

Chapter 6 pivots from an ideological project to analyze a set of public controversies surrounding the role of nuclear power and the threat of radioactive contamination within the Ministry of Economy, Trade, and Industry (METI), one of Japan's most influential ministries. The chapter investigates how the generic language of uncertainty can be deployed to render otherwise incommensurable risks commensurable (e.g., energy risk, financial risk, health risk) in order to create hierarchies of urgencies, which in turn serves to depoliticize debates about radiation danger. I demonstrate that for some state agencies the potential uncertainties linked with the abandonment of nuclear power could trigger political turmoil of a higher order than that linked with Fukushima's radioactive contamination. In this context, a form of double depoliticization took place, wherein Fukushima's radioactive contamination was depoliticized through perceived priorities that were paradoxically depicted as an urgent need for immediate action and not open to deliberation. This hierarchization of uncertainties acted as an effective tool for managing controversies surrounding energy and residual contamination.

Chapter 7 explores complementary approaches to risk-communication strategies in which state expertise on radiation hazards was increasingly disseminated to the public via teaching infrastructures that were cute (*kawaii*), jargon free, and interactive. Through an ethnography of state-sponsored exhibits, hands-on activities, and didactic centers, I investigate how radiation-related information was strategically mobilized for partisan ends, namely, a state-laden politics of revitalization. While scientific hubs made information on radiation fun and easy to understand, they concealed troubling aspects of radiation dangers, disregarding sociocultural and gendered experiences of the disaster. This chapter theorizes how environmental hazards are materialized to support specific politics in postdisaster contexts, while providing sociocultural insights within historically established processes of control that aim to defuse societal unrest, pacify fearful publics, and reclaim economic stability.

Chapter 8 goes beyond Japan and the Fukushima nuclear disaster per se to examine how the governance of Fukushima has inspired global nuclear lobbies roughly ten years after the disaster. I focus on how certain aspects of civic society can support hegemonic understandings of radiation danger and normative visions of postdisaster recovery. This chapter argues that the growing impact of citizen science echoes a neoliberal shift in the management of contamination, leading to reduced public expenditure, minimal government intervention, and risk privatization—meaning that risk becomes a matter of personal issues rather than the state's or polluter's responsibility. In this context, the empowerment resulting from citizen-science practices shifts responsibility for ensuring radiological protection onto the shoulders of former victims. The danger lies in a normalization of risk that produces societies in which citizens care for themselves amid increasingly polluted environments while interpreting partial data about controversial environmental dangers. This view challenges the celebration of citizen science as a democratic endeavor and theorizes the neoliberal implications of its pursuit, as nonstate actors become an integral part in the management of risks.

In a brief conclusion I theorize the governance of contamination in the Anthropocene, when human activity has become the predominant driver of environmental change. Ultimately, the experiences gathered in this book provide crucial insights for navigating the uncharted, polluted seas of our age, while exploring the new ways of living in a future with which we will one day all reckon.

1

Nuclear Monsters and Nuclear Saviors

I wrote a good part of this book in Hiroshima, moving there after my fieldwork to live with my Japanese partner at the time. Our apartment was situated a mere fifteen minutes away from the Hiroshima Peace Memorial Park, where the atomic bomb named "Little Boy" was first dropped. When I could not write, I often gazed at the Children's Peace Monument, which commemorates the history of Sadako Sasaki, a young girl who died of leukemia caused by the radiation poisoning.[1] I also paid my respects at the Memorial Hall for the Atomic Bomb Victims, where the following inscription is found: "Mourning the lives lost in the atomic bombing, we pledge to convey the truth of this tragedy throughout Japan and the world, pass it on to the future, learn the lessons of history, and build a peaceful world free from nuclear weapons." Late at night, I would admire the Genbaku Dome, the only structure left standing near the center of the blast zone.

A visit to the Hiroshima Peace Memorial Museum presents an unremitting catalogue of the effects of nuclear harms, which include terrible keloids (scars), hair loss, cancers, and other sicknesses. I have never forgotten a particular exhibit: a long black fingernail (*kuroi shime*) with an information panel explaining that survivors grew abnormal fingernails due to thermal radiation. Sights like these are commonplace in the museum, which stresses the difficulties that irradiated victims (known as "*hibakusha*," literally "people exposed to the bomb") have faced. These included not only health problems but discrimination associated with the narrative that radiation causes multigenerational genetic damage. In the libraries of Hiroshima, foreign visitors can find English versions of *hadashi no gen* (Barefoot Gen), a *manga* that tells the fictional story of Gen Nakaoka, a six-year-old boy living in Hiroshima during the final days of the war. The horrors wrought by the bomb are graphically depicted: Hiroshima lies in ruins, full of corpses, with people dying from severe burns and radiation sickness.

Every year on August 6—the day the bomb was dropped—the park is transformed into a politically charged locus, where Hiroshima the *place* becomes Hiroshima the *event*. On that day antinuclear activists protest nuclear power while right-wing extremists blast anti-American slogans through propaganda trucks (*gaisensha*). The police make sure that any noisemakers suspend their activities during the Peace Memorial Ceremony, when the attendees pray for the repose of victims, the abolition of nuclear weapons, and lasting world peace. The *Chugoku Shimbun*, a daily newspaper based in Hiroshima, offered a glimpse of the terrors that people faced on the day of the bombing: "He was a boy of 17. Today he recalls, 'Charred corpses blocked the road. An eerie stench filled my nose. A sea of fire spread as far as I could see. Hiroshima was a living hell.' She was a girl of 18. 'I was covered in blood. Around me were people with skin flayed from their backs hanging all the way to their feet—crying, screaming, begging for water.'"[2] While museums, journal articles, and current-day commemorations make nuclear hazards viscerally apparent, such was not always the case. After World War II, American forces occupied Japan until 1952, and the effects of atomic bombing on human bodies were carefully withheld from the public view.[3] Secrecy was so powerful that many Japanese remained unaware of the victims' suffering.[4] Nowadays, the picture is quite different, especially with Barack Obama becoming the first sitting American president to visit the Peace Memorial Park in 2016, going as far as offering a wreath of flowers to the Cenotaph of the A-Bomb Victims.

My experiences in Hiroshima were stark reminders that nuclear tragedies dangle between historical repression and national commemoration. Making nuclear harms visible—as well as invisible—is a political process that requires much effort. Nowadays, these efforts have naturalized a strong politics of victimization in Hiroshima. As Lisa Yoneyama observes, "The memories of Hiroshima's destruction, secured within the global narrative of the universal history of humanity, has thus sustained, at least in the dominant historical discourse, a national victimology and phantasm of innocence throughout most of the postwar years."[5]

Similarly, this chapter examines how the 2011 Fukushima nuclear disaster cannot be approached without a sense of Japan's nuclear history, nor without a broader understanding of the global contexts that

Figure 1.1. Antinuclear demonstrations in Hiroshima. Photo by Maxime Polleri.

shaped nuclear power and radiation dangers. In doing so, I take inspiration from scholars of STS (science and technology studies) like Gabrielle Hecht, who argue that nuclear ontologies are multiple and that nuclear things are part of different and contradictory systems of classification.[6] Following that train of thought, I historicize the practices through which nuclear matters were defined in specific ways before and after 2011. Pragmatically speaking, I am also inspired by Michelle Murphy's notion of the "regime of perceptibility," which is defined as a framework for examining how different forms of knowledge are made visible or invisible within our societies.[7] In the context of my research, I engage with these findings to argue that nuclear power was perceived as essential to the socioeconomic prosperity of Japan and thus promoted since the 1950s through political agendas that aligned themselves with the interests of the liberal international order. The implementation of civilian nuclear power in Japan required the creation of particular "regimes of imperceptibility,"[8] in which the beneficial aspects of nuclear energy concealed the most disturbing characteristics of nuclear hazards.

A Short Primer on Radioactivity

Before exploring this regime, it is important to define the phenomenon of radioactivity, as the reader might not be familiar with its intricacies.[9] Radiation and radioactivity are often considered as synonyms, but they involve different processes. Simply put, radiation refers to the transmission of energy in the form of waves or particles, while radioactivity is the spontaneous disintegration of atoms, describing a process of decomposition in which unstable atomic nuclei (the region consisting of protons and neutrons at the center of an atom) transform themselves into more stable nuclei by emitting radiation.[10] In the scientific jargon, unstable elements are called "radionuclides."

For better understanding of the difference between radiation and radioactivity, a useful analogy can be found in an X-ray machine. An X-ray machine is not radioactive per se but has the potential to produce radiation when activated. However, unlike an X-ray machine, radionuclides released during a nuclear disaster have no "on and off" switches. They both are radioactive and produce radiation. In terms of origin, radiation can come from natural sources, such as cosmic rays, or from naturally occurring radioactive materials found in the air, soil, water, and even food.[11] Additionally, radiation is produced as a result of human actions, such as medical CT scans and nuclear power plants.

Beyond its natural or man-made aspect, radiation usually falls within two categories: nonionizing and ionizing. Nonionizing radiation is composed of the low-energy parts of the electromagnetic spectrum, such as the light that we see, radio waves, and microwaves.[12] Conversely, ionizing radiation is a form of energy strong enough to penetrate the body and cause adverse health effects. This is the form of radiation that concerns people after a nuclear disaster, since the radionuclides released from a power plant emit dangerous ionizing radiation. For instance, the major radionuclides of Fukushima are iodine-131, cesium-134, cesium-137, and strontium-90. Each has a different lifespan. Cesium-137 can be "present in the environment for about 300–600 years,"[13] while iodine-131 radionuclides "decay away completely in a matter of months."[14] To complicate the picture, because ionizing radiation occurs under different forms, each radionuclide produces different types of radiation: cesium-137 produces gamma rays and beta particles; strontium-90 releases beta particles; and plutonium, alpha particles. Rays and particles differ in their capacity to do damage, as well as in their ability to penetrate materials: while gamma rays can penetrate deeply into human bodies, beta particles only travel a little way into human flesh, and alpha particles are stopped entirely by the skin.[15]

Ionizing radiation poses a specific risk to human health by potentially causing cancers as well as immune system problems.[16] It does so by cutting the chemical bonds of molecules in biological cells. Indeed, ionizing radiation can damage the DNA, a molecule carrying information for the growth, function, and reproduction of living organisms. In trying to repair themselves from such harm, cells are prone to make mistakes, producing errors in the DNA.[17] This causes mutations in living cells, which permanently alter their reproductive outcomes. This alteration might result in somatic effects, which are limited to the exposed individual, such as cancers.[18] They might also result in transgenerational or hereditary/genetic effects, which are mutations present in the germ cells (eggs or sperm) transmitted from generation to generation.[19] While transgenerational effects are well known in animals, human studies remain shrouded in controversy.[20]

Currently, it is known that high doses of radiation predictably lead to organ malfunctioning and death. In other words, there exists a limit where radiation damage is so severe that no DNA repair is possible. This type of harm is known as a deterministic effect—a certain dose determines an outcome.[21] In the context of Fukushima, no deterministic effects have happened; people were not exposed to doses that were high enough to lead to irreversible damage and subsequent death.[22] However, lower and chronic exposure to radiation, which is the situation that faces the residents of Fukushima, can still increase the risk of developing long-term somatic effects as well as heritable genetic defects.[23] As the Canadian Nuclear Safety Commission explains, "The probability of this type of detrimental effect is proportionate to the dose."[24] These stochastic (i.e., randomly determined) effects are considered "chance events, with the probability of the effect increasing with dose, but the severity of the effect is independent of the dose received."[25] Stochastic effects happen at any level of exposure, and as a result there is no threshold at which radiation exposure is perfectly safe.[26] As an expert in radiation physics and biology explained during an interview with me, "The problem is that you don't necessarily need a lot of exposure to trigger a severe harm. The cell just needs to be damaged in the 'right way,' which can lead to the 'right kind' of event. Some people might be more prone to having the DNA mutation that will end up causing severe cancers, for example. That's what we call the stochastic level; it can happen or not and it is linked with probability. The probability is in the dose that you received, but the severity of the effect is not." Because of radiation's stochastic nature, it is "scientifically impossible" to determine whether a given exposure dose is safe or dangerous for an individual.[27] To add to the complexity around radiation, a potential delay exists "between the start of the exposure and the observed health effect."[28] This state of uncertainty is precisely what the exposed population of Fukushima has been dealing with.

In terms of measuring radiation exposure, different units are used to monitor radiation.[29] A unit referred to recurrently in this book is the Sievert (Sv), a value that represents the radiation effect on the human body while considering the "type of radiation and sensitivity of tissues and organs."[30] Since the Sievert represents a large value, radiological safety uses smaller values, like the millisievert (mSv) (1/1000 of an Sv) or the microsievert (μSv) (1/1000 of an mSv). These values are frequently expressed through the rate at which a dose is delivered (e.g., mSv per year or μSv per hour).[31] Another unit, the becquerel (Bq), expresses the amount of radioactivity released by the decay of radioactive material per second.

Lastly, an individual can be exposed to radiation or contaminated by radioactive materials. For instance, during a dental X-ray, radiation passes through your jaw and disappears when the dentist turns the machine off. A dental X-ray does not make you radioactive, and no trace of radiation remains inside your body. To be contaminated, radioactive elements need to be on or inside your body.[32] Radioactive contamination therefore works externally, if the body is affected by nearby residual radioactivity, and internally, if radioactive elements are ingested or inhaled.[33] In the latter case, radioactive materials can accumulate in specific organs, remaining active for different periods of time, while causing unique types of harms like thyroid or bone cancers.[34]

Radiation hazard is a complex phenomenon. Not only is it invisible to the naked eye, but it takes the form of rays or particles, comes from natural or man-made sources, can be deterministic or stochastic, can be internal or external, and can have effects that stretch for generations. As the remainder of this book reveals, these characteristics have been mobilized by scientific organizations, expert bodies, and nation-states in calculated strategies to shape the governance of radioactive contamination from Hiroshima's atomic bombing to Fukushima's nuclear disaster.

Cementing Nuclear Power in Japan

At the end of World War II, General Douglas MacArthur—the Supreme Commander for the Allied Powers—controlled the occupation of Japan under US forces. Until 1952, MacArthur launched a series of political reforms aimed at transforming Japan into a liberal democracy. Amid attempts to mediate an understandably tense relationship, it appeared wiser to forget about the atomic bombings. Consequently, the United States regularly censored discussions surrounding radiation harm while prohibiting nuclear science in Japanese society.[35]

Japan might well have remained a nonnuclear nation were it not for the geopolitics of East Asia changing drastically in the 1950s. The first Soviet nuclear test of 1949, the rise of communist China, and the Korean War epitomize the geopolitical tension known as the Cold War. Under such pressures, transforming Japan into an ally with nuclear power plants could strengthen the global strategic nuclear balance in favor of the liberal international order by showing that an American ally could make nuclear weapons if the need ever arose. Wary of the rise of communist powers in the East, American forces once again introduced nuclear power in Japan, but this time under the promise of the peaceful goals of nuclear energy. But how could American forces convince a country that had suffered from two atomic bombings of the need to embrace nuclear power? To do so, they decided to shift the image of nuclear things from a power that obliterates life to a power that benefits the free world.

In 1953, President Eisenhower famously launched the Atoms for Peace program. Under the auspices of the IAEA, the Atoms for Peace program was dedicated to promoting the peaceful pursuits of nuclear energy, such as clean energy, agricultural benefits, and helpful medical radioisotopes.[36] As part of an American geopolitical Cold War propaganda strategy, the Atoms for Peace program "emerged from the need to control public anxiety about atomic energy, to discourage other countries from developing atomic bombs, and to take steps toward disarmament."[37] Within Japan, it strove to soften the image of America as "a military menace responsible for dropping atomic bombs."[38] Eisenhower's political advisors expressed reservations about the "dubious economic viability of civilian atomic power," and the program was primarily viewed in terms of its uses for foreign policy while preserving American superiority in nuclear science.[39]

In the official discourse of the program, nuclear power was manifested in tropes of peace, scientific advancement, and technological wonder. Within this new imaginary, American leaders began to frame Japan as a "democratic model for Third World countries that might be attracted to communism."[40] To facilitate this agenda, US forces financially backed political parties that shared their convictions. Founded in 1955, the Liberal Democratic Party of Japan (LDP) was just such a party. The LDP won the 1955 general elections, becoming Japan's first government with a strong nuclear-oriented agenda. It was the majority government for almost forty years and remains one of the strongest factions within Japanese politics to this day.

Notwithstanding the advances in developing nuclear power throughout the 1950s, resistance to nuclear energy grew steadily within Japanese society.[41] Antinuclear sentiments came to a head on March 1, 1954, when a Japanese fishing boat—the *Lucky Dragon Five*—was contaminated by nuclear fallout from a US thermonuclear test. The death of a crew member and the contamination of fish products sold on Japanese markets brought awareness about radiation dangers.[42] The incident produced a rise in antinuclear sentiments, leading to the creation of the Japan Council Against Atomic and Hydrogen Bombs (*gensuikyo*), which sought to ban nuclear weapons.[43] Subsequently, nuclear fears seeped into popular culture, best epitomized by the figure of Godzilla, a dinosaur-like mutant monster born from the radiation exposure of nuclear tests.

To reverse this "allergy to the atom" (*genpatsu arerugii*),[44] American and Japanese elites embraced a series of tactics aimed at changing the public understanding of nuclear power. Their first step was the creation of a clear separation between atomic weapons and nuclear energy. While atomic bombs were associated with a hurtful legacy, nuclear energy

TABLE 1.1. A timeline of Japan's embrace of nuclear power

1952	The Japan Science Council states the three guiding principles of nuclear power: liberty (jiyū), democracy (minshū), and public openness (kōkai).[a]
1954	The first nuclear research budget is passed throughout the Japanese Diet.
1955	Creation of the Atomic Energy Basic Law.
1956	Creation of the Japan Atomic Energy Research Institute.
1966	Japan's first commercial nuclear power plant produces energy in Tokai City, Ibaraki Prefecture.
1967	The Power Reactor and Nuclear Fuel Development Corporation is created to develop advanced thermal reactors and breeder reactors.
1973	The Oil Crisis cements the necessity of nuclear power for Japan. Nuclear power stands as a symbol of energy independence.
1977	Creation of the experimental Jōyō breeder reactor.
1986	Construction of the Monju reactor, a sodium-cooled fast breeder reactor.
1993	Construction of the Rokkasho Nuclear Fuel Reprocessing Facility, which separates fission products and unused uranium from spent nuclear fuel.
2011	Japan has fifty-four nuclear reactors and plans to increase its reliance on nuclear power.

[a] Philippe Pelletier, "De la guerre totale (1941) à la guerre de Fukushima (2011)." Outre-terre 1,35–36 (2013): 418.

stood as a developmental force to revitalize Japan. In public discourses, the division between the peaceful use of nuclear power and the danger of nuclear arsenals was as strong as the Iron Curtain, even though scholars argue that Japanese politicians showed interest in evolving the civil nuclear program into a military one.[45]

In this new imaginary, the peaceful aspects of nuclear power were linked with modern lifestyles. Historian Morris Low describes the efforts that shaped this vision, as public fairs, exhibitions, and science films contributed to the acceptance of nuclear power by nurturing a technology-oriented Japan.[46] Quickly promoted as an integral part of national policy, sustained by the development of economic measures, and endorsed by the nation's legal framework,[47] Japan's nuclear industry was on the rise to conquer the world.

The Nuclear Safety Myth

The revamping of a collective imaginary around nuclear power spearheaded the creation within Japanese society of a "myth of nuclear safety" (*genshiryoku anzen shinwa*)—the belief that nuclear power is inherently safe and clean and that disasters are impossible.[48] The "nuclear village" (*genshiryoku mura*), an assemblage of heterogenous actors consisting of politicians, bureaucrats, energy lobbies, mass media, and scientific experts, further cemented a strong consensus around nuclear power.[49] These actors have historically mobilized different strategies to advance their goal, leading nuclear power to be embedded in a strong culture of collusion, national education programming, regimes of acceptable expertise, selective mass media communication, and affective tropes of love for nuclear things. The next sections briefly examine the scheme that led to a myth of nuclear safety within the archipelago.

From State Regulation to Regulatory Capture

First, Japanese political elites supported nuclear energy as part of their national vision of recovery via strong economic policies. For instance, the Ministry of International Trade and Industry (MITI)—a powerful agency within the economic bureaucracy—deployed "vast government resources and subsidies" to make nuclear power a national priority in a country that lacked energy resources like oil.[50] Under the "government policy, private management" motto, MITI retained administrative guidance over nuclear power, while delegating costs to electric power companies.[51] By gaining control over nuclear issues, MITI expanded "its influence on matters of nuclear safety" and began to oversee "nuclear power regulation, licencing and safety."[52] This negatively affected nuclear safety culture and created troublesome instances of collusion through the cultural practices of *amakudari* (descent from heaven)—where bureaucrats from nuclear regulatory agencies retired to work in the private energy sector—and *amaagari* (ascent to heaven), which refers to employing nuclear industry members in regulatory agencies.[53] Therefore, regulatory agencies soon became dominated by the very industries they were supposed to regulate.[54] The strong ties between regulators and the regulated also implied that nuclear industries could count on the state to tame opposition around nuclear projects. For instance, when the nuclear industry faced civic backlash over the construction of new power plants, MITI developed economic policies that rewarded cooperation with energy lobbies.[55] As many authors explain, the state presented nuclear power as a way of preserving the lifestyle of rural regions affected by depopulation and poor economies.⁵⁶ Fukushima was one such region, and its residents had to accept the potential dangers of nuclear power "in order to acquire revenues and jobs."⁵⁷

Educational Agenda

Once the basis of Japan's nuclear program was firmly set, educational infrastructure and nuclear lobbies played a key role in making nuclear power socially acceptable, especially for a younger generation that was too young to remember the horror of atomic bombings. Since nuclear power was part of a national policy, it was imperative that education programs in Japan solidified the discourse of nuclear safety within the rising generations. Consequently, numerous education programs have attempted to build a foundation of pride around nuclear power. State ministries would regularly distribute pro-nuclear textbooks to elementary and high school children with appealing titles such as "The Exciting Nuclear Power Land" (*waku waku genshiryoku rando*) or "Challenge! Nuclear World" (*charenji! Genshiryoku wārudo*). These textbooks stress the superiority of Japanese nuclear technology and the impossibility of accidents like Chernobyl.⁵⁸ The "teacher editions" (*kyōshiyō*) of such textbooks are particularly telling, as they reveal clear indications that educators should make their students think about the advantages (*riten*) of nuclear power.⁵⁹ The Ministry of Education, Culture, Sports, Science, and Technology (MEXT) also promoted nuclear power through a series of educational activities, such as a "nuclear power poster contest" (*genshiryoku posutākonkūru*) in which children sent their best drawings depicting the useful aspects of nuclear energy.⁶⁰ Similarly, METI's Agency for Natural Resources and Energy created educational websites like "Nuclear A to Z" that allowed children to deepen their understanding about nuclear energy (*enerugī genshiryoku ni tsuite rikai o fukamete itadaku tame*) in what they described as a fun (*tanoshiku*), easy (*yasashiku*), and accurate (*tadashiku*) manner.⁶¹

Nuclear organizations have created their own televisual programs aimed at children. In one (in)famous cartoon developed by Japan Power Reactor and Nuclear Fuel Development Corporation, the radioactive element plutonium appears as a cute little figure aptly named Mr. Pluto (*pluto kun*).⁶² In the cartoon, Mr. Pluto claims that he is not a monster (*obake*) and that he is working toward peace (*heiwa*).[63] Against the stereotypes (*osoroshi imeji*) and bad rumors (*warui uwasa*) that affect nuclear energy, Mr. Pluto's mission is to tell the "true" and "safe" story of plutonium, which is unrelated to health scares like cancer. Mr. Pluto begs to be controlled by the "wonderful wisdom" (*subarashii chie*) of humans, indicating that his purpose is for high-tech projects like space satellites. To demonstrate how safe it is, a child is shown happily drinking a plutonium-laced soda. The subtext is clear: Not only is nuclear power safe, but a little radiation can be refreshing and even good for you.

Scientific Ostracism

While the aforementioned actors provided a strong basis for the nuclear safety myth, the overall acceptance of their enterprise would never have occurred without the support of scientific expert bodies. Unfortunately for the proponents of nuclear power, not all scientific experts were convinced of the safety of building nuclear power plants on an archipelago that is routinely prone to violent earthquakes and tsunamis. Consequently, an efficient way of repressing antinuclear sentiments within the scientific community was not necessarily through disciplinary measures but via gate-keeping tactics. In that regard, Jeff Kingston argues that the nuclear village acts as a kind of "gate community," where cooperation prevails over disagreement, thereby representing a modern version of *murahachibu*—the practice of village exclusion that ostracizes naysayers by denying certain benefits.[64] Similarly, scientists who have historically criticized nuclear power have faced the consequences of ostracization, which include unsuccessful grant applications, denials of academic tenure, and difficulties publishing scientific papers.[65] In sharp contrast with these struggles, pro-nuclear scientists have reaped the benefits of cooperating with energy lobbies, by accessing research funds and appointments to major centers of academic prestige.[66]

Censorship and Media Control

A similar way of controlling information about nuclear power was with mass media, a tactic that censored the more troublesome characteristics of nuclear things, while selectively amplifying nuclear power's useful aspects. Censorship and media control—under different forms—are indeed inseparable from the history of nuclear power in Japan. Initially, US forces employed more than eight thousand censors to silence the voices of *hibakushas*.[67] A strong hold on nuclear narratives was further facilitated by the CIA, which famously recruited media tycoons such as Matsutarō Shōriki to disseminate pro-nuclear propaganda, thereby painting a positive image of nuclear technologies.[68] Energy lobbies later developed similar extensive ties with newspapers and television networks by offering generous payments for advertisements that made the media wary of criticizing nuclear power.[69] In this more subtle form of media control, nuclear power became part of everyday life, normalized in the form of commercials during the breaks of one's favorite TV shows, as full-page ads within magazines, or as celebrities' endorsements during special events. During my fieldwork, many citizens complained that this culture of media control had created a tainted legacy, which discouraged further reporting on nuclear dangers. In 2016, I interviewed members of the Citizens' Nuclear Information Center (*genshiryoku shiryō jōhō-shitsu*), a Tokyo-based civic organization known for its thorough analysis of nuclear incidents. The center was famous for exposing the insufficient investigation during a hydrogen explosion at the Hamaoka nuclear power plant. Junpei Nagai, a core member of the organization, explained that governing power (*shihai kenryoku*) and huge financial capital (*kyodai shihon*) had created a powerful organization reluctant to share information with the populace. In fact, Nagai argued that the known nuclear incidents in Japan were probably only the "tip of the iceberg" (*hyōzan no ikkaku*):

> Enabling information to rapidly become public has never been a part of the government's mentality. We have always faced problems in trying to access nuclear-related information. A lot of data is simply never made public. For example, information surrounding physical protection, or the data gathered by private contractors, is almost impossible to obtain. Many companies refused to share this information under the pretext that it falls under "industrial secrets." Of course, we understand that such needs exist, but there needs to be a little bit more balance. How can you create appropriate policies and law if things are never made public?

Affective Structures

The creation of affective structures that permeated the imaginary of Japanese people was arguably more important than any policies in garnering not only cultural acceptance but in fact love for the infrastructure of nuclear power. By affective structure, I refer to an arrangement of interrelated elements, such as emotions, sensations, and imaginaries, that make people feel a particular way about nuclear power and radiation.[70] The story of a nuclear engineer named Yukio Hatayama is illustrative in this regard: "When I was young, I was first interested in geology, that's what I wanted to do. But in the sixties, the 'nuclear era' [*genshiryoku jidai*] was beginning, and nuclear energy was present everywhere. Tōkai was built during this era [Tōkai Nuclear Power Plant]. Coal and oil were described as archaic sources of energy. Even in cartoons, nuclear power was everywhere; for instance, think of Astro Boy! I was seduced by the promise of nuclear power. It was labeled as something that was completely safe and peaceful, something that was different from nuclear arsenals." As Hatayama explained to me, nuclear power quickly won the heart of postwar youngsters who followed the adventures of Astro Boy, a fictional character born under the pen stroke of cartoonist Osamu Tezuka. In the cartoon, Astro Boy is a little android created by the fictional Dr. Tenma, a roboticist working for the Japanese Minister of Science. Astro Boy possesses an artificial heart powered by nuclear energy, reflecting the dominant narrative of the sixties, in which nuclear power was no longer associated with the scars of atomic bombings. Indeed, where nuclear power once took life, it now protected it; in the comics, Astro is constantly shown as fighting against evil and injustice. Even the Japanese name for Astro (*tetsuwan atomu*), or Mighty Atom, is devoid of any association with negativity, and embodies a new political environment exempt from nuclear fear.

Joseph Masco has discussed the importance of affect in nationalizing images of nuclear apocalypse.[71] In the United States, one can think of the terrifying mutant ants from the 1954 movie *Them!*, which represent the perils of communism.[72] Comparing popular depictions of the nuclear imaginary between US and Japanese popular culture reveals a different portrait. In the North American imaginary, radioactive elements have a central role in the creation of heroes and saviors. In postwar cartoons, radioactive elements endow human beings with supernatural powers. Peter Parker gets bitten by a radioactive spider and becomes the Amazing Spider-Man. The scientist Bruce Banner gets exposed to gamma radiation during a failed experiment, transforming into the Incredible Hulk. The X-Men are literally mutants who possess diverse abilities, such as regeneration capacities or laser vision. Dr. Manhattan is a scientist who is trapped in a radioactive particle test room, only to become a living god. These are but a few examples of how radioactive elements create heroes in the US imagination.

But in Japanese culture radioactive elements do not empower human beings with such feats of strength. Indeed, there is a clear-cut separation between the human realm and the technological one. Astro was intentionally *created* by human scientists, because in Japan radioactivity is a nonhuman entity that remains under the control of human agency, harnessed for the well-being of the Japanese nation-state. Radioactive elements are never subject to an accidental situation where a radioactive spider escapes to bite a human. Moreover, Astro is "immunized" to the potential harmful effects of radiation exposure. While Astro takes the appearance of a young boy, he does not have sexual organs under his black metallic trousers. This suggests that Astro is not affected by the radiation illness, which, as Masco summarizes, "includes a displacement in time (sometimes occurring decades after exposure) and a potential to be genetically transferred across generations."[73] As an android that is neither boy nor machine, Astro stands as a hybrid, which, as Masco highlights, is an uncanny offspring stuck in "a form of generational stasis, allowing one to separate analytically the distinct genetic lines that came together to create the infertile being."[74]

As Hatayama further explained to me, Japanese nuclear science was immersed in carefully crafted images of little androids invulnerable to radiation. Within this context, nuclear power incited seductive feelings of limitless energy, heroic saviors, and the promise of what Lauren Berlant calls the "good life."[75] The experience of Hatayama demonstrates that nuclear power did not simply create material infrastructure; it also gave birth to an affective infrastructure that disregarded certain forms of hazards.[76] Nuclear power, which promised clean and limitless energy, became a domain of technical expertise that Japanese scientists could be proud of.

Yet, amid the radiance of such tropes, Hatayama began to see crucial flaws in the safety system of nuclear power. As he emphasized, "Even the laws that surround nuclear infrastructure were created to first promote nuclear advancement. They have never been created for public safety [*minkan hoken*]!" The constant promotion of nuclear power (*genshiryoku suishin*) over matters of technical safety became more problematic when Hatayama discovered data falsification and cover-ups of radioactive releases. The people living near power plants were ill prepared in the case of a disaster. Safety drills were nonexistent as government officials feared that these exercises would "affect the promotion of nuclear energy policy."[77]

Similar discoveries led Hatayama to become an ardent critic of nuclear power. His worries culminated in the creation of a research group composed of like-minded scientists, who began to investigate the potential risks and corruption practices of the nuclear industry. At the time, embracing this path was not a popular choice. Indeed, since nuclear science was a tool for forging a strong nation-state, nuclear scientists were expected to be the comakers of a strong, modern, and energy-independent Japan. As Hatayama explained, "As a young student, when I first started to study nuclear engineering, we were supposed to be doing research *for* the country; questioning the safety of nuclear power always created a lot of tension." In her study of the Brazilian nuclear power program, Donna Goldstein highlights how cultural and affective connections with nuclearity drastically influenced "moral public concern" around issues of nuclear power.[78] In fact, she demonstrates that the aura and prestige associated with nuclear energy even bypassed serious accusations of governmental corruption.[79] Likewise, denouncing nuclear power in Japan was tantamount to attacking Japanese modernity, economic recovery, and nationalism. The predominantly positive feelings associated with nuclear power were so powerful that they even reshaped the image of Godzilla. In the 1970s and 1980s—at the peak of the promotion of nuclear power—the role of Godzilla subtly shifted from that of a bad monster that ravaged Japan to that of a protector of the nation-state, fighting evil and horrendous creatures. From monstrous beginnings, nuclear energy had truly become a radiant savior.

The Illusion of Control

In the end, the myth of nuclear safety epitomized a recurrent trope of modern governance: the illusion of control. Timothy Mitchell argues that the politics of the twentieth century corresponds to the attribution of human agency over any other forces.[80] This was precisely the politics of nuclear things in Japan. For nuclear power to gain acceptance after Hiroshima, Nagasaki, or the *Lucky Dragon Five*, radioactive elements had to fall under the control of human agency at all costs. From something that produced tremendous pain, radiation was reincarnated as something under the control of Japanese scientists, who harnessed its power for the grandeur of Japan. This was a vision that could only exist by "designating certain costs as external, certain claims as secondary."[81] Amid the political propaganda that surrounded the peaceful use of nuclear power, the dangers of radiation were not necessarily brushed off, but rather depicted as the results of the unpeaceful use of nuclear energy. The history of nuclear power was not idiosyncratic, but met the path of an "unbridled industrial growth," wherein pollution is a necessary sacrifice.[82] However, nuclear power was a sacrifice unique to Japan, as the only country that suffered from the wrath of atomic bombings. Industrial factories stood as icons of progress for Japan, but nuclear power was *the* ultimate icon of progress. It was the electricity produced by nuclear power plants that enabled factories to produce much-needed chemicals and commodities. While industrial chemicals such as methylmercury or cadmium had not yet seeped into popular consciousness,[83] nuclear power was already associated with tropes of annihilation. Thus, strenuous efforts were required to shift this imaginary.

In postwar Japan, nuclear power was part of a nuanced atmosphere of both good and bad things. Most of the time, these contradictory discourses coexisted and evolved in tandem. Yet, specific categories of harms had to remain invisible in the official discourse. As opposed to the experience of Cold War Americans, nuclear power in Japan was not part of the brinkmanship between East and West. It was devoid of an imaginary of mutual assured destruction. War, nuclear arsenals, and radioactive hazards confronted peace, dreams of infinite energy, and economic miracles. Recognizing nuclear power as a source of harm—rather than an icon of progress—would go against Japan's modernity.

Governing this imaginary was a complex political project, but human interests, fears, and desires shaped the perception of radioactive dangers. In the end, expertise surrounding nuclear matter consisted of "a certain way of organizing the amalgam of human and nonhuman, things and ideas, so that the human, the intellectual, the realm of intentions and ideas seems to come first and to control and organize the nonhuman."[84]

Radiological Safety: An International Perspective

Beyond Japan, international forces have shaped the understanding of radioactive dangers in their own ways. The politics of radiological safety is highly complex and riddled with scientific controversies. Currently, the field of radiological protection adopts a linear nonthreshold (LNT) model. This approach argues that there is no safe threshold of radiation exposure. It states that risk is proportional (i.e., linear) to the level of exposure: "A lethal dose will produce a lethal effect, half of that dose will produce half of that effect, and so on, with no level being completely harmless."[85] The Committee on the Biological Effects of Ionizing Radiation supports this model, claiming the "presence of an increased risk of developing radiation cancer with increased exposure at low levels."[86] The International Commission on Radiological Protection (ICRP) also agrees, arguing that "in the low dose range, below about 100 mSv, it is scientifically plausible to assume that the incidence of cancer or heritable effects will rise in direct proportion to an increase in the equivalent dose in the relevant organs and tissues."[87]

However, alternative models variously argue that a threshold exists, that low doses are beneficial, or that chronic low doses are more harmful than one-time high doses.[88] To complicate matters further, the concept of a "low dose" is itself controversial, since there is "no universal agreement on the definition of low dose."[89] Indeed, there are more than nineteen different estimates from around the globe for what constitutes a low dose—ranging from 3,000 mSv down to 20 mSv.[90] As a result, understanding disasters like Fukushima requires grasping how international factors have shaped the governance of radiological safety.

Radiation and Calculating Risk

Before 1945, radiation risk was just a national affair, reserved for a community of professionals who used radiation in limited capacities.[91] The situation changed drastically with the advent of the nuclear age, best epitomized by an emerging nuclear industry and the Cold War arms race.[92] These events released tremendous quantities of radioactive materials into the environment, transforming radiation regulations into a matter of "global risk."[93] To control transnational risks, international institutions began to turn "data about radiation exposure into 'global' knowledge."[94] As Gabrielle Hecht argues, their aim was to create "working limits on occupational exposures to radiation," which were "crucial for nuclear power to overcome the fears generated by atomic bombs."[95]

Initially, the effort to articulate a protection culture in the form of working limits regarding radiation risks faced a seemingly immovable obstacle. Since all exposures are, according to the LNT model, detrimental to one's health, how could "permissible" risk thresholds be set in ethical ways? To deal with this problem, in the 1970s international expert bodies promoted an exposure philosophy called "as low as (is) reasonably achievable" (ALARA).[96] As Sven Ove Hansson explains, "ALARA is often described as a principle of optimization, by which is meant that some sort of compromise between dose reduction and cost containment is aimed for."[97] In this understanding, nation-states weigh a trade-off between the benefits of nuclear things (e.g., electricity, national security, medical isotopes) and the costs of potential exposure (e.g., health hazards, environmental contamination, large-scale disasters). The calculation of this trade-off is set by nation-states, resulting in different "politics of permissible exposure."[98] For instance, US nuclear employees have a higher dose of permissible exposure than UK workers do.[99] Differences in exposure are also justified between occupational and nonoccupational exposure. Because civilians do not reap the same benefits as occupational workers (e.g., a salary), they generally tend to have a lower permissible threshold.

The ALARA philosophy initiated an important shift regarding radiation risk. From a harm that was formerly ungovernable, where every dose represents a hazard, radiation became a "socially acceptable risk."[100]

Scholars of nuclear studies have criticized the ALARA philosophy, not for the balance of risk and benefit per se—which is inherent to modern life—but for how the optimization principle is impacted by secrecy, ignorance, and power.[101] For example, much of what is known about radiation hazards comes from the atomic bombings of Hiroshima and Nagasaki, which tragically produced the opportunity to study the effect of radiation exposure on human beings. Under US authority, the Atomic Bomb Casualty Commission (ABCC) and the Radiation Effects Research Foundation pursued studies on *hibakusha* survivors and their children.[102] Their research—known as the Life Span Study (LSS)—represents the "gold standard" of radiation exposure studies,[103] and it was instrumental in producing safety standards for the nuclear infrastructures of the world.[104] A major conclusion of the LSS is that certain doses of radiation exposure (those above 100 mSv/year) correlate with a significant increase in harmful effects (most famously cancers). However, the LSS never established a firm link between adverse health effects and doses below 100 mSv per year.[105] Furthermore, the LSS was unable to find genetic effects in the offspring of *hibakusha* survivors, even though Hermann Joseph Muller demonstrated that genetic mutations can be inherited due to radiation exposure.[106] As a result, endless debates have emerged around the risk of low-dose exposure and its inheritable genetic mutations.

As more documents have become declassified over the years, academics have challenged the integrity of the LSS, pointing out its methodological shortcomings.[107] For instance, ABCC was founded in 1946 and did not include people who passed away from the effects of radiation. Physician and epidemiologist Alice Stewart famously claimed that this omission led to an unrepresentative cohort of healthy survivors.[108] Moreover, the assessment of *hibakusha* radiation dose remains disputed. In particular, the LSS produced dosage estimates based on the recollection and memories of *hibakusha*, creating a study that was "aspirational rather than factual."[109] Lastly, the LSS only focused on external exposure caused by radiation rays. As Susan Lindee summarizes, the LSS failed to consider "estimates of internal radiation, that is, inhaled or ingested radioactive particles, in their calculations. Nor did they include estimates of exposure to residual radiation, even for those near the hypocenter who might have remained in the area for some time after the bombings."[110]

These drawbacks have led to claims that the LSS cannot be used to understand case studies associated with low-dose exposure.[111] Indeed, after an atomic explosion, individuals are exposed to short-term high external doses of radiation. This represents a different risk than the hazards of nuclear disasters, which are often associated with lower doses and internal contamination (given the nature of the radiation released). Notwithstanding this fact, the LSS is still mobilized to make sense of the aftermath of nuclear catastrophes, including the one at Fukushima.[112]

The Impact of the Cold War

The Cold War nuclear arms race also had a dramatic influence on the acceptable boundaries of radiation hazards—perhaps even more than the LSS. It did so by promoting the interests of national security over the well-being of communities affected by radioactive contamination.[113] By now, scholars have well documented the devastating effects of radioactive exposure on First Nations, Marshallese descendants, or Downwinders who either lived near nuclear test sites or worked in uranium mining.[114] Kate Brown has also documented the secrecy of knowledge that characterized the production of plutonium for weapons arsenals in both Soviet and American communities, as well as the dismissal of those who spoke about its danger.[115] In the context of the Cold War, "safety" was inseparable from wartime imperatives, a situation that impacted debates on low-dose exposure. This point is evident in the hardships that many US scientists encountered when trying to lower the permissible threshold of exposure, an effort that was vehemently contested by the Atomic Energy Commission.[116] John Gofman, an outspoken critic of the US federal safety guidelines for low-level exposures, gave voice to the systematic downplaying of radiation risk, noting how it was a consequence of the growing problem of nuclear waste (an unfortunate by-product of the nuclear arms race):

> No problem—there's a safe dose, nobody's going to get exposed to more than the safe dose. The clean-up and disposal of waste has been estimated to be in the billions, if they're really going to clean up Hanford [a site manufacturing plutonium for nuclear arsenal] and Savannah River and all the rest. . . . You won't have to bury things in these fancy vaults. You

won't have to worry about transport. You can even dispose of it in ordinary landfills. That will be the result. That's what the future will be. If low doses don't matter, the workers can get more and their families can get more by being in the vicinity. That's what we face.[117]

These practices of risk rebuttal and scientific muzzling created a legacy that still lingers to this day. In Goldstein's view, the Cold War generated an "atmosphere that at some level discourages the study of a broader range of contemporary illnesses that might be traceable to past contamination, or similarly discourages litigation using public health concerns against the government or its corporate partners from this era."[118]

The Role of Nuclear Disasters

In the midst of fears surrounding global nuclear war, the advent of civil nuclear disasters required novel ways of governing radiological risks. The 1979 Three Mile Island accident provided a foretaste of larger crises to come. While there was no cover-up surrounding the release of radiation into the environment, Three Mile Island revealed the enormous difficulties of managing a nuclear disaster, as well as the confusion of planning evacuation measures.[119] It notably created citizen mistrust in the state, generated anxiety around health effects, and led to tremendous cleanup and decommission costs that drastically curbed US nuclear growth.[120] Yet the event that forever crystallized the pitfalls of civilian nuclear power was the 1986 Chernobyl disaster.

Initially embedded in Soviet secrecy and state control, the Chernobyl disaster resulted in the evacuation of hundreds of thousands of individuals who never came back to their homes. Nuclear fallout also contaminated vast portions of Europe, leading to the realization that nuclear disasters had global consequences. The legacy of Chernobyl further created tense scientific quarrels about the dangers of chronic low-dose exposure to residual radiation.[121] Beyond an increase in cancer rates, survivors from Chernobyl have claimed to suffer from a range of symptoms, including "malaise, headaches, lower work capacity, loss of appetite, sleepiness during the day, insomnia at night, bleeding gums, disorders of the liver, kidneys, thyroid, menstruation cycles, tonsillitis and chronic gastritis."[122] This constellation of health effects—believed to be the result of years of low-dose exposure—has come to be known as "chronic radiation syndrome."[123] Throughout history, this diagnosis was dismissed by Western scientists who contended that Soviet research was simply "politically and ideologically tainted."[124]

While controversies remained around the number of deaths associated with Chernobyl,[125] international organizations like the IAEA contended that the most significant health impacts of the disaster were psychological.[126] Emphasis on the psychological nature of radiation harm led to the notion of "radiophobia," which was "first recognised by science experts and industry specialists after the 1986 Chernobyl disaster in Ukraine and used to describe public reaction considered out of proportion to the real risk of the accident."[127] Depicting radiation harm as a form of "mental disorder" proved useful in reducing or outright eliminating the impending costs (such as financial compensation) associated with a civilian nuclear disaster.[128]

Following the fall of the Soviet Union, more knowledge about Chernobyl became available, creating a reticence toward nuclear power worldwide. In this context, proponents of nuclear energy became increasingly worried that another civilian nuclear disaster might permanently thwart any ambition to increase nuclear power. These fears led to what Valerie Arnhold calls a "normalization of nuclear accidents," a process that attempted to transform nuclear disasters into events that are manageable, especially via internationally shared regulatory approaches to nuclear safety.[129] As Arnhold explains, a consequence of this internationalization was the fact that nuclear disasters became perceived as manageable events, even in the case of future large-scale accidents.[130] This change is evident in IAEA's International Nuclear and Radiological Event, which is a "tool for communicating the safety significance of nuclear and radiological events to the public."[131] Created in 1990, the scale is divided into seven levels: anomaly, incident, serious incident, accident with local consequences, accident with wider consequences, serious accident, major accident. The wording used to describe these levels is revealing, since it denies the possibility of nuclear accidents being global disasters (e.g., "accident with *wider* consequences").

The internationalization of nuclear safety also changed former imaginaries of apocalyptic nuclear disasters—best associated with stereotypes of Soviet "poor" managerial culture leading to Chernobyl[132]—to tropes of technological incidents that could safely be governed by experts perceived to be politically neutral.[133] Moreover, in the aftermath of the Cold War, newly formed states like Belarus were left to manage the aftermath of the disaster, especially the troublesome residual contamination. Amid the incremental costs and technical impossibility of decontaminating territories, a novel form of risk management emerged called "participatory governance."[134] Taking its cue from the idea of public participation in governmental affairs, the concept of participatory governance aims to empower victims of a disaster by providing tools to improve life in radioactive-tainted areas.[135] Scholars like Seizin Topçu have, however, criticized this principle as a form of governance that attempts to "delegate risk management to the private sphere."[136] As we will see, participatory governance proved itself to be a popular concept in the management of Fukushima.

In conclusion, the value of a historical approach lies in highlighting the context by which certain distributions of the sensible gain predominance. What is deemed safe, dangerous, or (im)permissible is the complex and messy result of scientific limitations, economic necessities, and political struggles. While we have learned much about radiological injuries, the science around radiation harm is never neutral. By saying this, I am not suggesting that we live in a post-truth world where everything is subjective. Rather, I am acknowledging that what is called "science" is a product of historical contingencies, which prioritize certain values in managing disasters. Fukushima provides a novel context in which to study these debates. The ensuing chapters highlight the structural factors that shape the governance of radiation hazards in ways that harken back to previous events while uniquely contextualizing them within Japanese society, ultimately facilitating a politics of revitalization.

2

The Theater of Expertise

At the opening ceremonies of the International Symposium on Disaster Management and Recovery for Children and Communities in the region of Soma, a coastal district of Fukushima harshly hit by the tsunami, an audience composed of both nursing students and international experts enjoyed a performance of *kyōgen*, a form of traditional comic theater.[1] During the performance called *bo shibari*—meaning "tied to a pole"—the *kyōgen* master declares that attendees should "enjoy the show and feel free to laugh!" The list of invited speakers for the two-day event was eclectic, but like the *kyōgen* master, everyone was there to reassure the audience. Many experts contended that "no statistical significance" existed for an increase of cancers and that the health impact of radiation risks was nonexistent. Everyone could rest easy and laugh.

During the symposium, Professor Ryugo Hayano, an expert in theoretical physics, explained how he had invited foreign students to spend time in Fukushima. He argued that the dose of radiation accumulated during their trip was not much different from the natural radiation of other countries. While showing his data, he underscored the fact that the external exposure of Fukushima was not particularly higher than in other parts of the world: "In fact, you can see that their highest peak is due to the natural radiation that children received during their plane trip to Japan!" Similarly, Dr. Gerry Thomas, an expert in molecular pathology of cancer, explained that the apparent increase of thyroid cancer among children was the result of a "screening effect," wherein high-tech equipment detected thyroid abnormalities that would not have been discovered prior to the invention of that equipment. To encourage the audience, Dr. Thomas stated that thyroid cancer was not a death sentence and explained the high rate of survival after thyroid surgery. For many experts present during the symposium, the nuclear meltdown was an "accident that killed nobody," as opposed to the tsunami, which had taken the lives of tens of thousands.

But in Tokyo, during a symposium called "Facing the Reality of Fukushima's Sixth Year," I encountered quite a different narrative.[2] Partly sponsored by an antinuclear organization, the symposium had invited Hiroaki Koide, a retired professor of nuclear engineering from Kyoto University, to speak. Known for his long-standing critique of nuclear power, Koide belonged to the Kumatori 6, a group of six researchers who created the Nuclear Safety Research Group. Among antinuclear activists, the Kumatori 6 were the stuff of legend, with its members being nicknamed the "Six Antinuclear Samurais of Kyoto University." On February 20, 2016, at the Mitaka City Social Education Center, Koide painted a very different picture of the radioactive contamination Fukushima faced:

> In some parts of Fukushima, everything has been contaminated. Try to imagine for an instant the scale of such contamination. Think of this building and its surroundings: the roof, the windows, the parking . . . it's an enormous scale. At the beginning of the disaster, I went into areas of Fukushima where people still lived. My jacket was so contaminated that I had to throw it away! It's important to communicate those risks to the population and to at least let the children evacuate from the contaminated areas in question. But when we talk about the risk of radiation, we are accused of impeding the revitalization of Fukushima [*fukkō no jama*].

Tetsuji Imanaka, another member of the Kumatori 6 and a second-generation *hibakusha*, offered a similar critique during two other conferences.[3] A nuclear engineer by training, Imanaka had conducted research on the environmental impact of residual radioactivity in Japan and Chernobyl. He had become involved in a survey of Iitate village, an area that was initially not evacuated, as it fell outside the official exclusion zone. There, he measured high levels of radiation, ranging from 30 µSv per hour to 150 µSv per hour (the predisaster background radiation levels of Fukushima ranged between 0.02 and 0.13 µSv/hour).[4] Residents of Iitate told Imanaka that "scientists in white suits with measuring devices" appeared in the weeks that followed the catastrophe. However, villagers never heard anything from these scientists, nor were they told to evacuate. Consequently, Imanaka warned them of the high level of exposure afflicting their village. His experience would lead him to clash with the radiation risk management adviser of Fukushima Prefecture, Dr. Shun'ichi Yamashita, who suggested that it was not necessary to evacuate beyond restricted areas. As Imanaka argued, "These [institutional] experts cannot even explain to people what they should eat or avoid. They will never be able to answer simple questions such as 'What do I do with my family?' The only thing they were able to say after the disaster was 'to not leave Fukushima.'"[5] He went on to offer this assessment:

> People often ask me if they can live in Fukushima or not. Honestly, it's not a question that can only be answered by science. I can tell you what the levels of radiation are, and my role is to provide as much information as I can on the risk of radiation exposure. But a Geiger counter cannot evaluate the sheer magnitude of harms brought by radioactive contamination. Moreover, you need to realize that a nuclear expert is something that does not exist! When we refer to someone as a "nuclear scientist," we are in fact referring to fragmented expertise. Most of the time, we are talking about nuclear engineering, which is obviously a by-product of the science of engineering. It comes with its own paradigm and has its own limitations. Be careful of people who claim to be "nuclear experts." We do not think enough about what constitutes a science.[6]

Regimes of Expertise

As the fifth-year anniversary of the Fukushima disaster, 2016 was the year of endless symposia. During that time, I attended more than forty conferences, where different experts described very different disasters. This chapter focuses on the issue of expertise, which has become a contentious battlefield after Fukushima. In studying the divergence of expertise, I do not argue that one group of experts possesses the truth more than another. Rather, I am interested in underlining how a successful politics of revitalization was inseparable from governing certain regimes of expertise. I argue that "proper" expertise around radiation hazards was a political issue, heavily mediated by social pressures, reified cultures of science, and state-approved policies. Throughout this chapter, I use the term "expertise" to refer to a specific and authoritative way of knowing. In the words of Anna Tsing, expertise is the reflection of a body of people who have "trained themselves to see with a singular vision."[7]

In examining the regime of expertise that gained ground after this disaster, it is easy to embed expertise in a mere clash of pro- versus antinuclear actors. However, not all experts whom I encountered had clear-cut political positions, and many refused simple labels. Nonetheless, every expert faced the hardship of navigating a controversial landscape, where claims around radiation hazards quickly became polarizing. This dichotomy also paints knowledge and politics as mutually exclusive, characterizing "real" expertise as impervious to political influence. To move beyond this naïve viewpoint, I draw from the concept of "coproduction," which describes how scientific expertise is jointly produced with political practices.[8] As Sheila Jasanoff argues, coproduction explores how "knowledge-making is incorporated into practices of state-making, or of governance more broadly, and, in reverse, how practices of governance influence the making and use of knowledge."[9] This framework is useful for examining how states of knowledge around radiation hazards "come into being, what makes them persist or disappear, and how they shape and are shaped by people's deeper political and cultural, as well as cognitive and material commitments."[10]

Drawing from a rich tradition of anthropological works, I study expertise as a set of practices, networks, and power relations, rather than as a form of knowledge that people possess.[11] As Summerson Carr argues, "Across its many domains, expertise is both inherently interactional, involving the participation of objects, producers, and consumers of knowledge, and inescapably ideological, implicated in the evolving hierarchies of value that legitimate particular ways of knowing as 'expert.'"[12] In the context of Fukushima, understanding expertise as a practice allows me to study how knowledge about radiation is produced and mobilized within given cultural contexts. Through a focus on state-sponsored conferences, I analyze the characteristics of radiation that are portrayed as harmful or not by certain experts, while exploring how recovery is conceptualized. I document how, in tandem with a politics of revitalization, expert narratives stressed peculiar characteristics of radiation hazards as the "major" culprit of this disaster. Then, I focus on the work of scientific experts who criticized this politics by arguing for the risk of adverse health effects. On the basis of semistructured interviews, I reveal the pressures, criticisms, and ostracization that some experts faced in highlighting contradictory narratives about radioactive contamination. In the end, I reveal how a successful politics of revitalization was coproduced with a unique regime of expertise.

Delving into Urgency

To better understand epistemic disagreements, it is necessary to give a brief portrait of the unfolding of the disaster. Fukushima released significant amounts of radioactive pollutants, resulting in contamination of both the surrounding sea and the northeastern region of Honshu, the main island of Japan.[13] Initially, both the quantity and scale of contamination remained controversial topics, especially since the earthquake and tsunami "disabled most of the existing local monitoring equipment."[14] The dangers posed by the release of radioactive contamination led to a series of major evacuations, as well as the creation of different restricted areas. The unfolding of these measures is quite complex to follow, as evacuation procedures drastically evolved over short periods of time. Table 2.1, based on governmental and scholarly materials, summarizes the evacuation procedures and the creation of restricted areas.[15]

In defining evacuation zones, the Japanese state eventually modified the level of acceptable radiological exposure, leading to one of the most controversial decisions of postdisaster governance. Typically, public exposure to radiation should not exceed 1 mSv per year.[16] Yet, on April 19, 2011, a threshold of 20 mSv/year—a twentyfold increase—was used to designate acceptable levels of radiation exposure in the playgrounds of primary schools.[17] This decision created an unprecedented public outcry, forcing the government to return to the traditional standard for school playgrounds (1 mSv per year).[18] Nonetheless, the 20 mSv/year threshold remains the current limit used to define areas considered safe enough for evacuation orders to be lifted.

While the decision to change radiation thresholds appears reprehensible, it is important to note that an expert rationale supported this policy. Indeed, part of the Japanese decision to increase the levels of radiation exposure was based on the recommendations of ICRP, which set authoritative standards in radioprotection. In the advent of a nuclear accident, ICRP can propose a new threshold of radiation exposure. ICRP's

TABLE 2.1. Evacuation procedures and restricted areas

Date	Order	Description
March 11	Evacuation by concentric zoning	The government launches an evacuation order within a three-kilometer radius from the plant.
March 12	Evacuation by concentric zoning	The evacuation zone is gradually increased in size as more information becomes available and as the situation becomes dangerous due to hydrogen explosions. The evacuation order is expanded to encompass a twenty-kilometer radius from the plant.
March 15	Sheltering order	Creation of a "sheltering order" within a twenty- to thirty-kilometer radius. The government instructs residents to stay inside their houses so as to minimize exposure to radiation.
March 25	Voluntary evacuation	The "sheltering order" is redefined as a zone of "voluntary evacuation." Citizens living in the twenty- to thirty-kilometer zone can evacuate by themselves if they feel the need to do so.
April 22	Restricted areas, deliberate evacuation areas, and evacuation prepared areas in case of emergency	The twenty-kilometer evacuation order becomes a restricted area. The government prohibits citizens from entering the zone. As data surrounding contamination becomes clearer, the government launches "deliberate evacuation areas," where the cumulative annual dose of radiation is expected to reach 20 mSv/year. Residents in these areas are required to evacuate within a month. For the first time, evacuation measures are based on a given threshold of radiation exposure. The government also creates "evacuation prepared areas in case of emergency." Residents living in these zones are advised to remain prepared to evacuate if the situation worsens.
June 16	Specific spots recommended for evacuation	The government launches "specific spots recommended for evacuation"—areas that fall outside of previous evacuation zones. Known as "hot spots," these areas contain high levels of radioactive contamination (above 20 mSv/year).
December 26	Rearrangement of restricted areas and areas where evacuation orders have been issued	When the safety of the power plant is ensured, the government rearranges the evacuation zones according to different thresholds. One year after the disaster, in March 2012, the cartography of evacuated areas becomes a patchwork of three different zones based on the cumulative annual dose of radiation exposure.

reference levels are based on "planned exposure situations" (1 mSv per year), "emergency exposure situations" (20 to 100 mSv for one year), and "existing exposure situations" (1 to 20 mSv per year, with 1 mSv per year as a long-term goal).[19] According to ICRP, reference levels are not scientific claims of safety or danger. Rather, they are used to guide protection measures while aiming to keep the magnitude of exposure "as

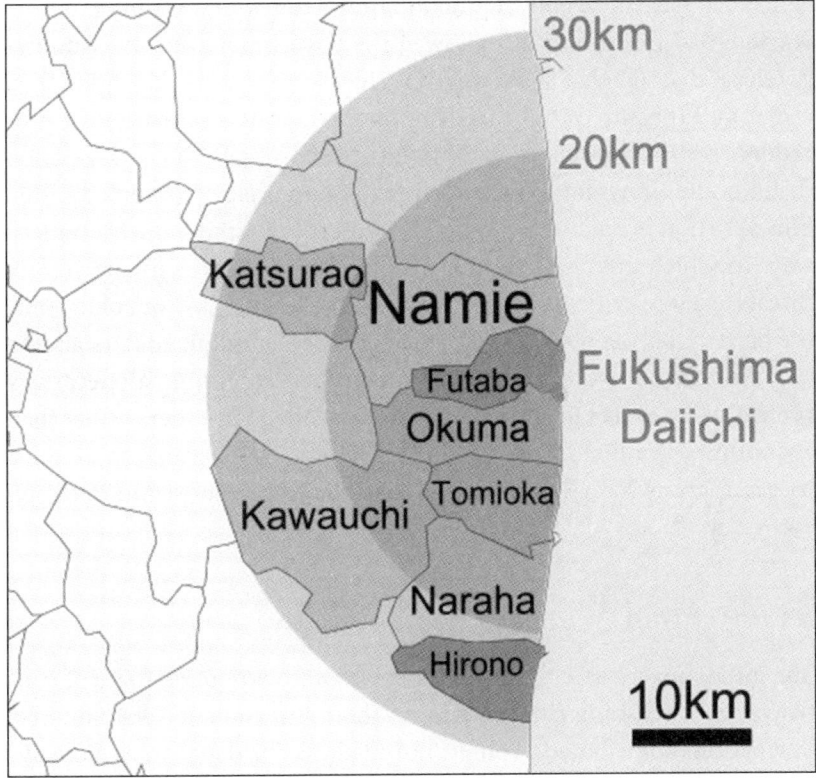

Figure 2.1. Initial evacuation zone. Map by Conrad Mayhew.

low as reasonably achievable, taking into account economic and societal factors."[20] Due to socioeconomic factors, ICRP argues that the "best option is not necessarily the one resulting in the lowest residual dose level for the individuals."[21] ICRP states that countries "generally cannot afford to lose a part of their territory, and most inhabitants generally prefer to stay in their homes rather than to be relocated (voluntarily or not) to non-contaminated areas."[22]

To better understand the dilemma of balancing risks and benefits, it is useful to consider the remarks of Prime Minister Naoto Kan, whose worst-case scenario included the possibility of fully evacuating Tokyo: "If 50 million people had to abandon their homes, leave their workplaces and their schools, and if patients had to leave their hospitals, there would have been many more victims during the evacuation, and Japan would not have been able to function fully as a nation for a long time."[23] A change of threshold thus allowed the government to avoid another potential disaster that some political elites saw as more damaging than radiation exposure. While this decision faced criticism, evacuation procedures are inseparable from an international system of risk regulation that literally allows for an increase in radiation pollution after a disaster. This situation is not unique to nuclear power but represents the modern ways in which nation-states govern pollution—by prioritizing certain threats as more critical to avoid than others.[24] In the case of Fukushima, the balance between risks and benefits shaped a unique understanding of long-term recovery by the government implementing "all necessary protective measures to allow people to continue to live there rather than abandoning [radioactive] areas."[25] The counterpart of this trade-off is that numerous individuals would "continue to be exposed to radiation every day."[26]

A Crisis of Trust

The initial governance of this disaster was not without its share of controversies, tarnishing citizens' trust in their government. First, multiple evacuations contributed to public unrest about the danger of radioactive contamination. The boundaries for evacuation became contested, especially when the US military recommended a much larger evacuation zone for its military and embassy staff.[27] Further anger ensued when the National Security Council of Japan, the Nuclear and Industrial Safety Agency (NISA), and MEXT failed to share the results of a high-tech system called SPEEDI, designed to predict the dispersion of radioactive contamination.[28] As a result, many citizens were evacuated to areas with higher levels of radiation exposure.[29] These incidents created an air of public suspicion of state experts.[30]

Additionally, the allowable threshold increase caused an uproar among the population, who criticized this decision as placing economic considerations over the well-being of vulnerable members of the population, like children and pregnant women.[31] Famously, Toshiso Kosako, an expert in radiation safety serving as the government's special advisor, resigned in protest of the 20 mSv increase. Bursting into tears on national television, he vocally decried the threshold as intolerable for children.[32] His resignation proved to be a "major blow to the government."[33] To rebuild civil trust, the government drastically altered its risk-communication strategies by notably choosing experts who supported its policy of increased threshold.[34] One such expert was Shun'ichi Yamashita, a medical doctor who became the radiation health risk management advisor of Fukushima Prefecture, as well as an advisor for Fukushima Medical University. In 2011, Dr. Yamashita became (in)famous for comments such as the following: "The effects of radiation do not come to people who are happy and laughing, they come to people who are weak-spirited" and "The people are suffering, not only because of the earthquake and the tsunami, but also from severe radiation anxiety, real radiophobia."[35] Dr. Yamashita faced worldwide criticism for his comments, as well as for his advice to not distribute iodine pills, which are used to reduce the amount of radioactive iodine taken into the thyroid.[36] Nonetheless, Dr. Yamashita's narrative was "compatible with government policy,"[37] since he attempted to lower panic and public disorder over concerns of radiation risks.[38] Increasingly, a specific regime of expertise became coproduced with political practices, resulting in a form of communication that produced reassuring messages around radiation hazards.

Health Effect of the Disaster

In the subsequent months and years that followed the disaster, experts like Dr. Yamashita announced that "the doses to a vast majority of the population in Fukushima were not high enough to expect to see any increase in the incidence of cancer and health effects in the future."[39] Similarly, many expert bodies asserted that the major sources of harm would result from psychological fears linked with radiation. As an official report from the Japan Cabinet Office explained, "In the short term, it is believed that the most serious and significant health effects of the nuclear accident will be related to mental health [*seishin eisei*] and social problems [*shakai fukushi*]."[40] International organizations echoed similar conclusions. For instance, the IAEA contended that "no early radiation induced health effects were observed among workers or members of

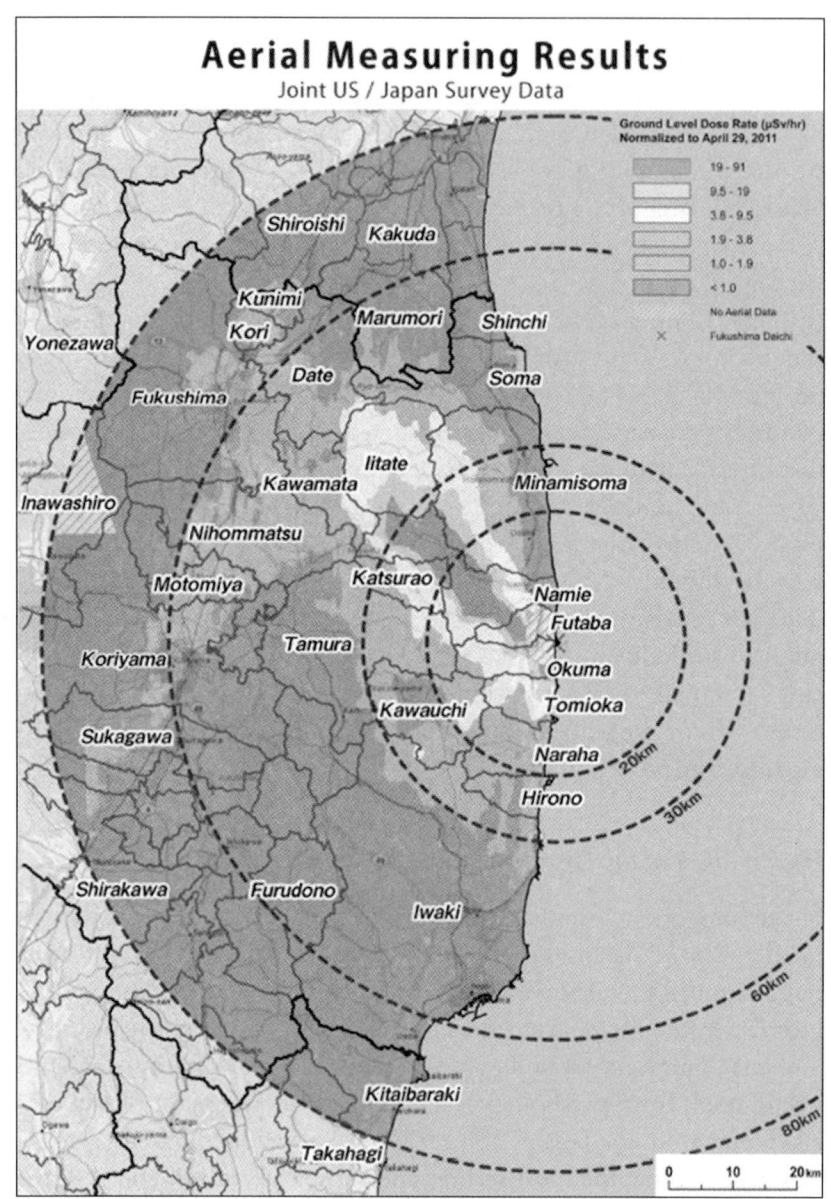

Figure 2.2. A map by the US Department of Energy showing the extent of radioactive contamination.

the public that could be attributed to the accident."⁴¹ A report from the United Nations Scientific Committee on the Effects of Atomic Radiation (UNSCEAR) similarly maintained that "no discernible increased incidence of radiation-related health effects are expected among exposed members of the public or their descendants."⁴² A health risk assessment produced by the World Health Organization (WHO) concluded that "outside the geographical areas most affected by radiation, even in locations within Fukushima Prefecture, the predicted risks remain low and no observable increases in cancer above natural variation in baseline rates are anticipated."⁴³ In the end, the most significant and far-reaching health effects were deemed to be on "mental and social well-being, related to the enormous impact of the earthquake, tsunami and nuclear accident, and the fear and stigma related to the perceived risk of exposure to ionizing radiation."⁴⁴

To monitor the potential long-term health effects of radiation exposure, the government launched a vast epidemiological study called the Fukushima Health Management Survey (*kenmin kenkō kanri chōsa*) (FHMS).⁴⁵ Its goal was to assess the health status of two million people, while providing long-term care.⁴⁶ Eventually, the survey led to the discovery of an increase of thyroid nodules and cysts among children aged eighteen or younger. By 2016, the survey diagnosed 113 children with malignancies, with surgical resection revealing "95 cases of papillary thyroid cancer."⁴⁷ While some experts explained this increase by radiation exposure, the state embraced another narrative, in which a "screening effect" led to the detection of thyroid cysts and nodules that would not otherwise have been discovered.⁴⁸ The survey concluded that it was "hard to believe that radioactivity had affected the population's health [*Hōshasen ni yoru kenkō higai ga aru to wa kangae nikui*]."⁴⁹ The state narrative of minimal risk was nonetheless challenged, most famously by the official report of the Fukushima Nuclear Accident Independent Investigation Commission, a commission set up by the Diet of Japan to investigate the causes of the disaster. The report recognized that "the residents in the affected area are still struggling to recover from the effects of the accident. They continue to face grave concerns, including the health effects of radiation exposure, the dissolution of families, disruption of their lives, and the environmental contamination of vast areas of land. Victims are still forced to live in shelters and no path to decontamination and restoration has been shown."[50]

Academics, NGOs, and independent organizations further criticized the safety narrative.[51] Scholars underscored the incomplete nature of data upon which expert risk assessments rested.[52] In many cases, the doses received by individuals were not empirically measured but calculated via computational models and then extrapolated to the whole population. They noted other shortcomings, such as the lack of dose assessment for citizens within the twenty-kilometer evacuation zone,[53] the absence of initial monitoring for internal contamination,[54] and the uncertainty surrounding the ingestion of contaminated food right after the disaster.[55] Due to such limitations, organizations like the Commission for Independent Research and Information about Radiation considered official assessments to be unrealistic.[56]

The groups also noted that the interpretation of radiation risks has been shaped by Cold War secrecy, as well as by the hegemonic standard set by the LSS, which has little to do with the risks faced during nuclear disasters. This legacy created skepticism toward scientific discourses that argue that radiation produces adverse health effects, particularly for ailments beyond cancer.[57] Some worry that the same legitimation of partial knowledge is happening after Fukushima.[58] They have also complained that the expert organizations that produced risk assessments and recommendations are not neutral arbiters of risk. For example, the Japanese Federation of Electric Power Companies lobbied ICRP to relax radiation protection standards.[59] The IAEA's main mission is to promote nuclear technologies,[60] while WHO is "bound by agreement not to publish anything concerning radiation without consent by the IAEA."[61] Even the Fukushima Medical University signed a memorandum of cooperation with IAEA.[62] This powerful network of shared expertise has created a strong consensus in defining the issue of radiation protection as "one of downplaying and managing risk to calm 'non-rational' public anxieties."[63] This partly explains why alternative narratives about health effects have failed to gather momentum internationally. The next section will examine how national politics further legitimized this regime of expertise within Japan.

Fukkō, or the Path Toward Revitalization

During the nuclear crisis, Prime Minister Naoto Kan governed Japan under a centrist political organization called the Democratic Party of Japan (DPJ). Amid a perceived lack of postdisaster leadership, Kan's approval rapidly tumbled, leading to his replacement by Yoshihiko Noda, another party member.[64] In 2012, the DPJ also lost the general election, leading Noda to announce his resignation. On December 26, Noda was replaced by Shinzo Abe of the LDP, a conservative and pro-nuclear party that previously had held majority control of the government uninterruptedly for almost forty years. While the politics of the DPJ attempted to manage the uncertainties of a nuclear crisis, Shinzo Abe inherited a Japan that was already post-Fukushima in outlook and no longer in a state of emergency. Abe's governance proved instrumental in promoting specific recovery policies that attempted to put the nuclear disaster behind Japan once and for all. The term favored by Abe's government was "*fukkō*" (revival, reconstruction, restoration), which evokes forward-thinking notions of revitalization and adaptation.[65]

Under Abe's management, the government's top priorities became the revitalization of Fukushima and more broadly of Japan. Pragmatically speaking, Abe's policies offered support to nuclear evacuees who wished to return to Fukushima. They also accelerated the reconstruction in the affected areas by promoting tourism, agriculture, and employment with socioeconomic incentives. A 2013 policy paper entitled *For Accelerating the Reconstruction of Fukushima from the Nuclear Disaster* epitomizes the importance placed on revitalization, stating that "the utmost efforts should be made for the reconstruction and revitalization of Fukushima after the nuclear disaster."[66] The policy underscores three principles: "(1) Back up Fukushima by offering support both for early return and for new lives; (2) Strengthen efforts for settling the accident at the Fukushima Daiichi Nuclear Power Station; (3) Accelerate the reconstruction of Fukushima after the nuclear disaster under the initiative of the national government."[67]

Shinzo Abe became well known for his "Abenomics," a series of 2012 economic policies that strove to restore Japan's economic competitiveness after the Triple Disaster.[68] This policy was crucial in shaping the understanding of "recovery" in Fukushima, which became dominated by socioeconomic considerations.⁶⁹ In 2013, Abe epitomized this economic enthusiasm when, during a successful pitch for Tokyo to host the 2020 Olympic Games, he argued that the situation at Fukushima was under control.⁷⁰ To facilitate recovery, the government also established the Reconstruction Agency (*fukkō-chō*) on February 10, 2012. As the principal apparatus of the government of Japan tasked with the reconstruction process of Fukushima, the agency acts as a "control tower" for all reconstruction efforts.⁷¹ Its function is to "accelerate structural reconstruction and revitalization in the affected areas by supporting the implementation of government policies and managing coordination of reconstruction strategy and initiatives between various branches of government at a national level and with local municipalities."⁷² According to a promotional video, five initiatives support the revitalization process: rebuilding homes and communities, reviving industries and livelihoods, supporting health and daily life, reconstructing and revitalizing Fukushima, and creating a new and more resilient Tōhoku, which is the northeast region of Japan where Fukushima is situated.⁷³

To learn more about the specifics around this initiative, I contacted Daisuke Tadanobu, an official of the Reconstruction Agency who was tasked with creating an "environment prompt for return" (*kaeru kankyō*) for the citizens of Fukushima. During our interview, Tadanobu explained that the state's revitalization efforts were currently hampered by the persistence of "harmful rumors" around radiation risks. These rumors, he argued, had created the avoidance of food products, as well as a decrease of tourism in Fukushima. In talking about the "harmful rumors," Tadanobu used the term "*fūhyō higai*." Consisting of "*fūhyō*"—which means "rumor or gossip"—and "*higai*"—which means "damage, injury, or harm"—the notion of a "harmful rumor" quickly became a staple of the politics of revitalization. As Tomiko Yamaguchi explained, "The government definition of *fuhyohigai* focuses on the damage done to businesses providing commodities or services in Fukushima, but does not identify precisely who is responsible for creating problems."⁷⁴ As she explained, the term underscores the "idea that someone is victimised or harmed by the rumours, and a concomitant implication that those who participate in the rumour-mongering are perpetrating harm."⁷⁵ The definition of "*fūhyō higai*" is highly nebulous and falls within what Swyngedouw calls the "postpolitical" enemy par excellence, where the target of concern is "always vague, ambiguous, unnamed and uncounted and, ultimately, empty."[76] When I asked Tadanobu for concrete examples of *fūhyō higai*, he handed me a pamphlet entitled *Eliminating Negative Reputation Impact*. However, the pamphlet did not contain any definition or examples of the nature of the rumors in question (for instance, it did not argue that radiation levels below 20 mSv/year were safe, nor that claiming the contrary was a case of harmful rumor).

The absence of guidelines as to what exactly constitutes a harmful rumor deserves more attention. While the term echoes a supposedly "irrational" fear of radiation, it differs from the notion of "radiophobia," which was historically framed as a "mental health issue."[77] Rather, the notion of *fūhyō higai* frames radiation hazards as a socioeconomic issue, where refusing to partake in Fukushima's commodities and services is akin to victimization. In this context, individuals who highlight narratives of radioactive contamination are depicted as lacking compassion for those who attempt to revitalize their region. By not providing the exact characteristics that constitute a harmful rumor, this concept successfully bypasses the scientific controversies surrounding low-dose exposure, transforming radiation harm into an issue that needs to be tackled through more than biological expertise.

Five Years Since the Nuclear Disaster

How did this peculiar understanding of recovery informed by *fūhyō higai* influence the expert framing of Fukushima at the crossroads of the disaster's fifth-year anniversary? To answer this question, I turn to two major symposia given in 2016: the Fukushima Medical University International Symposium: Five Years Since the Great East Japan Earthquake, Tsunami, and Nuclear Crisis and the International Symposium Disaster Management and Recovery for Children and Communities,[78] which was already mentioned at the beginning of this chapter. Both symposia happened in Fukushima Prefecture, involved the participation of major international organizations like IAEA, ICRP, WHO, or UNSCEAR, had numerous panels of experts, and were endorsed by local and national governments. In what follows, I provide a summary of the analysis employed in discussions of radiation hazards. I also highlight what counted as expertise, what kinds of disciplines were prioritized, and who was invited to official risk-communication symposia. Much like the official politics of revitalization, the symposia's expert panels had moved beyond narratives of damaged biology to stress posttraumatic disorders, reputational damages, and discriminatory practices as the "major" culprits of this disaster.

Anxiety, Depression, and Posttraumatic Stress Disorder (PTSD)

During the symposia, numerous experts regularly claimed that anxiety about radiation risks had resulted in family disintegration, the disappearance of confidence toward the government, and a feeling of loss of control within one's daily life. For instance, one panelist explained that mothers living in Fukushima were so concerned about radiation that they forbade children from playing outside. As the symposia experts explained, this decision added needless discomfort to children attempting to cope with the disaster. During one conference, a kindergarten teacher shared her experiences, explaining that children had become afraid (*kowai*) of nature (*shizen*) and that it was now perceived as something bad (*dame*). She emphasized that children had started to kill insects when playing outside—something that did not happen before the accident. As she explained, "Children are still unsettled after this disaster. They don't speak much, are demotivated, and demonstrate anger by biting and scratching at things." To make her point, the kindergarten teacher showed different pictures drawn by children. The paintings were dark, scary, and seemed to reveal high levels of anxiety. One panel of experts from Fukushima Medical University similarly explained that radiation-related anxiety had brought health problems of its own. Because of Fukushima's children staying inside too much, their physical abilities were purportedly underdeveloped, and many had scored poorly on the national physical ability test.

Discrimination

Marginalization of Fukushima's citizens was a recurrent theme of the symposia. According to many speakers, a gnawing fear of contamination had resulted in questionable practices toward the forced evacuees, which included bigotry, employment discrimination, and a refusal to marry those from the affected regions. These forms of discrimination further complicated evacuees' recovery. In that regard, the Nagasaki Association of Hibakusha's Medical Care had notably endorsed the Fukushima Medical University International Symposium, seeing echoes of the historical practices of discrimination against *hibakusha*. Following World War II, *hibakusha* suffered many social repercussions because of their "tainted" status, which included hardships when attempting to find employment, difficulty in getting married, and the fear of mutation in children—situations that mirrored what was happening in Fukushima. As a result, experts worried that a dark chapter of Japan's history was now repeating itself. Through this lens, radiation hazard was framed as a form of harmful discrimination based on historical misunderstanding and prejudice.

Reputational Damage

Beyond PTSD and discrimination practices, a major challenge of the disaster concerned reputational damage, especially regarding food production. After the disaster, people throughout Japan stopped consuming foods from Fukushima because of the fear associated with potential contamination. To promote the revival of agricultural industries, panelists explained, food produced in Fukushima was regularly tested and deemed safe for consumption. Much as in the state narrative, experts deplored the fact that harmful rumors and stigmatization were affecting rural production as well as local fisheries. One panelist argued that people who refused to eat food in 2015 were "still stuck in the mentality of 2011."

Miscommunication as Hazards

In contrast to autocratic leadership, many panelists deplored the authoritative nature of earlier state-sponsored communications, which had resulted in creating a gap between state experts and the population. For instance, a clinical endocrinologist involved in the thyroid ultrasound examination of children argued that poor communication about radiation exposure had created tremendous anxiety. She criticized the "impersonal" character of communication associated with FHMS, claiming that monitoring procedures created unwarranted stress for children. Since the risk of radiation appeared low, panelists argued for more appropriate forms of risk communication. As a local mayor in Fukushima claimed during the Soma Symposium, "We test the water, we tell them that it is safe, but there are still some people who refuse to drink it. We need a new environment for safety." Others lamented the presence of a strong taboo around radioactive contamination, leading panelists to argue for the need to create a welcoming place to address the topic of radiation (*hanashiaeru basho*). Experts also warned against a heavy focus on numerical values, which risked alienating citizens by providing hard-to-understand metrics. One panelist belonging to ICRP further explained that there was no point in starting explanations about radiation risks in terms of Sieverts, since these notions are foreign to the experiences of affected individuals.

People as Expert

A popular trope of the symposia was the need to move beyond the "top-down" governance approach that had characterized the earlier stage of disaster management. Panelists instead promoted the need to create "dialogue" between experts and citizens, stating that the former needed to learn from the latter. This approach echoed the etymology of the word "expert," which stems from the Latin "*expertuse*," meaning "I have experienced."[79] Panelists spoke about the importance of creating a "co-expertise with the population" while inviting them to share their postdisaster experience. This mobilization of citizen voices was apparent during a presentation entitled "*shimin no minasan kara no messāji*" (A Message from the Part of Every Citizen), in which a young mother from Fukushima conveyed her postdisaster journey:

> I just couldn't keep going. Moving from place to place after the disaster. Going back and forth between our house and the temporary housing. I couldn't continue the life of an evacuee, so I finally decided to return to Fukushima in the affected areas. At the beginning, I decided to take measurements near my home and the results that I saw were quite high: 3, 5, or even 30 μSv/hour. My family and I went on to decontaminate the house. We removed everything by ourselves. We've cut the trees, scraped

off the topsoil [of the garden], and cut some more trees. After all the emotional turmoil, I came to realize that living with your family members is the origin of happiness. I know that my children have been exposed to radiation during that time, but since they have a good metabolism, they can probably eliminate radioactive material from their body quite fast. I don't know if my children will face some problems in the future, but the world is full of other risks like food additives. Decontamination is not the most important thing for Fukushima. Now I've stopped measuring radiation levels. I think that with a lot of hugs it's going to be fine!

During the question-and-answer period, the mother explained that she did not disregard the impact of radiation, but that she wanted to transmit a message about what matters the most for the well-being of her children. While her experience undoubtedly is a legitimate narrative about the postdisaster recovery, it also represents a carefully selected discourse that suits the politics of revitalization. As Brian Wynne observes, "Deliberately or not, *invited* public involvement nearly always imposes a frame which already implicitly imposes normative commitments—an implicit politics—as to what is salient and what is not salient."[80] By inviting a former evacuee who "understood" that radiation exposure is not the prime factor of concern in recovery, the symposium promoted a specific distribution of the sensible around radiation-related behaviors, wherein anxiety (*fuan*) was more harmful than contamination. In the end, "A Message from the Part of *Every* Citizen" reinforced precise ways of speaking about the disaster. Those who argued for different understandings of recovery, such as mothers advocating for permanent evacuation, were nowhere to be heard.

Recoding the Narrative

Disasters resurface with periodicity, especially if they are framed around anniversary stories.[81] The official commemoration of a catastrophe is often the occasion to reshape collective memories or to imbue crises with new symbolic meanings.[82] Happening on the cusp of the five-year anniversary, the symposia became occasions to structure a novel narrative around the disaster by notably underscoring the persistent socioeconomic impacts of the nuclear catastrophe. These efforts are noteworthy, as such symposia created much-needed platforms for civilian voices, in contrast to the authoritative pronouncements of earlier state governance that disregarded them—especially when one considers the historical disregard of PTSD associated with nuclear disasters.

At the same time, these symposia were largely in the business of building a consensual narrative, where revitalization implied improvements for living conditions *in* Fukushima. Expert panels also shared an agreed-upon vision around radiation harm by overlooking the existence of controversies within low-dose exposure. For example, a physician present in the audience of the Soma Symposium tentatively tried to give his viewpoint on the increase of thyroid cancers, arguing that noticeable changes had happened since the disaster. But this "uninvited" form of public engagement was quickly brushed aside by the chair of the panel, who stated that "we have much more precise technologies now, so that explains why we have so many cases of thyroid cancer!"

On this matter, Sharon Stephens argues that a post-Chernobyl culture of radiation protection has resulted in "increasingly vigorous expert assertions concerning the solid scientific grounds for current policies and the expert control over areas of uncertainty."[83] Similarly, post-Fukushima symposia were not in the business of delving into areas of uncertainties and rarely provided detailed explanations about the more troublesome aspects of radiation exposure. Areas of certainty trumped the uncertainty of a subject that is still controversial (as well as historically bounded with secrecy and ignorance). Nevertheless, symposia did not merely restate expert-based claims of minimal radiological risks. They also provided a novel template for the recodification of this disaster narrative. By moving beyond tropes of urgency, uncertainty, or biological damages, symposia created the narrative of a *second* disaster, this time epitomized by PTSD, reputational damage, and ongoing discriminatory practices. Within this view, it appears that prejudice was the main hazard affecting Fukushima. Radiation? Not so much.

Othering Expertise

The fifth-year anniversary of Fukushima underscored an important shift in expertise, which changed from attempts to curb civilian panics to socioeconomic support for the revitalization of the region. But what happened to experts going against this distribution of the sensible? To answer this question, I draw from semistructured interviews with recognized experts in medicine and epidemiology. More precisely, I examine how a politics of revitalization hampered certain expert narratives from gaining authoritativeness in the official sphere, thereby creating powerful practices of "othering."[84] My analysis culminates in attention to how cultural forces have enabled, stabilized, and challenged the notion of expertise within Japanese society, leading to a unique form of social pressure and scientific ostracization.

"Radioactivity Is Not a *Fūhyō Higai*, It's a *Jitsugai!*"

Taking a set of slides from her nearby drawer, Dr. Haruko Kaneko began to explain the phenomenon of radiation harm to me: "Basically, the energy of radiation is stronger than the chemical bonds of our DNA. This energy easily produces complex double strand breaks in DNA. The cells, in trying to repair themselves from such harm, end up being more prone to making mistakes in their regeneration. This brings mutations and genomic instability. What you have is an accumulation of mutations that can end up causing cancer, even years after the exposure."

The former chief director of an important scientific institute in Japan, Dr. Kaneko was initially shocked by the state's decision to raise the acceptable level of radiation exposure by twenty times. As a physician specializing in radiation and cancer, she considered that this decision was based on economic motives rather than medical ones.

> I really don't understand what the government is thinking; it's just crazy [*kangaekata shinjirarenai, kurējī*]. Even now, the limit of radiation exposure is stricter in the medical domain than for this disaster; it makes no sense! As a scientist, I am really concerned about the potential health effects. The government has criticized the medical community by saying that we are "overdoing" it and that we are looking to scare people. . . . That's not our goal; we are simply explaining the basis of radioactivity's potential harm. The state keeps talking about the harmful influence of stress. Of course stress does play a part, but its harmfulness is nothing in comparison to radiation damage!

Dr. Kaneko was not a lone wolf in emphasizing the tropes of damaged biology. During my fieldwork, I heard similar arguments given by Dr. Rin Fujio, the medical director of a major hospital in the Greater Tokyo Area region. After Fukushima, Dr. Fujio had formed an association of doctors who opposed the increase of 20 mSv per year. Having done intensive thyroid screenings on children in Fukushima, Kanagawa, Tokyo, Ibaraki, and Chiba, Dr. Fujio also served as the caretaker of family associations affected by thyroid cancers. Like Dr. Kaneko, she believed that repatriating evacuees to Fukushima was a dangerous decision and contended that pregnant women, young girls, and children should permanently relocate to safer areas (*betsu no basho*). Kaneko and Fujio spoke of strong concerns around the danger of internal contamination, a subject that was seldom discussed in official symposia. For instance, Dr. Kaneko expressed worries about strontium-90, a radionuclide that mimics calcium, enters bone marrow, and weakens the immune system. Similarly, Dr. Fujio stressed the adverse health effects of ingesting radionuclides and remained unconvinced of the current standards for food consumption (100 Bq/kg). As she explained, "For old people, the 100 Bq/kg threshold might be all right, but for the young or pregnant women there can be risks. Even if the levels are low, they tend to accumulate in the body, and while some muscles might eventually expel some of the contaminants, other body parts don't. For example, radioactive cesium can enter the ovaries (*ransō*) of women and stay there without getting expelled; that's a risk that can be transmitted to the child and the future generations."

By insisting that their knowledge as physicians qualified them to criticize the state policy of radiation thresholds, medical doctors attempted to shift disaster governance toward their area of expertise: the body. Kaneko and Fujio repeatedly stressed how it could take decades for bodily ailments to develop while underscoring the transgenerational effects of radiation dangers, which warranted different recovery measures for them. By depicting bodies as sites of potentially damaged biology, they brought a different temporality to the distribution of the sensible, contradicting the state narrative of revitalization that emphasized past and current ailments (e.g., anxiety, fear, and discrimination).

Despite their qualifications, promoting a discourse of damaged biology was not without consequences. Dr. Kaneko claimed that her institute initially released a statement on its scientists' behalf, aimed at silencing internal conflict about radiation risks. When she became involved in an important study on radiation risks, superiors complained that her scientific opinion was "inconvenient" (*futsugō*) and threatened to terminate her research budget. As she shared to me, "This was a lot of pressure [*sugoku puresshā datta*]!" Dr. Kaneko complained that within the official narrative of minimal radiation risks, speaking of damaged biology was enough to warrant charges of spreading harmful rumors. In fact, both doctors were baffled by the use of "*fūhyō higai*." A perplexed Dr. Fujio once said to me, "The government keeps saying that Fukushima is suffering from 'harmful rumors' [*fūhyō higai*]. Why do they call it that way? Radioactivity is not a harmful rumor; it's a real harm [*jitsugai*]! There are true risks, the soil is still extremely contaminated."

Importantly, the notion of harmful rumors does not rely on whether experts like Dr. Kaneko or Dr. Fujio are scientifically right or wrong. *Fūhyō higai* is not concerned with science per se. Rather, it is used to govern "affective force[s] of shame and guilt,"[85] by painting certain individuals as "thoughtless, traitorous, and discriminatory."[86] As such, *fūhyō higai* is not about the slippery problem of scientific facts with regard to controversies around low-dose radiation but a problem of social behaviors and attitudes, in which certain discourses lack empathy and moral compassion for the victim of the disasters. In this context, scientific claims of damaged biologies are perceived as further increasing anxiety, discrimination, and marginalization, since they harm the financial recovery of Fukushima, the agricultural revival of the region, and the mental health of its residents. In contrast to radiophobia, which is considered a mental health issue and therefore an *individual* problem, the notion of *fūhyō higai* is a *collective* issue inseparable from a politics of revitalization that emphasizes socioeconomic factors as the prime issue of recovery. The very nature of *fūhyō higai* consequently enables the state to bypass scientific claims that do not fit with their politics of revitalization, even when such claims are produced by medical experts. By governing radiation under this form, certain expert narratives are rendered "inconvenient" (*futsugō*) instead of scientifically erroneous.

Against accusations of harmful rumors, medical doctors agreed that the debate around radiation risks had unfortunately become a political battle in lieu of a scientific one. Many deplored the fact that official risk symposia invited scientists whose views fell squarely within state policies rather than for their actual expertise on radiological science. As Dr. Kaneko critically observed, "There are a lot of scientists who are saying that the situation at Fukushima is all right, but they don't even have the slightest basis of knowledge on DNA damage!" One informant pointed to the example of Prof. Hayano, a theoretical physicist with an expertise in antimatter. In the aftermath of the disaster, Hayano had promulgated radiation information in a series of popular tweets, leading him to become an important public figure in state-sponsored symposia. While Hayano did not possess expertise in medicine, he nevertheless coauthored a much-downloaded paper that argued for minimal radiation harm.[87] At the International Symposium Disaster Management and Recovery for Children and Communities, he gave a speech entitled "Empowering the Young: Radioprotection in Fukushima." In his talk, he restated claims that radiation exposure was not particularly high and championed the empowerment of young people by having them involved in radiological protection. Beyond his participation in revitalization symposia, Hayano played a major role in communicating radiological risks, while conducting studies that were "used by the central and local governments as references to support policy making."[88] Years after this study, Hayano and his colleagues were accused of having drastically underestimated the radiation doses of affected individuals in Fukushima, reporting only one third of their actual levels.[89] The error was pointed out by Shin'ichi Kurokawa, a professor emeritus with the High Energy Accelerator Research Organization. In an article that probes this controversy, Kurokawa raises doubts about Hayano's data, hinting that he hid a "clear correlation between the external and internal doses with some residents showing internal exposure measurements of several thousand Bq even since 2015."[90]

As an anthropologist, my task is not to adjudicate among the nitty-gritty details of this controversy, which transcends my field of expertise. Nor am I advocating for a shift of expertise toward more sustained tropes of damaged biology, which are also problematic.[91] What I rather wish to highlight is how the politics of revitalization drastically shaped the regime of expertise that came to dominate official risk communication. This coproduction of expertise and politics resulted in creating a sharp dichotomy between scientists whose narrative supported a state-approved vision of disaster recovery and scientists whose critical view on Fukushima put them at odds with the government. Unsurprisingly, the latter group was pushed aside from official communication channels. Despite the expertise that people like Dr. Kaneko or Dr. Fujio possessed, I never once saw them speak in state-sponsored symposia. Their stories strikingly echoed the same politicization of expertise that followed Japan's postwar nuclearization, where nuclear engineers worked in parallel with nation-state priorities to successfully rebuff forms of expertise that were disruptive to its goals. In the aftermath of this disaster, expertise, much like radiation, also had its own half-life.

A Disaster Made in Japan?

Having booked numerous interviews with medical doctors, I initially expected to be lectured on the science of radiation harms. To my surprise, almost no informants spent time debating the subject. What grabbed my attention was how many experts constantly reinscribed the governance of this disaster within stereotypical notions of Japanese culture. For instance, Dr. Kaneko criticized the sheep mentality of her colleagues, claiming that "Japanese only move when they have an order from above" (*ue kara meirei sarete ugoiteiru*). Similar views were shared by Dr. Tatsuya Inaba, an epidemiologist who had criticized the state discourse of radiological safety. Although his research was published in a top international scientific journal, Dr. Inaba told me that he faced the wrath of state experts, who notably accused him of promoting erroneous findings that were not in accordance with the prevailing state-sanctioned outlook. Obviously shocked by such an attack, Dr. Inaba unsuccessfully tried to open a conversation with state experts, but to no avail: "These people don't even want to discuss matters with me! Simply because I have an opposite opinion. . . . Japanese don't debate [*giron*]. There's no dialogue or argument in the scientific community. When you go to a scientific lecture, most people simply say, 'Thank you very much for such an interesting presentation!' while bowing a lot. . . . If you have a different opinion, there's not much discussion that you can do. That's a sad culture for the world of science." Dr. Inaba deplored a culture of expertise that promoted allegiance to one's camp and the ostracization of dissenters, echoing the work of psychologist Takeo Doi, who described how groups exist in "concentric circles" without any interpenetration among them.⁹²

The "negative" impacts of Japanese culture on the governance of this disaster were further stressed when I interviewed Dr. Natsume, a professor of medicine and health policy based in Tokyo. Dismissing my initial questions about potential radiation risks, Dr. Natsume instead explained that Fukushima was caused by a Japanese desire for conformity, resulting in dysfunctional outcomes in the energy sectors. He argued that a culture of groupism, highly promoted by a normative preference for hierarchy and harmony (*wa*), had permeated the bureaucracy and scientific culture of the country. As he stressed, it was this that had expedited the culture of collusion in nuclear security: "In Japan, order works by structure, while in other countries order works more by function. Group thinking is not something uniquely Japanese, but we are more prone to it. We are even proud of this culture! Think for example of Japanese social system norms, such as lifetime employment in the same organization, seniority-based promotion before meritocracy, or even about *amakudari* [the revolving door between politics and business sectors]." For this medical expert, groupism had forbidden dissent, hampered transparency, and impeded accountability around nuclear security: "In such context, you're not able to say your opinion, you become obedient. . . . If you move outside of your group you'll be stigmatized!" Dr. Natsume further highlighted the downfall of a promising state policy called the Act on Promotion of Support Measures for the Lives of Disaster Victims to Protect and Support Children and Other Residents Suffering Damage due to the Tokyo Electric Power Company's Nuclear Accident (Act no. 48). On paper, the act provides freedom of choice for the victims of the nuclear disaster, such as the ability to permanently evacuate. However, this policy was never implemented, and the government quickly attempted to lift evacuation orders for the upcoming Tokyo Olympics. For Dr. Natsume, this choice emanated from the normative Japanese culture of group thinking: "We know that the government discourse makes no sense, but have you ever heard anyone complaining? Have you seen an attorney general coming forward? Have you seen the media talk about that? No one has moved. Why?" At the end of our interview, Dr. Natsume contended that the whole governance of this disaster had been staged and performed for mere political correctness. "It's a kabuki theater!" he bitterly said.

In the academic jargon, their discourse is known as "*Nihonjinron*" or "theories on Japaneseness." As Yoshikuni Igarashi explains, "*Nihonjinron* makes totalizing, essentialist claims regarding the unique quality of Japanese culture and distinguishes the Japanese from all other peoples."[93] In anthropology, *nihonjinron* has faced considerable criticism as a set of ideologies that downplay cultural diversity while defining Japanese people in standardized ways.[94] Most famously, *nihonjinron*-based explanations have appeared on the first pages of the *Official Report of the Fukushima Nuclear Accident Independent Investigation Commission*, which stated that "what must be admitted—very painfully—is that this was a disaster 'Made in Japan.' Its fundamental causes are to be found in the ingrained conventions of Japanese culture: our reflexive obedience; our reluctance to question authority; our devotion to 'sticking with the program'; our groupism; and our insularity."[95]

In line with *nihonjinron* criticism, scholars have criticized this report for providing cultural explanations that appear to dodge issues of accountability. As historian Naoko Shimazu explains, "Bringing out the 'made in Japan' argument is not helpful. It panders to the uniqueness idea and does not explain, but rather reinforces, existing stereotypes. Moreover, the supposedly Japanese qualities that the report outlines, such as obedience, reluctance to question authority, 'sticking with the programme' and insularity, are not at all unique to Japan, but are universal qualities in all societies."[96]

As a scholar of Japan, I agree with Shimazu, but at the same time deplore the fact that anthropologists might be unable to probe cultural issues without facing accusations of cultural determinism. As Yoshikuni Igarashi remarks in this regard, "It has today become almost obligatory both in the United States and Japan to disavow any claim of Japanese uniqueness if one wishes to claim a critical stance in the study of Japan."[97] For anthropologists, who shine in putting cultural specificity to the forefront, disavowing cultural factors is not only paradoxical but harmful to the discipline. Rather than brushing aside cultural discourses as irrelevant, I believe that the use of *nihonjinron* theories deserves more sustained attention. To be clear, I am not interested in understanding whether a so-called cultural desire for conformity explains the source of this disaster. Rather, I believe that the tropes of *nihonjinron* contribute to understanding the politics of expertise that surrounds Fukushima.

Importantly, the *nihonjinron* discourse employed by medical doctors should not be understood as a false consciousness on their part. Instead, such tropes are also strategies that enable medical experts to talk about the disaster in ways that might not otherwise be viewed as acceptable within Japanese society. As seen in the previous chapter, Japanese scientists criticizing nuclear power were historically labeled as unpatriotic individuals, while being shut off from major power centers. As the experiences of Dr. Kaneko, Fujio, and Inaba exemplify, something similar is occurring for those who speak about the risk of radiation. Criticizing a politics of revitalization has resulted in numerous difficulties, ranging from scientific ostracism to threats of funding cuts. In this context, mobilizing cultural discourses is a way to indirectly critique the governance of this disaster, rather than pointing fingers at specific political parties, scientific institutions, or corporate lobbies, which can result in both concrete and more abstract backlash. For the experts whom I interviewed, the narrow-minded framework of state bureaucracy was a much more virulent pathogen than radioactivity itself.

Drawing from the work of Dorinne Kondo, the discourse of *nihonjinron* is revealing when analyzed as a form of cultural talk embedded in a peculiar system of power relations.[98] As she explains, culture is "no reified thing or system, but a meaningful way of being in the world."[99] Igarashi argues that hegemonic ideologies like *nihonjinron* are thus better understood as historical realities that have everyday effects.[100] The appearance of *fūhyō higai*, which labels certain practices and discourses as "discriminatory," precisely relies on Japanese cultural pressure. Whether this *nihonjinron*-imbued discourse "represents" Japanese culture is beyond the point. What matters is that it creates a strong normative pressure, which Igarashi summarized as "behave like a Japanese if you are one."[101] In the case of Fukushima, this implies that proper expertise ought to support a politics of revitalization. As much as postwar nuclear expertise was put at the service of creating a strong nation-state, a post-Fukushima expertise was now at the service of revitalizing Fukushima.

The issue of *nihonjinron* reinforces the claim that expertise is coproduced with politics, and that the texture of politics is invariably shaped by unique cultural pressures. It is perhaps no surprise that Dr. Natsume compared the governance of this disaster with a dramatic performance unique to Japan: the *kabuki* theater. *Kabuki* is characterized by a focus on style rather than substance, and I cannot think of a better analogy to describe the politics of expertise after Fukushima. In the end, this chapter has demonstrated how state politics has drastically influenced the kind of expert narratives that guided recovery after Fukushima. In turn, this same expertise further reinforced a specific politics of revitalization, with the consequence of rendering certain forms of harms and certain discourses as more important than others. Experts who brought alternative claims toward hazards and recovery, such as those who stressed the biological dangers of radiation, have been unsuccessful in countering the official disaster narrative. Against the background of such epistemic battles, the next chapter analyzes how citizens dissatisfied with state experts mobilized knowledge about radiation to paint yet another representation of the disaster.

3

The Rise of Citizen Science

An elderly man once summed up the central challenge posed by radiation hazards: "With a knife you understand where the pain is coming from, but not with radiation." Against the intangibility of radiation, an array of grassroot movements began to rapidly confront the risks of residual radioactivity in the years following the disaster. Activities like radiation tracking, food monitoring, and scientific workshops organized by local organizations or in community centers ultimately led to the creation of what is now called "citizen science" (*shimin kagakusha*).

The phenomenon of citizen science existed before Fukushima, as well as beyond Japan. The origin of the term can be traced to the participatory engagement of civil society in scientific matters formerly reserved to a limited circle of experts. In the United States, a well-known example is the Cornell Lab of Ornithology, where members of the public partner with professional scientists to compile data on bird species.[1] In this context, citizen science is a form of cooperation between different actors.[2] It raises public awareness of science and fills in the gaps in state responses, leading to innovative forms of governance.[3] But citizen science also refers to alternative spaces of knowledge that have less to do with hand-in-hand cooperation and more to do with issues of public contestations, resistance, and mistrust. For instance, citizen scientists can collect data on environmental dangers to challenge claims of formal expertise associated with the state.[4] In these instances, citizen science resists a normalizing force.[5] It evokes a science that "assists the needs and concerns of citizens" and that is "developed and enacted by citizens themselves."[6]

In post-Fukushima Japan, most cases of citizen science fell within the latter definition, as data produced by citizen scientists led individuals to criticize state governance. I first witnessed this in a small citizen-science center based in Tokyo, where I encountered an array of technical devices that measured the level of radioactivity in different food samples. Over time, staff members of this center had taken on the responsibility of measuring contamination. They knew exactly the kinds of foods prone to radioactive contamination, like the sea cucumber (*namako*) or the sea weed (*wakame*). Taking a sample of food for testing, the director of the establishment shared that "so far postdisaster governance has been questionable at best. . . . All we want from our government is the truth and then we'll choose what is best for us! Their administration [*gyōsei*] [of this disaster] is scarier than radioactivity!"

Civic distrust toward the government was a recurrent pattern in my interviews with citizen scientists. Their discontent was often directed against scientists who worked for the state or for nuclear organizations. Many accused these experts of being "*goyō gakusha*," a derogative term that means "lapdog" or "government-patronized scholars."[7] As one citizen explained to me, "A lot of them are working for the nuclear lobbies [*genshiryoku mura*]. There's this guy, Shun'ichi Yamashita. He's a scientist for the government and he claimed that 'if one laughs, then radiation is not scary' [*waratte ireba hōshanō wa kowakunai*]. And that's what the government calls an expert!? This man is not an expert—he's a murderer [*satsujin*]!"

This vitriol echoes what Vincent Ialenti calls the "deflation of expertise"—a time characterized by global skepticism against expert-vetted knowledge and scientific authority.[8] Within this broader context, citizen science reveals a new facet of the governance of radiation hazards, especially when experts are perceived as failing societal needs. Against this background, this chapter looks at the factors that have led to a crisis of trust as well as a rise in citizen science. It examines how Japanese citizens produce data on radioactive contamination and whether citizen science successfully challenged a politics of revitalization.

Citizen Science After Fukushima

In the aftermath of Fukushima, Aya Kimura reminds us, the emergence of citizen science was not driven by a "single ideological conviction."[9] Rather, citizen science emerged from "people with various backgrounds, with varying motivations, and both with and without prior social movement experience and connections to existing organizations."[10] To further unpack her point, it is useful to deconstruct the categories of *citizen* and *science*. The notion of citizen does not represent a homogenous group, as "citizens" (*shimin*) differ widely in terms of gender, age, occupation, or political positions. These factors strongly influence who engages in citizen science, how science around dangers is mobilized, and how the same data can be interpreted differently. As Alan Irwin reminds us, the same holds true for the term "science." Its meaning ranges from visions of independent knowledge to a mere tool for assessing threats.[11] As I came to learn during fieldwork, different definitions of science (*kagaku*) could strategically be mobilized to fit the needs of different citizens.

Due to the range of grassroots actions involved in citizen science, this chapter targets a small spectrum of actors: Japanese mothers who have voluntarily evacuated from Fukushima and who became embedded in the realm of citizen science. Employing an ethnographical approach, I follow the story of one voluntary evacuee, a mother named Natsuo Amano, whose experience forms the primary analytical framework of this chapter. I use her background to highlight the numerous changes that citizens faced after the disaster, demonstrating how they lost trust in the government and reached toward citizen science as a means for agency. Amano's story, while unique, evokes the experiences of many citizens: Before the disaster she did not know anything about radiation, was not an activist, and had few reasons to doubt the expertise of state actors. Still, I do not simply center on Amano per se but use her story as a connective thread where other actors—ranging from scientists to lawyers—graft themselves onto her life. In doing so, I examine how she became embedded in a network of concerned citizens who attempted to evacuate children from Fukushima via the mobilization of scientific narratives and legal practices. My data was collected through interviews and from participant observation around Amano's attempts to rationalize the threats engendered by residual radioactivity. These included scientific workshops, radioactive tracking, food monitoring, public protests, and trial hearings for the evacuation of children.

In exploring the role that Japanese mothers play in assessing radiation risks, I draw on the work of scholars who focus on food monitoring. For instance, Sternsdorff-Cisterna examines how trust in the government was eroded when citizen scientists found contaminated food deemed safe by the government.[12] In this context, he argues that citizen science is an alternative route to state protection that creates a "sense of trustworthiness (*anshin*) in the production, consumption, and circulation of food."[13] Similarly, Kimura underscores the scientific enterprise of mothers embedded in citizen science, while highlighting the harsh social sanctions these actors have faced in testing food for radiation.[14]

My fieldwork with voluntary evacuees demonstrates another facet of citizen science. In contrast to the case of Sternsdorff-Cisterna, the results that citizens like Amano gathered were used to highlight the *dangers* of residual radiation. In other words, citizen science was not employed to create a feeling of safety (*anshin*) but was mobilized to promote permanent evacuation. Secondly, while I agree with Kimura that "radicalization through food politics did not take place in post-Fukushima Japan," I want to theorize a broader understanding of what counts as successful political action.[15] Drawing from the works of Dorinne Kondo, I argue that "resistance need not be seen as radical rupture or apocalyptic change in order to be effective."[16] While Kimura acknowledges that citizen scientists have sometimes "sought to do politics by science,"[17] her work highlights the structural factors that constrained the politics of citizen scientists. I pick up where she left off and examine how citizen science can sustain tropes of evacuation against a politics of revitalization that attempts to repatriate evacuees to Fukushima.

Natsuo Amano's Story

In a small coffee shop near downtown Shinjuku in 2016, Natsuo Amano ended our conversation by saying, "There's a giant incinerator burning decontamination waste near my home in Fukushima. . . . Ashes are falling on people's clothes, and when I made my concerns known to the local officials, I was told that I shouldn't worry, as they use special filters. . . . But honestly, how can you live in such conditions?" She no longer had the energy she had had two hours earlier at the beginning of our interview. Her brown eyes were seemingly lost in a not-so-distant past.

When the earthquake happened, Amano was working in the town of Fukushima, the capital city of Fukushima Prefecture. She recalled the sheer power of the event: "The whole office shook like hell; everything began to fall from the walls." But despite the quake's force, Amano was unaware of the damage to the nuclear power plant. At home in Koriyama City, she learned on TV that something "seemed wrong" with the power plant: "I tried to get as much information as I could, but the media weren't being clear on the situation. So, I began to investigate on the web, going on YouTube to access American news."

When it became clear that the situation was catastrophic, the Japanese state issued an evacuation order for everyone within a twenty-kilometer radius of the power plant. People forced to flee their residences became known as "compulsory evacuees" (*kyōsei hinansha*). Although situated within the prefecture of Fukushima, Koriyama City was sixty kilometers away from the plant, and so not evacuated. But Amano soon became wary of the overall situation. As she explained, "The foreign news advised a perimeter of eighty kilometers. . . . Why wasn't it the same for us? It didn't make sense to me."

Worried about her daughter's well-being, Amano left for Tokyo, staying with her sister in the hope that the situation would settle down. When her work resumed, she had to return to Fukushima. As she explained to me, "Of course, I was still worried about radiation. But in those days, I heard Dr. Yamashita, a well-known specialist on radiation exposure, saying repeatedly that it was safe in Fukushima and that no health effects would appear." In a speech entitled "Relationship Between Radiation and Our Health," given in Fukushima on March 21, Dr. Yamashita remarked that "if the dose does not exceed 100 µSv/hour, then it will not affect the health at all" (*100 Maikuroshīberuto/ h wo kosanakereba, mattaku kenkō ni eikyō oyoboshimasen*).[18] He encouraged people to not worry, claiming that the "effects of radiation do not affect people who are smiling" (*hōshasen no eikyō wa, jitsuwa nikoniko waratte iru hito niha kimasen*) and that "laughing takes away the fear of radiation" (*warai ga minasamagata no hōshasen kyōfushō o torinozokimasu*).[19] Temporarily reassured, Amano brought her daughter back to Koriyama to resume school, which in Japan begins in April. However, her daughter began to suffer from diarrhea, nausea, and recurrent nosebleeds producing blood that had "a very dark and unusual color." Children of her work colleagues suffered from similar ailments, and these symptoms planted a seed of doubt in Amano's mind.[20] Spurred on by her anxiety, Amano began a journey of self-education, reading everything she could find about the potential side effects of radioactive contamination. She even got her hands on a radiation-measuring device and began to track radiation in her house. As she explained, "On the first floor of our home the levels of radiation reached 0.6 µSv/hour and I measured 1.2 µSv/hour for the second floor.

Outside of our home, the radiation level peaked at around 2.7 μSv/hour. I did not know what those numbers meant at first, but when I searched on the Internet, I discovered that this was quite abnormal." Amano's actions highlight a unique aspect of the Japanese civic response, namely, access to technological infrastructure (e.g., Internet and monitoring devices). In 1986, victims of the Chernobyl nuclear disaster did not have similar opportunities.

In contrast to toxic disasters like oil spills, radioactive contamination is intangible, colorless, and odorless. As a result, there is considerably uncertainty related to its risk, especially when low doses do not produce immediate effects. These characteristics provide state experts with greater control over its governance, as they possess the technical tools to make it perceptible to the public. In Fukushima, civic practices of monitoring made the materiality of radioactive contamination perceptible in different ways. With her Geiger counter, Amano began to highlight the limits of state expertise. Alarmed by the levels of radiation that she measured in her house as well as the ailments her daughter was facing, Amano decided to permanently leave Fukushima in July 2011. In doing so, she became a "voluntary evacuee" (*jishu hinansha*), a term that "refers to people who moved from irradiated areas without being ordered to do so by the government after the nuclear disaster."[21] The division between compulsory evacuees and voluntary evacuees created a dichotomy between official and unofficial victims, which was criticized by the official report of the disaster for creating much confusion and inequality among citizens.[22]

As voluntary evacuees, Amano and her daughter were put on a waiting list for access to temporary apartments, because state housing supports (*jūtaku shien*) prioritized compulsory evacuees. Voluntary evacuees like Amano were "accorded little recognition and assistance by the authorities,"[23] who "defined only compulsory evacuees as 'real victims.'"[24] As Ayaka Löschke explains, "The popular view among Japanese people is that voluntary evacuees chose to leave freely and do not return out of personal preference, while compulsory evacuees were forced to leave and cannot go back, and that voluntary evacuees should take 'self-responsibility' (*jiko sekinin*) for their voluntary evacuation."[25]

After months of waiting, Amano and her daughter were assigned to an apartment in Kanagawa Prefecture, south of Tokyo. Unfortunately,

Amano's daughter, who was temporarily living with Amano's sister in Tokyo, was already enrolled in a junior high school and could not move to Kanagawa. Meanwhile, Amano's husband remained in Fukushima for his work. While he was supportive of his wife's efforts, leaving his employment would have jeopardized the family's economic situation. Japanese fathers were not necessarily indifferent toward the risks of radiation exposure, but gendered expectations limited their agency. According to Rika Morioka, "Most fathers did not actively participate in the efforts to guard their children from harmful radiation, because protecting children's health was not within the realm of their masculine role. State-sanctioned gender expectations about what it means to be a good father, namely to be a good worker, powerfully dictate what constitutes masculinity in Japan and may even prevent men from fulfilling the most fundamental responsibility of fatherhood—protecting the lives of their children."[26]

Similarly, traditional roles associated with womanhood structured responses to radiation risks. In Japan, the category of woman is constituted through a variety of different subjectivities and cultural pressures, such as the historical figure of the "good wife and wise mother" (*ryōsai kenbo*).[27] While other social roles exist, many mothers were forced to "make impossible choices between supporting the economic rebuilding of their communities and protecting their children from the threat of radiation."[28] These tensions routinely culminated in a series of separations, a phenomenon known as "atomic divorce" (*genpatsu rikon*).[29] While Amano's marriage survived this test, she knew too well the difficulties associated with trying to combine different social roles. Indeed, as a "mother and child evacuee" (*boshi hinansha*), Amano rarely got to see her husband, lamenting that "our family has become fragmented" (*bara bara*).

Worried about the health effects of radiation, Amano sought medical advice, but the state limited which doctors people could see for medical screening.[30] To receive information about their exposure, citizens had to participate in the 2011 Prefectural Survey. But Amano was dissatisfied with the way the survey determined external exposure levels. Much as in the LSS, exposure levels were calculated on the basis of the recollections of victims. For Amano, there was nothing scientific in this process. "Calculating on your own memory is not enough," she told me angrily. "Especially for evacuees who might not remember the whole sequence of events clearly." Unsure of her memory, Amano believed that her real dose of external exposure to radiation would never be known. Even though external exposure means that the radiation passes through the body, Amano found it worrisome because of the potential for genetic damage. In that regard, medical anthropologists have argued that the design of research projects and the knowledge they produce can sometimes be "reductionist and potentially dehumanising."[31]

Likewise, Amano was disappointed that the survey did not take into consideration the risk of internal exposure for voluntary evacuees like her. She believed that this represented a separate hazard in addition to external exposure: "If they had been really concerned they would have taken urine samples to gauge internal contamination." To make matters even worse, data would later reveal that the state initially underestimated the spread of the radioactive plume throughout Fukushima. As Amano lamented, "Now we know that the radiation level in Koriyama was quite high after March 15. If we had been given accurate information from our government, I would not have made my daughter come back. I truly regret what I did."

Scholars share her concerns, pointing to the survey's limitations by underscoring its low response rate (below 30 percent),[32] the lack of data on internal contamination,[33] and most of all what they see as its main purpose—reassuring people—which implies an "a priori conclusion that there is no problem."[34] Amano concluded that she and her daughter were unnecessarily exposed to radiation and believed that the dosage estimates she received were inaccurate due to governmental failures. As she remarked, "How can you trust experts in such conditions?"

Two years after the disaster, Amano became sick with Reiter syndrome, a type of reactive arthritis that occurs from an infection. "Usually, it's supposed to leave after one year, but I still haven't recovered from it, and it's been more than three years." None of the tests that Amano took pinpointed the cause of her disease. Doctors later diagnosed her with a form of autoimmune disorder involving chronic inflammation of the thyroid. Could her ailments be linked with radiation contamination? Amano has come to believe so, although no one would ever know for sure: "When you're sick from the flu, you know that your sickness is coming from it, but not so with radiation. You don't get sick right away; you might not even be sure of the real cause. Even the experts can't know for sure." Amano was not the only person who complained of mysterious ailments. During my fieldwork, I had informants bemoaning heart problems that they attributed to internal contamination by cesium-137. One young man claimed that he had the "same heart disease that people developed after Chernobyl." Even medical doctors struggled to make sense of post-Fukushima ailments. As Dr. Rin Fujio remarked, "I've been hearing a lot of complaints from people in Fukushima, Tokyo, and Kanagawa, often about children being prone to nosebleeds, weakened immunity systems, repeated cases of stomatitis, skin disorders.... There's still no clear scientific consensus on that. Could it be that the doses were higher than we thought? Could microparticles of cesium be involved? I don't know, but I have to listen carefully.... Otherwise, I might miss the truth. When clinicians close their eyes and their ears, it's the end."

These experiences point toward what Murphy calls "dual uncertainty," in which "any incidence of chemical exposure is difficult to pinpoint" and "experts disagree about the import and even the existence of widespread, low-level exposures."[35] Amano was trapped between a past when her original exposure remained uncertain and a future in which she worried that her ailments might potentially worsen. This situation reflects what Kim Fortun calls the "future anterior."[36] As she explains, "The future inhabits the present, yet it also has not yet come—rather like the way toxics inhabit the bodies of those exposed, setting up the future, but not yet manifest as disease, or even as an origin from which a specific and known disease will come."[37]

From Evacuee to Citizen Scientist

As the years passed, Amano became increasingly distrustful of official statements that claimed that "no discernible increased incidence of radiation-related health effects are expected among exposed members of the public or their descendants."[38] Nor was she alone in her doubts. In September 2011, a survey concluded that 73 percent of citizens did not trust their government.[39] Among the items covered within Amano's narrative, many factors explained this disintegration of trust, as summarized in table 3.1.

These sources of mistrust prompted Amano to learn more about radiation, resulting in her decision to permanently evacuate from

TABLE 3.1. Causes of mistrust following 3.11

Causes	Examples
Inability to obtain rapid information	As Amano's experience epitomizes, citizens were unable to obtain concrete information about the disaster in a timely manner.
Confusion surrounding evacuation orders and radiation-related metrics	The rapidly changing emergency orders, different types of evacuation zoning, and risk communications conducted in hard-to-understand metrics (e.g., Sieverts, micro-sieverts) caused confusion among members of the population.
Contradictory international assessments	The United States advised a perimeter of eighty kilometers for the evacuation of American personnel, as opposed to twenty kilometers for the Japanese government. This decision created mistrust toward the Japanese decision.
Self-assessment of radiological risk	Numerous citizens had to self-assess radiation dangers. For instance, the government "instituted a completely different response for residents within the twenty- to thirty-kilometer radius zone by forcing them to assess the degree of risk caused by radioactive substances by themselves and to make the decision to evacuate on their own."*
Poor risk communication	The cherry picking of experts to convey radiological risks resulted in a lack of trust in scientific authority. Terms like "lapdog scholars" (goyō gakusha), "nuclear village" (genshiryoku mura), and "nuclear mafia" (genshiryoku mafia) became popular in public discourses.
Failure to predict the disaster	Before 2011, citizens never considered the possibility of a nuclear disaster. Few had reason to doubt a state that had repeatedly assured the population of the safety of nuclear power.
Changes of standard	The change in radiation threshold (from 1 mSv per year to 20 mSv per year) further contributed to increasing mistrust of the government.
Perceived adverse health effects	Symptoms such as nosebleeds as well as the apparent increase of thyroid cancer in children created anger toward a government claiming that no adverse health effects existed.

* The National Diet of Japan, The Official Report of the Fukushima Nuclear Accident Independent Investigation Commission—Executive Summary (National Diet of Japan, 2012), chapter 4, 22.

Fukushima. Dissatisfied with the state's replies and wanting to protect her daughter, Amano began to look for citizens who shared her concerns. She eventually discovered a network of concerned citizens based in Tokyo. Initially, this network was created to support a legal case filed on behalf of several children who needed a court to rule in favor of their evacuation from Fukushima. In June 2011, fourteen children in Koriyama City filed a lawsuit at the Fukushima District Court, demanding the right to study in a safe environment where the annual dose of radiation received would be less than 1 mSv per year. Their plea turned out to be unsuccessful, forcing members of the network to diversify their mandate and become a rallying center for compulsory and voluntary evacuees living in the Greater Tokyo Area. Many of its members were active in the realm of citizen science, mobilizing discourses and practices that promoted tropes of permanent evacuation.

Within the network, I quickly noticed that most members were women, often mothers and grandmothers. The absence of young men was not particularly surprising, especially if one considers the pressures of "normative gender roles" around the denial of contamination.[40] In Japan, the construction of masculinity, which is "historically linked to the economic interests of the nation state,"[41] explains the lack of male "breadwinners" within the citizen-science networks that advocated for evacuation. Indeed, embracing this path would clash with a politics of revitalization, which is itself intertwined within the masculine ethos of work and its socioeconomic value. In the next sections, I underscore the network's activities in greater detail, focusing on how Japanese mothers like Natsuo Amano mobilized knowledge about radiation hazards for specific advocacy purposes.

Sievert Hunters

Members of the network often told me that the scariest thing about radiation was its invisibility—the fact that you "can't feel it" (*kanji nai*) or "really cannot understand it" (*mattaku wakan'nai*) without some form of technological prosthesis. As one informant explained, "When you burn yourself it hurts [*itai*], but with radiation it's very hard to understand the situation directly [*donna jōkyō . . . chokusetsu ni wakaranai*]." Monitoring devices brought a radical change to this imperceptibility by making part of radiation hazards visible to the naked eye. For citizen scientists, this was done via the help of Geiger counters, which were bought on the Internet, provided by NGOs, or lent from grassroot organizations. Amano had never seen any radiation data for her hometown until she began to measure radiation by herself. The initial absence of data is not necessarily due to secrecy but a function of the fact that state monitoring stations were destroyed after the disaster.[42] As Thomas Feldhoff explained, "It took some time for new monitoring systems to be installed that allowed for the gathering, publishing and regular updating of comprehensive data about radioactivity and radiation effects."[43] When I came to Japan in 2015, the government had by then established a network of fixed sensors throughout Fukushima. These sensors took the form of big, white, metallic tubes that measured the external dose of radiation in the air while displaying results on an electronic board. The information provided by these sensors was subsequently used to interpolate radiation levels in terms of municipal averages.[44]

However, in the time it took for the state to set up monitoring posts, many citizens had already become accustomed to tracking radiation by themselves. Even five years after the disaster, Amano kept the habit of monitoring radiation, especially when she came back to Koriyama to see her husband. By sticking to this practice, she continued to find hot spots of radiation around her house, which ranged as high as 2.26 μSv per hour. Amano perceived these levels as too high for her to ever return to Fukushima, since just 0.6 μSv per hour is considered a "radiation-controlled area" where it is forbidden to enter without protection.

For citizen scientists, the power of citizen science lay not simply in making radiation visible but also in the ability to test radiation *wherever* mothers like Amano wanted to do so. This form of agency made a crucial difference in understanding the scale of contamination, as citizens could monitor radiation beyond the state's network. Often, the results that citizens measured further increased the lack of trust in the state. Members of the network routinely argued that governmental sensors were unrepresentative of the "real" scale of contamination found in Fukushima. During a meeting, one mother contended that these sensors were "strategically placed" and that "the areas around them are constantly cleaned so that the levels of radiation will appear lower!"[45] Other mothers explained that children were at risk of playing in contaminated areas since residual radioactivity accumulated in higher concentrations in the soil than in the air levels monitored by the state.

As a result of their efforts, members of the network believed that governmental monitoring only served the purpose of reassuring a gullible population. Eager to show me the difference between fixed sensors and their own measurements, a group of volunteers arranged for a trip to

Figure 3.1. Citizens testing radiation with a Geiger counter in Fukushima. Photo by Maxime Polleri.

Fukushima. On March 6, 2016, I drove around Fukushima with other citizen scientists. Armed with Geiger counters, we became "Sievert hunters," measuring the levels of residual radioactivity in public parks and school playgrounds. It quickly became apparent that a mismatch clearly existed between our data and that produced by the state's fixed sensors. The fallout had produced patches of contamination beyond the range of the fixed sensors. For example, while a monitoring post displayed a level of 0.374 μSv per hour, moving a few footsteps away produced a tenfold increase of 3.604 μSv per hour. One young woman dutifully compiled the results in a notebook, and widespread discrepancies like these made citizen scientists critical of the official mapping that separated Fukushima into well-defined zones based on homogeneous levels of radiation. Self-monitoring practices created a novel distribution of the sensible that was twofold: It made a former invisible harm perceptible and underscored the limits of state expertise.

Food Monitoring

Food security became a sensitive issue for many citizens and, over time, one of the most controversial topics. By March 17, 2011, the government established the "first provisional regulation values for radionuclide levels in food and drinking water."[46] Thresholds were gradually revised, with the state implementing one of the strictest limits of allowable amounts of radioactivity in the world. Currently, the upper limit for radioactive cesium is 100 Bq/kg in general food, 50 Bq/kg for infant food, and 10 Bq/kg for beverages.[47] These measures and inspection mechanisms have enabled different state agencies to "guarantee" the safety of food available on the market. For example, the Ministry of Health, Labour, and Welfare concluded that "radiation-cesium in foods distributed were all extremely low, thus food safety was ensured."[48] As a result, the government (through a series of public fairs) encouraged people to consume food produced in Fukushima.

However, as scholars have demonstrated, trust in state narratives crumbled when citizen scientists revealed cases of radioactive contamination.[49] Many members of the network were skeptical about food produced in Fukushima. Mothers explained their dissatisfaction by an initial lack of state-sponsored data surrounding food safety. Some of my informants restrained themselves from eating sea products, stating that fish could not "respect" areas marked for fishing exclusion. Consequently, many mothers dabbled in food monitoring, and even contributed to the creation of a small center located in a quiet residential neighborhood of Tokyo where food could be tested for a nominal fee. When I visited in 2017, the director of the center, an elderly woman named Emiko Araki, explained that many citizens wanted to measure radiation levels themselves after the disaster. Therefore, Araki had the idea of creating a nonprofit organization (NPO), which led her to buy a becquerel analyzer. The machine, a NaI (Tl) scintillation detector FNF-401S, could detect traces of gamma radiation from radionuclide iodine-131, cesium-134, and cesium-137 in food or drinking water. With the machine having a price tag of 4.5 million yen (roughly fifty thousand dollars), the center could only afford to purchase one. Still, as Araki explained, that single scintillation detector had been put to great use:

"Many people wanted to measure their food to know if they could sell it [on the market]. At the beginning, things like fruits, especially their skins, or the spinach [hōrensō] had very high levels [of becquerels] and no one could sell their stuff. Even now that six years have passed, there are still some foods that have high levels of radiation."

Practices of food monitoring allowed citizens to critically assess the official management of this disaster. Araki argued that while state officials first encouraged people to consume food, they rarely provided data to back up their claims. As another member of the center remarked, "It has enabled us to see that what the government was doing and saying was strange [okashii]. It forced us to ask things like, 'Is it really right [tadashii]?'" This constant questioning of state authority forced citizens to develop their own scientific literacy around radiation risks rather than wait for the state's explanations. During workshops organized by the network, I witnessed mothers speaking about the types of food that should be avoided, such as mushrooms, green, leafy vegetables, and citrus (yuzu).

Paradoxically, food monitoring also made citizens aware of the limitations inherent in technological devices. Citizen scientists told me that their faith in food monitoring was shattered when they realized that not all types of radioactive particles could be detected by the current technology.[50] They explained that it was impossible to test certain foods without cutting the sample into small pieces or pulverizing it into a paste, rendering food that is monitored impossible to consume under normal conditions. While monitoring is useful for providing an overall picture of the contamination of a given area, it does not enable citizens to know for sure the levels of contaminants that they ingest daily. Citizens like Amano therefore saw food monitoring as a symbolic gesture that could help lower exposure but that would never bring back predisaster levels of food safety.

Workshops, Gatherings, and Study Groups

Members of the network ran regular workshops to increase their knowledge of radiation issues. Wary of goyō gakusha, which they perceived as experts unable to speak out against the government's positions, citizen scientists organized their own lecture series by inviting experts that were critical of the state's "safety campaign" (*anzen kyanpēn*). Many mothers had developed an exhaustive knowledge of nuclear-related issues, which went beyond the phenomenon of radiation. Their knowledge encompassed the inner workings of the nuclear industry of Japan, an understanding of international regulatory practices, and the history of previous nuclear disasters. Through these workshops, citizens were engaged in trying to *critically* analyze the nature of information provided by their government. On a practical level, this meant probing where an expert was trained, what institution he was affiliated with, and how funding for his research was obtained. Experts associated with the "nuclear village" (*genshiryoku mura*) were deemed untrustworthy since their expertise was akin to serving the interest of corporate lobbies. Subsequently, citizens systematically engaged in deconstructing the state's information. As one mother explained to me, "The government keeps saying that radiation levels are below the standard of safety, but they keep changing the standards! Did you know that the standard for what is considered as radioactive waste has been raised by a factor of eighty [*anzen ni sairiyō dekiru kijun*]? When the standards of risk are being changed, it's quite easy to call a place 'under control.' People need to know!"

In sum, the consumption of radiation-related knowledge by citizen scientists was inseparable from a deeper issue of trust. This relationship was catalyzed by the acquisition of scientific expertise—what Sternsdorff-Cisterna calls a "scientific citizenship."[51] In a mere five years, Amano had discovered new ways of expressing herself in language that she would never have thought possible. "Cesium-137," "becquerel," "sievert," "alpha particle," and "gamma ray"—what was once foreign terminology reserved for specialists had become a new language used to make sense of a contaminated environment. Far from being ignorant, Amano revealed an impressive understanding of the extent of radiation harm. For instance, she made a clear separation between acute radiation sickness (*kyūsei*) and chronic low-dose exposure (*teisenryō*). In explaining the distinction, she observed, "When people think about radioactive exposure, the first thing that comes to their mind is cancer. But there's much more than that.... [With low doses] you don't die right away. It brings a lot of small problems." Her point was telling: Radioactive contamination affects not simply life but also the *quality* of life. According to Amano, it is precisely this subtlety that the state experts have never been able to grasp. In this view, radioactive harm is embodied not only as a potential increase of fatal cancer but also as a harm that makes the ordinary travails of existence more acute.

An Ibasho

Mari Kobayashi, one of the main representatives of the network, once told me that their Tokyo-based organization could never succeed in Fukushima: "We can't do what we are doing in Fukushima! The pressure is real. People don't want to talk about radiation, being a plaintiff [*genkoku*] is a secret. Other members of the community will tell you to stop spreading 'rumors.' So, it's quite hard to express oneself directly [*hakkiri*]. People from the Tōhoku have a high culture of endurance [*gaman suru*]." Originally from Fukushima, Mari Kobayashi had helped mothers like Amano to find a locus where evacuees could speak freely about their concerns without fear of reprisal. "It can be very difficult for mothers to raise their voices [*koe agetakunai*]. The risks are high. If you criticize the government you'll be labeled as a traitor [*hikokumin*]." Amano and Kobayashi explained that talking about radiation in Fukushima was seen as hampering the revitalization of the region. This discourse was not only backed up by the government but also cultivated by certain segments of the population. As Amano related, "There are a lot of old people who refuse to believe information that doesn't appear on television and it's very hard to convince them. They'll tell us things like 'this ain't true, this ain't true' [*son'na koto nai, son'na koto nai*] or 'The country is saying that it's safe, so why do you contradict them?'" Mari Kobayashi had equally faced such pressures, ironically from members of her family. "My son's wife is in poor health, so he doesn't talk to her about that [the risk of radiation]. He doesn't want her to worry. But he encourages me in secret." She paused briefly to play with her glasses and then suddenly burst into tears, exclaiming, "Even my own son can't understand what I'm doing."

Against this form of social and political pressure, the network was more than a place where people gathered to learn about radiation. It also acted as a safe locus, where evacuees and angry citizens could articulate a different distribution of the sensible. In talking about this distribution ("*partage du sensible*" in French), Davide Panagia reminds us that the word "*partage*" refers to the sharing of an experience "common to all."[52] A *partage* is a "principle of aggregation" that helps to structure participatory forms in given communities.[53] A former taxi driver from Fukushima who was forced to evacuate after the disaster exemplified this point during one meeting: "Three years after the disaster my wife asked me if we should go back to Fukushima. All I could reply was, 'Where? We don't have a home. . . . Haven't you seen how much the scenery of Fukushima has changed?' Before Fukushima I knew nothing of such organizations. But with you, I've finally found my home."

In talking about home, the man used the word "*ibasho*," which can be translated as a "place where one belongs, where one fits in, place where one can be oneself."[54] By bringing together the sharing of similar experiences, citizen science also offered an *ibasho*, a place where people felt at home in post-Fukushima Japan. This *ibasho* could transform a reified percentage of hypothetical increases of cancers into lively story—something that evacuees could relate to without fear of being judged. For instance, a woman belonging to the network once reflected on her lack of prospects for returning home. In a teary voice, she spoke about how she missed Fukushima's flower viewing and how it was impossible to see the tombs of her family to pay them homage. She deplored the ghost town that her village had become and expressed anger at the thieves who broke into homes. She explained how in Fukushima "people were anxious, but couldn't express their troubles" (*fuan kedo ienai'n desu*) and remarked on how young women worried for their future, believing that they could not marry (*mō kekkon dekinai*). Amid these hardships, one of the most popular topics of discussion was the apparent increase of thyroid cancers in children, associated with the intake of iodine-131.[55] As a mother complained during one meeting, "The Prefectural Health Survey has found that 137 children are suffering from thyroid cancer. However, they keep saying that thyroid cancer is not linked with radiation exposure in Fukushima, that it's the result of a screening effect. They tell us that they have done too much testing, that the tests are too precise and that's why there are many thyroid cancers. What does that mean? That doesn't mean anything, that's stupid. A cancer is a cancer!" Ironically, the thyroid is the endocrine gland that enables the growth of children, which is symbolically what these mothers felt they were being deprived of: the possibility of a bright future that will enable their children to flourish. For many mothers, long-term evacuation was the only reasonable choice by which postdisaster recovery could be understood.

A Politics of Victimization

Citizen science gradually enabled the creation of a different distribution of the sensible: a politics of victimization, wherein mothers like Amano perceived themselves as victims of postdisaster policies.[56] Discourses of victimology prompt inquiries into the political potential of citizen science, especially its ability to enact lasting changes. In talking about politics (*seijiteki*), I was struck by an initial paradox. Many members of the network told me that their endeavor was different from political activism (*sekkyokukōdōshugi*). Countless times, I heard things that appeared contradictory, such as, "Our organization is not political! We are only trying to change the current state of order!" Both Natsuo Amano and Mari Kobayashi emphasized that their network had no ties whatsoever with antinuclear activists or with political parties. As Kobayashi explained, "Political parties are too tempestuous [*hageshii*]; we don't want to be their ally."

Jonathan Cole has argued that this apparent allergy to politics in Japan is a product of a "tradition of restricted political participation" that discourages the "questioning of authority."[57] Yet the rich history of civic movements in Japan, such as the Anpo struggle (*anpo tōsō*) or the Minamata Convention on mercury poisoning, challenged this so-called allergy to the political.[58] Understanding the political potential of citizen science requires examining politics *within* Japanese society rather than through Western notions of political participation.[59] Scott Schnell provides a useful insight in that regard: "In a society like Japan's where harmony and cooperation have been relentlessly promoted as fundamental principles of social interaction, it is often difficult to pose a direct challenge to the authorities. . . . Thus when people feel compelled to express their opposition, they are likely to do so through less direct means, such as in the form of festivals that 'spontaneously' escalate into violence, or in invoking vague fears of upsetting the ancestral spirits."[60]

If one acknowledges this different texture of political resistance, then it becomes apparent that citizen science acted to legitimize a politics of victimization in opposition to the prevailing politics of revitalization. More importantly, it also reveals how citizens articulate political demands while paradoxically putting forward "apolitical" discourses. Historical precedents reveal the sensitive nature of "politics" (*seijiteki*) in Japan and how what is meant by "politics" is always performed within broader historical and cultural pressures. As one antinuclear activist explained to me,

> The current "apolitical stance" [surrounding the nuclear issue] is a consequence of political movements surrounding May '68. During 1968–1972, political movements were very intense, but they were efficiently repressed. After the tumultuous period of the student movements [*daigaku funsō*], there was a sort of "allergy" to politics. In the '80s and '90s, if you had an opposite [political] ideology [*datsu ideorogī*], you were inevitably depicted as someone who was against the government [*datsu seiji/datsu seitō*]. Neutralism [*chūritsu shūgi*] became the norm. Now, the word "political" [*seijiteki*] has become a sort of taboo [*tabū*], especially in the last twenty years. The Communist Party [*kyōsantō*] has also contributed to creating such an atmosphere. The Communist Party always had a very strong antinuclear position. Yet there were a lot of individuals who did not want to be associated with this party.

Many Japanese citizens therefore associate the word "politics" with more radical or reified forms of political organization, which do not speak to their daily lives.[61] Considering these factors, claims of apolitical discourse by citizen scientists make perfect sense and should not be equated with stereotypical tropes that Japanese citizens are nonpolitical. Rather, these claims are part of broader cultural strategies that enable citizens to avoid a backlash while expressing dissent. Although Kobayashi and Amano took on a *private* antinuclear stance following the disaster, they did not want to be *officially* labeled as antinuclear activists. They feared that doing so would jeopardize the legitimacy of their movement, by depicting their network as the byproduct of a politically biased ideology.

Politics by Science

In her study of citizen science, Aya Kimura argues that worried mothers struggled with contamination as a "private problem that had to be dealt with in a highly secretive manner."[62] My experiences highlight a different story, in which mothers like Amano did not always shy away from acting on the knowledge they gathered. In fact, Amano went as far as taking her struggle public. Between 2015 and 2016, I followed Amano and other members of the network in the streets of downtown Tokyo as they organized a series of public protests.

For many hours, members of the network made demands for permanent evacuation while criticizing the raised threshold of 20 mSv per year. They shouted slogans such as "Let the children escape from Fukushima!"; "We won't be silenced by the government!"; "The nuclear disaster is not over!"; "Radiation is still a problem!"; "End the state's brainwashing campaign!"; and "Nuclear matter has 'suddenly' become less dangerous, this makes no sense! Now we are all nuclear workers!" Yet, in making these sensitive public claims, many citizens were careful to anchor their critique around a scientific narrative. During public protests, one could hear complaints like "Professionals in the radio-medical domain are not allowed to receive a dose that is higher than 0.2 mSv, but mothers and children can live in an area of 20 mSv? What is wrong with Japan!?" or "This time the number of thyroid cases has reached 172 cases! One hundred and thirty-one children have already been operated on and forty-one are awaiting their turn! All of that in a screening of thirty thousand people! This is not normal!" Citizen scientists equally backed their claims with banners that read as follows: "The incidence rate of thyroid cancer is fifty times higher in Fukushima!" or "The normal incidence of thyroid cancer is one individual per one million. Fukushima has 167 individuals in 380,000." Protests were the occasion to distribute flyers that scientifically attempted to explain the dangers of radioactive exposure. On a particular flyer, one could see a MEXT-produced map of the aerial dispersion of radioactive pollutants fragmented in colorful zones, each linked with specific levels of radiation. Below the map one could read the following: "The third zone corresponds to what nuclear workers call 'radiation-controlled areas.' In such zones, individuals need to wear special protection equipment as

Figure 3.2. Protest in Tokyo to evacuate the children from Fukushima. Photo by Maxime Polleri.

shown in this picture. It is also forbidden to eat, drink, and move objects from the site. As we can see on the map, places that fell within this zone are not just in the prefecture of Fukushima but also in Tochigi, Gunma, Ibaraki, Chiba, and Tokyo."

Members of the network also used scientific comparisons to tackle the controversial issue of food safety. For example, one flyer contained the predisaster level of radioactive cesium in a range of food products. In 2008, one could learn, the average value of radioactive cesium in rice was 0.012 Bq/kg. The flyer explained that the new food consumption threshold of 100 Bq/kg—one of the strictest in the world—still represented an enormous increase in comparison to the actual level of cesium that people had previously ingested. By resorting to scientific comparisons, citizen scientists attempted to highlight the arbitrariness of the claims surrounding food safety.

This articulation of politics through science is a tactic that has a long history in civic movements. In the context of Peruvian extractive mining, Stefanie Graeter argues that scientific documentation of contamination allows citizens to express political responses of "fundamental disagreement over the governance of life and death in Peru."[63] She highlights how scientific narratives formed the basis of political advocacy, thereby generating "conditions of political actionability—the ability to act on knowledge politically."[64] In an Indonesian context, Anna Tsing underscores how sociocultural practices linked with "nature lovers' clubs" act as strategies for becoming socially engaged without being perceived as explicitly political.[65] Andrew Mathews has examined how public performances linked with scientific knowledge around Mexican forestry seek to "define the contours of the political by making and remaking the boundary between science and politics."[66]

In the same way, the mobilization of a scientific discourse allowed citizens in Japan to express criticisms that would otherwise be quite hard to enact. As a vehicle for politics, science enabled members of the network to indirectly condemn the decisions taken by their government, while helping them to bypass accusations of ideological bias, which were often directed against antinuclear activists. Practically speaking, scientific narratives also appealed to broader audiences, such as mothers who wanted to hear alternative discourses, but remained wary of doing so through the prism of antinuclear sentiments. Indeed, one mother told me that antinuclear activists were "dreadful and scary" (*kowakatta*), which prompted her to ignore their claims. During my fieldwork with antinuclear organizations, I regularly witnessed violent vocal outbursts directed toward members of the government:

You will die [*shinimasu yo ne*]!
You've committed crimes [*hanzai*]!
Why don't you accept your responsibilities [*sekinin*]!?
Give us back our lives!
Give us back our clean water and pure air!
What about the children!?
Children are our treasure [*takaramono*]!
Do you hate Abe? I despise him! [*Abe wa kirai desu ka. Watashi wa dai kirai!*]

Many antinuclear pamphlets were written in an emotional register rather than a scientific one. I remember manifestos that depicted the prime minister in the shape of a slimy insect, with the caption "*kokumin mushi*" (the nation's larva), as well as drawings of Godzilla urinating on the shore of Fukushima, with three-eyed mutant dolphins jumping in a puddle of yellow water. As a result, antinuclear activists told me that ultranationalist groups routinely harassed them and that public security officers (*kōan keisatsukan*) scrutinized their every movement. In contrast, the "neutrality" of science stood as a more convenient medium to enact a politics of victimization, with the added benefits of mitigating some of the strong social backlash that activists experienced. Still, the line that separated both groups was sometimes thin. In their personal lives and private thoughts (*hon'ne*), many citizen scientists had clear political preferences about nuclear power, but their official discourse (*tatemae*) was epistemically anchored in scientific narratives.

Hibakusha Redux

As Amano painfully adjusted to her new life, the government announced that the financial help for voluntary evacuees would come to an end in March 2017.[67] This rent-free public housing acted as a "lifeline (*inochi zuna*)" for voluntary evacuees who received little compensation after the disaster.[68] Its termination would result in further financial difficulties for Amano, forcing mothers to return to their former areas of residence. Under the reconstruction policies of Shinzo Abe, the state made numerous comments that exhorted evacuees to return to Fukushima, often describing voluntary evacuation as an irrational choice.[69] Masahiro Imamura, the Reconstruction Agency minister, illustrated this sentiment when he said that voluntary evacuation was a problem of "self-responsibility" (*jiko sekinin*).[70]

Amano was understandably angry about the government's decision. Her ability to find a safe place for her daughter seemed about to disappear. In the years that followed her evacuation, Amano's daughter, who was originally an elementary student, became a young woman. She has become accustomed to their new life, and Amano feels that there is no point in her going back to an environment that would expose them (in her view) to dangerous residual radiation.

Amano saw radiation damage as an unwanted legacy for children, who are forced to bear a responsibility that should not be theirs. To change this narrative, Amano attempted to create a new legacy for her daughter. Specifically, she sought to create a diary (*techō*) that recorded one's personal history of exposure and sickness. In 2016, I followed Amano to an event in Koriyama City promoting the creation of an irradiation booklet society in Fukushima ('*Fukushima ni hibaku-sha techō o tsukuru kai' setsuritsu. Anata mo kaiin ni narimasen ka*). The event promoted the creation of an "irradiation booklet" for Fukushima's residents. According to the event flyer, the organization's aim was to secure public medical security for the victims of the nuclear disaster and the creation of a law based on the *hibakusha*'s experience, which had historically resulted in official recognition of nuclear victimhood. During the opening remarks, the founder of the organization, a woman from Koriyama named Kumiko Mita, explained the rationale behind an irradiation booklet: "This organization was established by a group of citizens who want to minimize their health damage caused by the residual radioactivity of 3.11. It's not only for those who have already become ill from radiation, but it's also for citizens who suffer from anxiety in regard to potential illness, especially for those who are worried about the future of their children. We want to secure the same kind of public medical insurance [*kōteki iryō hoshō*] received by the A-bomb survivors in Hiroshima and Nagasaki."

To make their case, the assembly had invited a *hibakusha* from Hiroshima, an elderly woman named Eiko Ono, who spoke about her personal experience of being exposed to the atomic bomb's radiation. In front of an audience composed mostly of young women, she described the ailments suffered during her lifetime: the decaying of her teeth, numerous eye problems, bone injuries, Basedow's disease, and thyroid cancer. "My body is full of numerous small illnesses," she explained. "A lot of *hibakusha* were never able to work because of these illnesses. Some of my health problems appeared late in life and these are the kinds of health conditions brought on by radiation."

As a victim officially recognized by the state, Eiko Ono possessed an "A-bomb survivor health notebook" (*hibakusha kenkō techō*). This notebook certified that Mrs. Ono was exposed to radiation and guaranteed government coverage of her medical costs in case of illness. Mrs. Ono believed that her lifelong illnesses were linked with her radiation exposure, and she encouraged mothers present at the assembly to begin tracking their health histories as soon as possible. She explained that the notebook had relieved her worries about financial matters, and supported the creation of a similar handbook for the residents of Fukushima. Waving her notebook in the air, Mrs. Ono asked mothers if they had savings in case of illness, stating that "a lot of *hibakusha* suddenly became unable to work, and this is a condition that didn't come right away. Now it might be all right, but who knows what can happen?"

After hearing her speech, Amano agreed that the evacuees from Fukushima needed something similar. She stood abruptly and said, "I believe that this is absolutely necessary, and I want that for my daughter!" Her activities as a citizen scientist had already laid the ground for such advocacy; with a Geiger counter, she had measured the radiation levels around her house, dutifully compiling these results in a personal notebook. Moreover, she had also documented the medical ailments faced by herself and her daughter. But an irradiation booklet stood as something completely different than her own *individual* record. Such a booklet, modeled upon the one that former *hibakusha* received, could enable individual accounts to stand as potential archives of this disaster and ensure state recognition of the effect of radiation on the residents of Fukushima.

In her study of American slavery, Ellen Garvey explains that anecdotes and personal vignettes were successfully recontextualized as the "containers of data" that served a political purpose—which in her case exemplified the brutality of slavery.[71] She contends that for the abolitionist movement, "marks, scars, and shackles that slaveholders noted as a means of identifying individual runaways became the individual, incremental indictments of slavery that might be systematically collected and analyzed."[72] In a similar fashion, a Fukushima health notebook might legitimize personal stories as aggregated data that would bear political weight. According to Amano, this endeavor had the potential to transform voluntary evacuees into recognized victims of the disaster. The prospect of this notebook was further enhanced through its association with the *hibakusha* movement, which has a history of state compensation due to the A-Bomb Survivors Medical Care Law of 1957.[73] As STS scholar Kyoko Sato argues, "Official certification has also allowed survivors to develop political identity, individually and as a collectivity."[74] In this context, having a figure such as Eiko Ono on her side strongly legitimized Amano's quest. While citizen science had given Amano novel forms of agency, the *hibakusha* connection had the advantage of mobilizing recognized cultural tropes of nuclear victimhood. Science and history were suddenly merging, transforming Amano's personal sense of victimhood into an official politics of victimization.

Children Don't Understand . . .

Beyond public protests and assemblies for the creation of health notebooks, many members of the network joined a collective lawsuit against the government, which demanded their right to permanently evacuate from Fukushima. In 2016, I followed Amano during one of these trials, which happened at the Fukushima District Court. There, I met Masuji Takeda, one of the lawyers for the defense. He explained the hardships of trying to accumulate enough legal proof to validate the necessity of permanent evacuation: "Radiation harm is more than thyroid cancers. The risk of radiation exposure is not simply linked with strong illnesses. There's a panoply of other 'smaller' ailments: dizziness, tired eyes, and a sore body (*karada ga darui*). These ailments represent a kind of liminal space between health and sickness. It's a kind of 'pre-sickness' period. Below a certain level, it's easy to pretend that radiation effects are simply psychological, since you don't have an immediate cause and effect."

To bypass this problem, Masuji Takeda articulated the case he would make around the precautionary principle, which defines actions on issues considered to be still uncertain (e.g., low-dose exposure). As he explained, this principle is used to justify discretionary decisions in situations where there is the possibility of harm from living in low-dose irradiated areas. Accordingly, Takeda framed his argument around three points: the uncertainty of risk, the potential irreversibility of health damage, and the late occurrence of low-dose danger. Because of the uncertainty surrounding low-dose exposure, Takeda argued that radiation health effects could not be rationalized through a dualistic pattern of safety or danger: "We can't calculate the risk of radioactive contamination and the health damage with the tools of present-day science. So much of this is a problem of the limits of science [*kagaku no genkai*]. I don't see our case as a problem of scientific argument, but as a discussion of another dimension based on the outcomes and limits of science."

To further prepare his case, Takeda and his colleagues had modeled their defense around the Chernobyl Law, which stipulates that individuals have the right to evacuate from a place that is radioactive above a certain level. As Löschke explains, the Chernobyl Law was "enacted in Ukraine, Belarus, and Russia in 1991 and has compensated residents remaining in areas with an estimated annual exposure of one to five millisieverts, and also people who moved from these areas."[75]

During the hearing, Takeda presented a thick document that revolved around the uncertainties of radiation exposure, such as unknown past levels, the possibility of internal contamination, and the presence of radioactive hot spots. In addition, two mothers were invited to share their experiences. The first speaker was Natsuo Amano. Assembling the knowledge she had gathered as a citizen scientist, she offered a very technical speech, describing the level of μSv/hour that she measured in her house, while explaining in detail the adverse health effects she and her daughter had faced since the disaster. If I had not known Amano, I would have mistaken her for a scientist. Distancing herself emotionally, she relied on a scientifically infused argument to highlight legal transgressions linked with the state threshold of radioactive exposure. The second speaker was a young mother from Fukushima named Akane Kajiwara. With her baby gently resting on her shoulder, she gave a very emotional speech by emphasizing her maternal fear of radioactive contamination in Fukushima:

> Children don't understand why they always need to wear a mask. They don't understand what a hot spot is. . . . All they understand is that they can't play outside, that they are not allowed to do this or that, and that they can't have fun! They can't do anything! And that's what you call protection? I'm always thinking about radiation: Is there some radioactivity on those flowers, can I let my baby touch them? Children can't protect themselves. I used to love Fukushima so much, but now it has been dirtied! We can't enjoy nature as we did!

Amano's and Kajiwara's narratives highlight the Janus face of women's roles regarding radioactive protection, as well as how victims of nuclear disasters "can exercise their agency by taking on multiple subjectivities."[76] While Amano stood as the rationally calculating citizen scientist,

Kajiwara embodied the logic of affective motherhood. Their narratives underscore the polarized facets of women's role in post-Fukushima Japan, where mothers navigate between "emotional" claims of well-being toward their children and the "cold" language of radiological science. These experiences also exemplify how women mobilized normative roles of femininity to their own advantage.[77] For instance, Kajiwara had drawn on the traditional role of motherhood to legitimize a political critique. As Morioka explains, "Motherhood, empowered by the moral imperative to protect children, gives women a license to trust their feelings and challenge other prevalent cultural norms of obedience to governmental and corporate authorities."[78] On the other hand, Amano had opted for a different tactic, not relying on emotional tropes to ensure she would be perceived as a legitimate speaker of science. This did not imply that Amano rejected the logic of motherhood. For her, being a "good" and "wise" mother now means becoming experienced in an array of novel practices, such as measuring radiation with a Geiger counter, testing food for radioactive contamination, and creating a health notebook. Science and motherhood were not antithetical but strategic discourses that complemented each other in both the legal and cultural realms. Against tremendous pressures to come back to Fukushima, a politics of victimization had to be carefully navigated, with all the political tools available to citizens. Amano's and Kajiwara's claims precisely highlight the range of tactics and the contradictions that women faced in navigating the aftermath of a nuclear disaster. They performed motherhood to their own advantage and in tandem with citizen science, to authorize demands for evacuation within the broader cultural context of Japanese society.

Protecting Life

While the endeavors of mothers like Amano are inspiring, citizen science has had limited success in challenging a politics of revitalization. Members of the network failed to change state policies regarding the raised threshold of exposure. They were unsuccessful in stopping the financial cut for voluntary evacuees. And the endless legal activities quickly eroded their network's meager finances, primarily supported by public donations. In line with Kimura's argument, these findings pinpoint how citizen science was "significantly constrained by the limiting normative parameters for citizens, women, and politics."[79] While this is undeniable, a broader conceptualization of political resistance also sheds light on a different interpretation of the situation. Abu-Lughod asks how a theory of politics can give women credit for "resisting in a variety of creative ways the power of those who control so much of their lives, without either misattributing to them forms of consciousness or politics that are not part of their experience—something like a feminist consciousness or feminist politics—or devaluing their practices as prepolitical, primitive, or even misguided."[80] This inquiry brings a different understanding to the phenomenon of citizen science. While citizen scientists failed to bring about drastic governance changes, they nonetheless promoted alternative understandings of recovery from those of the state. In the process, citizen science forged new communities, often participating in disaster governance by reimagining shared identities and values amid toxic legacies.

Combining a politics of victimization with the issue of citizen science might have sounded like an oxymoron for some scholars working on citizen science, especially since the field is not always associated with victimology but is instead linked to the idea of taking back one's life through direct action. However, there is a powerful form of ethnocentrism that rests in the Western concept of victimhood, which is too often perceived as a submissive state. By actively seeking to be recognized as full-fledged victims, Japanese citizen scientists were looking to bring forward their own understanding of postdisaster recovery, which drastically differed from the state policies. Their politics of victimization was not one of inaction but a politics of active resistance that put forward the creation of alternative storytelling about Fukushima. Importantly, their practices demonstrate that affected citizens do not have to position themselves as passive victims; they can also transform themselves into what Japanese refers to as "*tōjisha*." As Löschke explains, "'Victim' has a negative connotation, implying people who have been stripped of agency and control, whereas '*tōjisha*' has a quite positive connotation in the research context of social movements in Japan, insofar as it refers to agents who are seeking redress for damage on their own initiative. . . . Since then, the term has referred not to victims passively awaiting relief but to *committed victims* who are seeking redress for damage on their own initiative."[81]

Following this line of thought, citizen science enabled individuals to probe the kinds of values (*kachikan*) that they wished to see in a post-Fukushima Japan. Amano, Kobayashi, and I often spoke about radiation hazards, yet we spent most of our time debating broader political issues, such as the place of democracy in Japan, how money was a poor form of compensation, and the kind of legacy that they hope to bequeath to their children. Members of the network told me that their aim was to "protect life" (*inochi wo mamoru*). The term that numerous informants used for the word "life" was "*inochi*," which has archaic meanings of "foundation" and "core." As a member explained, "*Inochi* is more than the biological understanding of life. It's more than physical harm [*kenkō higai*]; it is also the mind, the soul, the heart, and the ethos [*seishin*]. But the ethos [of Japan] is becoming weird after Fukushima."[82] In this light, citizen science is a locus for rethinking the kind of *inochi* worth fighting for—especially during a normalized state of emergency. As Brodkin argues, "What makes a social movement a *movement* is the vision of something better and the sense that we can make it happen."[83] After Fukushima, this vision is inseparable from the new forms of knowledge that citizens must master to navigate an unfamiliar life. Following Sherry Ortner, citizen science demonstrates a political locus "in which resistance can be more than opposition, can be truly creative and transformative."[84]

In the years since the disaster, Amano experienced an array of changes and has discovered new ways of articulating her life—ways that she could never have imagined. "Microsieverts" and "transgenerational effects," once obscure terms reserved for a few scientists, are now part of a new political vocabulary that she must master. Without a doubt, Amano's experience as an individual, mother, wife, and citizen is socially and symbolically different from what it used to be. These changes have strong political dimensions, but understanding their potentialities requires a move beyond conventional understanding of politics and governance.

In this chapter, citizen science perhaps best demonstrates how lay people can directly draw from their own experience to provide concrete solutions beyond traditional top-down governance measures that too often epitomize postdisaster policies. Against a politics of revitalization that has systematically downplayed the fight of citizen scientists, new forms of political subjectivities are arising, which might one day bear fruit in the recognition of nuclear victimhood. When I last saw Amano in 2017, it was still too soon to know how civil society would successfully manage different political representations of the disaster and of recovery. However, since collective memory around nuclear disasters is a shifting process inseparable from numerous exercises of power, one can expect citizens like Natsuo Amano to play a key role in keeping different discourses alive. At the end of the book, we will come back to the multifaceted issues of citizen science, by looking at how this phenomenon can also reinforce a politics of revitalization aligned with the state rather than merely opposing it. But we will leave Geiger-wielding mothers for now and focus on one of the most powerful tools of the politics of revitalization: state-sponsored programs of radioactive monitoring and decontamination.

4

Everything Is Under Control

Situated in the city of Minami-Sōma, the Environmental Radiation Monitoring Center (*kankyō hōshasen sentā*) was a newly created facility that oversaw the tracking of residual radioactivity in Fukushima. Since the tsunami's damage to the coastal region's train infrastructure was still not repaired, the center rarely received visitors. This made my guide, Ken'ichi Kurozawa, even more eager to give me a tour of the state-sponsored center. An expert in radiation monitoring, Kurozawa explained that the center was composed of an analysis section (*bunseki*), which investigated the presence of radionuclides in samples collected throughout Fukushima, as well as an observation section (*kanshi*), tasked with the monitoring of restricted areas.

Every time we entered a room with radiation devices, I was forced to follow a strict containment procedure. As Kurozawa explained, this was to make sure that no contamination got in or out of the laboratory. First, a patch of blue sticky tape collected the dust on the soles of our shoes. Secondly, we had to take off our shoes before putting on special slippers. Lastly, we stepped on yet another piece of sticky blue tape before finally receiving our laboratory coat. As we exited a room, the pattern had to be followed again. No one was allowed to drink, eat, or smoke, and testing samples—from tree pine needles to sea water—were sealed in appropriate containers. No details were omitted; even taking a single pen out of the lab was forbidden for fear of cross-contamination. In the Environmental Radiation Monitoring Center, I could physically see the boundaries that separated me from the imperceptible harms of radiation.

Yet, outside the laboratory, such boundaries are far less tangible. In the convenience store's parking lot near Minami-Sōma, I saw decontamination trucks filled to the brink with bags of tainted radioactive material. While it was forbidden to take a single pen out of the laboratory, a decontamination truck could freely roam the streets of Minami-Sōma, where people lived and children went to school.

On Monitoring and Waste

This chapter explores the governance of radioactive risks through technical fixes, where monitoring and decontamination practices are perceived as the ideal solution to address contamination. I argue that these measures are governance techniques whose function is not only pragmatic but also symbolic. While both practices are limited in their effectiveness, they create specific narratives of governmental control, which are used to legitimize a politics of revitalization.

First, I define monitoring as an activity that implies the systematic surveillance of radioactive contamination. Far from being a neutral activity, monitoring is also a "socially negotiated and organized cultural practice."[1] For instance, monitoring produces symbolic meanings by "imposing a particular framework of theoretical assumptions, standards of evidence, and styles of interpretation."[2] In the context of Fukushima, monitoring is inseparable from managing a specific imaginary around the scale of contamination.

Second, I define decontamination as the removal of hazardous substances, in this case residual radioactivity. In analyzing practices of radioactive decontamination, I draw from a rich literature that focuses on waste, contamination, and toxicity. In *Purity and Danger*, anthropologist Mary Douglas argues that pollution works on pragmatic and symbolic levels.[3] She theorizes pollution as part of a system of classification that expresses unique cultural values: "Dirt then, is never a unique, isolated event. Where there is dirt there is a system. Dirt is the by-product of a systematic ordering and classification of matter, in so far as ordering involves rejecting inappropriate elements. This idea of dirt takes us straight into the field of symbolism and promises a link-up with more obviously symbolic systems of purity."[4]

In that regard, Douglas's approach highlights how decontamination is not a mere technical issue but also an exercise of symbolic classification. In the case of Fukushima, decontamination potentially transformed former images of nuclear wasteland into the vision of a region that can become "pure" again. Scholars of discard studies have further highlighted the unlikely promise of decontamination and its specific cultural imaginary.[5] As Liboiron, Tironi, and Calvillo argue, "Management via separation, containment, clean up and immunization—the hallmarks of

20th-century pollution control—are premised on a politics of material purity that is no longer available or was never viable to begin with."[6] Radioactive decontamination exemplifies this false premise, as there is no way to halt radiation once and for all. Radioactive waste can be buried in the ground, diluted by the oceans, or reduced in size through incineration, but none of these processes stop the phenomenon of radioactivity. Waste buried is still radioactive, radionuclides disperse themselves in the ocean, and incinerated waste creates radioactive ashes, which need to be managed. Only time lowers the amount of radioactivity emitted by harmful radionuclides.

Drawing on observations and interviews conducted in radiation-monitoring centers and scientific conferences, I begin by describing the practice of radioactive monitoring. Then I analyze decontamination policies through the lens of state-sponsored centers and firsthand observations of decontaminating practices in the urban and rural areas of Fukushima. In the second part of this chapter, I examine citizens' dissatisfaction with state-sponsored monitoring and decontamination practices. Using a comparative approach, I highlight how local experiences of contamination often clash with the overall narrative of technical control emphasized by the government.

Mapping the Disaster

Following the release of radioactivity, prevailing winds protected most residents from harmful fallout by blowing pollutants out to sea. Without such luck, a significant portion of Japan might have remained uninhabitable for the foreseeable future. The Japanese nicknamed this lucky wind "*kamikaze*" (literally "divine wind") in reference to the legendary storms that allegedly saved Japan from Mongol invasions in the thirteenth century. Yet the result of this "luck" was still quite devastating to Japan. The coastal region (*hamadōri*) and middle valley (*nakadōri*) of Fukushima Prefecture were tremendously affected by residual contamination.[7] Radiation also settled away from Fukushima Prefecture, reaching areas as far away as Tokyo.[8] Major pollutants included cesium-134, cesium-137, iodine-131, silver-110m, niobium-95, strontium-89, strontium-90, and plutonium.[9]

In total, the amount of radiation "released by the Fukushima accident placed it at 10 percent of the Chernobyl radiation."[10] To better understand the scale of contamination, the US Department of Energy and MEXT jointly conducted aerial tracking of radioactivity. These efforts established the first maps of radioactive contamination, demonstrating that radioactivity had not followed the initial concentric evacuation pattern.

When I arrived in Japan in 2015, the government was tracking radioactivity through the more than thirty-six hundred monitoring devices installed all over the prefecture of Fukushima. Each post, called a "real-time dosimeter," provided measurement of gamma radiation, while displaying the current atmospheric level on an electronic board. An advisor working for the state explained that radiation data was transferred wirelessly to provide constant monitoring. Witnessing my interest in this technology, the advisor prompted me to visit a network of laboratories that fell under the Center for Environmental Creation (CEC) (*kankyō sōzō sentā*). Created in 2015, this central organization aimed to create and restore a beautiful environment (*utsukushiku yutaka na kankyō o kaifuku sōzō suru*) in which affected citizens could live worry free (*anshin shite seikatsu*).[11] To make this goal possible, the organization undertook different activities, emphasizing the importance of monitoring (*monitaringu*) for a politics of revitalization.[12] In terms of radiation tracking, the organization provided detailed gamma ray monitoring and analysis of alpha- (e.g., plutonium) and beta-particle-emitting radionuclides (e.g., strontium).[13]

Throughout Fukushima Prefecture, CEC possessed different laboratories, such as an aquatic center in Inawashiro, a wildlife symbiosis center in Otama, a main branch in Fukushima City, and the Environmental Radiation Monitoring Center of Minami-Sōma. The purpose of the Minami-Sōma center was to ensure the safety of residents and workers living near the damaged power plant by conducting meticulous and continuous (*komayaka de keizokuteki na*) monitoring of radioactive materials.[14] Kurozawa further explained to me that his center specialized in different monitoring methods, including telemetry systems and unmanned helicopters. Bringing me in front of the center's main interactive screen, he explained the situation in Fukushima: "You can see that the radiation levels of Fukushima are represented by different colors: green, blue, and red. Right now, we've been doing a lot of observation in the red areas, which are still restricted, especially Namie, Futaba,

Figure 4.1. A monitoring post in Fukushima City. Photo by Maxime Polleri.

and Okuma. These towns will have high levels for a very long time, and we don't think that they will lower much." Since the creation of the center, Kurozawa and his team had continuously tested radioactive contamination in sea water, soil, dust, agricultural products, livestock products, plants, and marine wildlife. During our tour, I was taken to an annex with a strong, ubiquitous scent of burnt ash, reminding me of a crematorium. Kurozawa explained that this smell was the result of huge commercial incinerators, as every sample needed to be dried out before testing. The next room had an even more pungent smell—one of rotten guts and putrid flesh. Pointing at a chrome table filled with light films of stinky oil, Kurozawa explained the source of the odor: "That's the table where we dissect the fish to test them. Radioactive contaminants have also fallen in the seabed, and the species that live there are more prone to bear high levels of exposure. There's still a lot of bottom fishes that we can't eat."

During the tour, a clear expression of pride could be read on the face of Kurozawa, who was keen to show me the center's complex technological abilities. I was often told remarks such as "There are only six machines like this in Japan" or that this is the "latest technology." Kurozawa then proceeded to show me the calibration and control room. As I looked at a series of metallic tubes from which emanated a brown and murky substance, he enumerated the technical names of every machine. He underscored the fact that their center possessed one of the few devices that measured the level of tritium in the sea, a pollutant that cannot be removed from water as it is a radioactive isotope of hydrogen. Kurozawa explained that no solution existed for properly disposing of tritium-contaminated water: "Right now, contaminated water is stored in tanks. The government wants to dump it into the sea, but the fisherman unions are against it." The last room was reserved for high-tech machines that monitor internal exposure. These noisy machines resembled square metallic vacuums and continuously sucked down the ambient air through special filters. It was then possible to estimate the internal level of contamination by measuring the contaminants in their filters.

The Environmental Radiation Monitoring Center also shared its office with the Japan Atomic Energy Agency (JAEA), an independent agency conducting research and development (R&D) in the field of nuclear energy. Designated as the main R&D institute by the government of Japan, JAEA was heavily involved in developing technologies for the environmental recovery of Fukushima. In their hangars, which were filled with the strong smell of gasoline, I had the opportunity to speak to engineers working on sensor drones and unmanned aerial vehicles. As we approached a small helicopter, Kurozawa began to ask numerous questions, seeming even more interested than I was. "What kind of motors does this helicopter have?" he asked. "It's a 250 cc!" replied one of the engineers, who also shared Kurozawa's enthusiasm regarding technology: "But wait, we've got something much more interesting. It's a new model of a guided plane. It's still not assembled, but you can see the wings over there."

Beyond these centers, I witnessed a similar atmosphere of excitement during scientific conferences that unveiled the latest findings in the field of environmental remediation. For instance, during the Radiation Measurement Forum Fukushima and the International Symposium on Decontamination of Radioactive Material, many scientists boasted about computer codes that simulated the movement of radionuclides in the environment.[15] Other scientists presented calibration software that eliminated the need for traditional calibration in gamma sample assays, introduced novel analog circuits for radiation measurement development, or claimed that they had a "bit of fun" while flying radiation-tracking drones. During the Radiation Measurement Forum Fukushima, members of the audience were presented with the digital image of a cesium ball. Immediately, every scientist started to giggle in their chairs, trying to snap a picture of this ball, which ironically shared a similar look to the numerous bald heads present in the room. Displayed by a supercomputer and made possible by 3D modeling software, the strangely beautiful image of radioactive cesium offered a weirdly exciting experience, echoing Joseph Masco's notion of "nuclear technoaesthetics," wherein nuclear materials are experienced through the lens of an "aesthetic-intellectual project."[16] Was this really the famous culprit responsible for so much of the contamination that followed from this disaster?

My fieldwork in laboratories and scientific conferences represented a sharp affective contrast with the experience of worried mothers like Natsuo Amano, for whom radioactive contamination dramatically altered their environment. I was especially surprised by the different symbolism that monitoring represented. For Amano, monitoring had served as proof of Fukushima's contamination and was used to promote a politics of victimization. But for state experts like Kurozawa, monitoring was entangled in the realm of scientific innovation and pride, while serving the revitalization of Fukushima—even though their practices *also* demonstrated the presence of residual radiation. How could monitoring technologies tell such a different story despite reporting the same findings? How did the state mobilize monitoring to support its politics of revitalization?

I got my answers at the end of the visit, when Kurozawa brought me back to the center's main interactive screen, which subdivided Fukushima into different affected areas. Glancing at the colorful map, I began to understand the power of monitoring and how it enabled state experts to fragment ubiquitous radiation into something more manageable. The word "monitoring" is derived from a Latin term that describes a senior pupil charged with keeping order at school.[17] For the state, radiation monitoring acts in a similar way, creating order where there was once chaos. As exemplified by the endless samples of air, soils, foods, animals, plants, and marine life tested in the center of Minami-Sōma, monitoring provides a method by which to "clearly" judge the scale of contamination.

Anthropologist Tania Li argues that to "render a set of processes technical and improvable an arena of intervention must be bounded, mapped, characterized, and documented; the relevant forces and relations must be identified; and a narrative must be devised connecting the proposed intervention to the problem it will solve."[18] In that regard, state monitoring practices literally transform the distribution of the sensible around radiation. One passes from a "matter of concern," that is, matters that have "no clear boundaries, no well-defined essences, no sharp separation between their own hard kernel and their environment" to a "matter of fact," or matters with "*clear boundaries*, a well-defined essence, well-recognized properties."[19] While the emergence of "matters of concern" is associated with crises, "matters of fact" belong "without any possible question to the world of things, a world made up of persistent, stubborn, non-mental entities defined by strict laws of causality, efficacy, profitability, and truth."[20]

Via monitoring, the crisis of ubiquitous radiation subsequently becomes a testing sample, a piece of dried fish, a murky substance boiling in a tube, a snip of dead pine needles, a sampling of seabed soil, a slight film of oil, a plastic cup on a conveyer belt, or the dusty filter of a metallic lung. Fragmented under these forms, uncertainties surrounding the initial scale of contamination can be weighed, measured, estimated, and ultimately opened to governance. Residual radioactivity was no longer mere "contamination" but precise amounts of becquerel in the bark of a tree or quantifiable amounts of cesium in persimmons (*kaki*). The point is that state monitoring involves a shift from qualitative concerns (e.g., is my environment safe, can I eat the rice?) to quantitative facts (e.g., radiation in the air is X µ/hour or cesium in rice is measured at X Bq/kg). While matters of concern are hardly governable, matters of fact lend themselves to state management and expert narratives.

Pragmatically speaking, monitoring enables the state to eliminate the former concentric zone of exclusion by subdividing Fukushima into three specific areas, which were themselves open to their own speed of revitalization. These areas were represented by different colors (green, orange, and red) and corresponded to the annual dose of external radiation residents were projected to receive if they remained within these zones.[21] Area 1, in green, consisted of zones where the evacuation order was ready to be lifted (*hinan shiji kaijo junbi kuiki*). Atmospheric radiation levels there fell under 20 mSv/year, allowing citizens to return home temporarily to conduct business or resume certain activities. Area 2 in orange consisted of restricted zones (*kyojū seigen kuiki*). They had atmospheric radiation levels falling between 20 and 50 mSv/year, which allowed citizens to temporarily return to their home on a need-to-enter basis. Lastly, area 3 in red (*kikan konnan kuiki*) consisted of the difficult-to-return zones. They had atmospheric radiation levels of over 50 mSv/year.[22] Citizens were required to permanently evacuate these areas, which were surrounded by barricades.

The division of contamination under three specific areas demonstrates that monitoring acted as a "zoning tool," enabling radiation to become a localized risk, which in turn became open to different types of mitigation practices.[23] Importantly, areas 1 to 3 were not depicted as dangerous or safe per se. Rather, they were simply areas open to different *repatriation* schedules. The etymology of zoning reveals that even the most contaminated areas (*kikan konnan kuiki*) were perceived not as permanent zones of exclusion but as "troublesome" areas (*konnan*) to return to.[24] Consequently, state monitoring transformed a territory that was believed to be ruined by the nuclear disaster into a region that could eventually recover, and the tool to enable such a recovery was decontamination.

Decontaminating Fukushima

On August 26, 2011, the government of Japan enacted the Act on Special Measures Concerning the Handling of Radioactive Pollution.[25] The purpose of this policy was to create remediation programs in the areas affected by residual radioactivity. In 2012, the Ministry of the Environment (MOE) became the responsible authority for decontaminating Japan's urban and agricultural areas. To do so, MOE divided the decontamination program into two distinct areas.[26] First, it created Special Decontamination Areas, consisting of zones falling under the initial evacuation orders (Naraha, Tomioka, Okuma, Futaba, Namie, Katsurao, Iitate, Tamura, Minami Soma, Kawamata, and Kawauchi).[27] Then it created Intensive Contamination Survey Areas, representing more than

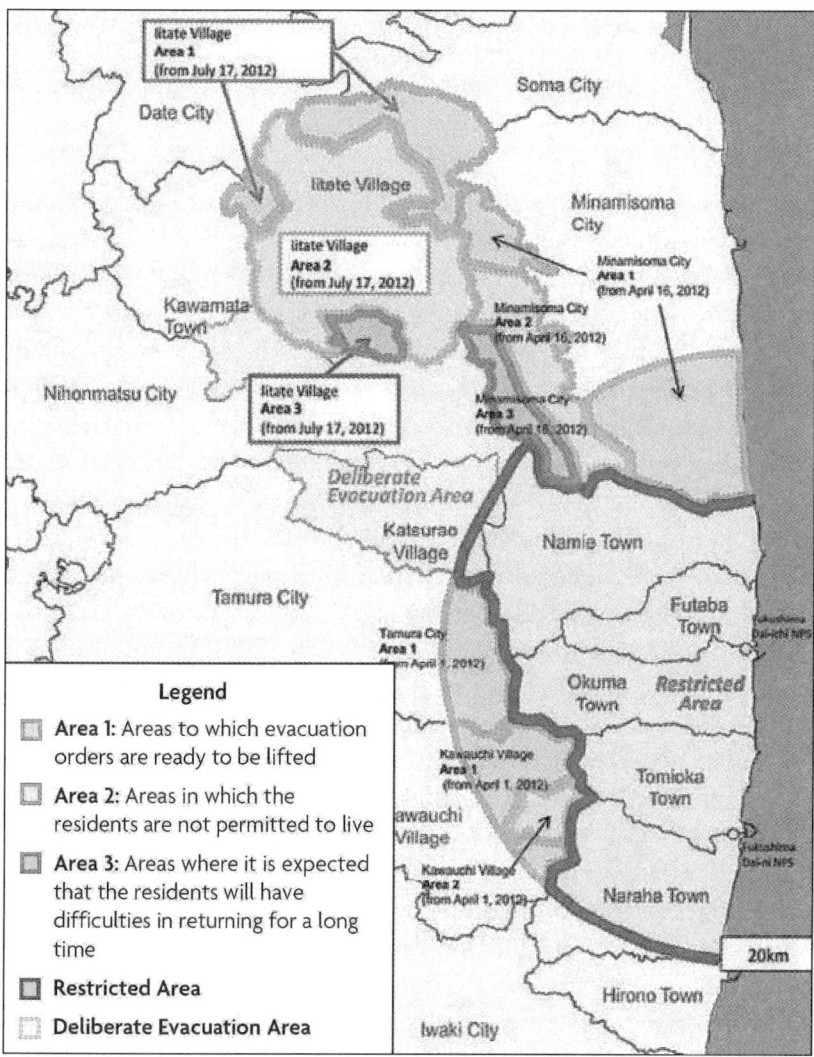

Figure 4.2. Rearrangement of Evacuation Zoning. Map by METI.

one hundred municipalities outside the official evacuation perimeters.[28] These areas included cities in Fukushima but also areas in other prefectures, such as Iwate, Miyagi, Ibaraki, Tochigi, Gunma, Saitama, and Chiba.[29] While Special Decontamination Areas were specified by the government of Japan, the Intensive Contamination Survey Areas were identified by local municipalities. The state took care of all expenses, and the budget for promoting decontamination measures reached 254.5 billion yen in 2016 alone—the equivalent of two billion US dollars.[30]

To learn more about decontamination policies, I spent a good part of my fieldwork in the Decontamination Info Plaza (*josen jōhō puraza*) (DIP), a governmental center established in January 2012 as a joint program between MOE and the prefecture of Fukushima. Located in the town of Fukushima, DIP was a center point for the dispatch of experts, who presented decontamination as the key remediation strategy to return Fukushima to a livable state. As the center explained, decontamination procedures consisted of a series of activities that aimed to eliminate pollutants. First came the "removal of radiation-contaminated objects" (*torinozoku*), which included the collection of radioactive-tainted materials (e.g., soils, fallen leaves, shrubs, grass) in different places (e.g., parks, schoolyards, street gutters, paved roads, and building rooftops). The second part, called the "blocking of radiation" (*saegiru*), aimed to transfer contaminated material in large plastic bags to prevent seepage. With an inner layer coated with thick rubber, decontamination bags were described as sturdy in the open air while ensuring maximum durability. A technical advisor assured me that there was no need to worry about potential tearing. The last step consisted of "keeping" radioactive waste in temporary storage spaces (*toozakeru*) before their final disposal in a permanent facility. Bags were then covered with a thick layer of thirty centimeters of uncontaminated soil to seal them completely in order to prevent seepage and reduce the risk of exposure.

In 2014, Fukushima Prefecture approved the creation of an Interim Storage Facility around the crippled power plant, where decontaminated soil and other radioactive-tainted materials were transported.[31] At DIP, scale models provided explanations of temporary storage spaces, which consisted of volume-reduction facilities, twenty-four-hour monitoring, R&D laboratories, and public information centers. There I found the following message: "The risks of radiation weaken with distance. Temporary storage spaces must be located at a safe distance from the nearest houses and workplaces. Temporary storage spaces are surrounded by fences to keep people out." These spaces were described as using the latest insulation methods until the government could find a final disposal place for radioactive waste. Models also underscored how decontamination had drastically reduced radiation exposure—sometimes by more than 45 percent—while safeguarding the health of residents.³² As an advisor of DIP explained, "The situation is getting better day after day and people will be able to come back to their beloved Fukushima!"

Following Fukushima, the general director of the French Institut de radioprotection et de sûreté nucléaire (Radioprotection and Nuclear Safety Institute) has argued that "a nuclear accident is like a war, you may lose some territories."³³ Yet, for a country like Japan, an island nation with little territory and long-held tropes about the value of its land, adopting measures that would lead to the abandonment of precious national territory was simply unthinkable. Christine Fassert and Reiko Hasegawa argue that the Japanese government had to prove that contaminated "territories were not 'lost' and could indeed be 'reconquered.'"³⁴ Decontamination measures served this purpose since they allowed the state to set aside more troubling narratives of disaster governance like full-scale evacuation. Pragmatically speaking, decontamination allowed for drastic reductions in areas of concern by lifting restrictions on formerly restricted zones. Working in tandem with monitoring practices, decontamination transformed "Area Where Residents Are Not Permitted to Live" into "Area Where Residents Have Difficulties in Returning for a Long Time," and ultimately into "Area Where Evacuation Orders Are Ready to Be Lifted." The pace of this process was quick during my fieldwork, and I had to keep up with the ever-changing map of Fukushima.

Monitoring and decontamination measures were key to the politics of revitalization, since they created a strong narrative of control and safety, enabling the state to put the disaster behind it. For instance, in informational pamphlets, MOE explained that citizens could now play in parks and schoolyards without any worries, since these areas had been thoroughly decontaminated (*kōen ya kōtei wa hajimeni josensareta kara, soto de genki ni asoberu yo ne*).³⁵ This official discourse of safety was then picked up by different state agencies and ministries, and filtered down to the level of newspapers and even travel guides: "The no-entry zone around the nuclear plant makes up less than 3% of the prefecture's area, and even inside most of the no-entry zone, radiation levels have declined far below the levels that airplane passengers are exposed to at cruising altitude. Needless to say, Fukushima is perfectly safe for tourists to visit."³⁶

In the end, remediation measures echoed expert practices that successfully monitored, controlled, and isolated radioactive risks. Yet, how did this carefully woven discourse of containment hold beyond laboratories and scale models?

Beyond the Lab

Monitoring and decontamination made perfect sense in laboratories, governmental white papers, and scale models. However, the limits of remedial measures were apparent in Iitate, a small hamlet heavily affected by radioactive contamination. As of June 2015, MOE had completed most of the decontamination of residential areas in Iitate and aimed to finish it by 2016.[37] When I first came to Iitate in 2016, the village was still a patchwork of different zones, with difficult-to-return areas, restricted-residence areas, and areas where the evacuation order was about to be lifted. While these divisions made sense on governmental maps, it was sometimes difficult to know the exact location of a given area, except for the "difficult-to-return areas," which were fenced off. Amidst the six thousand original residents of Iitate, only a few hundred citizens returned to the village. Many returnees were elderly male farmers who hoped their beloved region could return to its former uncontaminated glory. To keep residents safe, the government had tracked contamination through a network of fixed monitoring posts, while promising to decontaminate the region further. At the time, the possibility of a pristine Fukushima seemed within reach. However, all the farmers I spoke with echoed a clear dissatisfaction with the state monitoring and decontamination practices, which were supposed to provide them with a clean environment for their return.

The Limits of Monitoring

As a farmer, Atsuo Tanizaki did not care much for the state's maps of radioactive contamination. He was not a lone wolf in this regard, as other farmers also criticized the state's monitoring efforts. Many complained that the state's network of fixed monitoring posts only provided so much information, often in the form of the average radiation level of their village. Yet, this information was rarely useful for farmers, since the dispersion of contaminants was heavily heterogeneous. Indeed, areas deemed safe were often filled with spots that had levels falling within evacuation measures. In Tanizaki's village, the monitoring of airborne radiation produced measurements that were not precise enough to give a picture of shifting contamination. Villagers initially lived with constant uncertainty: Is the garden contaminated? Are the trees behind the house safe? Are mushrooms in the forest still edible? Color-coded zoning restrictions might make sense for government workers, said Tanizaki, but real people did not experience their environment through shades of red, orange, and green. Instead, they navigated the landscape one field, one tree, one measurement at a time. "Case by case," he said, grimly, as he guided me along the narrow paths that separated his rice fields, on the outskirts of his village. With a Geiger counter, Tanizaki began taking measurements, showing me how contamination was structured in a way that no state was prepared to solve. For MOE, a successful remediation equaled the reduction of the air dose rate of a given area—that is, the amount of radiation level in the air, per hour or per year. But monitoring rates were often unrelated to the actual levels of contamination found in farmers' paddy fields or in the forested areas of their region, where no monitoring posts were installed. When farmers drove me around the village, my Geiger counter gave drastically different radiation readings than what was displayed on the few monitoring posts. In this context, maps produced by institutional experts soon proved to be completely useless for the returnees.

As Tanizaki came to learn, a peculiar characteristic of radioactive contamination is that it does not follow a clear-cut pattern. Displacement over a few meters gave very different measurements due to the presence of "hot spots"—places where one could find an accumulation of radioactive material. Contamination was more akin to the fur of a leopard, filled with numerous such spots. Because of the perceived inefficacy of state measures, residents had decided to track radiation by themselves, notably to keep the map of their village relevant. In one farmer's house, I witnessed self-made models that exhibited the topography of Iitate's geographical landscape. These models had been made through 3D printers, and the level of radiation had been monitored by the citizens themselves with Geiger counters. In particular, the local knowledge of the geography of Iitate had helped citizens attain a level of precision vastly superior to that based on the network of fixed monitors. Citizens had soon learned that radiation doses could be higher at the bottom of a slope or that the woods behind one's home might impact the radiation level inside one's house. This was a form of pragmatic monitoring that attempted to serve their needs, not that of the politics of revitalization.

In the southern part of Iitate village, state barricades blocked access to highly radioactive areas (*kikan konnan kuiki*), where the annual cumulative radiation dose was too high for reopening (50 mSv/y). A lonely policeman acted as a guard by the gate, trapped in a small wooden cabin. The gate, which was three meters in length, was supposed to separate people from an environment considered problematic, but anybody could easily cross the forbidden zone. In fact, farmers like Tanizaki had access to the areas to check on the condition of their houses. Cars and small pickups went in and out without any form of decontamination, their wheels clearly filled with radioactive mud. As I took a picture of the gate, a farmer looked at the guard with a perplexed smile, telling him, "He's a foreigner [*gaijin*] you know, he just wants to see." Looking at the guard squeezed in the small cabin, I could not help but ponder the meaning of these gates. It was forbidden for a *gaijin* like me to enter the area, but the same interdiction did not apply to local people. One man was harshly critical of this double standard, arguing that "the people of Fukushima are no longer normal people [*Fukushima no hito, ippan no hito ja nai*]." While maps, monitoring, and gates were supposed to lend a sense of control by demarcating which areas were accessible or not, their function appeared more symbolic than pragmatic. Radiation does not have much to do with such clean-cut delimitations; borders are human decisions.

In Fukushima, I also had occasion to witness the scale of devastation near Tomioka, a city situated on the coast of the prefecture. On an unusually cold March morning, I left Tokyo on a bus with members of an organization that advocated for permanent evacuation. As we came closer to Tomioka, road panels announced that the radiation levels could oscillate between 0.1 and 4.4 μSv per hour (3.8 μSv/h is equivalent to 20 mSv per year). The scene outside the windows looked like a battlefield: broken houses, abandoned storefronts, faded colors in shades of gray, long patches of dying grass, and offerings of teas or flowers for the numerous victims of the tsunami.

Figure 4.3. The gates of Iitate. Photo by Maxime Polleri.

Within our group, a former nuclear subcontract worker argued that the network of fixed monitors could show only parts of residual radioactivity. The man explained to me that the number displayed by the state's monitoring posts were deceptive: "Those posts only measure external radiation levels, like gamma rays. . . . They don't consider the dangers of internal contamination, which is one of the main risks in the case of a nuclear incident." While the numbers displayed by monitoring posts in Fukushima were not high enough to cause acute radiation poisoning, the former worker argued that the primary danger for people living in Fukushima came from internalizing alpha- or beta-emitting particles. For him, state maps created via the monitoring of external radioactivity produced a false sense of security.

The danger of internal exposure is indeed dependent on the toxicity of each radionuclide and its interaction with specific body parts. For instance, the toxicity of alpha particles is twenty times greater than that of gamma rays, and many radionuclides adversely impact body organs when internalized.[38] As fixed monitoring posts do not consider these dangers, different forms of risk are not necessarily factored into the current radiological maps of Fukushima, which are based only on external radiation levels, mostly emanating from cesium-134 and cesium-137.[39] Scholars have also underscored the limits of radiation monitoring. Alexey Yablokov, a professor of the Russian Academy of Sciences, argues that "official dose calculations were based on cesium-137, but in some places, americium-241, plutonium-238 and -240, and strontium-90, which are more difficult to detect, can be the main factors in overall internal and external irradiation."[40] In 2018, scientists found novel forms of radioactive contamination—glass-like cesium-rich microparticles.[41] These microparticles contain dangerous radioisotopes that do not dissolve easily and that are small enough to be ingested, potentially causing long-term health risks.[42] As professor of chemistry Bernd Grambow explains, "Assuming that residents of Fukushima—or residents of Tokyo—have inhaled cesium microbeads and that these have remained in their lungs for a long time, local damages, fibrosis or even necrosis, are theoretically possible."[43]

At the train station of Tomioka, our group began to put on masks and plastic coats to protect ourselves from radioactive dust. "Be sure to tighten your mask and wear your raincoat! When you're done, put them in the plastic bag that was given to you; we don't want to bring radioactive contamination on the bus," shouted the organizer of the tour. After visiting the abandoned city, we began to dispose of our masks and raincoats in a sealed garbage bag. However, a quick look at the floor of the bus revealed a nonnegligible amount of dust. Few measures seemed to successfully prevent the entrance and exit of radioactive pollutants. Next to me the former nuclear worker explained that Fukushima had transformed itself into an enormous open-air nuclear plant, freely accessible to anyone. As he claimed,

> In any nuclear power plant, or rooms with radiation devices for that matter, you basically have a "controlled area," a place where radiation levels are controlled. Take a bottle of water, for example; it's like if the radiation levels were controlled inside the plastic bottle and radiation can't get out. We're bringing all that contamination with us. Nothing prevents the entrance and exit of radioactive pollutants in Tomioka. I mean, just look

at your boots: they are full of dust and mud. It's the same for everybody. It's already all over the bus. It's in the air that we are breathing right now.

The way back to Tokyo was a long one. Hungry, I began to unwrap a sandwich until someone tapped my shoulder: "Maybe you shouldn't eat that," the man said, "in case you have radionuclides in your beard." We had almost arrived in Tokyo, an area officially deemed clean, but the certitude of radiological safety maps now seemed to merely hold on paper.

While monitoring is certainly useful for understanding *part* of the scale of contamination, it also creates what Michelle Murphy calls "regimes of imperceptibility," rendering some hazards invisible.[44] Similarly, what cannot be problematized on state maps, such as internal contamination by alpha and beta particles, is often sidelined from the overall narrative of remediation and control. This imperceptibility echoes Scott Frickel and Vincent Bess's notion of "ignorance by design," which refers to "a form of organized ignorance that, among other things, masks ecological complexity."[45]

In sharp contrast to state maps, different scales of contamination became visible after Fukushima through alternative means, such as artistic exhibits. In 2016, I went to an exhibition entitled *Radiation Image: Visualizing Radioactivity* (*hōshasen-zō, hōshanō wo kashika suru*),[46] and became acquainted with the work of Masamichi Kagaya, an artist who became famous for literally photographing residual radioactivity in Fukushima. Such a feat is made possible by autoradiography, a form of nuclear emulsion produced by the pattern of radioactive decay.[47] In simpler terms, autoradiography creates images on an X-ray film (or specially produced photographic plates) by using the energy emitted from a radioactive substance. Because autoradiography plates come in close contact with different samples, and because they are sensitive to beta particles, the process of autoradiography detects amounts of radiation that are not picked up by airborne monitoring.[48] Radioactive pollutants that have adhered to or penetrated organisms' bodies are made visible with this process.

Traveling across Fukushima with Satoshi Mori, a professor emeritus from Tokyo University specializing in plant nutrition, Kagaya and his team began to collect dead animals, plants, insects, wild boar excrement, and many other things. In the process, they not only tested the level of radiation found in these things, but produced beautiful autoradiograph plates. The result became a series of phantomatic-like photographs showing signs of radioactive contamination. As Kagaya explains on his website, "The radioactive contamination continues to be hotly debated throughout Japan and is a recurring topic in the media. And yet, very few have taken on the task of capturing a visual image of the harmful radiation for the public to see, such as enabling people to see the radiation emitted by objects directly subject to the fallout, to see where the radiation is concentrating in the food chain and in contaminated foodstuffs, and how the flora and the fauna living in radioactive areas take in radioactive substances and where these substances accumulate inside them."[49]

During a conference entitled "Visualizing Radioactivity" (*hōshanō wo kashika suru*), Prof. Mori showed a picture of a small bird, a swallow that had gone through the process of autoradiography.[50] The result was a ghostly halo, a phantomatic doppelgänger of the bird, filled with numerous small black spots (*butsu butsu supotto*) representing traces of contamination. One could see the stomach and intestines of the bird, places that had accumulated high doses of radiation. Another picture was the radiography of a snake. With a body mostly composed of muscle, it had absorbed lots of radiation. All these dead animals seemed, for a short instant, to be brought back to life, haunting the audience with the proof of their contamination. Other pictures included bird nests, coins, foot slippers, temple stones, a radiator from the girls' bathroom of a school, the bark of trees, dragonflies, frogs, a butterfly, and a pair of boots. In their book, entitled *hōshasen-zō* (Radiographic Images), Kagaya and Mori provide "before" and "after" images of contaminated objects.[51] While "after objects" invariably have the same form as "before objects," the process of autoradiography demonstrates that their substance has changed permanently. All radio-pictures are also labeled and dated, acting as proof of the level of contamination. These artistic efforts reveal a different scale of contamination, one that state monitoring and color-charted maps paradoxically make imperceptible. Their work is a haunting testament to the pervasiveness of residual contamination, which slowly moves up the food chain, to gradually end in the lungs, guts, intestines, and stomachs of living things. At odds with the recalcitrance of state maps, the specter of radiation keeps haunting diverse forms of life, like the soft, almost inaudible murmur of a vengeful ghost. Marilyn Ivy argues that ghosts haunt us because they reveal the "impossibility of stabilizing meaning."[52] Against claims that the nuclear disaster is under control, Kagaya's pictures act as phantomatic evidence of the perniciousness of contamination.

The Limits of Decontamination

Beyond monitoring, many citizens were dissatisfied with decontamination policies. At the beginning of the disaster, the government applied a cookie-cutter approach to decontamination, and blue Prussian—a chemical used for decontamination in Chernobyl—was sprayed throughout Iitate village. Unfortunately, blue Prussian was unsuccessful at dislodging radioactive cesium. Farmers explained to me that this was the result of the specific soil of Iitate, which is rich in vermiculite, a hydrous phyllosilicate mineral that impedes cesium from dispersing. As one man explained, "The cesium gets trapped in a sandwich kind of way, between minerals. That's a specific problem linked with our soil."

During a symposium entitled "Let's Not Forget Fukushima" (*Fukushima wo wasurenai*), a former dairy farmer named Ken'ichi Hasegawa also criticized the decontamination procedure: "They wipe our roof with paper towels and call that decontamination!"[53] In Iitate, I heard similar comments, as farmers complained that "house sanitization" was a mere synonym for washing houses with pressurized water jets. State decontamination had yielded unsatisfactory results for farmers, as such practices rarely lowered their house level by half.[54] Even decontamination workers criticized the effectiveness of decontamination policies. During a conference at the No Nukes World Social Forum, Minoru Ikeda, a former Japanese decontamination worker, argued that decontamination (*jōsen*) was nothing more than "weeding" (*josō*), claiming that it consisted of putting contaminated grass in plastic bags.[55] While "radioactive decontamination" sounded highly technical on paper, Minoru Ikeda's narrative demonstrated that decontamination was akin to shoveling contaminated materials elsewhere. In Tomioka, I witnessed decontamination workers put heavily contaminated bricks, soil, and other debris into plastic bags, with mountains of them lying about as far as the eye could see. Decontamination did not resolve the problem of residual radioactivity per se, as the lifespan of radioactivity is longer than the lifespan of plastic bags. In fact, many bags had already broken down, once again spilling their radiation-laced materials over "freshly decontaminated" lands.

At DIP there was no sense of the aftermath of decontamination, as figurines and scale models do not talk back. But in Iitate, I quickly realized that decontamination policies had changed the social landscape of the village, creating considerable anxiety for returnees. By 2019, decontamination practices had generated more than twenty million cubic meters of soil waste.[56] In Iitate alone, farmers had to deal with the presence of more than 2.3 million bags. To demonstrate the drastic alteration of their life, Tanizaki showed me two pictures of the village. The first one, taken before the disaster, consisted of golden-brown rice fields with wonderful hues of green—a postcard-perfect picture of what life used to be like. The second picture, taken after state decontamination, showed a vastly different sight: torn-down landscapes filled with bags of radioactive soil and gray-looking mountains.

In Iitate, the sheer magnitude of plastic bags was simply astonishing. While experts at MOE contended that plastic bags should be stored in spaces located at a safe distance from the nearest workplaces, the reality was otherwise. Bags were literally everywhere, stacked upon each other, like skyscrapers of modern contaminated times. Citizens who had returned to Fukushima complained about this daily eyesore and the lack of a permanent disposal site. Five years after the disaster, the government had still been unable to secure an area for a final disposal site, since it had only purchased 2.3 percent of the land necessary for a storage facility.[57] As one man from Fukushima angrily told me, "Waste disposal is one of the biggest problems. Bags are always moved from a temporary site to another temporary site. It's temporary over temporary over temporary." To alleviate the vast quantities of waste in Fukushima, MOE had allowed farmers to rent their plots of land as temporary disposal sites, a decision that further fueled tensions within the village of Iitate. As a local official explained,

> I don't know what kind of impression [*inshō*] you have of Iitate. . . . Iitate used to be in the top ten of the prettiest villages in Japan. Now, there are

1.5 million bags all across it. They are left right next to the paddy fields. Citizens are seeing these bags every day and ask themselves, "Can we really go back?" They are being told that everything is safe, but when they see those bags, how can they be sure? Currently, there are four hundred persons of the original six thousand that have come back to the village. Most of them are old [*kōreisha*]. People have started to plant flowers, as well as growing rice. But it [the recovery] will probably take a lot of time.

Notwithstanding these problems, Iitate was indeed a pretty village that had all the charms of the Japanese "countryside" (*inaka*), but as soon as one left the mountains, the endless rows of plastic bags brought one right back into the world of contamination. Bags were even near cemeteries, impeding citizens from visiting family graves. On state-sanctioned maps, clearly divided in chromatic palettes, there was no impression of the texture of life amid pyramids of radioactive-laced bags. As one informant commented, "I can understand the mothers that don't want to come back to the village. Just look at that [the bags]. Who would want to raise a child in this environment?" A popular saying in the village of Iitate echoed this feeling of abandonment amid radioactive debris: "First we were victims, then refugees, and now abandoned people" (*hajime wa hisaisha de, jikini nanmin to nari, korekara wa kimin desu*).

A decade after the 2011 meltdowns, Iitate remained contaminated by industrial pollution. Though attempts at removing pollutants continue, a new realization had taken hold among many of Fukushima's returnees: there is no going back to an uncontaminated way of life. When people like Tanizaki returned to their village, many expected a thorough decontamination of mountain and forest areas. Yet, there are no decontamination activities in such areas, which cover 75 percent of Fukushima Prefecture.[58] This is due to the risk of soil erosion, potential landslides, and the cost of decontamination. As a local official explained, "When the decontamination started, about two years ago, we were told that we would be able to come back. But the government can't decontaminate the mountains and that puts a lot of stress on the citizens. . . . The official evacuation of Iitate is supposed to be lifted next year, but there are so many things left to do that I don't know if it will be possible. There are a lot of parts that are still very contaminated."

Figure 4.4. The result of decontamination. Photo by Maxime Polieri.

In rural Fukushima, the mountains and forest are integral to citizens' lifestyle, and discouraging people from entering them is simply impossible. "Many citizens are probably never going to come back to Iitate if they don't decontaminate these areas," a villager shared. As opposed to the clear boundaries present in the radiation laboratories that I visited, the residents of Iitate experienced their environment as interconnected: "We can't go into the woods to hunt, pick foods, or do any kind of forest management [because of the contamination]. So the population of wild animals, vermin, and pests has risen. They constantly destroy the renovations that we make. Every time people come back to their house they find rat feces. It's really a kind of vicious cycle."

Similarly, the rise of wild boars had become problematic in Iitate, as many destroyed farmhouses, while leaving behind radioactive excrement. MOE's documentation explained that while wild boars are usually cowardly (*okubyō*), the disaster resulted in low human activity, which drastically increased their numbers.[59] Radiation had toppled a specific ecosystem that simply could not be revitalized by putting contaminated topsoil in vinyl bags. Things that look as insignificant as moss ended up representing an important vector of contamination, creating a vicious cycle. As a scientist in Iitate explained, "Moss is one of the most radioactive things in the forest. Its concentration of cesium is ten to one hundred times higher than wild grasses, which themselves vary from 500 to 8000 Bq/kg. Of course, we don't eat moss, but the animals do and we eat those animals. It causes a lot of bioaccumulation in the muscles of wild beasts. Even after thirty years, moss is still going to be very radioactive." Being fond of things like moss, earthworms, and mushrooms, wild boars had accumulated high levels of contamination, sometimes reaching 15,000 Bq/kg. Their migratory pattern also meant that they could travel far beyond the vicinity of Fukushima, where their contaminated flesh risked being eaten by unsuspecting hunters. Adding to these difficulties, decontamination policies view irradiated topsoil as unwanted and needing to be promptly removed. But for many farmers, land has historically been passed down from generation to generation, and topsoil is anything but "waste" in their minds.[60] Symbolically speaking, the discarding of precious soil is akin to losing one's identity—even more so when one considers the Japanese concept of the family household (*ie*), which encompasses both past and future generations. Returnees like Tanizaki were then forced to ask themselves difficult questions about their homes, livelihoods, and identities: What will happen if farming is impossible? What does it mean to be a rice farmer when you can't grow rice? What if life has been irrevocably altered?

A former way of life may be impossible to retrieve, and state decontamination may have failed, but farmers like Tanizaki have also learned to form new relationships with this irradiated environment. Rather than giving up, some took matters into their own hands, embracing novel practices for living alongside toxic pollution. These practices go far beyond traditional farming. One method involved planting sunflowers, which were believed to absorb radiation as they grew. Yellow flowers bloomed across the farmlands of Fukushima. However, the results proved to be unsatisfactory. During my time in Japan years after the disaster, I still saw dead sunflowers rooted in irradiated fields—withered emblems of early dreams to retrieve a predisaster Fukushima. When this failed, farmers collaborated with agricultural scientists, beginning to grow silver grass as a potential source of biofuel that would provide energy for their region. "If we can't grow food, we can at least make energy!" one scientist told me.

Traditional farming also continues, albeit in a different way. For instance, during one trip to Fukushima, I visited a long plastic greenhouse where a group of farmers and scientists were cultivating fire-red strawberries. Inside, I saw rows of strawberries growing on the ground, fed by filtered water from a system of tubes. This watering system ran in and out of soil that was thick with pebbles, which a scientist told me were "volcanic gravel from Kagoshima" on the other side of Japan, hundreds of kilometers away. According to him, they were using gravel because the soil in Fukushima was "too contaminated to harvest safe products." In fact, almost everything that the strawberries needed to grow, from the plastic greenhouse to the filtered water, had come from elsewhere. For some, new products like little red strawberries grown with imported soil became symbols of resilience, adaptation, and recovery—part of the fabric of solidarity in a new Fukushima.

Still, many farmers learned to accept that life in Fukushima will never be the same, even with monitoring and decontamination policies. Small details were constant reminders of that transformation, like the library in Tanizaki's home, which is now filled with books on Chernobyl, nuclear power, radioactive contamination, and food safety. Even the mushrooms tasted different. One farmer, Takeshi Mito, told me he had learned to grow shiitake mushrooms on artificial tree trunks, since forest trees were too contaminated to produce edible fungi. "Now the taste of the shiitake has changed," he mumbled, a strange sadness filling his voice. The real trees had given the mushrooms a special flavor, just like ageing a whisky in a sherry cask. "Yeah," he said, pausing to remember. "They were good." Nuclear mushrooms in the form of atomic bombs or edible delicacies keep haunting Japan.

Radioactive Flowerpots

To govern radiation, the Japanese state opted for a set of narratives and practices that sought to manage the uncertainties of residual contamination. It did so by transforming the nature of radiation risk as a biophysical entity that can be isolated from the human environment. Under this language, radioactivity became accessible to governance. Yet, as exemplified by the lived experience of citizens, remedial measures had limited efficacy. While technical measures were seen as an incentive to make people come back, many citizens also chose not to return.[61]

Notwithstanding these shortcomings, both monitoring and decontamination remained powerful symbolic measures that suited governmental needs. They enabled the state to reduce evacuation areas, cut financial compensation, and promote a narrative of "cleanliness," where Japan was no longer contaminated. In terms of symbolic power, these practices were highly successful. They showcased a Japan on the verge of recovery and enabled the nation to even host the Olympic games. The symbolism behind the decision to start the torch relay in Fukushima was lost on no one.[62]

Outside Fukushima, few citizens were aware of the difficulties that rural returnees like Tanizaki faced. Remediation measures looked good on television programs and created the narrative of a disaster that was now over. Yet, as one local official from the village of Iitate explained to me in 2016, "Now we are entering the sixth year of the disaster. Many people might be surprised at how quickly time has passed by. But let me tell you that for us, it has been a very, very long five years." Radioactive contamination, as experienced in the environment, clashed with the politics of revitalization promoted by the state. But by configuring access to knowledge about radiation hazards, state experts projected a particular narrative of control. Remedial measures were not necessarily those that led to actual decontamination but rather those that gave an appearance of control.

Even as I write these lines, the reality on the ground is far from pretty, as contaminated materials are piling up more quickly than expected. Decontamination wastes currently account for more than eleven Tokyo Domes, or roughly 305 hectares.[63] MOE promised local governments to eliminate all that waste by 2045, but the ministry faces the legal challenge of finding a final disposal site outside of Fukushima.[64] Unsurprisingly, no prefectures have volunteered to host such wastes. Against the failure of decontamination measures, it appears that even state ministries are starting to acknowledge the shortcomings of traditional waste governance, built on the false promise of isolation. For instance, MOE has begun to promote alternate governance schemes, one of which implies the "recycling" (*sairiyō*) of decontamination waste. Faced with the impossibility of proper disposal, MOE is attempting to reduce the amount of waste by launching recycling demonstration projects in the Nagadoro district of Iitate village.[65] The ministry wishes to "recycle" radioactive-tainted soil and debris as construction materials that can be used in farmlands, embankments, or construction projects.[66] Their plan is to "transfer soil containing less than 8,000 Bq/kg to be used under roads and in building levees not only in Fukushima but all over Japan."[67] Current exhibits of "potted plants using removed soil from Fukushima Prefecture" are even visible in "the Prime Minister's office, Reconstruction Agency, the head office of the Liberal Democratic Party of Japan, Shinjuku Gyoen National Garden, the National Institute for Environmental Studies, and other locations."[68] This diffusion of radioactive waste throughout the archipelago of Japan is officially touted as an effort to "eliminate" misconceptions about Fukushima.[69] Now that narratives of isolation no longer work, a new nationwide strategic plan of waste management attempts to transform the symbolism of waste into "recycling" materials. Ironically, a new Japan is literally being constructed on the contaminated ruins of its former self. In this radiant narrative, radioactive waste is no longer "matter out of place."[70] Rather, it finds its place alongside the most common decoration of everyday life: the office potted plant.

5

Commodifiable Phantasm

Five years after the disaster, I found myself driving from Tokyo with volunteers to visit a temporary housing complex. We were en route to speak to the displaced residents of Tomioka, a small city situated within the former twenty-kilometer exclusion zone of the power plant. Its residents were still forbidden to return (excluding short trips to retrieve personal items). As we entered the abandoned city, the highway's electronic board solemnly reported the radiation level of 2 μSv per hour.

The place was a ghost town. With phantom-like eeriness, the storefront windows were stuck in time, exhibiting the same household items from five years earlier. Pictures and posters of politicians had faded, reinforcing the spectral appearance of the town. A child's bicycle lay across the road with shattered glass nearby. The most striking sight was the pervasive rust, as if the brittle skin of the town was crumbling apart. Houses had begun to collapse due to neglect and the passage of time. Further down the road, we stumbled upon an abandoned school. The grass was long, rust covered the playground, and a huge stone pillar lay across the building's entrance, toppled during the earthquake. Inside the school, nothing had changed except for a few millimeters of dust covering the whole place. The clocks had all stopped at the exact same time.

For the displaced resident, Tomioka represents what the Japanese call "*furusato*." As Jennifer Robertson explains, "*Furusato* literally means 'old village,' but its closer English equivalents are 'home' and 'native place.'"[1] In this chapter, I explore how postdisaster governance has been inseparable from managing the imaginary of the *furusato*. I underscore how state performances, especially those associated with the Reconstruction Agency, played on tropes of resilience and nostalgia for one's native land to promote a politics of revitalization. By focusing on the narratives of state officials, forced evacuees, and voluntary evacuees, I explore how different understandings of the *furusato* influenced the interpretation of radioactive contamination. I argue that engaging with the *furusato* was a political touchstone for speaking about recovery. For some, the phantasm of a place that was pure before confronted the phantasm of a place that can become pure again, and thus opened the ground for the discourse of revitalization, repatriation, and economic commodification.

In describing this political touchstone, I introduce the concept of "commodifiable phantasm," which refers to the mobilization of nostalgia as the driver behind idealized reconstruction paths in Japan. By resorting to this imaginary, the government was raising the specter of a precarious *furusato* that was affected by harmful rumors and in ways that reinforced the trope of a strong, resilient, and unified nation-state. Instead of embracing the diverse realities of the *furusato*, the state phantasm of citizens' longing for their native homes conveyed commodified notions of the *furusato*, which had little to do with the lived realities of evacuees, and which ended up being open to marketable practices and socioeconomic policies.

The Marketing of Nostalgia

Following the nuclear disaster, the Japanese state mobilized the imaginary of the native land to promote a policy of repatriation to Fukushima. As Tom Gill argues, "*furusato*" became a key term for the LDP 2012 election platform with the motto "'First, recovery. Bring back the hometown' (*Mazu, fukkō. Furusato o, torimodosu*)."[2] In my interviews with government officials, the repatriation to former restricted areas was explained by the fact that evacuees longed to return home as quickly as possible, with officials emphasizing the psychological suffering of evacuees induced by the separation from their native land of Fukushima.

In a pamphlet entitled *Five Years down the Road to Reconstruction*, produced by the Cabinet Office of Japan, one could find statements like the following from evacuated children: "I want to return home" and "I want to spend more time with my family."[3] In another publication entitled "What Is Happening in Fukushima" (*Fukushima de, hajimatte iru koto*), METI explains how it is actively "working on various issues so that residents can choose to return in the future" (*shōrai-teki ni jūmin ga 'kikan' no sentaku ga dekiru yō, tayō na kadai ni torikunde imasu*).[4] Similarly, a technical advisor working for MOE once explained to me that "people in Fukushima love their native land [*furusato*], their home sweet home." MOE's materials emphasized the joys of nature and the traditional foods available in the different *furusatos* of Fukushima. To explain the phenomenon of radioactivity and to fight the presence of "harmful rumors," MOE had even created a little mascot called *"furusato midori"* (literally "green *furusato*"), who took the form of a little boy with olive-colored hair and a green jacket. Within this narrative, the state discourse presented repatriation (*kikan*) as a desire of residents to return to their native land, which helped to support decontamination and revitalization projects.

Historically speaking, the term *"furusato"* has a rich tradition of political mobilization, since it is a cultural notion imbued with deep nostalgic feelings for one's native place. In talking about nostalgia, I refer to a feeling of yearning for an idealized past, while keeping in mind that nostalgia is always a "cultural practice, not a given content."[5] As many authors explain, cultural practices surrounding the nostalgia of the *furusato* evoke traditional images of a rural idyll, which are predominantly linked with agricultural labor or natural landscapes.[6] Thus the notion of the *furusato* does not represent "a specific location but rather a pervasive, nostalgia-driven ideal—one that represents whatever is felt to be lacking in contemporary industrialized society."[7] The travel industry successfully mobilized this perceived lack to offer "pseudotravel experiences for busy urbanites,"[8] despite the irony (pointed out by scholars like Tom Gill and Marilyn Ivy) of urban citizens predominantly consuming this nostalgic yearning for a more traditional lifestyle.[9] Similarly, financially strapped municipalities have used *furusato* movements to rebrand themselves and promote revitalization via tourism.[10] These movements culminated in 2008 with the creation of a "hometown tax" (*furusato nōzei*), which acts as "a way for people to channel part of their taxes to help rural areas struggling with falling populations and shrinking revenues."[11]

But there is something deeper going on with this mobilization of nostalgia, especially regarding nation-state making and essentialist features of Japaneseness.[12] In highlighting the role of yearning, I draw from Tim Choy's analysis of nostalgia, which denotes a "kind of painful homesickness."[13] As he argues, "If we remember this sense of nostalgia, we might see that nostalgic discourses of endangerment do not simply bemoan the passage of time, but are sick, instead, from the loss of specific, meaningful spaces."[14] Similarly, by mobilizing tropes of "a pre-Western, pre-industrialized, and nonurban past,"[15] Millie Creighton argues, the *furusato* asserts "a unique Japanese heritage in the face of an increasingly Westernized lifestyle,"[16] often to the detriment of social difference.[17] From a political viewpoint, the *furusato* successfully imbues "whatever it names or is prefixed to with traditionalness and cultural authenticity."[18] Nuclear lobbies have made use of this concept by presenting nuclear power as a way to revitalize the economy of struggling rural regions, thereby "allowing" local population to save their native land.[19]

In conceptualizing the *furusato* as a form of "commodifiable phantasm," it is important to define what is meant by both "commodity" and "phantasm." First, while the *furusato* is not a thing per se, it takes the characteristics of a Marxist commodity—a good or a service that results from human activity and is sold on a market.[20] Marx famously argued that a commodity encompasses a shift from the *use* value of a product (which satisfies a basic need) to the *exchange* value of a product (which can be traded for something else), thereby creating a process of alienation. As Benoît Heilbrunn summarizes, "Alienation is what separates the object from its manufacturing process, leading to a fetishism that conceals relationships between men, mediated by objects that have a life of their own, but one that is artificial."[21] In post-Fukushima Japan, similar processes of alienation are happening, as radioactive contamination forces social actors to drastically rethink what their native land stands for while leading to a nostalgic fetishization of past ways of life.

Secondly, in talking about phantasm, I refer to an "epistemological object whose presence or absence cannot be definitively located."[22] This definition echoes the understanding of the *furusato*, which can be regarded as a figment of imagination, a sought-after utopia—in brief, a product of fantasy. However, while phantasms are illusory things, anthropologists have argued that they produce concrete social effects.[23] Similarly, the phantasm of the native land was shaping the governance of post-Fukushima disaster recovery in specific ways. One of these effects was the creation of a nostalgic discourse about former ways of life, which was turned into commodifiable practices, best exemplified by expensive decontamination procedures.

Before Fukushima, nostalgia for the native land was linked with the disappearance of Japanese tradition (such as in the cases of rural depopulation) and with efforts to maintain cultural homogeneity.[24] Yet, in post-Fukushima Japan, the vanishing of the *furusato* was not the result of foreign Western influences but rather the result of the specter of radioactive contamination brought about by Japanese elites. As a result, this phantasm longs not for a pre-Western archipelago (resulting in the marketing of tourism) but for a pre-Fukushima Japan, which can perhaps become uncontaminated again, either by technical fixes (e.g., decontamination) or by permanent evacuation practices (for voluntary evacuees). While the *furusato* was always depicted as something vanishing, radiation politics opened a novel phantasmagoric space for its commodification practices.

The Phoenix of Fukushima

In this section, by focusing on the Reconstruction Agency, I examine how tropes of resilience (*rejiriensu*), hope (*kibō*), repatriation, and technological innovations have become key values in the post-Fukushima *furusato* of the Japanese state. Through public performance and revitalization projects playing on affective tropes of nostalgia for one's native land, the Reconstruction Agency began to govern the understanding of Fukushima beyond scientific forms of expertise. In 2016, this approach was epitomized during a forum organized by the Reconstruction Agency whose title translates as "Great East Japan Earthquake Fifth Anniversary Reconstruction Forum: Toward a New Stage of the Reconstruction/Creation."[25] In the opening keynote, Tsuyoshi Takagi, the minister for reconstruction, emphasized the remarkable revitalization that followed Japan's Triple Disaster: "Many people wondered if Japan would be able to return to its former self. But Japan is back, Japan is revived with an indomitable spirit and will lead the world again. . . . We will continue to decontaminate and restore the living infrastructure, to create an environment where people who want to return to their hometown [*furusato*] can do so."[26]

During the forum, Fukushima was described as quickly recovering from the nuclear meltdowns, with Minister Takagi explaining that the atmospheric level of radiation had decreased by more than 65 percent since 2011. In a pamphlet created by the Reconstruction Agency, the state of radiation levels at that time in the cities of Koriyama (0.12 μSv/h) or Naraha (0.10 μSv/h) was shown as being "about the same levels" as in Munich, Shanghai, or Paris, implying that radiation had returned to normal levels.[27] The audience was reminded that the only deaths from the nuclear disaster were caused by the evacuation procedures and not by radiation exposure. In like spirit, the governor of Fukushima, Masao Uchibori, joyfully declared the following: "I want to give you two numbers: seven percent and zero percent. Seven percent is the current area of evacuation among the whole prefecture of Fukushima. People that have evacuated because of radiation and that are not able to live there. Zero is what we are aiming for! That seven percent should be brought down to zero!"

The audience burst into energetic applause upon being told that a "normal life could be recovered!" The governors of Iwate and Miyagi, the adjacent prefectures of Fukushima, shook their heads in approval while declaring that a resilient spirit was necessary to overcome the disasters: "We cannot just walk away even if it seems impossible! One small light is enough to enable us to advance in a tunnel!" The governor of Fukushima then introduced the audience to the concept of Fukushima Pride (*Fukushima puraido*), which consisted of two points: "First, we want to turn the negative into zero, and secondly, turn that zero into something positive." The "negative" in question was not explained, but Uchibori's narrative implied that it was not the residual radiation that he was referring to but instead the notion of harmful rumors.

The Reconstruction Agency also introduced its vision for a "New Tōhoku" (*atarashii tōhoku*), wherein Fukushima and its adjacent prefectures were slated to become leading models of Japan. The five pillars of this New Tōhoku consisted in creating "a reliable society to promote the safe and healthy growth of children, a vibrant super-aged society with 'the elderly people as standards,' a society with sustainable energy, a leading society introducing robust and highly resilient social infrastructure, and a society with wide appeal in utilizing regional resources."[28] In this scenario, Fukushima and Tōhoku would become the "world's 'ideal' place to be," providing a model that could be applied nationwide wherein resilience was a key value for the future of Japan.[29]

During the forum, the need for repatriation was explained by the claim that forced evacuees were longing to return to their *furusato*. Because of the long-term evacuation, there was also the fear that children might forget about their native land and that the traditional heritage associated with local regions might disappear. Therefore, the agency promoted local initiatives that aimed to restore *furusato* culture, where children could learn about their hometown (*furusato o manabu kodomo-tachi*).[30] For instance, the agency created a nationwide writing contest for schoolchildren, with themes such as "our thoughts toward our hometown and the progress of our reconstruction" (*watashitachi no fukkō no ayumi to furusato e no omoi*).[31] It also implemented a "reconstruction of the heart" project (*kokoro no fukkō*) to record local memories of *furusato*.[32]

Accordingly, speakers invited to the forum were not nuclear scientists or medical experts but rather citizens who faced the potential disappearance of their *furusato*. Speakers included a famous violinist, members of a women's association of traditional handicrafts, as well as representatives of the local workers and farmers from Fukushima. Many shared their postdisaster discourses of resilience, expressing confidence that their *furusato* would recover from the nuclear catastrophe. For instance, upon seeing the state of devastation in Fukushima, the violinist burst into tears, muttering, "Oh, what has happened to my dear *furusato*!" To contribute to the revitalization project, a TV anchor also told the audience to enjoy the rich cultural traditions of Fukushima and to "spend your money, have fun, and buy souvenirs! That's the best thing you can do for the people of Fukushima!" Since tourism had sharply decreased after the disaster, the Reconstruction Agency promoted the cultural heritage of different *furusatos*, regularly profiling traditional foods such as frozen rice cake (*shimi mochi*) or buckwheat noodles (*soba*).[33] In their print material, the agency further highlighted the rich natural beauty (*utsukushī midori*) of Fukushima, praising the possibilities of ecotourism (*ekotsurizumu*),[34] as well as initiatives that encouraged the "regeneration of the *furusato*" (*furusato saisei*).[35] To fight against an increase in obesity that had followed the disaster, the Reconstruction Agency stressed the importance of doing sports in one's hometown, highlighting the "fun of jogging in one's native land" (*furusato wo hashiru tanoshisa*).[36]

During the forum, a young woman shared her dream of getting married in Naraha, a small town situated within the exclusion zone of the power plant. While the disaster had led to numerous atomic divorces, it now appeared that a resilient *furusato* could become the locus where marriage would once again become consumable. To make this revitalization possible, the forum eulogized the need to lead a "normal life" (*futsū*) and invited a singer to compose a song that praised reconstruction efforts. It went like this: "We have rebuilt our homes to be as beautiful as in our memory!" By mobilizing a specific understanding of the native land, the government framed the return of evacuees as a question of returning to one's *furusato*, where nostalgia was seen as a form of collective loss. As Lindsey Freeman observes, "Nostalgia is often mistakenly believed to be a solely individual experience, but like memory it is also a deeply social phenomenon. Nostalgia is sociologically relevant because it works as a conduit to show collective ideas about the present, while simultaneously revealing shared past desires, giving new insights into the practices, structures, and institutions those desires created."[37]

By framing nostalgia for the *furusato* as a form of communal loss—ironically performed for an audience of Tokyoites and foreign ambassadors—the forum revealed much about the political potential of the native land. Jennifer Robertson has long argued that the Japanese state successfully mobilized the *furusato* imaginary to reinforce nativist political values against a fear of Westernization.[38] But in the context of Fukushima, it is the qualities of proper civic duties in postdisaster recovery that are reinterpreted rather than nativistic meanings. In other words, "proper" Japanese citizens were individuals who were nostalgic for their hometown, did not abandon their *furusato*, and stuck with their community to revitalize their region.

The Reconstruction Agency ceaselessly encouraged this form of community-based resilience. For instance, it underscored the story of selected citizens who had revitalized their *furusato* by creating start-up companies, moral support initiatives, and tourism improvements.[39] Moreover, it endorsed economic projects like donations (*kifu*) or citizen-based crowdfunding (*kuraudofandingu*) for *furusato*-related projects.[40] These included the creation of rice-based alcohol breweries (*sake*) and hometown folk song collections. In this context, proper citizens were not victims who expected monetary indemnity from the state but individuals who could economically support the revitalization of their own region, thanks to their love for the native land.

In the end, the *furusato* became a notion drenched in images of tradition, resilience, and local consumables. By emphasizing the affective connections that citizens maintained with their native land and by raising the specter of a *furusato* affected by harmful rumors, the Reconstruction Agency reinforced images of a pure and unified Fukushima, rather than a space whose tensions were exacerbated by contamination. On paper, recovery policies were supposed to consider the different intentions of evacuees, such as returning to Fukushima or permanently settling elsewhere.[41] Yet, by performing a nostalgic story of the *furusato*, the agency was the driver of a politics that did *not* support long-term evacuation. The speakers present during the forum only included individuals who felt saddened for their beloved *furusato* while hoping for its prompt recovery. A utopian future was modeled through the figure of a carefully selected "imagined community."[42]

Consuming Furusato

Beyond the forum, the state deployed numerous efforts to revitalize regions affected by the disaster. For instance, in the Tokyoite district of Chiyoda, the Reconstruction Agency arranged food fairs, cultural workshops, and art exhibitions that enabled urban citizens to enjoy the "flavor of *furusato*."[43] In the train station of Fukushima City, Kibitan—the yellowish mascot of the prefecture—welcomed visitors, while cartoon characters provided information about radiation to fight "harmful rumors" about contamination. At the entrance of the train station, the charms of the native land were presented under colorful kiosks and interactive stands that made use of pictures and art projects. All these exhibits promoted the food terroir, traditional hotels, cherry blossom viewing, hot springs, and historic festivals of the region. A new baseball team had even been created after the disaster under the strategically chosen name of "Fukushima Hopes." An enormous signboard at the station told of the promises of happiness: "Toward Fukushima's future! Fukushima is also happy, everybody is happy!" (*Fukushima no mirai ni mukatte! Happy Fukushima, Fukushima mo happy, min'na happy!*). Not far from the signboard, a Renewable Energy Information Center (*saiseikanō enerugī jōhōkan*) underscored the use of clean energy in the region. A little robot explained how wind, biomass, hydro, or geothermal power could produce electricity for everyone. By pressing a button, one could activate either a fan that made a small wind turbine move or a lamp that activated solar panels. In transforming a nuclear-stricken region into a pioneer of renewable energy, people could rest assured that a disaster like Fukushima would never happen again—at least not in their native land. Part of these activities fell under an important project called the "Innovation Coast Framework" (*Fukushima inobēshon kōsuto kōsō*), which is a national project "designed to build a new industrial infrastructure in the coastal region of Fukushima Prefecture."[44]

Consequently, events such as Robot Festa Fukushima were held to increase interest in robots among returnees and citizens. During these events, one could learn about snake-like robots that wiggle through complex pipe structures for inspection purposes in the power plant, thus leading the robotic industrial revolution of Japan.[45] The subtext was clear: Fukushima was a desirable place to live, with traditional charm and soon-to-be-blooming industries standing at the cutting edge of technology. The Innovation Coast demonstrated that one's *furusato* does not need to be an archaic place, a trope that younger generations often associated with their hometown. Indeed, one of the main aims of the Reconstruction Agency during its forum was to make "Fukushima attractive to young people" (*wakamono ni totte miryoku aru Fukushima o mezashite*).

During my trips to the prefecture, I observed other revitalization practices, especially in the village of Iitate. Of particular interest was a newly constructed roadside station called "Michinoeki Madeikan." There I found souvenir kiosks that sold locally produced goods and memorabilia, while being greeted by Ītane-chan, the big plant fairy mascot of Iitate village. In talking about the commodification of Japanese travel, scholars have underscored the importance of "local dialect" within the *furusato*.[46] Similarly, it was possible to purchase different products of Iitate and to enjoy the peculiarities of their *furusato*, which was known as "*madei*," a term that implies a slow and joyful life movement.[47] As the website of the *Michinoeki Madeikan* further explained, "The word '*Madei*' is defined as 'slow life' and represents the ideology and way of thinking of the people of Iitate Village. The word itself comes from the word '*Mate*,' which means to place your hands together. This local word encapsulates ideas such as thoughtfulness, respect, taking one's time, sincerity, and living life to the fullest. At Michinoeki (Roadside Station) Madeikan, '*Madei*' embodies trends seen around the world towards a slow and sustainable life. The people of Iitate village have been leading this '*Madei*' lifestyle, so please feel '*Madei* welcome' at Michinoeki Madeikan."⁴⁸

In Iitate, I also visited the Yamatsumi Shinto Shrine, famed for its 240 paintings of Japanese wolves. While much of the shrine was destroyed during a fire in 2013, Tokyo University art students reproduced many of the paintings as part of a revitalization project. As the *Japan Times* explained, "Now the shrine is refitted with wolf art on the ceilings. One wolf is seen sleeping in the bush, while another gazes at a blue waterfall. 'I hope the paintings of these happy wolves will lift the feelings of viewers,' said Keisuke Kato, a staffer at the shrine. 'I hope the art will give more people a chance to visit the village, and help with its reconstruction.'"⁴⁹

However, despite these revitalization efforts, few tourists flocked toward these regions. The many pictures of wolves made me think about the Japanese subspecies of wolf (*Canis lupus hodophilax*) that became extinct due to the same capitalist practices responsible for the nuclear disaster. What else had become extinct in Fukushima? Many of the ghost towns and abandoned houses that I saw seemed to point toward its former citizens. For a town that had roughly six thousand living souls before the disaster, only four hundred people—mostly all elderly men—had come back to Iitate by 2017. Outside "tourism" sites like the Madeikan, the only things visible were closed convenience stores, rusty houses, abandoned fields, and rows of plastic bags. As one of my informants said, "This is a revitalization without people." The state phantasm of the native land appeared disembodied from its social means of production—a *furusato* alienated from its former people. Within a specter of radiation and without those six thousand souls, would the *furusato* of Iitate still be able to function as a tourist attraction?

Decontaminating the Furusato

A significant number of financial subsidies were injected into the revitalization of Fukushima, as the Japanese state promoted a nostalgia for the *furusato*. By way of explanation, Marilyn Ivy states that "dominant ideologies in Japan still depend on a politics of nostalgia suitable for an advanced capitalist polity: a nostalgia for a Japan that is kept on the verge of vanishing, stable yet endangered (and thus open for commodifiable desire)."[50] The commodifiable desire that Ivy highlights is exactly what was at stake in the state-sponsored revival of Fukushima's *furusato*, whether in terms of tourism, jobs, R&D, or reconstruction policies. An extremely lucrative market was available for actors who pretended to make contaminated areas into habitable zones. In 2014, the national government budget for radioactive decontamination was an astonishing 1.9 trillion yen (or nineteen billion US dollars).[51] Decontaminating the *furusato* became big business for many industrial companies, but their profits rarely trickled down to the people living in Fukushima. Decontamination contracts exemplified this, as local contractors could not compete with those from Tokyo.[52]

The national government also claimed that Tokyo Electric Power Company (TEPCO), the electric utility holding company responsible for the Fukushima Dai'ichi power plant, would cover the cost of the decontamination and decommission measures.[53] What they failed to mention is that TEPCO was nationalized in 2012,[54] and thus while the profits went to corporations, the costs ultimately fell on the shoulders of taxpayers—all for a false simulacrum of decontamination, according to Greenpeace:

> The decontamination program is motivated by the political agenda of Prime Minister Abe's government and corporate interests. The original Japanese government cost estimate of 2.5 trillion yen for the Fukushima decontamination program was revised in 2016 to 4–5 trillion yen . . . [H]owever, independent assessments have estimated that the total cost could reach 30 trillion yen (271 billion dollars). For Japanese contractors, hundreds of subcontractors (and organized crime) this is a source of enormous profit at the taxpayers' expense. All for a program that fails to decontaminate 70% of the most contaminated areas of Fukushima and that violates the rights of workers.[55]

Cases of collusion were rampant in decommissioning projects, where, paradoxically, the companies responsible for the disaster were making profits by revitalizing Fukushima.[56] For instance, a high-scale subsidy project on contaminated water was won by a joint bid from TEPCO and Toshiba Corporation, joined by Hitachi-GE Nuclear Energy Ltd.[57]

In his study of climate change, Erik Swyngedouw argues that CO_2 functions as a commodity that inserts itself within a "complex governance regime organized around a set of technologies of governance."[58] Similarly, the commodification of the *furusato* was inseparable from technologies of governance that surrounded postdisaster revitalization, successfully commodifying the imaginary of the native land into something that was tangible and open to marketable practices. In heavily contaminated areas where the *furusato* as a tourist commodity no longer worked, the native land became the driver of a phantasm that had consequences in terms of "disaster capitalism" (which refers to how elites profit from catastrophes).[59] The Innovation Coast Framework, decontamination contracts, and decommission projects demonstrated that Fukushima had become recommodified as a place of high-tech resilience.

The governmental take on the *furusato* itself became a phantasm that acted as a substratum upon which revitalization projects were implemented. In this commodifiable vision, lucrative postdisaster measures acquired exchange values by highlighting the vision of a homogeneous and resilient nation-state. In talking about a nuclear arsenal, Masco argues that the atomic bomb is not a commodity in the strict Marxist sense,[60] yet as a "national fetish," the bomb maintains a "magical hold on people's thinking, and in doing so, energize[s] very specific national-cultural imaginaries."[61] In post-Fukushima Japan, the governmental practices of reconstruction articulated a similar national fetish of the native land based on spatiality, thereby opening the *furusato* to commodifiable gains, but also to a specific phantasmagoric vision of the nation-state. Alf Hornborg states that "Marx's seminal insight was that objects such as money tokens and commodities are incorrectly understood as autonomous sources of productivity and agency, whereas they in fact signify social relations of exchange."[62] What was being exchanged after this disaster was the phantasm of a contaminated place that can become pure again, or if not radiation free then at least worry free for consumption as usual.

In the end, tropes of nostalgia for one's *furusato* were supposed to provide an environment for return—but one should ask, For *whom* exactly? In Tomioka, I witnessed giant incinerators burning irradiated debris. On its front, the logos of Kajima Corporation, Mitsubishi, and MOE were inscribed. Under those logos one could read "*ganbarō tomioka machi*"

("Let's do our best, city of Tomioka!"). This "*ganbarō*," which can be translated as "perseverance" and which is a common term for effort used in government slogans, has proven to be highly profitable for Mitsubishi, the conglomerate that provides nuclear services and reactors, as well as for Kajima Corporation, a Tokyo-based super-general contractor. But for former residents, could one really come back to a place where radioactive waste was being burned and call that one's *furusato*? Like a phoenix regenerating from its (contaminated) ash, this "*ganbarō*" seemed to promote an ironic twist for the residents of Tomioka.

A Paper Rice Cake

Between 2016 and 2017, I made several visits to a temporary housing complex situated in the southern part of Fukushima. Residents consisted of young families and elderly individuals whose houses were located within the exclusion zone. I first went there with a group of volunteers who provided moral support for the evacuees. We did activities such as storytelling (*kamishibai*), pounded fresh rice to make sweet cake (*mochi tsukuri*), and produced musical shows. Often, these activities were the only sources of distraction that evacuees had in their temporary housing complex.

As I came to gradually know the residents of this housing complex, especially the same group of elderly women, many talked about how their current life was deprived of the joys of their former *furusato*. After the disaster, very few of the elderly women believed that the evacuation order would have lasted for so long. Three months after March 2011, some evacuees were able to briefly return to their houses to retrieve important personal belongings. On their farms, they discovered starved pigs eating away the flesh of their dead horses. This was a harsh welcome, rendering the original *furusato* inseparable from such haunting images.

Life in Temporary Housing

As opposed to city dwellers, residents of the complex were born in the countryside and were used to living in spacious environments. As one volunteer explained, "Living in a cramped space is even harder for those evacuees; nights are long and they feel trapped." Many regularly complained about the lack of privacy in the complex. Barracks were constructed right next to each other to save on construction and heating costs. The resulting paper-thin walls produced buildings that were badly insulated. One day, our group of volunteers tried to make a batch of miso soup only to realize that the pipes were frozen. "It happens every winter," explained an elderly woman. The situation was no better in summer, as the heat and humidity became intolerable.

Many spoke negatively about life in the complex, arguing that there was nothing to do except drink every day (*sake nomu shika nai*). The police often came because of alcohol-related problems like domestic abuse. The continuous strain of living in cramped spaces created a lot of pressure on family ties, with divorces becoming common in the complex. Ironically, radiation not only cut chemical bonds but also marital ones. What used to be forever no longer held together after this disaster.

These kinds of problems made evacuees particularly nostalgic about life in their former *furusato*. The main subject of conversation usually gravitated around radioactive contamination. For example, I repeatedly heard elderly women criticize the state as well as TEPCO. In opposition to the enthusiasm of state officials, forced evacuees were harshly critical of the decontamination processes supposed to provide a clean *furusato* for their return. "They don't tell us the before and after difference of radiation levels when they do the decontamination! We had to do this by ourselves," claimed a resident of the center. "I don't know how to do this!" Her nearby companion added, "They spray our roofs with water to get rid of the radioactive pollutants, but the water just falls right down near the house with all the contaminants in it." Other evacuees explained how decontamination work was subcontracted to local mobsters (*yakuza*), which made them anxious regarding a potential return. Residents claimed that they found people squatting in their former homes and that burglary was a recurrent problem in their village.

When I first visited the housing complex in March 2016, evacuees could still not return to their original hometowns. This was either because radiation levels were too high or because their houses had crumbled down due to the passage of time. In the former house of one evacuee, Setsuko Yamaguchi, everything had broken down: "Rain has passed through the roof, the house is falling apart. . . . I didn't have any other choice but to start building a new one." Yet TEPCO, which took care of radiation-related compensations, refused to compensate Yamaguchi for her damaged house, claiming that the destruction resulted from natural causes (e.g., the earthquake) and not from radioactive contamination. Angry, Yamaguchi argued that she had to flee her house because of the evacuation order linked with radioactive contamination and that her home gradually fell apart since no one could maintain it: "TEPCO, they see a wall that has fallen and they say that it's a consequence of the earthquake or the tsunami. . . . It has absolutely no link whatsoever with the earthquake and the tsunami. But the people at TEPCO don't understand, no matter how many times I've tried to explain it! I've gotten so angry at them!"

On the other hand, life elsewhere was made impossible by a lack of proper financial support. Indeed, some evacuees were facing problems in receiving compensation for their losses. "We have never been paid, but they [the government and TEPCO] keep saying that they have done so," one evacuee told me. "How can we trust them after that!? All they want is to cut all potential links with us as soon as possible." To make matters worse, many had to rely on their meager pension (*nenkin*) to survive. The termination of financial subsidies was due to the fact that compensation was based on evacuation zoning rather than on the necessities faced by evacuees.[63] Unfortunately, unequal compensation quickly "triggered a feeling of injustice among the affected population."[64] In that regard, I can still hear the complaints of an elderly woman whose compensation had been cut: "People from Futaba still have theirs, why was ours cut? We are victims also!"

Gradually, the notion of one's hometown became a concept upon which evacuees no longer had a strong hold. It had been replaced by what Anne Allison calls "social precarity"—a "sense of being out of place, out of sorts, disconnected (*fuan, fuantei, ibasho ga nai*)."[65] Amid these hardships, evacuees were getting accustomed to a supposedly temporary home by individualizing their barracks and by making the complex feel more like their former *furusato*. For example, evacuees were particularly happy when we made gelatinous rice cakes (*mochi*) in a traditional manner. On a cold day in January 2017, our group brought a batch of fresh rice with the intention of making *mochi*. One must continuously pound the rice with a big wooden sledgehammer. A few seconds after the hammer pounded the rice, an old lady expertly tossed it upside down before the hammer struck again. After a few good strokes, we molded the pummeled rice into small cakes and dipped them in various sugary coatings. In rural Japan, making *mochi* in this manner is a form of work that reinforces the community—a performative act of what the *furusato* used to be about. On that day residents appeared nostalgic for the time when they could carry out such activities in their own hometown.

In front of her barrack, Yamaguchi even made her own little garden amid the hard rock pebble of the housing complex. "I've scraped all the pebbles by myself and filled the hole with soil. It took seventeen bags!" she proudly said, while showing me tiny vegetables. In many ways, this garden was the reflection of a nostalgia for a former way of life that some hoped to recover. Many evacuees had lived in this complex for more than six years. Children were even born in this center. Under such conditions, one could not help but ponder the meaning that the term "temporary" embodies. Radioactive contamination was altering the very conception of time, producing a sense of homelessness that went beyond the loss of a physical *furusato*. The so-called temporary was now home to normalcy, where the emergency became an integral part of everyday life. People were living in a temporality that should not make any sense, becoming refugees of a kind of permanent temporary. This had become their home, the temporality in which many were prisoners. No bright future ahead. Living day to day. Surviving.

This specter of an uncertain future provoked the image of a past *furusato* that was pure and untouched, as echoed by the common refrain of evacuees ("What happened to our *furusato*?"). Still, scholars have argued that pre-2011 Fukushima was never an idyllic *furusato*, since it was caught in multiple forms of precarity, like a poor economy, aging population, and rural exodus.[66] The small garden of Yamaguchi can thus be seen as what Robertson calls a "nostalgia for a nostalgia," which is "a state of being provoked by a dissatisfaction with the present on the grounds of a remembered, or imagined, past plenitude."[67] Still, this new kind of garden is also a phantasm that provides a commodified notion of the *furusato*—monetarily deprived in this case—but with tangible values to hold onto, as a "form of bargaining with what is overwhelming about the present."[68]

Figure 5.1. The garden of Mme. Yamaguchi. Photo by Maxime Polleri.

Coming Back?

One day evacuees learned that their temporary housing complex would close in March 2017, thereby enabling (or forcing) them to return to their *furusato*. While some residents were happy about this news, others were also critical of the revitalization process. As one volunteer from our group told me, "The government wants to repatriate them as quickly as possible to show that Japan is safe for the 2020 Olympics." Yamaguchi offered a similar remark: "People keep talking about the upcoming Olympics. . . . What's the link with us and our village? The country and the *furusato* need to be clean so that they can go on with their Olympics, but we surely don't see that revitalization money." During a quiet afternoon, as Yamaguchi and I watched television, we saw an ad for the Olympic games. She suddenly became angry, wondering why so much money was poured into the games, while her hometown was still hurting. "Where does all that money go?" she asked. After this ad, we saw a special program promoting the revitalization of Fukushima, filled with city folks attending a traditional festival. Many were exclaiming, "It's so great! It's so great!" (*subarashii, subarashii*). Yamaguchi shook her head in disapproval: "These people just don't understand, they just don't know."

When I asked residents of the complex what they would do after the expulsion deadline, many were unsure of what would happen to them. "Well, maybe I'll live with my daughter," replied a woman with a perm. "But I'm unsure if it will work. . . . I've tried in the past and it didn't go well." A lot of elderly people share similar concerns of being a nuisance to their children and preferring to live alone. Due to the impact of radiation, their children and grandchildren had started their life elsewhere. "Our families have become fragmented [*bara bara*]," claimed Yamaguchi. Evacuees complained about the fact that they rarely saw their family, but they also believed that children should not grow up in Fukushima. Many were in favor of the evacuation of children from the prefecture: "It's important," said the lady with the perm, referring to an upcoming evacuation trial. But if those elderly people returned to a hometown where no young people lived anymore, social problems would likely emerge and their *furusato* might disappear again. As Tom Gill summarizes, there comes a threshold "where the ageing and dwindling of the community reaches the point where it is no longer viable," rendering the town "a 'marginal settlement.'"[69]

In Hirono, a former hometown to which some evacuees will return, there are still places with low radiation levels and other places with higher levels. Therefore, not all evacuees will be able to go back to their former areas of residence, and crucially, to their original *furusato*. In the end, many will return, but to a *furusato* that now has little meaning (*imi*) for them. The former connections and human relationships (*ningen kankei*) that used to be a part of their former *furusato* are no more. One man who oversaw the temporary housing wondered how citizens could come back to a town that was falling apart, especially without a strong workforce of carpenters and artisans. Others complained that electricity was still not available everywhere, that there were no doctors, no services, and no public transportation whatsoever. "What kind of well-being will we have in this context?" asked a resident. At Hirono there were many problems to be taken care of. "When I need to go to the hospital, I have to take a taxi," said Yamaguchi. In Japan, taxis are especially expensive, further adding to the financial difficulties of returnees. "Honestly, I feel like I want to punch the people of TEPCO sometimes."

Citizens like Yamaguchi wondered about the kind of *furusato* they would come back to. In some parts of their hometown, many could not grow rice, pick forest mushrooms, or eat wild boars; the contamination levels were too high, they told me. Yet a self-sufficient life, exemplified by picking wild foods and selling vegetables, was an important part of their *furusato* culture—a culture that no longer existed because of residual radioactivity. Some worried about the continuous testing that needed to be done to ensure that food was not contaminated. Evacuees told me that most tests used to detect radioactive contamination were done for free in Hirono. However, this was not without problems. As an old man explained, "We need to chop everything in small cubes of one centimeter; that's fine for vegetables that are big and soft, but for the ones that are harder it is quite difficult to do so. Also, we used to need to send about one kilogram of foodstuff for testing. Now they can do the test with a minimum of five hundred grams, but it's still a lot. . . . Five hundred grams of *daikon* [a big, soft radish] is fine, but for the small stuff, like mushrooms or garlic, it's impossible or too expensive."

The precious food that ended up being wasted during testing was money that came directly out of citizens' pockets, further making their *furusato* more precarious. In this context, I cannot help but remember Yamaguchi saying, "This revitalization is like a painted rice cake [*e ni kaita mochi*]; you can't eat it"—implying that revitalization policies had no substance and that they were merely performative acts. As emphasized by the Reconstruction Agency, many residents longed to come back to their *furusato*, which was indeed true. Still, their longing was not for a place per se but for a temporal locus found *before* the disaster—in other words, a *furusato* that could only live in their memory, echoing the "impossibility of return that rests at the painful core of contemporary nostalgia."[70]

Losing Home, Once Again

In the housing complex, many residents were evacuees from different parts of Fukushima. In talking about catastrophe, Kim Fortun argues that once sociogeographical boundaries are destabilized, it can be difficult to "discern what a community is and who is part of it."[71] While this was initially the case after the disaster, evacuees had also created a new community for themselves. "We are all from different regions," said an elderly woman. "At first, we did not know each other, but now we are friends [*nakama*]." When the center closes, this new community will dissolve itself and home will once again break apart. These evacuees were constantly deprived of an *ibasho*, "a space where one feels comfortable and at home."[72] The predisaster nostalgia imbued in the concept of *furusato* will confront the nostalgia of a future disrupted environment, as the new social relations that evacuees created will disappear.

Still, many residents of the temporary complex were tired of living there. "There is always one problem after the other," mumbled a woman. Children were often the trigger of such difficulties. As one lady told our group one day, "There was some big altercation with kids playing around and making noise. . . . That bothers people and everybody gets angry at each other." In this environment, children could not play in nature, something that was a crucial aspect of *furusato* life. Evacuation caused by radioactive contamination brought more than a physical displacement; it also brought a displacement of childhood itself. In their new home, children were taught to stay put and to act like adults. Upon leaving the complex, our group stumbled across three children who had put rubber bands around broken chopsticks, imitating a gun and firing imaginary shots at each other. The world of handheld videogames, which was not so long ago the second strongest economy of the world, was absent from this picture.

The children kept on playing as if everything had always been this way. This new environment had become normalized to a point where they simply regarded it as their hometown. For these children, the *furusato* will remain a phantasm. It is a concept that they did not experience or recall through the nostalgia of a place per se. How can they yearn for something that they have no knowledge of? Ivy states that "the *furusato* resides in the memory, but is linked to tangible reminders of the past; when the material, palpable reminders of one's childhood home no longer exist, then the *furusato* is in danger of vanishing."[73] Many of the volunteers were aghast at the eeriness of this place, a feeling that crept beyond normalcy. This was precisely what home had become for those evacuees: uncanny. As Ivy argues, the uncanny is "the strangeness of that which is most familiar"—in other words, "place out of place."[74]

Leaving One's *Furusato*

In July 2016, I visited an NPO that provided a home for children who wished to evacuate from Fukushima. As opposed to the temporary housing complex, this organization was situated far away from Fukushima, in the Chūbu region, which is part of central Japan. The organization was created for voluntary evacuees, and attempted to provide a place where children could safely play, live, and study. In 2016, numerous children from Fukushima were under the care of this NPO. They resided year-round in a dormitory while attending local school in Chūbu. After contacting the NPO, I was invited to visit the establishment by its director, a tall, strong, and well-tanned man called Shinobu Ueno.

When I first met Ueno, he was wearing long rain boots, a green bog hat, and a working jumpsuit, giving him a very militaristic appearance. He was once part of the Self-Defense Force (*jietai*), which explained his self-assured look. As we drove toward the dormitory, I asked Ueno to tell me about his life story. Before the nuclear disaster he had lived in Koriyama, a small city situated outside of the mandatory evacuation zone. When the nuclear meltdown was confirmed, he decided to leave Koriyama for Tokyo. As he explained, "As soon as it happened, I decided to flee with my family. I didn't care about the money; health was more important!" Looking back, he believed that his decision paid off, since the radioactive contamination went beyond the initial evacuation zone. Like other evacuees, he reported stories of weird ailments, such as children who had thick, continuous nosebleeds of a very dark color. "And the government calls that 'damages by rumors' [*fūhyō higai*]," he said. "What is wrong with them?" While looking at the bucolic landscape of his village, I asked Ueno how the idea for his NPO came to mind. To evacuate children, he initially reached out to different organizations: "I called, sent mail, but no one was listening to me," he explained. To raise the specter of radiation in Fukushima was to impede the collective effort of revitalization. As he said, "So, it became apparent that it was something that I simply had to do by myself. And that's what

I did! The government will fund any organization helping people to stay and live in Fukushima. But for those who want to leave there's nothing. We don't receive a single yen from the government."

A New Furusato

It took a good forty minutes before we arrived at the main center, a beautiful wooden house typical of the Japanese countryside. There I was introduced to the staff and residents, including a child who had just come back from a hiking trip. Seeing the child's happily exhausted face, Ueno commented, "Here children can have fun, they can play in nature, and hike in the mountains! None of this is possible in Fukushima without exposing oneself to radiation." During our conversation, Ueno repeatedly stressed the importance of a "worry-free life" (*anshin shite seikatsu*) associated with an "environment free of radioactive contamination" (*hōshanō osen no nai kankyō*). Talking about the natural richness of the region, he explained that the green mountains of Chūbu region look a bit like Fukushima: "There's a girl that came from Iitate village in Fukushima and here it's actually quite similar to her former place."

In the afternoon, members of a local farming union surprised the children by bringing fresh watermelons. We played a traditional game called "*suikawari*," involving the splitting of a watermelon with a stick. As with a piñata, we were blindfolded and made to rotate until dizzy. The first shots missed by a few, but the green fruit finally cracked under a couple of strong strikes. Later we went to a nearby hot spring (*onsen*), which transformed the complexion of my fair skin to the color of a boiled lobster, making everybody laugh. Afterward, we dined in the back yard of the center on fresh food graciously brought by the farmers. "People bring us so much food that we have cucumbers for months!" said a volunteer working for the NPO. "There is a limit to how many vegetables children can eat!"

During my fieldwork, this was one of the rare moments when I put the notebook aside and started to enjoy my stay. I did not stress about radioactive exposure, nor did any thoughts of the presence of possible harmful radionuclides cross my mind while I was biting into a juicy piece of watermelon. Ueno argued that it was likely the same for children living

Figure 5.2. The game of *suikawari*. Photo by Maxime Polleri.

there. The center was a place where children could be children again, forming a sharp contrast with my experience at the temporary housing complex. As Ueno later told me, "Here children don't have to wear masks or long clothes to protect themselves from radioactive dust. In Fukushima, they are constantly reminded of radiation. It takes a lot of energy out of a person." I asked him if the children had ever faced discrimination (*ijime*) since they moved from Fukushima, but he replied that it "never happened. On the contrary, people have been very nice!"

Later, when the children were sleeping and Ueno and I shared a nightcap, I realized the sacrifice parents had made, not seeing their children in the prime of life, in the process of becoming the man or the woman that he or she is destined to become. They had accepted the necessity of sending their children far away to live with a stranger. This was how anxious many were for the safety of their children. Ueno explained that many parents wanted to leave Fukushima and start a life elsewhere, but were bogged down financially. The desire to leave as one united family remained a phantasm. For many, home in Fukushima had become a locus of chronic low-dose exposure. It was precisely in this context that worried parents had been willing to send their children away from their former *furusato*. This was the story of many children then staying in the NPO. "Some kids have been here for almost three years," mentioned Ueno. Since the NPO was far from Fukushima, they rarely got to see their parents. The center was slowly becoming their new home and the rural area of Chūbu region their new *furusato*.

In the aftermath of Chernobyl, Petryna highlights how the socioeconomic conditions of a post-Soviet era "continue to lead individuals to neglect their bodies in exchange for something: the stability of a household, authority over the 'facts,' survival."[75] The situation in the NPO pointed to the opposite. For parents sending their children away, Fukushima had transformed itself from a locus of family ties to an area perceived as dangerous. In Japanese, two words are used for safety regarding radiation harm: "*anzen*," denoting the pragmatic aspects of safety, and "*anshin*," which refers to an affective safety.[76] For Ueno, postdisaster recovery had to rest on both pillars, but *anzen* came first, supporting *anshin*. Amid worries of adverse health effects, the nuclear family was taking on a different meaning. Radiation is known to affect the genetic material of one individual, the biological bastion upon which the transmission of kinship is founded. Like the forty-year-old house mortgage passed on to children (a common practice in Japan), the risk of radiation is leaving an unwanted legacy. Against these fears, the new *furusato* of Chūbu acted as a place of *anzen* and *anshin*, gradually supporting novel forms of family ties. This was notably epitomized by the faceless conversations that parents had with their children over the phone. Ueno told me about the letters of support that he received from grateful parents. In one of them, a mother extolled her happiness about the fact that her daughter regained her strength and had a good appetite. Marx claimed that one of the main characteristics of a commodity is its exchange value.[77] As opposed to Petryna's account of "biological citizens" who made use of their damaged biologies to access state compensation,[78] the precarity of biological risk had not become a commodity in Fukushima. In this NPO, what was turned into a tangible driver was the perception of an irremediably contaminated *furusato* exchanged for the idea of a new and pure one.

A Critical Nostalgia

After evacuating, Ueno's marriage surprisingly grew stronger. "It was the right thing to do for us," he claimed. "My wife and I can work on many projects together." One of these projects included the tending of grape fields. Part of Ueno's village is famous for its *kyohō* grape, a Concord-like variety whose name literally translates as "giant mountain grapes." On a sweltering hot summer day, I worked alongside Ueno, carefully wrapping countless bunches of grapes to protect them from crows and rodents. The grapes of Ueno represented more than food; they also stood as the symbol of a new *furusato*, a new rural idyll that produced safety for him. This work would not have been possible in many parts of Fukushima, as forests and mountains were out of the jurisdiction of decontamination processes. The ideas of a pristine natural environment, enjoying the fruits of nature without worrying, or hiking through mountains in search of wild mushrooms were parts of this imaginary.[79] For Ueno this culture could not live with the effects that radioactive contamination brought. The disappearance of that culture implied the disappearance of what the Japanese state was precisely looking to save: the *furusato*. But tellingly, Ueno argued that his former *furusato* could never be brought back, for symbolic reasons that were equally as important as the material risk of radiation. Following the disaster, he became disgruntled by state policies, especially regarding the change in the allowable radiation threshold. He was critical of revitalization projects that argued for a safe living space by alleviating other risks via the consumption of healthy food, staying away from tobacco, or teaching children not to worry about radiation.

For Ueno this was nonsense, and he refused to participate in knowledge-based institutions at the local scale, like citizen science initiatives sponsored by NGOs or the Japanese state. Ueno maintained an ambivalent relationship with these scientific approaches; although he did not disregard radiological science, he had no use for citizen science, having already evacuated elsewhere. As opposed to farmers in Iitate, technoscientific practices could not re-create a connection with his former *furusato*, nor infuse a feeling of belonging to a community. Designed to reduce risk, devices like a Geiger counter acted instead as a *constant* reminder of contamination. For Ueno, his *furusato* could not be a place where children wore dosimeters, nor where radioactive contamination was normalized to the level of a weather forecast on the highways of Fukushima. This was a *furusato* alienated from its true values. In contrast, the new *furusato* of Ueno enabled him to develop a "critical nostalgia."[80] As Freeman explains, a critical nostalgia "allows for an imagination of a future that is better, where tradition and history are experienced not as a nightmare ... but as dream-images of possibility, capable of embracing a bit of healthy disorientation and destabilization on the way to something better."[81] Creating a radiation-free environment was the only way to create a new *furusato* that Ueno could perhaps, one day, regard as his own. For him, an environment under limitations, best emphasized by the constant monitoring of one's doses and movements, was no place to raise children.

After working in the grape field, Ueno brought me to a panorama up in the mountain. He was bitter about the amount of money poured into the revitalization efforts. "Right now, Fukushima is like a bubble," he said, "but it's going to pop one day." In his view, this bubble was akin to the Japanese economic bubble (*baburu keiki*), which brought down the archipelago's economy during the 1990s. "Money is like a drug," he claimed. "A lot of people will come back to Fukushima because the government is promoting employment and kickbacks, but honestly ... what is more important?" Upon leaving this scenery, I could not help but think about the *panorama-kan* of Meiji Japan, which consisted of 360-degree entertainment rotundas, filled with scenic historical paintings that praised the glories of the Empire of Japan.[82] As Machiko Kusahara explains, these panoramas performed a propaganda function regarding the modernization of Japan as a powerful new nation-state.[83] Were post-Fukushima revitalization practices a modern version of *panorama-kan*? Mr. Ueno seemed to believe so.

A Political Touchstone

An engagement with the *furusato* was a political touchstone that remained trapped in a double bind; the phantasm of a place that was pure before confronted the phantasm of a place that can become pure again. Both phantasms were differentially articulated and remained important windows into the political sensibilities of Japanese elites and citizens. For the state, the native land acted as a return to normality, a political project that echoed the normalization of life in the radioactive-tainted areas of post-Chernobyl Europe.[84] This *furusato* was understood as a delimited physical space and via tropes of economic commodities, such as a decrease in tourism. The proliferation of commodifiable *furusatos* can be linked to both the failure of state economic policies, which forced poor rural communities to market themselves, and the failure of the state to manage the consequences of a nuclear disaster.[85] Within a politics of revitalization, the native land was transformed into a commodity imbued with particular social meaning: a place of resilience, hope, and prompt recovery.

In *Discourses of the Vanishing*, Ivy argues that the notion of modern Japan was inseparable from mourning the loss of its rurality, perceived ethnic homogeneity, and so-called millennium traditions.[86] The nuclear disaster interrupted these narratives of vanishing to create novel fears of disappearance. From the state's perspective, Fukushima's *furusatos* appeared in need of revitalization, so that they could continue to vanish in expected ways, rather than from the specter of radiation.[87] By revitalizing contaminated regions, everything was done to engineer a form of future nostalgia, so that children who had ironically never known Fukushima would one day be able to experience their own yearning. Yet, for many evacuees, state-sponsored performances did not acknowledge the fact that the *furusato* is also a sociocultural conceptualization lived and experienced in ways that have no longer been possible since 2011. If some evacuees were nostalgic for a return, their nostalgia was for a locus that now only existed in the realm of their memories. As the evacuees of this chapter highlight, the state *furusato* was a mimicry devoid of the meaning that supported their former *furusato*—a *furusato* that did not have use value for them anymore. The nostalgia of a former *furusato* was now exchanged for the new social relationships and imaginaries that one found in temporary housing complexes or in the grape fields of Chūbu region.

The experience of evacuees demonstrates that the essence of one's *furusato* was decaying at a faster rate than cesium-137. Against these hardships, the native land was being reimagined, often to the advantage of polluters. As Ivy observes, "The notion of the *furusato* has thus proved to be a labile and shifting one, open to conservative political uses as well as to sharply antiauthoritarian attempts to reimagine the democratic possibilities of community."[88] Between the state narrative and the evacuees' viewpoints, political resistance to the specter of radiation hazards was inscribed in the same term, but nonetheless viewed through different politics of harm and recovery. On the one hand, a utopian future was modeled through a resilient and unified *furusato*, like the nation-state itself. On the other hand, a contaminated *furusato* articulated one's political standpoint toward the perceived inequalities of revitalization practices as well as the risks of radioactive contamination.

Cultural narratives of a place, such as the ideas of the American frontier or the wilderness, serve to form powerful national imaginaries, creating specific representations of nature and the Other.[89] In studies surrounding technological disasters, much has been written about the strategic mobilization of science to suit specific understandings of risk or recovery. However, managing a place's cultural imaginary is sometimes as powerful as science—if not more so. This forces to the fore questions such as whose imaginary counts and how different forms of nostalgia are governed, legitimized, or contested after disasters. In Japan, the native land opens different notions of political imaginaries for governing what matters after Fukushima. As an archaic word, "*furusato*" once meant "ruins, historic remains." On the ruins of a former *furusato* undercut by Westernization practices and the specter of radiation, the post-Fukushima *furusato* was now being built.

6

Postpolitical Uncertainties

It took three minutes to reach our destination. This does not sound like much, but when one is trapped in a cage-like elevator descending three hundred meters below the ground, time passes slowly. This harrowing journey led us to the Mizunami Underground Research Facility (*mizunami chōshinchisō kenkyūjo*), a state-of-the-art R&D facility for the safe geological disposal of high-level radioactive waste (HLW). Situated in Gifu Prefecture, this project was led by the Nuclear Waste Management Organization (NUMO), a Japanese entity created in 2000 by METI.

The events that led me to visit this site were a series of state-sponsored speeches presented in 2016. Entitled "National Symposium: Let's Rethink Geological Disposal" (*zenkoku shinpojiumu: ima aratamete kangaeyō chisō shobun*), this lecture series explained the long-term safe management of HLW in Japan, as well as where it would be stored.[1] In one speech, the state minister of METI (*keizai sangyō fukudaijin*), Yōsuke Takagi, proudly described the research and development that surrounded this technological project: "France and Finland have already done successful waste repositories. We were told that we could not do such a project in Japan [because of the seismic activity], but we have the scientific expertise to do so!" These presentations were not mere narratives but also, as the speech of Takagi highlighted, assertions of Japan's technical prowess in the nuclear domain compared to other countries. From such a viewpoint, nuclear waste products were transformed from a problem into a scientific opportunity and a source of national pride.

Yet that enthusiasm often came crashing down during the period of public questions that followed every presentation. The lecture series happened five years after Fukushima in a highly politically charged environment. Japanese society was confronting the future of its nuclear industry head-on since nuclear power plants had been shut down or suspended for safety inspections after 2011. Before the disaster, Japan had fifty-four nuclear reactors, providing more than 30 percent of the nation's electricity.[2]

An atmosphere of uncertainty surrounding both Fukushima's radioactive contamination and the role of nuclear power in Japan was particularly tangible amid the crowd that attended the symposium. For instance, one elderly lady grabbed the microphone and inquired, "You have been evading one of the main questions linked with geological disposal. What are we going to do with nuclear power plants? We can't put waste forever in the ground! If we keep going with nuclear power, it will become very hard." Other attendees also expressed their frustration with the country's focus on HLW, arguing that it made no sense since Japan was currently grappling with radioactive contamination caused by the Fukushima nuclear disaster.

No state actors seemed to know what to say to the people asking questions about the future of Japan's nuclear policy or about the management of radioactive contamination in Fukushima. The state minister of METI had made his point clear on the issue of HLW: "I know there are some antinuclear voices in the room today, but no matter where your political allegiance stands in viewing nuclear policy, this is an issue that we have to deal with together." In a similar manner, Iwao Miyamoto, the director of radioactive waste management technology at METI, acknowledged that nuclear power had caused much harm to Fukushima. Yet, for the present conference, the audience was told to concentrate on the urgent problems of HLW. The plan for geological disposal was described by METI's officials as done for the sake of Japan's future. Yet few people applauded at the end of these meetings, and most left with scowls on their faces, continuing the discussion by themselves.

Nuclear Uncertainties and Nuclear Controversies

In this chapter, I explore a set of controversies around the role of nuclear power and the threat of radioactive contamination by focusing on METI, one of Japan's most powerful state ministries. METI is the heir to MITI, which was fundamental in cementing nuclear power in Japan. More importantly, METI had been the former regulator of nuclear energy before Fukushima. While the ministry no longer served as a regulator, it remained one of the main governmental actors in the recovery process,

Figure 6.1. The Mizunami Underground Research Facility. Photo by Maxime Polleri.

sanctioning and rejecting the evidence linked to the disaster as well as being in charge of reconstruction policy and the decommissioning of nuclear power plants.[3] In the aftermath of Fukushima, I argue, METI reframed nuclear power as an apolitical necessity for the well-being of the Japanese nation-state and its citizens. It did so by mobilizing categories of uncertainty around specific political issues, such as energy security or global warming. For METI, the potential uncertainties linked with the abandonment of nuclear power had the power to trigger political turmoil on a larger scale than those uncertainties linked with Fukushima's radioactive contamination. A form of double depoliticization took place, in which the issue of Fukushima's radioactive contamination got depoliticized through perceived priorities that were paradoxically depicted as "postpolitical" (i.e., in urgent need of action and not open to in-depth deliberation).[4] Throughout this chapter, I refer to this process as generating "postpolitical uncertainties."

To introduce the notion of postpolitical uncertainties, I first draw from Erik Swyngedouw's "post-political condition," in which "debate, disagreement and dissensus" are replaced through "a series of technologies of governing that fuse around consensus, agreement, accountancy metrics and technocratic environmental management."[5] In a postpolitical moment, any issue becomes political, but always in a harmonious way that is exempt from conflict.[6] To examine the nature of nuclear-related uncertainties, I bring into conversation a range of works that see uncertainty through the lens of an ethnographic approach, tracking how (in the words of Gregory Button) "politically generated uncertainty reconfigures both the landscape of disaster and our social arrangements."[7] In this view, uncertainties are mobilized as part of strategic and ideological tactics, especially when particular interests are threatened.[8] This framework is useful in order to open "an inquiry into how different sources of uncertainty, danger, and liveliness come to be known and managed while suspending the question of whether an area of uncertainty should be characterized as a sociotechnical risk, a political drama, or a financial risk."[9] Furthermore, in talking about controversies, I draw from Sarah J. Whatmore's analysis of how specific knowledge claims and policy practices become "subject to public interrogation and dispute."[10] As Robert Proctor explains, controversies are not simply the result of "imperfect knowledge but a political consequence of conflicting interests and structural apathies."[11] Depending on the specific stakes of METI, uncertainties can thus be manufactured for specific reasons, such as to downplay a controversy or to keep one alive.

To date, numerous scholars have focused on the role of nuclear energy in Japan,[12] on regulations that led to the disaster,[13] and on the failure of nuclear policy reforms.[14] Other critiques have examined the contradictory scientific and civic narratives that made sense of the scope, character, and tangible effects of radiation dangers.[15] However, the emphasis is focused on one facet of nuclear controversies, such as nuclear power policies or Fukushima's radioactive contamination. In that regard, an in-depth exploration of the broader network that links nuclear infrastructure and radioactive contamination has rarely been sustained. To borrow from Jasanoff and Kim, in this context the "relationship of science and technology to political power has tended to remain undertheorized."[16] As a result, there is a need for more dialogue on how nuclear infrastructure, its governance, and the rationalization of radioactive contamination risks are enmeshed, as well as for empirically mapping how this relationship continues to unfold in postcrisis contexts.

Following the disaster, some scholars have argued, the interpretation of uncertainty around the danger of radiation was marginalized through a series of tactics.[17] Others have provided overviews on how nuclear controversies are embedded in socioeconomic contexts with clear pro-nuclear overtones.[18] These researchers have illustrated an important relationship between a specific part of the Japanese nuclear infrastructure and the current rationalization of radiation risk. But rather than depicting pro-nuclear agents' influence in the radiological safety domain, this chapter takes a different path. It explores the normative framework ingrained in nuclear power and highlights how a particular vision continues to affect the basis of expert authority through which state actors handle post-Fukushima controversies and their subsequent uncertainties.

To probe these connections, it is useful to bring to the conversation what Jasanoff and Kim call "sociotechnical imaginaries," which consist of "collectively imagined forms of social life and social order reflected in the design and fulfillment of nation-specific scientific and/or technological projects."[19] Through focusing on a "comparative examination of the development and regulation of nuclear power in the U.S. and South Korea,"[20] Jasanoff and Kim associate sociotechnical imaginaries "with active exercises of state power, such as the selection of development priorities, the allocation of funds, the investment in material infrastructures, and the acceptance or suppression of political dissent."[21] Throughout history, sociotechnical imaginaries' relative stabilities have been "invoked and re-performed at key turning points in policy formation."[22] I contend that the theoretical approach of sociotechnical imaginaries can be strengthened through an ethnographic focus that examines the mobilization of nuclear uncertainties. To do so, I pay close attention to the areas of uncertainty linked with specific sociotechnical imaginaries in nuclear power, highlighting how these are framed as postpolitical. I offer a series of critical but situated insights into METI's politics of expertise, allowing me to explore other facets of nuclear governance in the wake of this disaster. My aim is to examine how postpolitical uncertainties are important tools for managing controversies surrounding energy and pollution. Ultimately, I highlight how controversies surrounding Fukushima's radioactive contamination are prevented from becoming the subject of public interrogation and political disputes through the mobilization of postpolitical uncertainties. This kind of depoliticization raises ethical questions surrounding meaningful public participation in decisions that happen at the intersection of politics, science, and technology studies.

METI and Nuclear Power

Like its forefather, METI occupied a very conflicted position, as it was promoting nuclear energy while serving as its safety regulator. Before the disaster, nuclear safety was under two umbrellas: the Nuclear Safety Commission (NSC), under the authority of the Japanese Cabinet, and NISA, under METI's jurisdiction.[23] Fukushima's events threw Japan's nuclear infrastructure into turmoil, debunking the myth of safety that had prevailed while forcing economic bureaucracies to rethink the future of nuclear power. Indeed, before the disaster, METI had plans to "increase nuclear power to more than 50 percent of Japan's total energy consumption by 2030."[24]

The catastrophe destroyed these ambitions and caused the gradual closure of nuclear power plants for safety inspections.[25] METI, as a promoter of nuclear energy, initially attempted to circumvent this decision by issuing "public reassurances" about the safety of nuclear reactors.[26] However, Prime Minister Naoto Kan "produced the first major breach in the elite consensus in July 2011 when he called on Japan to plan its complete exit from nuclear power."[27] Kan's successor, Yoshihiko Noda, equally supported a nuclear phaseout, and the DPJ went as far as to undertake a deliberative polling.[28] As Naoyuki Mikami summarizes, "The government presented three policy options proposing different levels of nuclear energy dependency by 2030, including a zero-dependency (0%) scenario, and called for, what it termed, a 'National Discussion' on the matter."[29] A change in government, in which the more conservative LDP replaced the DPJ, led to the abandonment of this approach. The pro-nuclear administration of Prime Minister Shinzo Abe quickly reinstated nuclear power as an important element within Japan's energy policy, with METI and business groups raising concerns about the problems that a zero-nuclear policy would produce.[30] The restarting of some nuclear power plants in 2015 caused vocal public criticism and led to major antinuclear demonstrations. It also illustrated that Japan had not abandoned nuclear energy. To avoid future conflicts of interest and the clear case of regulatory captures that arguably had led to the Fukushima disaster, NSC and NISA were replaced in 2012 by the Nuclear Regulation Authority as an administrative body of the Cabinet of Japan.[31] While METI lost its role as a nuclear safety regulator, it nonetheless remained a powerful actor in the governance of this disaster. It controlled revitalization policies, designated and rearranged areas of evacuation, and fought the spread of "harmful rumors" via economic initiatives.[32]

Japan Without Resources

In 2012, METI released one of its first public documents, Japan's Challenge Towards Recovery.[33] Throughout this document, the triple disaster was predominantly analyzed in terms of economic factors, while issues of recovery focused on the safety of nuclear power, the environmental challenge of fossil fuels, and the practical use of renewable energy. In its thirty-eight pages, there is no mention of the potential adverse health effects of residual radioactivity. The only thing alluding to the issue is a grid explaining the different radiation doses that one can find on Earth. At the top of the grid is Guarapari Beach, one of Earth's most naturally radioactive places. At the bottom is the standard dose received around a light water nuclear plant, with a parenthetical explanation stating that the actual results are far below the given value. The grid contains no explanation of the numerous man-made radionuclides released during the disaster. If one looks only at this document, the uncertainties of radiation hazards seem to have failed to materialize.

At the beginning of 2016, I attended a series of public talks produced by METI and witnessed a similar pattern. The series was delivered all over the country and included prominent experts in business and the economy, and policy planners. Entitled "Japan Without Resources: A Symposium Toward the Shape of Our Future Energy" (*shigen no nai nihon, shōrai enerugī no sugata ni kansuru shinpojiumu*), the series of speeches was explicit in presenting nuclear power not as an option but as a necessity, even in the aftermath of Fukushima.[34] In these speeches, Japan was stereotypically compared to Easter Island and its former residents, who supposedly used all of their natural resources to a point of no return. The energy problems of the archipelago were depicted as being intrinsically different from the problems faced by European countries; Japan was an island nation and thus unique among modern Asian countries. The subtext was clear and reminiscent of the 1973 Oil Crisis that had cemented the necessity of nuclear power for Japan: the black swan of Fukushima should not impede rational thinking in energy matters so as to avoid turning to expensive oil and natural gas. Since all of its nuclear power plants were closed after Fukushima, the audience was told that Japan was in a very precarious situation. For the sake of the nation, nuclear power should be fully restarted as soon as possible. According to the panel of experts, the shutting down of nuclear power had resulted in creating a climate of uncertainty regarding Japan's future.

The first uncertainty was linked to energy security. According to the symposium, Fukushima had led to a decrease in the self-sufficiency rate of electrical resources, as well as an increase in power costs. As the panel members explained, this was the case because Japan had to import costly fossil fuels and gas to compensate for the shutdown of nuclear power plants. Kyōji Yoshino, the policy planning coordinator of the Agency for Natural Resources and Energy at METI, was quick to make this point by highlighting Japan's deficit trade balance and claiming that the nation suffered from one of the highest levels of dependence in its history. Indeed, an unstable supply of electricity led METI to fear a scenario where business could not proceed "if blackouts frequently occur."[35] Furthermore, given its long-term tense relations with neighboring Asian countries, it was seen as unsustainable for Japan to depend on external supplies. In contrast to the oil and gas that came "from unstable parts of the world,"[36] nuclear power provided a stable, Japanese-made energy and a self-sufficient vision of the future. After Fukushima, the government applied strict energy-saving measures to overcome the electricity shortage. For instance, METI's action plan included restrictions on electricity usage (e.g., turning off unnecessary lights, reducing printer use, and stopping elevator services), as well as the promotion of the Cool Biz policy (*kūrubizu*), which advocated for lighter summer dress codes (e.g., short-sleeve shirts and no ties) to save on air conditioning.[37] These measures created a 14 percent drop in electricity consumption between 2011 and 2014.[38] Yet, rather than praising such savings, METI'S bureaucrats told the audience that the quality of life in Japan had decreased. Energy security in Japan was depicted as being on a crisis level—not in regard to the country's actual needs but in comparison with the electrical consumption of other countries.

The second uncertainty was linked to the future of Japanese expertise in the domain of technological innovation. According to Ryūzō Yamamoto, a professor of business administration at the University of Tokoha, the decrease in electrical independence led Japan to fall behind internationally: "If we continue in this actual way, Japan will lose much of its expertise to China. We are even behind Korea in terms of innovation!" Japan was depicted as at the cusp of a critical turn. "If Japan opts for the wrong energy politics, the country will end up being lost (*ushinawareta*) for another thirty years!" insisted Yamamoto. These concerns were also apparent in R&D projects that focused on the safe geological disposal of HLW, since such technological ambitions would only be viable through a thriving nuclear industry. A nonnuclear Japan would prove itself unacceptable to METI, an institution that viewed technology as a "game changer" nationally and internationally.[39] In that regard, depriving Japan of its nuclear expertise was seen as preventing the nation from leading the Asian market during a period of geopolitical tension with East Asian countries. Members of the nuclear village echoed similar concerns: "If Japan were to abolish nuclear energy, nuclear equipment manufacturers and energy companies would be deprived of their technological expertise, with negative consequences for the country's international competitiveness."[40] During an interview, one high-level official in the executive board of TEPCO also explained to me that nuclear expertise was at risk of being cornered by the Chinese and the Russians if Japan decided to phase out nuclear power.

The third uncertainty for Japan was associated with an apparent increase in carbon dioxide, described as an "urgent global issue" (*sekaiteki na kikkin no kadai*). After the release of radioactive pollutants, METI could no longer play on the trope of clean energy and resorted to a different rhetoric: global warming. Following the moratorium on nuclear power in Japan, Yoshino and other speakers argued that emissions of carbon dioxide had increased dramatically due to reliance on fossil fuels. As Vivoda and Graetz observe, "Japan's carbon dioxide (CO_2) emissions increased by 2.1% in 2011, and with most nuclear reactors offline in 2012, CO_2 emissions increased by a further 6.7%."[41] During the symposia, renewable energies (such as solar panel technology) were depicted as inefficient measures for tackling an uncertain energy future. "In winter and during the night there's just no light. The risk with renewable energy is that we don't have any control over it [*kanri dekinai*]," claimed the businesswoman and author Kazuyo Katsuma. After Fukushima, renewable energy was shown as receiving unjustifiable preferential treatment (*yūsenteki*), as well as something that could not be economized (*keizai dekinai mono*). "We need to be more realistic and to look at it from a bigger scale," claimed the panel of experts. Notably, not a single speaker invited by METI had expertise in global warming or renewable energy. However, global warming was taken as a "black box" and presented as a "total threat" that only nuclear power could ward off.[42]

Nuclear Imaginaries After Fukushima

To counter these problems, a new energy policy was proposed under the abbreviation "3E+S." This policy emphasized (1) energy security (*antei kyōkyū*), (2) economic efficiency (*keizai-sei*), (3) the environment (*kankyō*), and (4) safety (*anzen*). The 3E+S perspective was said to be the most realistic policy through which to tackle the three future uncertainties surrounding post-Fukushima Japan. More interestingly, the policy relied on an energy mix that aimed for a restart of nuclear power; by 2030, 22–24 percent of the produced energy would come from nuclear power. Under the difficulties enumerated, a 0 percent nuclear option was deemed hardly realistic, with METI promoting a "safe restart" (*anzen saikadō*) of nuclear power.

What was striking about these public declarations was how nuclear power was seen as a key factor in the resolution of many uncertainties arising after the disaster, including energy security, technological expertise, and, ironically, environmental safety. In this context, nuclear power was not depicted as an option—in contrast to the 2012 National Discussion—nor as a by-product of a political choice or cultural preference. Instead, it was reframed as an apolitical necessity that had to be enacted for the well-being of the nation and Japan's citizens. During one symposium, METI had invited a cultural critic, Emi Kawaguchi-Mahn, who argued that the nuclear phaseout in Germany was unrelated to the risk of nuclear power; it was simply a by-product of a foreign political culture permeated by the strong antinuclear presence of the Green Party. The Japanese context was different and unrelated. These narratives notably highlighted three specific elements of a larger sociotechnical imaginary around nuclear power.

First, they demonstrate that for METI, nuclear power is more than electricity per se; it stands as a perceived symbol of Japanese independence. Many of the speakers did not want to depict Japan as a nation that was saving energy or—worse—depending on other countries like China. Nuclear power was seen as a pillar on which a strong, modern nation-state should rest. Historically speaking, this imaginary can be tied to stereotypical tropes of the "nation island" (*shimaguni-ron*), which depict Japan as a culturally unique land that struggles for resource security.[43] This imaginary has always been part of METI's vision, resting on the belief that "Japan is a country with very few natural resources, making it highly dependent on overseas imports of fossil fuels."[44] In fact, as early as the 1970s, this imaginary was mobilized to sustain the importance of nuclear power for the growth of Japan's independence.[45]

Secondly, METI's series of symposiums reveal that nuclear power remains a form of technological pride, wonder, and challenge. The Japanese state has always embraced technology to create and maintain a gap between itself and other countries; the *wakon yōsai* idiom of prewar Japan, translated as "Japanese spirit and Western techniques," is a good example of this outlook.[46] While some scholars argue that nuclear power in post-Fukushima Japan will "no longer be a 'baseload' source of electricity, capable of supplying a reliable load,"[47] the technological expertise associated with the nuclear industry was seen as essential to maintain for METI. Indeed, shutting down nuclear power would deprive the country of an important part of its knowledge economy. While nuclear power infrastructure was widely viewed as crumbling after Fukushima, officials in METI spoke of dealing with technical and scientific challenges as simply needing adjustment. The fear of losing this expertise was apparent in the 25 percent decrease in students with nuclear-related majors between 2011 and 2021.[48] This was bad news for a state that had long prided itself on creating "science-oriented citizens" (*kagakuteki na kokumin*).[49]

Lastly, the third imaginary demonstrates a fetishization of nuclear technology as the only fix that can ward off an environmental crisis—in this case, epitomized by global warming. Nuclear power exemplifies broader imaginaries around a "consensual vision of the urban environment presenting a clear and present danger" (i.e., the rise of CO_2).[50] In contrast to the residual radioactivity in Fukushima, which was depicted as gradually disappearing, experts at METI wrapped global warming in a different temporal imaginary, one in which things would gradually get worse. This was done to the point where political elites paradoxically stressed the same technology that brought a nuclear disaster. The global and pending nature of climate change subsequently transmuted the story of Fukushima into an accident that was merely local in consequence and bounded to the past. METI's "nuclear green energy" agenda also gained support when the European Union Taxonomy Delegated Act announced that nuclear energy would be marketed as a "green investment" starting January 1, 2023.[51] As part of its "priority areas" for carbon neutrality by 2050, METI was exploring new generations of nuclear power plants, such as Small Modular Reactors.[52]

Electricity in the Air

These three elements rendered addressing some uncertainties more important than addressing others. Issues of science and technology linked with nuclear infrastructure did not simply "encode and reinforce particular conceptions of what a nation stands for," in contrast to Jasanoff and Kim,[53] but were also associated with specific categories of uncertainties that drastically differ among countries. The specific future uncertainties of METI—increased dependence, negative consequences for technological competition, and global warming—stood in sharp contrast with the German nuclear viewpoint, in which "the rule of law and the risks of legal irresponsibility remain live and urgent topics of debate,"[54] or with the US vision of "a potentially runaway technology that demands effective 'containment.'"[55] For METI, perceived uncertainties were closer to the Korean imaginary, in which the "risks and benefits of nuclear power were framed in terms of their implications for the nation's future."[56]

However, uncertainties surrounding the nation's future were not generally shared by members of the audience of the symposia. Indeed, a heated discussion always ensued at the end of these speeches. During one presentation an enraged elderly man shouted, "Why are you putting us right back into that mess after Fukushima! We won't be able to live in Japan for twenty-five hundred years if another nuclear disaster happens!" Another argued, "You want to know what's the 'best energy mix'? It's to cut all nuclear power! I was always told that nuclear power was safe and good for the environment, but that was all false! You are going to do the same thing again! You spend all your time saying that it's safe, but there is a gap between what you are doing and what you are saying!" Everybody applauded the man while the expert panelists fidgeted in their seats. The last speaker claimed that radioactive contamination from Fukushima had already polluted a good part of Japan and that nuclear power should be stopped before it was too late. The only thing Yoshino could say in response was that it was the only solution to take care of global warming. The dissenter was subsequently cut off and told that he could ask questions after the meeting: "You bet for sure, I'm going to ask some questions!" he replied. Electricity had been the main subject of the presentation, and amid such tensions one could equally feel it in the air. At the end of the discussion, the panel of experts was surrounded by members of the audience, who eagerly tried to redirect the conversation to the contamination of Fukushima. They fought over technical matters, stating that the problem of radiation was far from being over, invoking for example the long lifespan of certain radionuclides.

In his study of Mexican forestry, Mathews argues that state officials silenced public opposition by "claiming to translate generalized knowledge to local contexts, seeking to imprison their audiences in a slot of local knowledge."[57] However, even in this context, Mathews notes that officials faced a feeling of "uncertain authority" as "translating between the general and the local makes them vulnerable, worried about their lack of local knowledge."[58] Mathews's definition of expertise, in which experts are troubled by public resistance, stands in contrast with Timothy Mitchell's conceptualization,[59] in which an expert "seamlessly enlists audiences and produces subjectivities."[60] By focusing on public performances linked with scientific knowledge, Mathews argues that technical knowledge does not necessarily silence the political. Instead, he contends that each redefinition of technical knowledge "redefines expertise, the role of audiences, and forms of witnessing" while also redefining "how and where political debates about justice can take place."[61] Similarly, the dynamic present during these public talks in Japan did not imply a unidirectional relationship in which participants merely listened to expert teachings. It also involved a back-and-forth exchange about which future uncertainties should receive the lion's share of attention. Both sides tried to mobilize different categories of uncertainty around the controversies caused by the nuclear disaster. While none of the presentations were designed to address the topic of radioactive hazards, the question-and-answer periods were spaces of intense political debates in which the audience tried to reframe the problem produced by the disaster, not around a politics of uncertain trade level, power costs, or global warming but around the threat of radioactive release, which many saw as imperiling the future of Japan. Members of the audience were trying to make "visible what had no business being seen"—radioactive contamination.[62] Yet these concerns, which challenged the very framework of what could be discussed or not after Fukushima, were unconditionally ignored by the panel of experts, who put forward energy security, technological expertise, and global warming as the only issues that had to be dealt with.

The disregard for radioactive risks was also made apparent during an interview conducted with Junsō Nishimura, an informant formerly employed by METI and TEPCO. Nishimura had notably been involved in the negotiations surrounding the reorganization of evacuation zones with the local municipalities of Fukushima. He explained to me, "Even after I was able to build trust with the local people, I had difficulty dealing with people from outside who refused to see the real ongoing situation because they benefit from thinking about imaginary damages." Nishimura was careful to emphasize that the only cases of disaster-related deaths were caused by the stress of evacuation and not by radiation exposure. In his narrative, radioactive contamination was clearly a postpolitical problem that was not contestable. If uncertainties did arise, they were of an "individual" nature raised by outside people who "refused to see the real ongoing situation." As Fisker-Nielsen explains, these outside people were perceived as an anomaly in Japanese normative culture: "At the local level in Japan, the individual is normally understood as standing in the way of collective national, political or economic interests. This is increasingly seen as political rhetoric devoid of substance which caters to elite interests."[63]

In inquiring about radioactive contamination, I was struck by a series of contradictions rarely problematized by my interlocutor. For instance, Nishimura did not believe that current technology for tracking radioactive contamination was advanced enough, that a complete decontamination of Fukushima was possible, and that absolute safety could exist in terms of nuclear power—issues that the experts at METI's symposia had equally embraced. Yet amid those contradictions, radioactive risk was not a form of potential uncertainty that demanded the same amount of focus as energy security or global warming. Why was that so? Some have argued for explanations that highlight Japan's conventional political culture, stating that "men working for dominant institutions that prioritize the economy have built the system that created nuclear energy plants. They believe in the system and have invested their life work within the system. If radiation from Fukushima proved to be harmful to their families and could eventually destroy the economy, they would have to fundamentally re-evaluate their role. To consider the threat of radiation from the technology they have created is to doubt the system . . . which they help maintain, as well as their values and life choices."[64] This is clearly a part of the story. However, mentioning Japanese specificities as the single factor for the mitigation of hazardous pollutants forecloses the complexities of postdisaster management politics, with the additional effect of removing the responsibility of governments or industrial polluters.[65] Homogeneous behavioral traits cannot fully explain the entanglement of science and society.[66] Furthermore, beyond a cultural deterministic approach, deeper structural factors mitigate the risk of radioactive contamination in a post-Fukushima scenario.

Instead, METI's understanding of the controversies linked with this nuclear disaster ought to be seen as coproduced with specific sociocultural imaginaries, where knowledge and order co-evolve.[67] This was particularly apparent in the picture given by Nishimura, whose expertise around nuclear matter was couched in what Carol Cohn famously called "technostrategic language"—terminologies that disregard particular realities and values in the face of nuclear risks.[68] Nishimura described the problem of radioactive contamination by referring to terms such as "negotiation," "due diligence," "agreement," and "transaction"—imaginaries that prioritize certain forms of uncertainties as being more important than others. This makes perfect sense for a state agency like METI, which has jurisdiction over industrial policy and energy security, and for whom abandoning nuclear power has the potential to trigger tremendous political risks. To address "more urgent" uncertainties, METI had to temporarily "stabilize" the risk of radiation.[69]

Some readers might argue that this is not particularly problematic, since other state ministries are implicated in managing radiation hazards. Indeed, different views on the management of uncertainties requiring remediation are found among various state agencies. For instance, an important conflict between METI and MOE emerged around the government expenses surrounding Fukushima's decontamination.[70] These internal tensions within the Japanese state are reinforced by bureaucratic problems of "vertical administration" (*tatewari gyōsei*), where different ministries defend their field of competence, sometimes without coordination with other ministries. The vertical administration of different problems demonstrates that the state views nuclear power versus radiation exposure as different kinds of politics. Energy security, technical expertise, and climate change reside in the realm of international geopolitics for METI, while radiation exposure resides in the realm of local environmental politics for MOE. In this case, postpolitical uncertainties are also instances when the state seeks to separate these kinds of politics. While METI does not produce nor track data relating to radioactive contamination, the practical operations for designating areas under which evacuation orders are issued fall under its jurisdiction.[71] Accordingly, METI possesses one of the strongest influences on the governance of this disaster. If radioactive contamination is depicted as an important problem, it will impede the reopening of nuclear power plants across Japan, the R&D of NUMO, and the economic policies previously highlighted in the 3E+S.

Bulldozing Uncertainties

In light of METI's depoliticization of radioactive hazards, many citizens had found alternative venues to express their frustration. An important gathering point during my fieldwork was the Antinuclear Tent (*datsugenpatsu tento*), a small wooden shack built near the bureaucratic office of METI in the governmental district of Kasumigaseki, Tokyo. Literally translated as the "gate of fog," Kasumigaseki was an ironic name for the location of an antinuclear movement mostly ignored by the state.

The tent had been established to protest nuclear power and the health danger of radioactive contamination after Fukushima. Next to the office of METI, the tent displayed slogans such as "Don't erase the voices of Fukushima!"; "Don't trust the government and the big media!"; "Save the children of Fukushima!" As I spent time interviewing members of the tent, I soon learned that many protestors were once part of the All-Campus Joint Struggle League (*zenkyōtō*), the Japanese equivalent of May '68. This social movement consisted of a series of student protests against the traditional values of capitalism, consumerism, and perceived American imperialism. Therefore, even before 2011, many members of the tent had already developed a strong antinuclear agenda, as well as a distrust of their government. They believed that Japan was not a democracy but, as a member called Tetsuo Kawabata explained to me, a "police town."

For members of the tent raised in the tumultuous period of May '68, nuclear power was an undemocratic source of energy. Many argued that nuclear energy was never developed to produce stable electricity, but rather to create the atomic bomb.[72] Therefore, for members of the tent, nuclear power plants were born not for the *demos* but for the *polemos*, or for militaristic purposes. For them, the history of nuclear energy was embedded with mass destruction and inequality. Similarly, Kawabata was convinced that the government had minimized the harmful influence of radioactive contamination in order to restart nuclear power as soon as possible. Stating his disdain for capitalism, he explained to me that nuclear power had built a needless dependence on electrical consumption: "We waste too much electricity and the government makes us believe that we need more of it! The neon in Ginza—is it really necessary? And the LED all over the city? We have become too comfortable. This consumption is not even linked with our actual needs! When the power plants stopped after Fukushima, we still had light! It was enough! The restart of nuclear power is simply for the financial sake of the electrical companies and for the benefit of the government. It's not for the well-being of the population!"

Kawabata was not lying; scholars have underscored how "the Japanese economy has not collapsed without nuclear power and [how] there have been no largescale power outages despite the delicate energy security challenge."[73] Yet, the theoretical point of interest lies in the fact that antinuclear activists had developed their own sociotechnical imaginaries around nuclear power, molded in a very different context than those of METI. For these antinuclear activists, nuclear power was experienced as a problem of extravagance (*zeitaku*), as well as reflecting undemocratic values that put the utilitarian interests of electric companies above the welfare of citizens. Radioactive contamination was the extension of an already established precarity. When I interviewed antinuclear activists, it was not unusual for me to hear phrases such as "Radioactivity [*hōshanō*] is the devil [*akuma*]!" or "The atom is wicked [*kaku wa aku*]!" Similarly, in describing the contamination of Fukushima, activists resorted to the word "*yogoreta*," which can mean "dirtied," but equally "corrupted," or "*kōgai*," which means "pollution" or "public nuisance." Many lamented the fact that ultranationalists harassed them: "They came not so long ago and broke our door," related Kawabata while pointing at the tent entrance. "It's the third time that we had to replace it! Be careful if you ever see some right-wing propaganda truck [*gaisensha*]!" Moreover, members of the tent told me that METI had forbidden them to wear antinuclear signs during a public conference. Before I attended the symposium, METI reminded participants that they should not wear or wave political signs. Many activists were outraged by this and gave me endless stickers of the famous antinuclear logo "Smiling Sun," stating that METI's decision was a slur on their democratic rights to show dissatisfaction in a free country. My interviews with members of the tent and antinuclear activists demonstrate that nuclear power was portrayed via three specific imaginaries: (1) a ubiquitous threat to life, (2) a dirty and polluting form of energy, and (3) the bastard product of an undemocratic legacy born from the union of warfare and capitalism.

Consequently, members of the tent mobilized their own categories of uncertainty in a post-Fukushima Japan. The uncertainties that demanded urgent action were unrelated to energy security, technological expertise, or global warming. Rather, they were associated with uncertain health hazards from radioactive exposure, ecological collapse from radioactive contamination, and the downfall of democracy throughout Japan. Many informants were worried about the uncertainty of a democratic future for Japanese society. Talk of a country that was returning to "the old imperialistic history of Japan" was rampant. As one man explained,

During the war, you had the *kamikaze*, you had to die for honor, for the country. Now, it's the same, people are told to be resilient to this disaster. . . . We need to prepare the way for the future. We can't prepare ourselves against the threat of nuclear power—it's the evil of humans. We cannot stop earthquakes or tsunami, but we can stop nuclear power. *How* to live is the most important thing, but right now, we are not living—we are surviving! It's easy to stop all that. The government just has to say a few syllables: STOP! [in Japanese, *ya-me-ta*]. How many years will be necessary for them to be able to say those three mere syllables?

Both METI and members of the tent were concerned by the uncertain path of a post-Fukushima Japan. Yet, the categories of uncertainty mobilized to advance their vision were utterly antagonistic. Still, what happened to the uncertainties put forward by this small antinuclear organization, mainly composed of elderly individuals? How did the state reply to them? Erik Swyngedouw has argued that the postpolitical moment "relies on either including all in a consensual pluralist order and on excluding radically those who posit themselves outside the consensus. For them, . . . the law is suspended; they are literally put outside the law and treated as extremists and terrorists."[74] By resisting the "noncommittal way" and the path of "non-conflict,"[75] the members of the tent had positioned themselves outside the consensual pluralist order that emphasized the safe restart of nuclear, as well as the recovery of Fukushima. State replies precisely echoed the postpolitical moment.

Indeed, members of the Antinuclear Tent faced a Strategic Lawsuit Against Public Participation (SLAPP) brought by the government. A SLAPP usually aims to silence critics by burdening them with the cost of a legal defense until they abandon their opposition. As Kawabata told me, "The government is trying to burden us with the cost of a legal defense, so that we will stop our fight. They are claiming 110 millions of yens. But we won't be intimidated!" When many people began to support the tent with financial donations, the government claimed that members of the tent were illegally occupying private property by sitting next to the offices of METI and ordered the "dismantlement" of the Antinuclear Tent. In the small hours of August 21, 2016, a bulldozer came and swiped the small barracks clean off the ground.

Figure 6.2. The Antinuclear Tent in downtown Tokyo. Photo by Maxime Polleri.

Members of the public could participate in discussing post-Fukushima nuclear controversies during the question period of METI's symposia. Yet they had to follow political-participation procedures considered valid by the state, which usually fell within the configuration that actors like METI recognized as legitimate (or not). When public actors tried to mobilize different uncertainties around nuclear policies or radiation harm, they faced the real risk of being trapped in a postpolitical moment, where less urgent uncertainties were depoliticized by bulldozers.

Long Live the King!

It is a well-known fact that uncertainties can be manufactured or mobilized to suit the needs of political actors.[76] This is even more true when uncertainties "seek to maintain the asymmetrical balance of power by protecting corporate and state interests over the public good."[77] This chapter emphasized that managing uncertainties is much more efficient in controlling public controversies when combined with a postpolitical moment. The officials whom I met clearly realized that the myth of nuclear safety was detrimental to the well-being of the Japanese nation-state. They transformed it into a question of weighing the risks and benefits of a post-Fukushima scenario—one in which radiation danger did not tip the balance against nuclear power. METI's definition of what counted as a higher risk was not shared by the public, as exemplified by the tension-filled debates of their public talks or the Antinuclear Tent. Only through the instantiation of specific categories of postpolitical uncertainties around nuclear power could METI enact its Japanese vision of the future.

In the context of the Chernobyl disaster, many scholars have focused on the strategic mobilization of uncertainties regarding health risks.[78] For instance, Petryna argues that a "catastrophe whose scale was unimaginable, difficult to map, and 'saturating' became *manageable* through a particular dynamic: non knowledge became crucial to the deployment of authoritative knowledge, especially as it applied to the management of exposed populations."[79] Similarly, secrecy around radiation harm became a primordial part of the collapsing Soviet regime. The "politics of invisibility" that followed radioactive contamination was enacted by the production of scientific uncertainties around low-dose exposure, the use of deceitful dosimetry, the delegitimization of local expert voices, and the branding of the local population as suffering from radiophobia.[80] While these forms of secrecy and ignorance are also present in the official governance of radioactive contamination after Fukushima, the notion of postpolitical uncertainty highlights a different technique of governing, where specific categories of uncertainty can be mobilized to foreclose in-depth political deliberations around controversial issues. Rather than resorting to nonknowledge or secrecy, as in the case of Chernobyl, the management of nuclear controversies through postpolitical uncertainties acts as a specific distribution of urgencies that contain disruptive uncertainties.[81]

By relying on postpolitical uncertainties, METI foreclosed the very possibility of alternative viewpoints around revitalization in a post-Fukushima Japan. This has led to a form of double depoliticization, wherein radioactive hazards are depoliticized through more important priorities that are depicted as postpolitical and not open to discussion. Still, postpolitical uncertainties are enacted not in a vacuum but in given sociocultural relationships and exchanges among different groups. In recognizing this, we need to acknowledge that while particular forms of uncertainties cannot merely be explained by cultural determinism, they are always in dialogue with prior sociotechnical imaginaries and cultures, making their enactment quite different across societies. In that regard, Strathern notes, "If we think of present-day cultures as the 'offspring' of past ones, we see new combinations forever being put together out of old cultural elements."[82] What then becomes pertinent is to target the areas of uncertainty linked with a postpolitical moment, examining how these uncertainties are differently articulated. The relationship of postpolitical uncertainties with changing visions of the Japanese future highlights a shift from postwar narratives of economic and technical advances (the idea of unlimited nuclear energy) to a contemporary sense of national vulnerability (climate change, economic turmoil). With the failure of the postwar nuclear narrative, METI's mobilization of postpolitical uncertainties can be seen as closely tied to this shift.

Postpolitical uncertainties show how controversies are managed in a liberal democracy that nominally relies on public participation but constrains the public so that it is not disruptive. In this way, political leaders and technical experts encourage limited forms of public participation as ends unto themselves rather than as a means for actually affecting policy. In this way, the concept of postpolitical uncertainties inscribes itself in the broader critique of "participative turn," which restrains citizen participation to block radical change in the status quo.[83] Democracy risks becoming mere public participation as opposed to participation in actual decision making. This remains an important inquiry for the field of science and technology studies (STS), which has argued that "more public participation in technical decision-making improves the public value and quality of science and technology."[84] Accordingly, STS researchers should explore how postpolitical uncertainties create a semblance of political participation, which not only stands as a form of tokenistic participation but contributes toward the marginalization of science and democracy.

In the end, myths are myths for a reason: they resist the test of time, define ideal stereotypical cultures, create affective structures, and are constantly reconfigured in response to present societal needs. Japan's nuclear infrastructure of regulatory capture is perhaps no longer present, but its legacy is still alive. The nuclear safety myth has not died per se; it is instead taking new forms and even mutating toward the rationalization of radioactive contamination. As Thompson argues, change does not imply that the "legacies of older representations, identities, discourses and institutions disappear, but rather that they realign and reemerge."[85] The changes following nuclear controversies in a post-Fukushima Japan reflect a perpetuation of similar structural harms that made this disaster possible while continuing to mitigate radiation hazards, echoing the continuity of monarchy amid ever-changing kings: The nuclear safety myth is dead! Long live the nuclear safety myth!

7

Radioactive Performances

While radiation risk is often described as invisible, odorless, and intangible,[1] signs of a nuclear disaster were clearly present in Fukushima. Citizen scientists had adopted diverse technoscientific practices with the hope of making the radioactive threat visible with electronic pocket dosimeters. Often these devices were more than tools, functioning as bodily prostheses to augment corporeal senses in irradiated environments. And then there were just the scenes of utter desolation—abandoned streets whose traffic lights aimlessly changed from yellow to red.

Yet, in the scope of my fieldwork, radiation never seemed more tangible than in Miharu Town, where CEC had created a vast, government-sponsored scientific hub to explain the phenomenon of radiation to the population of Japan. At this center, members of the public could learn about radiation through interactive games, fun activities, and cute presentations. For instance, children read *manga* (Japanese comics) that tackled questions about radiation, such as food safety or health effects. Written by a local entertainer, these *manga* adopted an approach of adorable and charming aesthetics.

Within the politics of revitalization, the CEC of Miharu Town is emblematic of a specific form of risk-communication strategy that attempts to promote the understanding of radiation by way of jargon-free explanations.[2] Through an ethnography of state-sponsored exhibits, hands-on activities, and didactic centers providing radiation information, this chapter examines how state expertise on radiation hazards is increasingly disseminated to the public via a teaching infrastructure that makes radiation easy to understand, interactive, and even enjoyable. I argue that the educational infrastructure in post-Fukushima Japan fostered a process of "radioactive performances," where radiation is presented as nonthreatening and even beneficial. These performances promote asymmetrical information about radioactive risks, taking a partisan stance toward the state's politics of revitalization. While providing comprehensible information, this form of risk communication is partial in nature, omitting controversial aspects of radiation phenomena, as well as different understandings of what counts as recovery.

To introduce the notion of radioactive performances, I take a cue from theories of performativity that focus on understanding the normalization of violence and gender roles. I first draw from Eyal Ben-Ari and Sabine Frühstück, who critically examine how violence is "concealed and exposed" in public demonstrations surrounding the role of Japan Self-Defense Forces (*jieitai*).[3] By highlighting the specific actions, spatial arrangements, displays, and theatrics of a live-fire demonstration by Japan's military, they demonstrate that militaristic violence is successfully transformed into "an object of fascination, enjoyment, and celebration."[4] Far from being neutral, these performances sustain a specific purpose: to legitimize and normalize the role of the Self-Defense Forces in a country that still bears the harms of its military past.[5] I also draw from Judith Butler's analysis of the performativity of gender, which argues that the normative power of performance lies in a process of reiteration, not only through a repetition of norms but also through exclusion.[6]

In a context of teaching infrastructure, a focus on performativity highlights how specific reiterations materialize and explain radiation hazards for the public. During my fieldwork, I noticed that three elements of radioactive performances were repeatedly promoted over other ones. First, they emphasized the naturalness of radioactivity over man-made radioactive pollutants. Second, information about radiation was enacted through cute aesthetics and games. Third, these performances fostered the amazing and useful aspects of radioactivity in the domains of scientific and medical technologies. These iterations are not random processes, as there is always a politics behind making certain aspects of radiation hazards visible or not.[7] For instance, after Chernobyl, Petryna examined how knowledge about radiological injury was strategically made visible as a form of political power to negotiate public accountability, financial revenue, and medical compensation in a post-Soviet Ukraine transitioning from communist to capitalist ideologies.[8] Following the same disaster, but in the context of Belarusian society, Kuchinskaya highlighted a different story, where invisibility around radiation risk is produced due to particular structural conditions that serve the interests of the nuclear industry and the state's economic needs.⁹ In a similar vein, radioactive performances in post-Fukushima Japan are associated with politics that sustain policies of recovery, such as full-scale repatriation.

Ethnographically speaking, this chapter draws from direct and participant observation in state-related centers that explain radiation, as well as from interviews with technical advisors and scientists present during public activities. I also highlight the visitors' interactions with the materials that explain radiation, focusing on the prevailing narrative that is propagated through such experiences. To track which aspects of radiation hazards are prioritized or not, it is useful to bring into the conversation Gabrielle Hecht's concept of "nuclearity," which unsettles classificatory schemes by examining both the banality and the exceptionalism of nuclear things.¹⁰ I engage with this concept to historicize the practices through which radiation hazards are defined as exceptional, banal, or nonexistent—before and after Fukushima. Combined with a focus on performativity, this frame looks at how radiation phenomena get stylized through repetitions, which assumptions about risks end up being normalized, as well as whose voices get marginalized in the process. It sees radioactive performances not as all-encompassing state replies but as part of a set of diverse strategies for information delivery about radiation hazards.¹¹

While it is easy to critique shortcomings in risk communication, especially from the viewpoint of a non-Fukushima resident, there is a logic associated with radioactive performances. For the Japanese state, an important part of radiation hazard is associated with unwarranted stress, where the fear of radiation might be more damaging than exposure to certain levels of radiation. As noted earlier, the state has identified the major risks of this disaster as mental health problems, social problems, and the stigma associated with radiation. Against this background, radioactive performances attempt to alleviate the fear of radiation for the benefit of the public. Yet performances also imply an audience, and scholars working on risk communication have argued that there is no such thing as a homogeneous public.¹²

While some citizens I interviewed were happy that the state embraced a jargon-free approach to radioactive risk communication—making it easier for them to understand a difficult phenomenon—responses to these centers were polarized. For instance, members of an organization wishing to evacuate children from Fukushima argued that the endeavor was little more than a "safety campaign" (*anzen kyanpēn*) and a form of "brainwashing" (*sennō*). Accordingly, it is important to keep in mind that the state materialization of radioactive risks sometimes differs from the lived experience of affected individuals, such as evacuees, citizen scientists, farmers, and medical doctors. Radioactive performances can therefore clash with alternative understandings of risk and recovery.

Radioactive Risk: Between Exceptionalism and Banality

Many tropes associated with post-Fukushima radioactive performances were molded through specific historical and political contexts. As emphasized throughout this book, the atomic bombings of World War II have represented a foundational core in the Japanese imagination of nuclear risks. The Hiroshima Peace Memorial Museum is filled with narratives that capture the "inhumane nature of nuclear weapons,"[13] such as drawings made by the *hibakusha*, which depict burned and bloodied survivors walking around like zombies. Powerful emotional reactions are generated within such an imaginary; one can even "experience" the bombing of Hiroshima and the suffering of *hibakusha* via interactive virtual reality tours.[14] These depictions constitute a case of what Hecht calls "nuclear exceptionalism," which demonstrates the specific harm brought by nuclear things.[15] In Japan, nuclear exceptionalism has been linked with a politics of victimization (*higaisha*) to highlight the unique status of the nation as the "only country in the world hit by the atomic bomb (*sekai yuiitsu no hibakukoku*)."[16] Yet, by making nuclear risks "hypervisible,"[17] the Hiroshima narrative also conveniently casts a shadow over Japan's past as a former military and colonial aggressor. As Philippe Pelletier explains, it erases the fact that Hiroshima was precisely chosen because the town was an important military target filled with armament factories.[18]

At the other end of the spectrum, nuclear exceptionalism confronts "nuclear banality,"[19] the latter being used to downplay radioactive risks and promote nuclear infrastructure. In that regard, one could think about the (in)famous Mr. Pluto and its thirst-quenching plutonium-laced soda (see chapter 1). "This clever down-playing of the dangers of plutonium," notes Morris Low, "was part of the campaign to counter public opposition to the building and 1993 start-up of the plutonium-fuelled Monju prototype fast breeder reactor by PNC in Fukui prefecture."[20] Mr. Pluto advanced this agenda by making nuclear risks visible and banal for a different politics: the promotion of nuclear power.

After Fukushima, nuclear risks were initially embedded in both exceptionalism and banality, but the latter narrative quickly began to gain ground.[21] A few days after the disaster, an artist named Kazuhiko Hachiya released a four-minute video animation that explained the nuclear disaster to the children of Japan.[22] The video introduces "Tummy Hurting Nuclear Boy," a cute little animated character who stands for the Fukushima power plant. It explains that Nuclear Boy (*genpatsu kun*) suffers from tummy aches (*onaka ga itaku natta*). In the video, one can see Nuclear Boy, crouching down, holding his belly and saying, "Ohh! I hope that it's not a big poo poo [*unchi*] . . . but I can't hold it anymore . . . !!!" A "big sound" is eventually released from the rear end of Nuclear Boy. Soon after the suspicious sound, a character with a big nose called *Nioi kakunin man* (literally: the man who can confirm the smell) comes to examine what happened. "Ohh, fortunately it was not a poo poo, but only a big fart [*onara*]!" To prevent further unfortunate but harmless "farts," Nuclear Boy is fed with some medicine. Viewers are then told, "Nuclear Boy might release some other little farts [radioactive pollutants], but there's no need to worry—the odor will soon fade away and far-away people won't even notice it! The smell of fart will leave after one week!" Nuclear Boy is seen smiling while wearing a big diaper (*omutsu*) to prevent further leaks. The message is clear—the nuclear disaster is a minor incident that should not cause adverse health effects. Nuclear risk from Fukushima is not exceptional but merely as banal as passing gas.

The Japanese state put forward its own discourse, which, much like Nuclear Boy, often leaned toward banality. At first, in a model case of "knowledge deficit" (which implies that the public is deficient in understanding the consequences of given risks),[23] the state engaged in a traditional communication strategy, bringing its own experts to dole out information about radiation. This risk communication was criticized for its disregard of uncertainties, as well as for its sole purpose of mitigating fear.[24] One of the major problems of this communication approach was the delivery of data in a dry and unclear manner, often through "number-drenched information."²⁵ Citizens I interviewed echoed their initial confusion associated with trying to make sense of radiation risks through complex quantitative explanations made in interchangeable units of radioactivity. In response to this public frustration, the state embarked on creating a more effective form of communication, mobilizing activities that were participative in tone, rather than simply top-down.

While this change can be applauded, it is important to remember that the purpose of risk communication, as Kim Fortun reminds us, is often one of "assimilation."²⁶ Indeed, risk communication, which is homogenizing in its treatment of hazards, falls within governance techniques that attempt to "secure or repair credibility, without fundamentally questioning the forms of power or social control involved."²⁷ Therefore, it is important to consider that so-called novel forms of communication do not simply provide basic information (*kisoteki jōhō*) about radiation. Rather, they are also "subtly performative," and such communication "reflects and tacitly projects models of the human subject into the public world."²⁸

The remainder of the chapter focuses on how radioactive performances support an attempt to rebuild life in post-Fukushima Japan. I examine three cases. The first case study focuses on DIP, which was established in January 2012 as a joint program between the Prefecture of Fukushima and MOE. Situated in Fukushima City, DIP provided information about radiation in general, as well as explanations about monitoring methods and decontamination practices. Another important educational infrastructure was the CEC of Miharu Town, which was inaugurated in July 2016. The center was established with the financial support of the Japanese government to conduct research and provide education on radioactive contamination. It possessed numerous facilities, and its public halls could accommodate hundreds of individuals. The last case study concerns the National Institute of Radiological Sciences (NIRS) (*Hōshasen igaku sōgō kenkyūjo*), a world-leading radiological institute with a mandate to study the effects of radiation on the body. After 2011, it assisted in the restoration of the areas affected by radioactive contamination by managing research projects that addressed concerns like "harmful rumors" (*fūhyō higai*).

The Naturalness of Radiation

During the spread of commercial nuclear power, the banalization of nuclear things through natural comparisons was a tactic used by the industry, which insisted that "radioactivity was part of nature" and that "nuclear power [was] just a form of energy like all others."[29] Similarly, in the post-Fukushima teaching infrastructure, the phenomenon of radiation was explained through the use of comparisons that highlighted its naturalness (*shizen hōshasen*), whether conferred by cosmic rays, radioactive rays emanating from the earth, radon gas in the air, or even in foods. Such an emphasis was particularly present at DIP, as well as in the CEC of Miharu. Both venues had facilities that promoted the understanding of radiation with familiar examples to raise awareness regarding the environmental recovery efforts in Fukushima.[30]

At CEC, the most popular attraction was the Environmental Creation Theater (*kankyō sōzō shiatā*), where young families immersed themselves in a 360-degree multisensory experience that explained the phenomenon of radiation in under ten minutes. The theater's narrator argued that radiation was part of daily life: "It can be found everywhere! From the sun's rays to the minerals in the earth. . . . Without radiation, no life would exist." After these explanations, an enormous Boeing jet passed over theatergoers' heads in the cinematic sky. The film went on to argue that the amount of radiation exposure received during an intercontinental flight (mostly from cosmic rays) was higher than the level of radiation found in Fukushima. With necks strained upward, children and parents present in the theater mumbled words of apparent relief. To make radiation phenomena easier to understand, NIRS similarly provided "mini-lectures on radiation all around us" (*minomawari no hōshasen ni tsuite mini kōgi*).

In addition to the theater and lectures, particle detectors used for visualizing the passage of radiation—such as a cloud chamber (*kiribako*)—allowed visitors to literally see radiation emanating from natural sources. These particle detectors were popular with children, as they allowed them to see a phenomenon associated with tropes of invisibility, in this case, energetic ionizing particles. As a little mascot explained, "You can see that it's flying!" (*pyunpyun tte tonde iru no ga wakaru yo ne*).[31] Cloud chambers were also used to convey the fact that radiation naturally exists in other areas, such as in Osaka or Fukuoka.³²

At DIP, visitors could manipulate radiation-measuring devices, such as the scintillation radiation counter PA-1000 or the semiconductor radiation counter PDM-122. With these devices, technical advisors encouraged visitors to test the amount of naturally occurring radioactivity in commonplace materials gathered on a table (e.g., a bag of rice, a piece of granite, or an iron plate). Beyond interactive displays, many pamphlets emphasized the fact that food produced in Fukushima was regularly tested, with results falling under the strict limits of allowable amounts of radioactivity. These pamphlets explained that radiation naturally exists in our food, such as the potassium ingested in bananas: "Foods will bring us effects of natural radioactive rays, one of which is the element K [potassium] that is indispensable to us."³³ In light of this optimistic portrayal, a technical advisor at DIP argued that "there is absolutely [*mattaku nai*] no need to worry about the food we ingest." The same advisor also told me that the "Ultraman Stamp Rally" was about to take place in Fukushima, where children could collect virtual stamps of their favorite superhero, whose superpower stems from another type of natural radiation: the sun.

At CEC, visitors could search for and display the current atmospheric level of radiation in Fukushima Prefecture through an interactive "radiation measurement map" (*hōshasen sokutei mappu*). With the help of a touch panel, visitors witnessed how much the radiation levels had changed since the accident, as well as how much they differed from overseas areas. In July 2016, it was possible to compare the radiation levels in Fukushima with other locations in the world, like New York, Brazil, or Iran. In doing so, visitors learned that many places had naturally occurring radiation levels (called background levels) higher than what had been detected in Fukushima. Such background radiation is often due to naturally occurring terrestrial or cosmic radiation sources.

These comparisons all provided optimistic views of radiation levels in Fukushima, and visitors playing with the radiation measurement map could see that radiation exposure had seemingly reached normal levels. When I questioned a radiation scientist about the heavy emphasis on the naturalness of radioactivity within the teaching infrastructure narrative, I was told that radiation is "a bit hard to understand" and that "you can't explain it from nothing, you can't explain it without at least some kind of basis that everybody can understand." While the emphasis on naturalness makes the presence of radiation banal to the point of being easy to understand, these comparisons also perform specific semiotic materialities. The constant iteration of the naturalness of radiation conveys that radioactivity is a common occurrence, rather than something mysterious associated with the by-products of nuclear power. As Hansson argues, the term "natural" has strong values of approval and was regularly used in pro-nuclear claims, which stated that "exposures of the same size as naturally occurring (background) radiation cannot be dangerous—presumably because they occur in nature."[34] Similarly, by saying that citizens are routinely exposed to radiation like that coming from cosmic rays, the teaching infrastructure of Fukushima performs a narrative wherein there is no need to worry about the exposure of the region.

Yet, performances surrounding the naturalness of radiation do not convey the sheer complexity of radiation dangers after a nuclear disaster. There is nothing natural about the radioactive isotopes such as iodine-131, cesium-134, cesium-137, and strontium-90, as well as the radioactivity stemming from plutonium. Repeated claims about the naturalness of radiation, such as saying that we ingest radioactivity by eating bananas, have little to do with the specific hazards of fission products from nuclear power plants, which "cause cancer, leukemia, genetic mutations, birth defects, [and] malformations."[35] Furthermore, all these radionuclides possess "unique biological signatures,"[36] which present particular risks if inhaled or ingested—a phenomenon referred to as internal contamination. For example, iodine-131 accumulates in the thyroid gland, causing thyroid cancers. Cesium-137, which causes pancreatitis, as well as cancers in the liver and kidneys, also tends to accumulate in muscles, exposing soft tissues to beta particles and gamma radiation.[37] Strontium-90 is particularly problematic as it mimics the function of calcium, causing "cancers of the bone, bone marrow, and soft tissues around the bone."[38] Plutonium-239 is arguably even more dangerous: "When plutonium particles are inhaled, they lodge in the lung tissue. The alpha particles can kill lung cells, which causes scarring of the lungs, leading to further lung disease and cancer. Plutonium can enter the blood stream from the lungs and travel to the kidneys, meaning that the blood and the kidneys will be exposed to alpha particles. Once plutonium circulates through the body, it concentrates in the bones, liver, and spleen, exposing these organs to alpha particles."[39]

Spending a weekend on Guarapari beach or eating bananas every day does not produce cancer. In fact, while bananas have naturally occurring potassium, it would require eating the astronomical sum of twenty million bananas for radiation poisoning to occur.[40] Nonetheless, the naturalness analogy is a powerful tool for a state that wishes to reassure the population of Fukushima's safety. It not only performs the materiality of radioactivity as a form of risk that has always existed daily but reimagines Fukushima as a region whose radiation levels appear normal, especially in comparison to other places with higher background radiation levels. Kuchinskaya argues that seeing an area as "no longer significantly contaminated" is equivalent to redefining the radiation risk as "in the past, thus canceling out the need for continued radiation protection work."[41] It comes as no surprise to note that evacuation zones in Fukushima were gradually lifted when the level of radiation appeared to be satisfactory. The analogy of the naturalness of radiation helps to facilitate this policy of recovery, but also conceals the specific risks of man-made radioactive pollutants, which will linger for decades and even centuries.

What should be criticized here is not the fact that naturalness is *indeed* a part of radiation-related phenomena but the misleading analogies that are mobilized to fit a politics of revitalization. While radioactive performances depict radiation as banal to the point of being naturally present in our foods, they neutralize the controversies over raising the threshold of exposure to man-made pollutants to 20 mSv/year. The naturalness of radioactivity thus makes radiation something that is normal for a city like Fukushima on the path to recovery. The coup de grâce of this performance is arguably found at the train station of Fukushima City, where visitors can buy radium eggs (*rajiumu tamago*) that are parboiled in the waters of the Iizaka hot spring, famous for its natural radium. Through such symbolic association, radiation is made completely palatable in a few delicious bites. *Itadakimasu* (*Bon appétit*)!

Nuclear Cuteness

At the entrance of CEC, a large-bellied hippopotamus-like mascot welcomed visitors while accepting hugs from children. The educational annex of CEC, known as the Environmental Innovation Center Exchange Building (*kankyō sōzō sentā kōryū-tō*), or more simply "Komyutan Fukushima," was primarily visited by young families. An advisor explained that the center's purpose was to "deepen the understanding of children about radiation" by making their experience enjoyable. With the help of the giant mascot, young visitors were primed to have a good time before even entering the center.

In their study of Japan's Self-Defense Force, Ben-Ari and Frühstück argue that military violence is often deproblematized via aestheticization, which refers to "the process by which violence is transformed into something to be contemplated or experienced in 'safe' conditions."[42] A striking fact about the teaching infrastructure encountered during my fieldwork was that information about radiation was similarly performed, presented under the auspices of cute aesthetics, displays, and games—something the Japanese call "*kawaii*."[43] In the context of nuclear science, facilitating the understanding of complex information has long relied on appealing explanations, sometimes blending education with propaganda. One could think about the endlessly cute nuclear mascots, such as *Gumo-kun*, the mole-like mascot of NUMO—which engages in the long-term management of HLW—or *Tsukaeru*, the smiling green frog of Rokkasho Village, where the Rokkasho Nuclear Fuel Reprocessing Facility is located.

However, in the aftermath of nuclear disasters, a cute and fun take on radiation is a wholly novel approach and not something witnessed after Chernobyl or Three Mile Island. In the case of the 2011 disaster, I argue that the cuteness aesthetic is used to support the normalization of life in Fukushima, especially for citizens who are worried about contamination and wish to learn more about radioactivity via simple explanations. From a foreign viewpoint, it is easy to criticize the use of cuteness as trivial, but this constitutes an ethnocentric understanding. Importantly, the Japanese notion of "cuteness" does not have the puerile significance that it possesses in the English language. And while "*kawaii*" is often translated as "cute," "adorable," "charming," "lovely," or "pretty," it also points towards behaviors and mindsets evoking notions that are better understood as joyful, nonthreatening, and fun. In Japan, making things cute is a well-accepted practice, encouraged within a diverse set of social contexts. In the present context, *kawaii* echoes the analogy of a "flavor-coated pill," in that it facilitates the integration of frightening information in an attractive way, bringing the user closer to the "desired frame of mind and attitude and then deliver[ing] content that might not otherwise be received."[44]

Indeed, one of the main aims of CEC is to "make invisible things visible" (*me ni mienai mono o mieruka suru*) and to replace "hard-to-understand numbers" (*wakarinikui sūchi*) with interactive playrooms that the medium of *kawaii* facilitates.[45] One way cuteness is used is through what anthropologist Shunsuke Nozawa calls "characterization," or the transformation of things into charming and lovely characters.[46] For instance, in many centers, visitors learned about the specific threats present in Fukushima, although representations of these perils were anything but threatening. At DIP, a series of cartoonish posters first explained the phenomenon of radiation. In them, a teacher—depicted as an old and wise owl—explained radiation to a bear, a rabbit, a squirrel, and a little girl. The wise owl pointed out that ionizing radiation could pose a biological threat to one's genetic material, but that the body's enzymes quickly repaired any damage. Alongside these scenes, a small, blue cape–wearing hero successfully applied a Band-Aid to the damaged body. Yet, what the cute hero failed to mention is that cells are also prone to making errors in regenerating themselves from DNA breaks. These errors risk generating mutations within living cells, which permanently alter the cell's reproductive outcome. An accumulation of mutations can cause cancers, immune disorders, and genomic instabilities even years after the initial exposure.[47]

Likewise, in a document produced by MOE, radiation phenomena were introduced by a set of two characters, a little boy with green hair called Midori and his blue dog, Ao.[48] In the booklet each radionuclide had specific characteristics like pronounced eyebrows, large ears, or notable hairstyles. For example, strontium-90 took the form of a friendly-looking yellow figure with eyes, a mouth, and an antenna on the top of its head. Although children interacted with these adorable anthropomorphic radionuclides, there were rarely in-depth discussions about how exposure to them caused specific bodily harm. In one of the few instances where readers learned about the problems of internal contamination, the dog Ao explained that food put on the market had passed the reference value for radioactive contamination, thereby alluding to issues around safety.[49] In talking about internal contamination, Ao argued that radioactive cesium was easily evacuated (*haishutsu*) through our sweat (*ase*) and our urine (*oshikko*).[50] Yet reference values for the safe consumption of foods are measured in a unit called the becquerel, symbolizing radiation emissions per second. This unit does not capture the potential adverse health effects from consuming contaminated food since it does not consider the toxicity and longevity of radionuclides. What the cute characters failed to explain is that citizen scientists have also found contaminated food by testing products themselves.[51]

Since they constitute an important interface that relays specific signs, Nozawa argues that cute characters are "specialized speech-actants" that produce performative effects.[52] According to the advisors employed in educational centers, anthropomorphizing radiation or giving it cute characteristics was a key step in rendering information accessible for those who interacted with the exhibits. Yet cuteness also performed a scenario that constructed an optimistic narrative of minimal risk, conveying a sense of safety around the controversial and uncertain topic of the dangers of low-dose radiation. Moreover, Carr argues that "expertise requires the mastery of verbal performance, including—perhaps most importantly—the ability to use language to index and therefore instantiate already existing inner states of knowledge."[53] At DIP, specific forms of cute verbal performance were used by the state. For instance, many radiation-measuring devices had honorific suffixes added to their names. The diminutive suffix "*chan*"—a cute pronunciation of the suffix "*san*," translated as "Mr." or "Mrs." to connote an amiable, childish, or feminine context—was present on monitoring devices (e.g., *arufa-chan*, *bēta-chan*). Numerous tactile electronic screens also displayed information about radiation in accessible language, like *hōshasen tte nani* ("What is radiation?"), with the Japanese particle "*tte*" indicating informally reported speech. Similarly, colloquial speech was present in different explanations, such as when the dog Ao stated that radioactive cesium is evacuated through our pee (*oshikko*). These cute and nontechnical

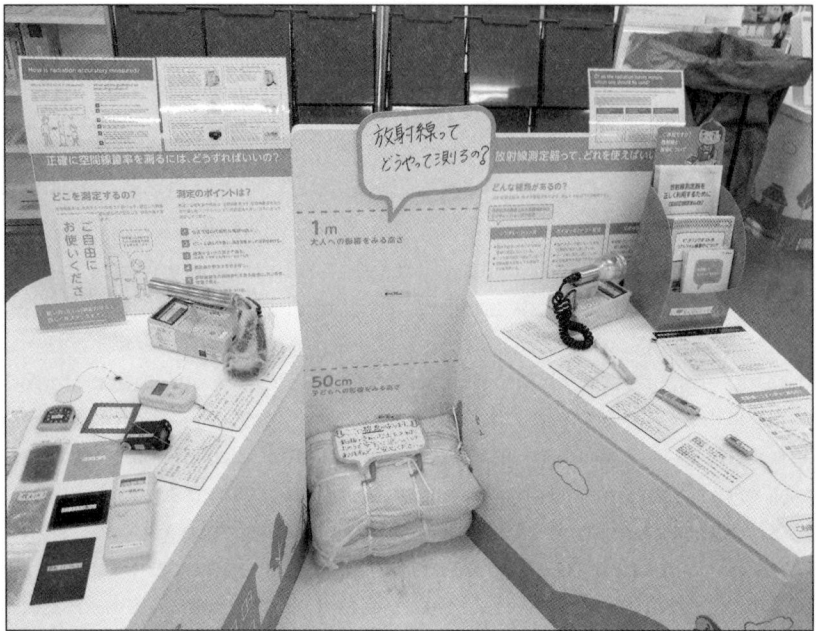

Figure 7.1. Teaching devices at DIP. Photo by Maxime Polleri.

verbal performances evoke a friendly feeling, indicating that the discussion is directed toward the public.

Such performances subsequently shift the topic of radiation from something formerly reserved to a body of experts toward information and practices that everyday people can understand and enact. According to the technical experts, it was important that measuring devices, described as educational tools (*kyōiku tsūru*), did not induce feelings of anxiety. Advisors argued that citizens had to become physically accustomed to testing devices and encouraged residents to touch their buttons and play with them during mock tests. These infrastructures attempted to convey that measurement was "the first step to protect yourself from radiation" (*'hakaru' koto ga hōshasen kara mi wo mamoru daiippo de aru koto wo tsutaeru*).[54] Through such technoscientific mobilizations, citizens could empower themselves by using these measuring devices as part of the minutiae of everyday living in Fukushima, while the aesthetic of *kawaii* promoted an experience of pleasantness and accessibility. As one technical advisor explained, "This learning process is the key to the reconstruction [*fukkō*] of Fukushima."

At DIP, cute and interactive models also helped younger visitors understand the process of decontamination, seen as having contributed to the sharp decrease of radiation levels. For instance, a model explained the decontamination process through playtime. It consisted of a miniature house in a transparent plastic box filled with small white and red balls. The white balls represented uncontaminated soil; the red balls stood for radioactive pollutants and were encrusted on the house rooftop, in the miniature trees, and amid the uncontaminated soil. With a toy shovel, it was possible to pick up the red balls and to dispose of them in scale-sized vinyl bags (*furekonbaggu*). Children could literally pick up the symbolic contaminants, conjured as a biophysical entity isolated from the human environment. Much like Latour's modern stance, the game created two distinct ontological zones: that of the human and that of nature.[55] Playing with the toy shovels and trying to get rid of the radionuclides in the plastic box environment gave decontamination a tangibility that made it feel like a game of sorts, trivializing the harsh reality experienced by workers subcontracted to carry out the actual work of decontamination.[56] Indeed, children did not need to put on protective suits before separating the red and white balls, and there was no recognition of potential health hazards. The game also performed decontamination as a successful technical fix (from contaminated to clean) and did not consider the fact that vinyl bags used for decontamination have broken down due to the build-up of gas released by rotten soil—nor that plants and flowers have grown inside the bags, tearing them apart and rescattering radionuclides.

Cute interactive games were equally popular at CEC. In front of a giant interactive screen called the "radiation visualization wall" (*hōshasen mieruka uōru*), children learned to block radiation rays or particles through the movement of their bodies. By selecting the proper material (e.g., a piece of paper), they had to block either alpha particles, beta particles, or gamma rays. Children collected points, and at the end of the game, the child with the highest score was crowned the winner. As exemplified by the happy faces of children I watched play the game, this aestheticization of scientific knowledge implied a profound sense of investment (as play) that dismantled the separation between the

Figure 7.2. The decontamination box model. Photo by Maxime Polleri.

individual and the fearsome agent of radioactivity. Furthermore, with radiation protection being transformed into a game, where external radiation was to be blocked, there was no mention of the risk of internal contamination from radioactive particles, which represent an important hazard. And because the children's game blocks radiation in "real time," there was no mention of delayed health effects of radiation exposure, such as potentially harmful genetic changes.

In the context of Cool Japan ideology (a form of economic soft power adopted by the Japanese state), Laura Miller argues that *kawaii* aesthetics were used to officially promote a "narrow model of cute femininity, thus maintaining and promoting structures of gender stratification."[57] In her study of Japan's military, Frühstück similarly examines how the "strategic use of cuteness serves as a tool for achieving a more sympathetic public response" toward the Self-Defense Forces, while normalizing the military through infantilization.[58] Cuteness in Fukushima had a parallel function, and was strategically used to perform radiation information in a manner that softened the former uneasiness associated with the complexity of knowledge about radioactivity. Yet the performance went beyond mere description, as it asymmetrically presented a nonthreatening atmosphere around radiation, glossing over the dangers of radiation hazards and the complexity of contamination in the lived environment. In this way, cuteness was part of radioactive performances put into service of a state politics of normalizing raising the threshold of exposure after Fukushima.

The Wonder of Science and Technology

Hecht argues that "the power of nuclear things depends on *both* exceptionalism and banality."[59] The same applies to post-Fukushima radioactive performances, which were also imbued with exceptionalism around the wonders of science and technology. In this context, the useful aspects of radioactivity were emphasized. Radiation was no longer a synonym for harm but instead was linked with the latest technological advances and scientific wonders. In her historical study of modern Japan, Hiromi Mizuno examines how a "sense of wonder" (*kyōi*) around the promotion of science was strategically mobilized by Imperial Japan to promote a form of "scientific patriotism" (*kagaku hōkoku*) catering to wartime needs.[60] Similar mobilizations around science's wonder happen in radioactive performances, albeit for a different objective.

Through my fieldwork, I witnessed state-sponsored open days and activities that allowed people to dabble with normally off-limit radiation-related technologies. For instance, on April 24, 2016, NIRS held a public open house entitled "I Want to Know More! What You Can Do with Radiation" (*Motto shiritai! Hōshasen de dekiru koto*).[61] At this open house, the research institute felt like a fairground. Hundreds of members of the public were invited to see the institute's research facilities, jostling each other to admire the latest PET scan technologies, radiation emergency instruments, and enormous cyclotrons used in nuclear medicine to produce radioisotopes. While waiting in line to be photographed in front of a high-tech minivan, children could try the equipment of the institute's latest task force, the Radiation Emergency Medical Assistance Team. Usually reserved for emergency situations, the van was the background for a role-playing scene (*kosupure*), with children wearing mock radiation emergency costumes. Children also collected as many stamps as possible during a "stamp rally," running between stands to see all areas of radiological interest, from the new therapeutic research facilities to the electrostatic accelerator building. At NIRS, a special elevator led to the Heavy Ion Medical Accelerator in an impressive subterranean facility. Walking through the underground maze of this metallic behemoth, families were overcome by the scale of the apparatus, whose interior looked like a sci-fi *anime* scene. I overhead visitors repeatedly say things like "Oh! This is so cool!" (*suge*) or "It looks like a spaceship, right?" (*Uchūsen mitai ne*). In this way, the experience of visitors to NIRS echoed Ben-Ari and Frühstück's concept of "spectacularization," which refers to how a "demonstration is turned into a grand and impressive spectacle that is entertaining."[62]

It is equally important to note that the NIRS's expertise first and foremost focused on radiation protection in the medical domain. The previous sections described how the boundary between the natural and artificial aspects of radioactivity was strategically mobilized to make radiation trivial. But at NIRS, man-made radiation was not synonymous with triviality. In fact, man-made technologies were affectively linked to technologies that sustained life. For instance, radiation-related devices exhibited by the institute were used to produce helpful particle therapies to treat cancer. Here, "radiation damage" was not something to be afraid of but a useful agent that killed harmful tumors, as demonstrated on medical dummies during the open day. In this instance, radiation education was channeled to sustain life in awe-inspiring ways. Yet, displays and technologies at NIRS asymmetrically performed information that selectively amplified the positive aspects of radiation over its negative effects. The result was a trajectory that promoted a pleasant atmosphere in which radiation was not a scary entity but something useful and wonderful.

Radioactive performance presents an image of radiation that is not merely beneficial (literally life-saving) but also carefully controlled by human actors. This conceals that there are no benefits per se from exposure to uncontrolled and long-lasting radionuclides escaping from nuclear power plants. As pointed out by Dr. Andreas Nidecker, a radiology specialist, "Radiation is of the *same* type in medicine and nuclear power but very *different*: small doses are used in a controlled way in medicine and dangerous long-lived radioisotopes are blown into the atmosphere in an uncontrolled way in a nuclear accident."⁶³ Still, this emphasis makes sense in Japan's precarious context surrounding nuclear-related technologies. Before Fukushima, Japan had one of the world's most well-respected radiological scientific communities, while being embedded in a nuclear power industry revival known as the "nuclear renaissance."⁶⁴ The disaster was a harsh blow to this expertise, causing the nuclear community to adopt a pessimistic vision of the future of nuclear research. Scientists to whom I spoke shared a common fear that good students might not come to work in nuclear-related research after Fukushima. In this context, members of the nuclear village have attempted "to encourage young people involved in nuclear power amid the hostile climate."⁶⁵ It is therefore not surprising that the NIRS open house had activities "recommended for children" (*okosama ni osusume*). Focusing on children is a way to revitalize nuclear-related interest in a generation that is too young to remember the disaster. In this way, radioactive performances also work for the future of Japan's nuclear policy, suggesting that the country might increase its reliance on nuclear energy and technology.

Moreover, to fulfill the need for knowledge in teaching infrastructure, the prefecture of Fukushima has turned to experts working in nuclear-related agencies. This has resulted in cooperation with IAEA and JAEA—organizations that promote nuclear power industries and their associated technologies. Because of such collaboration, an important pro-nuclear ideology permeated the teaching infrastructure. At DIP, a technical advisor whom I interviewed was critical of the antinuclear movement, arguing that "you cannot work on the problems that radioactive contamination has brought while being linked with an ideology.... The antinuclear activists are victimizing the people of Fukushima to suit their needs!" However, in criticizing this bias, the advisor was seemingly unaware of the pro-nuclear ideology present within his own center. In that regard, performances around science and technology do not lead to a rejection of the nuclear lobby but reinforce cooperation with agencies that have their own interests and for whom recovery lies in the revitalization of an industry affected by a nuclear disaster.

In her study of Japanese Self-Defense Forces, Frühstück argues that information about specific weapons and armed vehicles given to the public represents a "celebration of military technology ... associated with

Figure 7.3. NIRS's Heavy Ion Medical Accelerator. Photo by Maxime Polleri.

having the latest and most advanced equipment."[66] Likewise, radioactive performances celebrate radiation-related technologies in ways that make the revitalization of Fukushima possible through the latest monitoring technologies. For instance, at the NIRS, one of the most popular attractions was the whole-body counter (WBC), a machine that measures the internal level of radioactive contamination in a person's body. Visitors waited in line for their results as a technician stated that each body was "just fine" (*daijōbu desu*). While the WBC appears to be the epitome of radioactive risk monitoring, there was no discussion regarding what this machine could not measure: the potential for future genetic damage. The overall amount of radiation in a person's body can offer a misleading sense of security, as one expert in radiation/chemical carcinogenesis explained to me in 2016: "While the average result of a test might appear to be low, one particular spot in the body can have a very high amount of internal contamination. Even on a single organ, like the stomach, there can be a lot of heterogeneity. This is enough for a cancer to develop, as a cancer does not 'understand' the term 'average,' but concentrates itself on a spot. A result that is 'below average' does not imply a lack of risk—not at all."

A radiation biologist employed by NIRS tellingly (and unironically) explained the reasons for using a WBC: "We are doing those tests because we can do them. In theory, the screening can make people feel better." In talking about the management of radioactive pollutants, Hamblin argues that the term "monitoring" holds considerable power, since it suggests "a certain level of vigilance in scientific testing, thus ensuring safety."[67] In that regard, WBC tests were technological performances that acted as an assurance aimed at providing emotional safety (*anshin*) rather than only biological safety (*anzen*).

At CEC, visitors also experienced guided tours of the JAEA and the National Institute for Environmental Studies' research facilities. There, children were given white lab coats and introduced to brand-new instruments that monitored radioactivity in Fukushima. Technical advisors did not present monitoring machines as a sign that the prefecture was contaminated, but rather presented them as encounters that reflected the wonder of science and technology, arguing that these machines were rare and the most advanced of their kind. Such performances echoed the concept of "technophilia," which refers to the "fetishisation of technology in support of progress and modernity."[68] As Goldstein argues, technophilia is inseparable from a "rational march toward progress,"[69] thereby making it hard to criticize a politics of revitalization in Fukushima. Tropes of technological wonders were also present within the prefecture of Fukushima, which aims to lead Japan's robotic industrial revolution with machines used for radiation monitoring. These tropes are plainly part of the government's Innovation Coast framework: "This scheme has already started to produce results, as seen in the opening in rapid succession of hubs for development of cutting-edge technologies. These include the Fukushima Hama-Dori Robot Test Zone and Remote Technology Development Center to promote development of drones and other robotic devices. In January this year, a demonstration test was conducted in a section of the robot-test zone along the seashore, and it achieved the world's first successful long-distance air freight shipment by a fully autonomous drone."[70]

As the report concluded, "Rebounding from the disaster, the people of Fukushima are now striding vigorously toward the future."[71] That future includes advances in radiation-related science, such as mock-up facilities for "nuclear emergency response robots" (*genshiryoku saigai taiō robotto*) and training systems for decommission operators that used virtual reality (*VR wo mochiita sagyōsha kunren shisutemu*).[72] Every time I went to Fukushima, I found pamphlets that advertise a "robot revolution" (*robotto kakumei*), while being invited to witness drones (*dorōn*), exoskeleton suits (*massurusūtsu*), and land-based robots (*rikujō robotto*) during a "robot-test field symposium" (*robotto tesuto fīrudo shinpojiumu*). In this world, radioactive contamination was no longer a problem (*mondai*) but a challenge (*chōsen*) to be tackled by the next generation of scientists.

In the creation of modern Japan, Hiromi Mizuno argues, to "win the wars with China and the United States, the state needed to create imperial subjects capable of doing science and technology. And for that, it mobilized the sense of wonder, seeing, and doing science."[73] In post-Fukushima, where the Japanese state fears that confidence in national science and expertise is falling,[74] radioactive performances mobilize a similar sense of wonder but trace a different future: one where Japan can find its way back onto the international scene of top-tier scientific nations.

Performing Hazards

After the disaster, radioactive performances provided information that was easy to understand, interactive, and nonthreatening. This was achieved through three specific iterations that emphasized natural analogies, cute aesthetics, and the wonder of science and technology. Butler has argued that performativity is a "process of iterability, a regularized and constrained repetition of norms."[75] In this understanding, a successful iterability represents the capacity of specific tropes to be repeatable in different contexts; the naturalness of radiation, a cute and fun aesthetic, and a fetishization of nuclear technologies are all tactics that existed before Fukushima and beyond Japan. Yet each of these tactics is repurposed in the context of an ecologically and economically insecure Japan. Thus, this kind of risk-communication strategy does not merely depict the phenomenon of radiation exposure. Rather, what is being governed through radioactive performances is also an attempt at defining what radiation hazard is and is not—and for whom. Radioactivity is a process in which unstable elements gradually transform into more stable elements. Likewise, radioactive performances are performative processes—part of a broader form of radioactive governance—that transform the story of Fukushima from tragedy and anxiety into a narrative of revitalization and normalization.

In sharp contrast to the bodily artifacts of the Hiroshima Peace Memorial Museum, which transforms a former military aggressor into a victim of nuclear war, post-Fukushima radioactive performances eliminate the disturbing aspects of radiation exposure. They fall within historically established processes of control that defuse societal unrest and attempts to reclaim political control, economic stability, and public trust. A politics of victimization and relocation, as seen in Petryna's account of Chernobyl, has no place in this narrative.[76] Nor did Japan adopt the nuclear performances of the United States. Not too long ago, in the midst of the Cold War, American children were taught to "duck and cover" to protect their bodies against the effects of a nuclear explosion.[77] As Masco argues, these performances were integral to the expertise of nation-states, often with the effect of affectively managing the national community to install "structures of emergency into a deep future."[78] However, the radioactive performances seen in Japan embody a different politics entirely. They do not represent a normalization against potential annihilation from foreign enemies but a normalization of a Japan that is *already* post-Fukushima. These performances point toward a form of governance that reframes ongoing exposure as normal, while attempting to socialize the victims of a nuclear disaster into learning to live comfortably with the radiation that infests their environment. Consequently, radioactive performances skirt the "nuclear uncanny"—moments of disruption and anxiety associated with radioactive materials.[79]

Academics have long argued that risk discourses generate "right" or "wrong" ways of knowing.[80] Radioactive performances, while novel in their appearance, are not exempt from such a dichotomy. They have a real influence since they reinforce a structure of exclusion for those who experience risk and recovery differently than the policies of repatriation promoted by the government would have them do. As opposed to the initial crisis that followed Fukushima, fueled by anxiety, panic, and fear, technical advisors argued to me that information about radiation should now be shared in ways that did not instantiate fear. If fear was inevitable, it should be what they called a "proper fear" (*tadashiku osoreru*). Yet, this suggests that "the 'correct' fear is the one established by the authorities," and dismisses different opinions as being mistaken.[81] This was how Natsuo Amano, the evacuee mother from Koriyama, saw the government managing evacuees' fear. As she explained, "The government is constantly repeating the slogan of 'recovery and reconstruction,' and in doing so they encourage voluntary evacuees to return to areas of high risk. . . . Mothers who criticize how the Fukushima disaster is being handled are being called unpatriotic [*hikokumin*]." For Amano, this pressure had created a social atmosphere wherein avoiding exposure to low-level radiation for one's long-term safety was considered the wrong and even an irrational choice. When I last met her in 2017, she was appalled by the state-sponsored public exhibitions, which she saw as undermining her fight for the right to remain where she was, evacuated from an environment she considered dangerous. By emphasizing specific aspects of the phenomenon of radioactivity, educational infrastructure contributed to the strengthening of this atmosphere and encouraged the return of evacuees to their hometowns, especially as financial subsidies for evacuation were cut off.[82]

2:46 P.M.

Since the disaster, the Japanese state has doubled down on nuclear-related educational infrastructure. When I left Japan in 2019, the state was on the verge of inaugurating a new museum, the Great East Japan Earthquake and Nuclear Disaster Memorial Museum (*denshō-kan*), whose main aims are (1) "passing on to future generations and sharing with the world the records and lessons from the nuclear disaster and the recovery process," (2) promoting "disaster prevention and mitigation based on the experiences and lessons from the nuclear disaster that only Fukushima has encountered, and (3) "contributing to a faster recovery by uniting with people and organizations who want to help Fukushima and working to revive communities and local traditions as well as train people to take part in the region's recovery."[83] Through this museum, visitors can "inherit the lessons" (*keishō suru*) of Fukushima citizens, who are now "storytellers" (*kataribe*) rather than victims. Their stories are carefully systematized (*taikeika*) and used to promote a sense of self-responsibility (*jiko-sekinin*), where "things learned" (*mananda koto*) enable all Japanese citizens to "protect their own life" (*jibun no inochi wo mamoru*), "receive information and take action during a disaster" (*saigai-ji no jōhō no torikata to kōdō ni utsusu chikara*), and "trigger a change" (*kōdō suru kikkake to naru*) for disaster prevention.[84]

These forms of infrastructure attempt to create novel structures of resilience, representing an important shift from "passive" citizenship (e.g., awaiting help from the state in the case of a disaster) to more "active" citizenship (e.g., being self-reliant while helping one's community). Resilience discourses are used to promote responsibility because the Japanese state can no longer guarantee the impossibility of future disasters, in contrast to the former "safety myth" (*anzen shinwa*) in which a catastrophe was impossible (*sōteigai*). This promotion of national resilience transforms disaster preparedness, as citizens become responsible for "the unfolding of collective life."[85] Yet rarely are there spaces to criticize who or what resilience serves. Indeed, the *Asahi Shimbun* revealed that tour guides of the Great East Japan Earthquake and Nuclear Disaster Memorial Museum were "bristling" at instructions "not to criticize the central government or Tokyo Electric Power Co. when speaking to visitors."[86]

In a risk society, Ulrich Beck argues, "handling fear and insecurity becomes an *essential cultural qualification*, and the cultivation of the abilities demanded for it become an essential mission of pedagogical institutions."[87] This cultivation is exactly what we see in Japan today, which attempts to socially engineer postdisaster resilience. To understand the performativity of environmental hazards, it is essential to examine how former imaginaries get recycled within new political contexts, with the effect of reproducing social inequalities and propagandist forms of knowledge. The notion of radioactive performances reveals how subtle forms of governance give the appearance of openness and public participation while reproducing limited conventions of what counts as harm and recovery. While such forms of risk communication are innovative in their interactivity and freedom from jargon, they are less so in their content.

In the end, for a community where harmful residual radioactivity has become a public everyday concern, coming to grips with serious contamination requires more education than ever. This raises a set of conceptual and ethical questions: What can be considered an appropriate relationship toward long-lasting contamination? Who gets to teach about these problems, and what is presently being left out of the narrative? How do we define normality when attempts to recover former prepollution baselines are naïve nostalgic endeavors? Instead of a single narrative of recovery, answering these questions requires stories that embrace complex experiences associated with radioactive contamination. Yet it is doubtful that this will happen. Inside the educational annex of CEC stands an enormous black-and-white digital clock, showing the time elapsed since 2:46 p.m. on March 11, 2011. As one can read below the clock, "This is also the amount of time Fukushima has been working to recover and create the local environment. Fukushima will continue to advance this process step by step." Representing the ultimate trump card of radioactive performance, the clock normalizes hazards as temporal problems stuck in the past, while gliding over the potential genetic dangers associated with chronic exposure to radiation. And with each second passing, the prospects of those who still fight for permanent evacuation appear dimmer and dimmer.

8

Conflictual Collaboration

As I approached a metal gate near a small ditch, my Geiger counter began to register 13 μSv/hour, which was a high level of radioactivity. A tad anxious, I glanced at Tora Atsumi, my guide on this adventure. He was unperturbed. "See?" he said with a wry smile. "I told you the radiation level would be high near the gate!" Atsumi was not a nuclear scientist but a former farmer from a small rural village in Fukushima. He also belonged to a citizen-science network that aimed to revitalize the sociocultural life of the region.

To help residents shed light on the invisible harms afflicting their village, Atsumi's citizen-science network provided farmers with technologies to measure and analyze the residual radioactivity in the environment. Like Atsumi, many resident members of this NPO owned Geiger counters or dosimeters. Other members tested for radioactivity in rice paddies, which the residents decontaminated using processes they had developed independently. Farmers would flood their fields, and then use tools to mix the water with the irradiated topsoil below, stirring up and dislodging radioactive pollutants such as cesium. The muddy water was then pushed out of the field with large, stiff-bristled brushes.

Five years after the disaster, such citizen-led initiatives were thriving throughout Fukushima, even though MOE had ended much of the official decontamination in Atsumi's village, deeming it free of harmful radiation. These grassroots practices continued because rural residents were dissatisfied with how the state experts had assessed the radioactive contamination of their region. As one local man angrily told me, "The government has decontaminated a twenty-meter radius around our houses, but they didn't do any kind of follow-up. And every time it rains, the radioactive pollutants in the nearby mountains are washed down, and [the area] gets recontaminated." Against this backdrop, citizen science provided concrete answers that state officials failed to supply. As one resident summarized,

> This is a disaster that we couldn't see with our eyes, a problem that we couldn't smell or hear. At the beginning, we had no way of knowing if our radishes [*daikon*] were contaminated or not. And that's hard, because that's a big part of our culture. Everyone was wondering what life would come to under these conditions. That was our biggest problem. But by "seeing" the radiation through the data [that we have produced], we were able to know what to eat and what not to eat. We could know how dangerous it was. Our anxiety [*fuan*] has disappeared.

The kind of citizen science that I encountered in Atsumi's village was different from the one witnessed with evacuee mothers, wherein scientific practices were used to promote a politics of victimization. In Atsumi's village, I found citizen science hard at work with the aim of revitalizing life *within* Fukushima. As I participated in their network activities, I was struck by a paradox. Many citizen scientists harshly criticized state-sanctioned experts, who had been unable to provide clear guidelines on how to cope with the potential dangers of ionizing radiation. Yet the same citizen scientists were embedded in practices similar to the state-sponsored revitalization politics. Indeed, farmers used citizen science to *revitalize* local agriculture, to promote repatriation, and to lower the fear of residual radiation. As opposed to the worried mothers whom I met, farmers appeared convinced that the data they produced demonstrated that life in Fukushima was possible. Furthermore, resident-led radiation-monitoring practices were conducted in places that would have arguably been described as "uninhabitable" before the disaster. In fact, residents engaged with residual radioactivity even though it was "forbidden" for them to be living there in the first place—at least according to the previous safety standards of 1 mSv per year.

When I was invited by the NPO to help farmers decontaminate rice paddy fields, wearing only a pair of rain boots as protection, while my guides assured me it was safe (*anzen*) to do so, I began to ponder the Janus face of resistance and risk privatization that seemed to epitomize citizen science. As I watched farmers working with their feet in radioactive mud, I asked, how does this fostering of science in society intersect with official state politics of governing postdisaster Fukushima?

This chapter examines a different facet of civic participation in the tracking of radiation. I focus on how citizen science can evolve in collaboration with the official Japanese politics of radioactive governance, with the result of sometimes supporting hegemonic understandings of radiation danger and normative visions of postdisaster recovery. In many instances, citizen science involves what I call "conflictual collaboration." This concept captures how issues of resistance and collaboration are not always necessarily opposed but can happen at the same time. I argue that civic resources used to resist and reinterpret official narratives of contamination ended up reinforcing a state-sponsored normalization of the disaster. Later, I demonstrate how they became crucial techniques of neoliberal governance designed to govern the conduct of populations amid contaminated environments. While useful, the growing impact of citizen science echoes a neoliberal shift in the management of contamination, leading to reduced public expenditure, minimal government intervention, and risk privatization—meaning that risk becomes a matter of personal business rather than the state's or corporate polluters' responsibility. In such a context, the empowerment provided by monitoring capacities shifted state responsibility for ensuring radiological protection onto the shoulders of nuclear victims.

The danger lies in a normalization of risk that produces societies in which citizens must care for themselves in increasingly polluted environments, while interpreting partial data about controversial environmental dangers. As civil actors become integral to managing environmental risks, I challenge the celebration of citizen science as a de facto democratic endeavor and theorize the neoliberal implications of its pursuit. This contrasts with the vast literature on citizen science, which often theorizes it as a space of contestation or resistance.

The Neoliberalization of Citizen Science

At first glance, the rise of citizen science in post-Fukushima Japan was described as a "renaissance in civil society," especially since citizen scientists appeared to resist the normalizing forces of governmental, industrial, and academic expertise on radiological risk.[1] Within this view, scholars have depicted citizen science as an independent endeavor outside of official governing bodies.[2] This conceptualization echoes broader scholarship around public participation in science, where civic innovations are applauded as democratic ventures that provide empowerment against dominant forms of governance.[3] In this mindset, citizen science thus illustrates what Tania Li calls the "practice of politics"—the expression of a "critical challenge" to issues of governance and a "refusal of the way things are."[4]

As an anthropologist whose discipline has a long tradition of promoting local knowledge, I am perhaps expected to view citizen science as an epistemic activity that is "truer" than the state's knowledge. Yet, following Alan Irwin, I am mindful of producing an "uncritical (and perhaps romantic) espousal of all forms of contextual understanding as necessarily superior to more 'scientific' accounts."[5] As Irwin further explains, contrasting scientific and local knowledge is problematic for two reasons: "First, because the latter variety may . . . incorporate elements of the former as appropriate. . . . Second, because science is itself a form of contextualized knowledge."[6] Drawing from Jasanoff's and Martello's intellectual contributions, it is best to remember that all forms of knowledge have both "strengths and limitations."[7]

In post-Fukushima Japan, one limitation of citizen science is the pervasive influence of neoliberal ideology. Neoliberalism refers to market-oriented reforms (e.g., downsizing, offshoring, removing government regulations, privatizing public services) that reduce state influence on the economy.[8] However, academics have moved beyond economic policies to criticize neoliberalism as an ideology that permeates the social sphere and promotes tropes of individual accountability, self-responsibility, and risk management.[9] In this understanding, neoliberalism shapes the subjectivities of individuals in a Foucauldian way, according to which nation-states exercise political sovereignty by governing people's conduct.[10] As Miyako Inoue summarizes, "The individual becomes a rationally calculating and risk-taking entrepreneur who participates freely in the market and takes full responsibility in the case of financial loss."[11]

As Roberto Barrios explains, neoliberal influences are especially problematic in the aftermath of disasters since "all facets of human life are subjected to judgments of financial and biopolitical cost-benefit analysis at the expense of other meanings and attachments."[12] In Fukushima, neoliberal ideology not only limited the understanding of recovery but erased polluters' liability and shaped civilian responses in ways that rendered the concept of victimization troublesome. Part of citizen science subsequently falls within debates around neoliberalism, according to which the self-responsible citizen becomes an "entrepreneur of himself" amid contaminated landscapes.[13]

In the final analysis, I follow Erik Swyngedouw in tracing how "socially innovative forms of governance are both actively encouraged and supported by agencies pursuing a neo-liberal agenda."[14] In the context of Fukushima, I refer to how nuclear industries see citizen science's potential to serve their vested interests. On this view and in line with Philip Mirowski, citizen science enables "greater direct political control of the actual regulation of pollution, compared with an earlier regime that had to accommodate itself to the strictures of 'experts.'"[15]

Separate Projects, Common Agenda

In introducing the notion of "conflictual collaboration," I contend that merely seeing citizen science as a form of resistance is not only naïve but "foreclose[s] certain questions about the workings of power."[16] In public participation in science, there is the tendency to "think of 'top-down' as the way power operates oppressively, and of 'bottom-up' as revolutionary."[17] In contrast to this stereotypical view of power, I draw from a more nuanced understanding of power, which shows that people can "both resist and support the existing system."[18] Similarly, I see conflictual collaboration as a set of alternative practices of resistance that intersect with governmental tactics, straddling the gap between Foucault's governmentality ("the conduct of conduct") and Tania Li's "practice of politics," which challenges governance.

When different actors focus on a common project, they can sometimes maintain separate political agendas, as in the case of Tsing's forest industries or Hathaway's matsutake mushroom farming.[19] The notion of conflictual collaboration reveals a different story, namely, how *separate* projects lead to a *common* agenda. Pragmatically speaking, the citizen-science networks that represent the focus of this chapter share a similar characteristic: they were created by citizens who had no history of political activism and who were driven by dissatisfaction with the state's management of radioactive hazards. In terms of fieldwork, I interviewed core members of different networks and the citizens who participated in radiation-monitoring activities. I paid close attention to the factors that led them to initially clash with the state, while participant observation of their networks' activities allowed me to understand how data about contamination was collected, interpreted, and used. I learned that conflictual collaboration happened for three reasons: interpretations of "raw" data, specific understandings of social recovery, and neoliberal tropes of empowerment. The next sections examine each of these reasons in more detail.

The Interpretation of "Raw" Data

In 2016, on the top floor of a crowded building, I attended a workshop on do-it-yourself (DIY) radiation-monitoring devices organized by a network of citizen scientists. With a dozen participants, I had the opportunity to build a Geiger counter of my own from a kit designed by the network. Inside was a motherboard, an LCD display, resistors, and a low-voltage pancake mica window. There was a look of excitement on the faces of the participants—who included many Japanese and a few foreigners—as each of us received our kits and started to decipher the instructions.

After a few hours the task was completed—no small feat given that participants had to dexterously weld the right color resistors to the motherboard without burning themselves—and all of us proudly held our Geiger counters in the air as the organizers snapped a photo of our achievement. Workshop participants were invited to test their newly made Geiger counter on a contaminated piece of wood brought from Fukushima, which triggered an elevated reading on our screens.

Like many of the participants, I had become familiar with this network by hearing about its DIY workshop. Intrigued, I initially attended one of their conferences, where a founding member of the organization revealed why he became involved in citizen science: "There were a lot of problems with how governmental measurements were being conducted. For example, the measurements [of radiation levels] were taken thirty meters in the air and only concerned gamma rays, while we suspected that other rays, like beta ones, could also be present. Even when measurements were made public, through the United States military, for instance, it took more than a year before reaching the public! So this kind of data was useless."

Considering what they perceived as ineffective state measures, the DIY network members decided to measure radioactive contamination themselves and provide their measurements in real time on the Internet. To maximize the usage of their limited number of Geiger counters, they began tracking contamination with monitors attached to their vehicles, like the camera-mounted cars that capture images for Street View in Google Maps. Yet the scope of this work was overwhelming. As a result, the organization decided to focus on running workshops to enable local citizens to build their own monitoring devices. Throughout these efforts, Geiger counters were described as a Promethean gift that could produce essential data for a population urgently needing information. As one of the founders proudly exclaimed, "Citizen science has beaten the pre-planning of any government in a matter of weeks!" Members boasted that forty million measurements had been collected to that point—a shining example, they thought, of what citizen science can accomplish, even with its limited capacity.

In the aftermath of Fukushima, this DIY story is far from unique, as dozens of citizen-science organizations produced a plethora of data via an influx of different measures (*hakarikata*). In addition to Geiger counters, I witnessed other citizen scientists producing data via dosimeters or through food monitoring. And while each citizen-science network had its favorite way of producing data, I noticed that citizens rarely made explicit public claims about the data they produced.

For instance, during the DIY workshop, participants rarely remarked about the relationship between radiation risks and the measurements on the screens of our Geiger counters. No members of the network dealt with issues of scientific legitimacy regarding radiation hazards. Rather, the network was simply providing the technical means to generate raw data, which actors could then freely use and interpret. Many networks functioned similarly. For instance, the members of one network that produced data on food contamination restrained themselves from publicly saying whether the food was safe to eat or not. They simply provided monthly measurements on the network's website, letting users decide whether they felt confident in consuming Fukushima's products. In other words, citizen-science data provided quantification, but the qualitative interpretation of radiation numbers was often left to the individual. This outcome led to the first instance of conflictual collaboration, with the effect of downplaying and normalizing the extent of radiation dangers.

The reason for not publicly taking a stance on the safety or danger of residual radiation is easy to understand. Despite their success and spread, citizen-science networks have faced public and political pressure to clarify their position on radiological safety. For instance, worried that any sort of political affiliation might compromise the integrity of its data, the DIY network decided not to take an official position on the politics of radiation dangers. "We are often asked if we are antinuclear or not," the group's director said. "Well, we always respond that we are pro-data!" In this context, the narrative of apolitical data enabled citizen scientists to avoid the polarizing issue of activism in Japan, where a "pro-nuclear" position too often confronts an "antinuclear" one (see chapter 3). However, this discourse portrayed data as something that is factual, natural, and untempered at its core. It echoed the "commodity fiction of data," which is the "belief that data and context are separate-able, making data a free-floating, harvestable entity."[20] As Max Liboiron explains, "There is no 'raw' data or 'neutral' data collection that can bridge the gap between divergent concepts of disaster and recovery. A single common data set may not only omit questions of populations of interest to grassroots efforts, but may also obfuscate larger debates about power and representation that undergird all portrayals of . . . disaster[s]."[21]

One problem surrounding radiation information in citizen science is the fact that data is depicted as the building blocks through which an individual can make an *informed* decision. Yet, in practice, what data represents is left to highly divergent interpretations, which can be associated as much as with tropes of danger as with tropes of safety. For instance, during a conference, one resident from Fukushima, holding his own homemade Geiger, thanked the citizen-science network for helping him "see" radiation, which resulted in lowering his anxiety (*anshin*). Similarly, I noticed that many citizens using Geiger counters firmly believed that the data produced demonstrated a low and "common value" (*yoku aru atai*), which they interpreted as an undeniable sign of safety (*anzen*). Regularly, data collected with Geiger counters was used to compare background radiation levels worldwide, thereby depicting Fukushima as no more contaminated than elsewhere. According to this mindset, such measure was conflated with the fact that Fukushima was necessarily safe. In addition, some citizen-science networks had begun to visit high schools in Fukushima Prefecture, often to produce a series of DIY workshops. In collaboration with the science teachers of Fukushima schools, teenagers learned how to make their own Geiger counters. During these workshops, teenagers were asked if they knew about their locality's radiation level and then had the chance to measure it. Some citizen scientists even created smaller Geiger counters that elementary students could build. In this context, one individual explained that students had been surprised to see that the radiation level measured in their environment was often lower than the level of radiation detected during an intercontinental flight. This comparison made students feel confident about the safety of living in Fukushima.

As a result of their approach, citizen scientists ended up reproducing the same hegemonic understandings of radiation hazards as the state (e.g., a low dose is not dangerous), as well as the same misleading analogies used by nuclear-related educational centers (e.g., radiation in Fukushima is no higher than the exposure received during an international flight). This interpretation of radiation hazard was the result of three factors: (1) the partiality of what data represents; (2) a reified knowledge based on the monopoly of international experts; and (3) the importance of social factors, wherein health is not the prime element of concern.

Producing (In)visibility

Jalbert and Kinchy have argued that monitoring devices "always produce areas of ignorance by facilitating observations of some parameters and not others."[22] This was notably the case of measurements made by Geiger counters, one of the most widely used devices in citizen science. A Geiger counter is relatively cheap and easy to use. Simply point it toward a given area, and the device will tell you the radiation levels on its screen. Because of these characteristics, Geiger counters were very popular with citizen scientists. Yet, a major limitation of this device is that it only shows *part* of the actual scale of contamination. Importantly, Geiger counters are only useful for measuring external levels of radiation present in one's surrounding area. These machines were never intended to gauge the risk of alpha- or beta-emitting particles, which can cause cancers if inhaled or swallowed.[23] As medical doctor Helen Caldicott explains, "When these radioactive elements enter the lungs, liver, bones, or other organs, they transfer a large dose of radiation over a long period of time to a very small volume of cells. Although most of these cells are killed, some on the edge of the radiation field remain alive. They are often mutated, potentially causing cancer. Alpha emitters are among the most carcinogenic materials known."[24]

Furthermore, measurements produced by Geiger counters produce a limited *temporal* understanding of radiation harm, since they do not consider the displacement in time of radiation-induced illness. But perhaps most telling is the fact that Geiger counters do not inform users how different radionuclides will react within the bodies of real persons. In fact, as Shannon Cram explains, the science of radiation protection is generally based on protecting the health of the average individual (an adult male), which is a theoretical concept based on mathematical models.[25] Measurements gleaned with Geiger counters can lead citizen scientists to turn a blind eye to the risks faced by specific segments of the population (e.g., children) who are not appropriately represented in radiation-protection standards. While Geiger counters make certain forms of harm visible, they equally render other radiation hazards invisible. Unfortunately, not all citizens recognized the limitations of monitoring devices, especially children, who do not have the valence to understand the complexities of nuclear-related technologies.

Jalbert and Kinchy have put forward the need to challenge the assumptions that "putting monitoring devices into the hands of at-risk communities will lead to their empowerment."[26] Geiger counters, which are part of the same technological tools used by states, nuclear lobbies, and radiological protection agencies, do not produce "truer" data simply because citizens mobilize them. Much like the organizations they criticized, citizen science can and does reproduce an incomplete portrait of contamination by resorting to the same technologies hiding the more troublesome aspects of residual radioactivity.

Cold War Shadow

When "raw" data is produced, it is necessary to make sense of it so that affected individuals can make an informed decision about life in Fukushima. Yet, as Thomas Feldhoff argues, "The individual reception and evaluation of such information . . . requires a willingness to acquire some basic technical and scientific knowledge of how to analyze and interpret radiation exposure data."[27] In the aftermaths of nuclear disasters, making sense of "basic" knowledge is troublesome, especially in light of the long history of secrecy, denial, and propaganda that shaped the interpretation of radiation risks. In their interpretation of radiation-related data, citizen scientists do not escape this heritage, nor the tight control that international lobbies have in prioritizing political stability and economic benefits over the uncertainties of low-dose exposure.

In fact, while citizen scientists showed disdain toward the Japanese state and the nuclear lobby, many drew on epistemic knowledge produced by the latter to make sense of their data. For instance, citizen-science organizations gathered information from international expert agencies such as IAEA, UNSCEAR, or ICRP. Yet these are the same organizations that have been criticized for minimizing the gravity of nuclear disasters in favor of economic and social factors while promoting nuclear power.[28] The necessity of data interpretation can result in reliance on reified knowledge of experts, who, much like antinuclear activists, are prone to political biases and historical contingencies. While these epistemic associations are useful for grasping the fundamentals of nuclear science, I noticed that many citizen scientists ended up reproducing similar reasoning around risks found in the monopoly of international experts. For instance, one citizen argued to me that doses in Fukushima were simply too low to be dangerous and that the ungrounded fear of radiation was the real culprit of this disaster, reproducing the logic of "radiophobia" first pushed by members of the nuclear lobby. I also witnessed citizen scientists reframing radiation risks via natural analogies unrelated to the specific risks associated with Fukushima. One man argued to me that there was no need to worry about food security since bananas have naturally occurring radiation. A core member of a citizen-science network also tried to convince me that radiation at low doses could be beneficial. He was referring to the hypothesis of hormesis, a discredited theory that was nonetheless mobilized by the Japanese state after Fukushima.[29] Citizen scientists even offered school workshops in which they explained to children that radiation can be helpful rather than simply dangerous. In doing so, they replicated the radioactive performances used by the Japanese state in its educational infrastructure.

The notion of an informed choice via data interpretation remains a problematic concept within the scientific controversy of low-dose exposure, where ignorance and knowledge gaps still exist.[30] The former Cold War legacies of secrecy and partial truth do not disappear because citizen scientists mobilize radiation knowledge. As Olga Kuchinskaya concludes, "It is not enough for citizens to produce their own data; it matters how data are interpreted and who controls how that interpretation is undertaken."[31]

"I Don't Care About Radiation . . ."

In spite of such pitfalls, it is important not to depict all citizen scientists as actors who remain unaware of the aforementioned problems. Indeed, other factors significantly influence data interpretation, such as gender, social occupation, and cultural pressures. Nowhere was this more apparent than during my fieldwork with older Japanese farmers, who resorted to citizen science to revitalize their region. By spending time with them, I noticed that few interpreted the data that they produced as dangerous for themselves—in sharp contrast with the worried mothers who used citizen science to evacuate from Fukushima. This interpretation is not due to farmers' ignorance of the technical limitations of measuring devices. Rather, this interpretation resulted from their peculiar situation, in which their health was not a prime concern.

As a farmer best explained it to me, "I don't care about radiation. . . . I've got fifteen years left at best!" Farmers quickly understood from the data they produced that they faced no risk of acute exposure to life-threatening radiation. Many also understood the subtleties and uncertainties associated with chronic, low-dose exposure, which includes a displacement of harm in time. However, with their limited life expectancy, few interpreted low-dose radiation as a potential health threat that warranted tropes of damaged biologies. In this context, the recovery that was important for them was not the recovery of the body, which was already beyond remedy due to old age, but the recovery of their precious land affected by residual contamination. Consequently, they produced data with a clear goal: to revitalize their beloved region's social life. This specific understanding of recovery led to the second instance of conflictual collaboration.

"It Would Have Still Been in My Head..."

A foul odor greeted everyone who walked through the door of Naomi Kawashima's center. It was the smell of various foods waiting to be tested for contamination in the center's Food Radiation Screening System. Naomi Kawashima, the center's director, was a housewife before the disaster; now she runs one of Fukushima's most high-tech citizen-science centers financed by public donations. Before the center's creation, she was constantly hearing the same complaints from neighbors: "I don't know what's safe for my children to eat" and "Is it safe to live here?" In her mind, the government did not do much to alleviate the anxieties of residents: "The initial response was from municipalities, which are underprepared and unequipped to properly calculate radiation levels. Many only calculate radiation levels in terms of city averages or what is present in the air. And the official maps overlook a lot. They don't show hot spots [areas where radiation levels are significantly higher] or the range of radiation levels in a city. For example, levels might be very low on the right side of a road, but the left side can be a completely different story!"

Because residual radioactivity accumulates in ditches, drainages, and playgrounds, results near the ground were often higher than what state monitoring posts can detect. Consequently, many citizens were concerned that children would face higher levels of exposure since they are closer to the ground and tend to put things in their mouths. Kawashima explained how even the family dog was a vector of potential harm; by swooping itself into a hot spot, it risked bringing dangerous radionuclides home, where children would pet it. Soil samples tested by her center later proved that citizens' concerns were warranted. Some of Kawashima's tests revealed extremely high amounts of radioactivity in the ground, going as high as one million Bq/kg when the standard for radioactive waste is set at 8,000 Bq/kg.

According to Kawashima, these insufficient bureaucratic responses hastened the town's need for a citizen-science network. "It just came naturally, as something that we had to do!" she told me. Her center was initially created as a stopgap measure to fill the void created by a lack of governmental oversight, echoing cases in which citizen scientists work as governmental watchdogs.[32] Subsequently, the network began by demanding an administrative response whenever its data indicated a significant threat to local citizens. Yet, as Kawashima noted, this did not work as planned. "Initially," she said, "we conducted some tests and contacted the municipality, but they didn't pass on the results we gave them." As a result of unsuccessfully convincing the state to conduct more thorough monitoring, their network primarily focused on using its data to help residents become more aware of risks of exposure to elevated radiation. As Kawashima emphasized, "We want to know for ourselves [*jibun de shiru*] . . . to help people have safer and more comfortable daily lives." Now the center offered many services in that regard, such as a WBC to measure internal levels of contamination (cesium-137 and cesium-134), thyroid ultrasound screening, and food-contamination testing. The latter, in particular, kept them busy.

Worrisome Levels of Contamination

At the time of my research, the state guaranteed the safety of market products, but the food people brought to the network came from forests, home gardens, and the like—and the center's food testing revealed a wide range of radiation levels. Chestnuts, wood bark, mushrooms, citrus (*yuzu*), pine cones, and honey had high radiation levels that often exceeded the allowable becquerels for food. In contrast to other citizen-science networks, Kawashima's center tested residual radiation via an array of devices, using dosimeters for external radiation, but also scintillation counters and germanium semiconductors for food contamination. Her center possessed a liquid scintillation counter and a mass spectrometer for beta particles like strontium-90 or tritium-contaminated water. Kawashima complained that devices for beta-particle measurement were not available to citizens and that specialized institutions asked for expensive testing fees, which were close to two thousand US dollars (or two hundred thousand yen). This prompted Kawashima to purchase her own equipment that could track not only gamma rays but also beta particles. Testing was subsequently kept much more affordable, with a test costing between five and twenty US dollars (five hundred to two thousand yen).

With these machines, Kawashima's network found additional contamination by beta particles, such as tritium in rose petals (17.3 Bq/kg) and strontium in garden soil (10.3 Bq/kg). As opposed to other citizen scientists who never talked about the risk of such particles, Kawashima was clear-cut in her explanation. She provided pamphlets explaining that strontium-90 could accumulate in bones (*hone ni chikuseki shita*), where it caused serious internal exposure (*shinkoku na naibu hibaku*) and risks of bone tumors and leukemia (*hone shuyō oyobi hakketsubyō no kikensei*). Her pamphlet even underscored how internal exposure by tritium could cause devastating damage (*kaimetsuteki na daměji*) to one's DNA and RNA, causing concern about brain tumors (*nōshuyō*), congenital malformations (*sentensei kikei*), or childhood cancer (*shōni gan*).

Likewise, Kawashima explained how vacuum cleaner bags (*sōjiki no gomi*) and air-conditioning filters bore high levels of contamination, forcing residents to rethink their relationships with everyday objects. Indeed, many citizens were reluctant to turn on their air conditioning (used for both heating and cooling in Japan), knowing that doing so put them at greater risk of exposure.

Through its technoscientific practices, Kawashima's network gradually produced data that clearly contradicted the state's narrative of radiological safety. Many members also interpreted residual radiation as potentially dangerous for one's health. But despite gathering worrisome information and arguing that it was not normal for untrained citizens to be exposed to the same maximum annual dose allowed for radiation workers (20 mSv per year), Kawashima never took legal action on behalf of residents. This decision sharply contrasts with Ukraine's "biological citizens," who after the Chernobyl disaster used scientific expertise as a key resource in litigation practices.[33] Why is that so?

In the case of Kawashima's network, I learned that the consumption of citizen-generated data was embedded in a network of social relationships and cultural identities that promoted a specific vision of social recovery—a vision that existed in parallel with the state's politics of revitalization. While Kawashima was clear about the risk of radiation, she also explained to me that anxiety about health hazards was only one of the many problems facing Fukushima residents. Families had become fragmented (*bara bara*), social ties (*ningen kankei*) were severed, and rural traditions that brought neighbors together disappeared after community members evacuated. Some residents had produced their own food for over forty years before the disaster. "After Fukushima, this was no longer possible," explained Kawashima. "The culture of food exchange, giving and taking [*yaritori*], was slowly dying." However, trust was slowly being rebuilt through their network practices, and people were beginning to partake in *yaritori* again. Therefore, the data collected by Kawashima amounted to more than technical knowledge. They were part of the ties keeping this community together and revealed the experiences of the center's patrons. As Kawashima put it, "We see the people who come to our center, we meet them, we listen to their problems. Then we go out into the field and take samples." By being socially meaningful, the center's data contrasted with what she called "*gariben*"—ivory tower experts who produced paper-based evidence.

In many members' views, data used for political purposes would result in an even more fragmented community of people bound to remain in Fukushima by circumstance or social consideration. For instance, a technical member in Kawashima's network explained that using data on food contamination for radical action would risk hampering the economic recovery of the farmers living in the region. Accordingly, data was not used for evacuation purposes but to reduce the strains and anxieties of inhabitants while revitalizing life *in* Fukushima. Similarly, when asked if she had ever considered evacuating for good, Kawashima replied, "Of course, but you can't really escape. Even if I had moved to another country, it would have still been in my head." The proclivity of Japanese normative models was apparent in Kawashima's discourse. These forms of cultural pressures often stressed harmony (*wa*) and groupism (*shūdanshugi*) as ideal cultural values, according to which citizens are expected to stick with their group in times of hardship, remain attached to their native village (*furusato*), and uphold the kinship obligations of their household (*ie*). Often, these forms of social pressures were even stronger in small rural communities that faced postdisaster recovery hardships.

What Is Recovery?

What I came to learn during my stay in Fukushima was that citizen scientists have divergent understandings of "recovery." In rural contexts, some citizens could hold a vision of revitalization similar to the state's priorities, excluding other social perspectives on recovery. For instance, many farmers were more concerned with the revitalization of the rural economy than with the potential effects of chronic low-dose exposure to radiation. Consequently, farmers used citizen science to revitalize their area. This was notably the case of Atsumi's citizen-science network, which was created to revitalize agriculture-centered industries. Like other farmers, Atsumi had a deep attachment to his land, inherited from his family.

Many members of Atsumi's network put forward a narrative that emphasized the "blessing of nature" (*shizen no megumi*) and the beauty of natural landscapes (*sanrin no megumi*), as well as the hope for agricultural regeneration (*nōgyō saisei*). Consequently, citizen science became a means to realize the possibility of life in Fukushima. To navigate postdisaster recovery in this new irradiated environment, farmers created their own radiological maps while testing food to produce clean vegetables that could be confidently eaten (*anshin shite taberareru*). In this context, citizen science was not a tool that promoted evacuation but a set of practices that helped farmers transmit a "bright message" (*akarui messēji*).

Anna Tsing argues that populist alternatives to state power sometimes reproduce the same hierarchies of state political culture.[34] A similar but slightly different process happened within the aforementioned citizen-science networks, as specific visions of social obligation and recovery led them to share common ground with the state's attempt to reinstate life in Fukushima—*even* when the citizen science data ironically demonstrate a significant amount of contamination—constituting the second root of conflictual collaboration.

Still, according to Kawashima, there were two Japans: that of individuals (*kojin*) and that of the state (*kokka*). Despite apparent differences in views on radiation protection, there was a strong consensus that Fukushima's citizens wished to live there for the long term rather than be evacuated. As a result, official state views about recovery ended up being

Figure 8.1. Farmers creating their own radiological maps. Photo by Maxime Polleri.

reinforced (e.g., creating a stress-free life, reviving local community ties, or revitalizing rural traditions). While citizen scientists like Kawashima produced data that clearly showed high levels of contamination, they were reluctant to demand evacuation since they worked above all to reduce social fracturing. For former evacuees to return to Fukushima with some peace of mind, many would have to engage in citizen-science practices. This was essential in mountain and forest areas, which were not part of the state-sponsored decontamination policy. When I asked a technical adviser from MOE about the risks encountered in these areas, he optimistically pointed to the work of citizen scientists: "There won't be any additional dose if people don't enter those areas. If they do enter, at least they can measure the levels by themselves. They have the [technical] means to do so."

In the end, public participation in science became another instance in which the deployment of citizen-science data evolved in collaboration with the state's vision rather than in radical opposition to it. While Kawashima's network did not reproduce forms of ignorance, it held a vision of revitalization like the state's, excluding in the long run other social perspectives on recovery.

"It Can't Be Helped"

Every three months, Kimiko Sakaue organized meetings in her citizen-science network in a small rural part of Fukushima. There, residents discussed their personal levels of radiation exposure and shared tactics to lower their doses. Even though Sakaue's network had one of the smallest centers I visited during my fieldwork, it became famous for collaborating with an NGO called Ethos, known for having ties to the nuclear industry.

I first heard about this peculiar relationship at the 2016 Fukushima Medical University International Symposium, where Jacques Lochard, the chief representative of Ethos and a member of ICRP's Main Commission, came to discuss his NGO's work. During his speech, Lochard explained that Ethos was founded after Chernobyl, to improve the living conditions of victims of nuclear accidents. He argued that one way to do so was to involve citizens in postdisaster management. In Fukushima, Ethos's mission was similar: to empower the population with knowledge about radiation. Accordingly, Lochard stressed the importance of building resilient societies that could respond to disasters while explaining that empowerment gives affected citizens the opportunity to be transformed.

Launched in 1996, Ethos is an NGO that is described as an offspring of the European nuclear lobby, notably benefiting from the support of French nuclear-related organizations.[35] The organization is known to promote citizen empowerment in areas afflicted by chronic exposure, a project that led sociologist Seizin Topçu to criticize the "politics of empowerment" as a disguised means of decreasing the "state's burden in managing the risk society."[36] In Fukushima, the neoliberal implications of Ethos's agenda closely echoed those of Chernobyl, although critics assumed that Ethos seamlessly imposed its program of self-responsibility in a traditional governmental way.[37] However, unlike what it did with post-Chernobyl victims, Ethos never reached out to Fukushima residents with the aim of setting up its own network. Rather, as I learned from Sakaue, it was the citizens of Fukushima who initially contacted

Ethos, knowing full well the organization's mandate to revitalize the irradiated landscape and its ties with nuclear-related actors. After Fukushima, why would citizens do such a thing?

State Abandonment

To answer this question, it is important to consider that citizens' abilities to respond to issues of radioactive contamination are inseparable from the preexisting distribution of political power, as in the cases of northwest England,[38] Soviet Ukraine,[39] or Kazakhstan.[40] In Japan, bureaucrats had long developed policies that rewarded collaboration with the nuclear lobby, by presenting nuclear power as a way of saving the rural lifestyle of depopulated villages.[41] Peripheral regions like Fukushima consequently became energy producers for major metropolitan centers, creating an asymmetrical balance of power. As Yusuke Yamashita explains, "It is impossible for individuals to nullify the damage of nuclear accidents. Even the amount of damage cannot be determined without the help of expert knowledge. This means that Fukushima Prefecture, the local governments in the proximity of the accident, and the refugees from the radiation, cannot solve this problem. They must all turn to the Japanese government and experts in radiation and nuclear power. Thus, it is in the nuclear accident that the relationship of center and periphery emerges most clearly."[42]

Within this asymmetry, the resources that citizens of peripheral regions had for making sense of radiation hazards were extremely constrained. Moreover, the thinking of citizens like Sakaue evolved in a specific economic context, which was heavily influenced by the neoliberal policies that followed Japan's economic crisis.[43] Around the 1990s, rural regions saw public services and state responsibility gradually decrease, especially around disaster emergency response.[44] This neoliberal shift strengthened tropes of individual responsibility (*jiko sekinin*), which emphasized the responsibility of Japanese citizens. As Anne Allison summarizes, "Under its new banner of 'risk and individual responsibility' (*risuku to jiko sekinin*), the government asked its citizens to remake their subjectivity to become strong and independent individuals 'capable of bearing the heavy weight of freedom.'"[45] These events laid the ground for a specific conceptualization of citizen science.

When I first visited Sakaue's village, five years had passed since the official evacuation of the town on April 22, 2011. Yet, many citizens were still dealing with strong feelings of abandonment by the state. Indeed, when the evacuation order was lifted one month later, citizens were left with two options: they could come back to their village (which the state deemed safe) or flee as voluntary evacuees. Yet, because the livelihoods in this poor rural area were tied to food production, long-term evacuation was not a viable option for residents who did not receive financial support. As a former Fukushima resident explained, "All the rich have left Fukushima. It's easy to do so if you have money, but for the poor it's not the same!" Moreover, rural citizens had no access to preexisting information centers with radiation-monitoring devices, in contrast to technology-rich metropolitan areas.[46] The only information available was state-produced data. But as Sakaue argued, "These measurements didn't mean much to us. What was a high or low level of exposure? This was very ambiguous." Returnees were thus concerned about the adverse health effects of residual radioactivity, especially after the threshold for radiation exposure was increased. As Sakaue explained, the departure of the first government nuclear adviser, Toshiso Kosako, who resigned in protest of the state's policies of 20 mSv per year, further amplified citizens' anxieties and their feelings of being abandoned by the state.

Disappointed by the lack of support from her government, Sakaue invited academic experts to her village to gain general knowledge about radiation, but academics were unable to answer fundamental questions like "Can I eat the food produced in my garden?" Sakaue therefore began to educate herself on the Internet in search of proactive solutions. Eventually, she reached out to Ethos, taken in by their culture of radiation protection and the concrete steps they provided to improve the living conditions of nuclear victims. With the initial help of Ethos, the residents of the village created their own independent citizen-science network, where, as Sakaue put it, "radiation was no longer taboo" and "people could talk about radiation with a smile!" According to Sakaue, this was an environment that the state had failed to provide. While Ethos did not supply monitoring devices, it gave the villagers something that a poor and depopulated rural region did not have: global visibility and pragmatic knowledge. With the help of the Ethos international network, Sakaue was able to raise funds for radiation-monitoring materials while pressuring the regional government to provide dosimeters to its citizens. It was therefore the citizens' ongoing feeling of abandonment by their own state, coupled with the perceived inefficacy of academic experts, that forced them to collaborate with a nuclear-affiliated NGO and to mobilize resistance against the uncertainty brought about by radioactive contamination. Connecting with Ethos made sense, given that residents had few choices regarding disaster recovery. In this context of neoliberal precarity, the only option available was to monitor the radiation. As one member said, "It can't be helped [*shikata ga nai*]."

Practical Radiological Protection Culture

When questioned about the ethics of collaborating with Ethos, Sakaue told me that being pro- or antinuclear was not relevant to the network. "It's not linked to our reality or our lived experience," she said. "We might be receiving different experts, but in the end it is the individuals who make their choices." Still, processes of collaboration are never symmetrical, and collaborators can have different agendas when working together.[47] While citizens like Sakaue were looking to regain a sense of control over their lives, Ethos had its own interests and particular understanding of recovery, especially as an organization supported by the nuclear lobby.

Although Ethos does not force citizens to stay in contaminated environments, its main aim is to revitalize nuclear disaster areas, complementing the interests of the nuclear lobby. Its work aims to show that life within residual contamination is possible and that nuclear disasters are not an impediment to living well. Promoting evacuation would clash with the vested interests of the nuclear lobby by depicting nuclear power plants as dangerous technologies that create an irreversibly irradiated landscape.

To empower people after disasters, Ethos promotes a "practical radiological protection culture" (PRPC), which develops new lifestyle practices to reduce radiation exposure.[48] In this context, citizens who are worried about their food (*shinpai nara*) are told to thoroughly wash their fruits and vegetables (*shikari aratta*) and soak them in water to get rid of residual radioactivity.[49] Food must also be tested for contamination before consumption, and doses of internal contamination can be measured via WBC. Citizens are also encouraged to have their own dosimeters and wear them as much as possible daily (*narubeku mainichi*). Documents provided by Ethos explain that a reassuring radiation value (*anshin dekiru sūchi*) is a number that differs according to one's opinion. As a result, Ethos does not make claims of safety or danger but encourages people to decide for themselves (*jibun-tachi de kimeru koto ga dekimasu*) whether they feel comfortable eating particular foods. If one's goal (*mokuhyō*) is to lower internal contamination, citizens should eat commercially available products (*shihan-hin*) rather than food foraged in forest areas. In contrast, citizens who want to enjoy the "blessings of nature" (*shizen kara no megumi*) are told to resort to monitoring to lower their dose.

The philosophy of PRPC has important implications concerning the nature of risk. It echoes the ALARA principle ("as low as reasonably achievable"), which attempts to minimize radiation exposure in consideration with social factors. As Shannon Cram explains, this principle is based on a risk-benefit calculus that manages radiation exposure as "an unfortunate, yet necessary, part of modern life and work."[50] Within Ethos's philosophy, this risk-benefit calculus—initially contextualized in the realm of energy production (e.g., higher radioactive risks are accepted by nuclear workers because they receive a salary)—is reassigned to postdisaster contexts (e.g., some citizens are willing to accept higher risks to enjoy the benefits of nature). Subsequently, the nature of radiation harm becomes a subjective risk, as citizens can supposedly "choose" their own acceptable level of risk. Through this relativistic mindset, lowering exposure levels is not a fundamental human right but instead a private goal (*mokuhyō*). Against this background, radiation risk is no longer a hazard *imposed* by the nuclear industry but a matter of *personal* choice. Are you comfortable with eating contaminated food? Do the benefits of enjoying the blessings of nature outweigh their potential health risk (e.g., positive risk)? This is up to you.

While the PRPC framework might appear to provide agency, citizens' choices remained highly constrained by structural factors. For instance, embracing a complete monitoring agenda quickly becomes a full-time occupation, a task that is often impossible for most victims who struggle to make ends meet. Citizens are thus more likely to sporadically make use of monitoring practices, which only show parts of

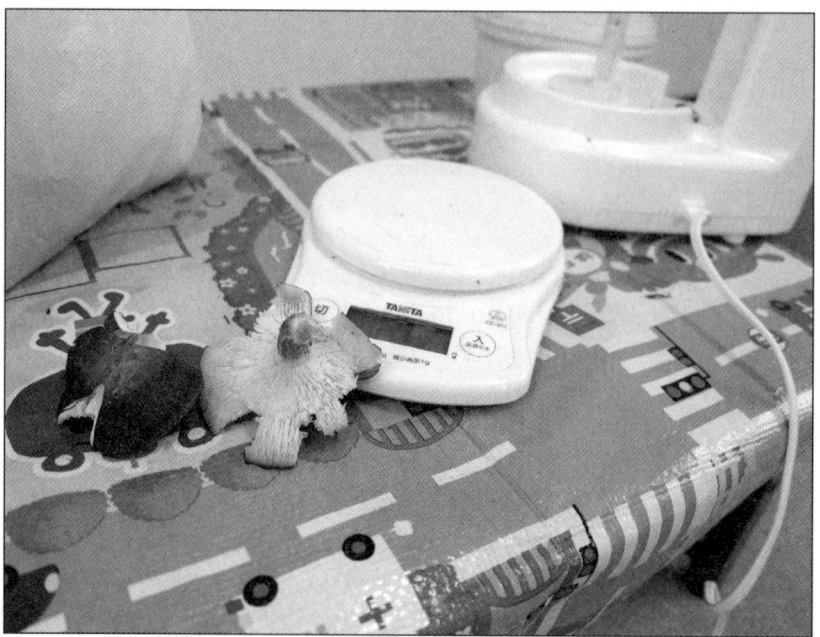

Figure 8.2. Testing wild mushrooms for contamination. Photo by Maxime Polleri.

the full scale of contamination. Moreover, regularly buying commercial products becomes too expensive for rural citizens, who historically produced or scavenged their food.

PRPC also depicts citizens as actors who can properly evaluate radioactive risks. However, most of the knowledge promoted by Ethos is heavily influenced by the organization's main goal, which is to make life possible in the aftermath of nuclear disasters. This led to questionable interpretations of radioactive danger. For instance, while I attended Sakaue's meeting in 2016, I noticed that members wore dosimeters to measure their cumulative dose of radiation, compiling data to follow their exposure histories. The citizens involved in Sakaue's network argued with me that their doses of external radiation were "low" because they were not much different from the background levels of other worldwide cities. They interpreted this analogy as a sign that radiation was safe "enough" to pursue their lives in Fukushima. During one meeting, I also witnessed an elderly man presenting shiitake mushrooms from the forest. "What is it? What is it?" asked one member's child. "Some mushrooms," replied the organizer. "We'll test them for radiation—but don't touch them before that, OK?" The mushrooms were sliced and put in a blender. "I want to press the button!" exclaimed the child. The resulting brown paste was then put into a device that measures radioactive contamination in food, and the child bounced excitedly, shouting, "Not yet? Not yet?" (*mada, mada*). Many members of Sakaue's network contended that Japan's current radiation threshold for food—100 Bq/kg—was the strictest in the world, and that tested foodstuffs often fell below this threshold. Yet the average amount of radioactive cesium present in food before the disaster was nearly nonexistent (rice, for example, had an average measure of 0.012 Bq/kg).[51] Thus, Japan's limit of allowable becquerels—which only considers cesium—was an important increase compared to the level of cesium that people previously ingested. Some experts stated that this increased ingestion presented a risk of adverse health effects.[52]

I Don't Think About TEPCO Anymore

Beyond influencing the nature of risk, PRPC has shaped postdisaster subjectivity by downplaying the concept of victimhood, using words like "stakeholder" instead of "victim."[53] As documents produced by Sakaue's network reveal, the point was to move beyond victimhood, that is, from a situation of anxiety (*fuan*) and dismay (*urotaeru*) toward a situation where one did not worry about radiation (*hōshasen-ryō ni ikkiichiyū suru no denaku*), controlled the situation (*jōkyō o kontorōru shite iru*), and lived independently (*shutai to natte seikatsu*). While monitoring practices lowered overall risk exposure, they deterred people from criticizing policies that fell outside their control, such as the increased radiation threshold, while reducing the liability of corporate polluters like TEPCO. As one mother who initially fled from Fukushima told me, "I was angry at everything. I felt so much rage and hate toward TEPCO. But I don't think about TEPCO anymore. It's just a waste of energy." In this neoliberal mindset, there is no place to blame the perpetrator of harm. This was evident in Sakaue's network, whose members had come to gradually blame themselves, saying things such as "I shouldn't have eaten those mushrooms" or "I shouldn't go to this area because of its high level."

In this way, PRPC is part of broader "participative" governance projects that individualize environmental risks at the expense of a critique of structural factors.[54] As STS scholars argue, "Such individualist approaches also carry a moralistic undercurrent that holds individuals responsible for their health status despite population data that demonstrate the importance of social structural factors in determining health and disease in populations."[55] Still, it remains essential not to depict citizens as naïve individuals who are simply coopted by these tactics. Within Sakaue's network, views on the normalization of radioactive contamination were not as optimistic as those of the Japanese state or Ethos. When questioned about the safety of their environment, Sakaue answered, "I think there are risks, even if some old people don't think so or don't care about [them]." In this context, members of her network also attempted to establish their homes as safe enough within the structural conditions that bound them to Fukushima. As Rebecca Lave reminds us, "Neoliberalization is not simply a result of top-down, structured processes, but also of individuals finding worth in and embracing particular components of neoliberal philosophies."[56] Amid the lack of state support faced by citizens, the embrace of PCRP is perfectly understandable. At the same time, this "stakeholder empowerment" remains tainted by an economic rhetoric that favors members of the nuclear industry.[57] This framework replicates a normative vision of radiation risk while promoting an increased normalization of contamination wherein self-responsible citizens take care of themselves. The irony of this conflictual collaboration is that preexisting neoliberal factors had forced nuclear victims to collaborate with doubtful actors—a collaboration that ultimately reinforced and expanded the neoliberalization of citizen science.

It is therefore no surprise that the government, keen to resettle the population in Fukushima, began to embrace this kind of citizen science. Indeed, in 2015, Sakaue's network was invited to become part of a consultation system for the Japanese government, and she began to give talks about their monitoring activities during state-sponsored symposia. This led their network to receive government funding, allowing them to pursue their work without seeking donations. Such funding is not unique, given that the Japanese state and international nuclear lobby are incorporating forms of citizen science into their agenda. For instance, some citizen scientists have been invited to nuclear security summits to discuss solutions for a safe nuclear future. Citizen scientists are even gaining recognition from IAEA, whose aim is to promote the "peaceful" use of nuclear power.

This collaboration represents a drastic departure from the traditional expert-led management model adopted in postdisaster Japan, where nuclear experts initially attempted to educate a population that knew little about radiation harm.[58] Within a crisis of expertise, citizen science allowed the state to bypass traditional forms of governance so that civilians themselves engineered the normalization of Japan's radioactive thresholds. Recognizing civic monitoring capacities was a means of shifting some of the state's responsibility for ensuring safe living conditions onto the shoulders of the population.

Collaboration or Cooption?

Complicating the binary between those working with or against contamination is how citizen science is increasingly coopted by the same actors responsible for the disaster. Japanese state ministries and nuclear-related organizations encouraged citizens to become responsible for keeping their radiation-exposure dose as low as possible. In this way, safe living conditions became the responsibility of citizens, as tropes of resilience were conveniently deployed while financial support for disaster victims was cut off. In this cooption, we find an unreflexive celebration of citizen-science empowerment—a celebration that served the status quo of state agencies, corporate polluters, and nuclear lobbies.

Another example of this delegation is found in the Nuclear Regulation Agency's decision to remove 80 percent of radiation-monitoring posts in Fukushima, arguing that the radiation levels had stabilized themselves—owing in part to the presence and efficiency of monitoring provided by citizens.[59] This decision was controversial, since problems of radioactive contamination persisted. Retiring these posts would force citizens to fully take on the burden of monitoring. The other reason for retiring state monitoring was the huge maintenance cost, which reached a total of five hundred million yen per year.[60] Through this logic, disaster could be mitigated, free of charge, by the victims themselves.

As a result, Japanese ministries encouraged citizen science. In fact, MOE had set up a series of "radiation classrooms" (*hōshasen kyōshitsu*) in close cooperation with citizen scientists. During these classes, parents and children could "learn about life without being defeated by radiation" (*hōshasen ni makenai seikatsu ni tsuite oyako de manabō*).[61] The Japanese nuclear industry also sang the praises of citizen science. For example, when I interviewed a high-ranking individual working at TEPCO, the latter championed citizen science: "I think that what people are doing is very good. Curie, Sieverts, and becquerels . . . it wasn't taught in Japan before. People only thought that radiation was scary. It was a hard topic to approach with Hiroshima and Nagasaki."

What is more, government publications indicated that the state was mobilizing citizen-science data to downplay the perception of radiation risks. Indeed, many citizen-science networks promoted the concept of "open data," which referred to the "act of making data available for others to freely use and re-use."[62] Communication scholars have theorized open data as one of the most promising contributions of citizen science, which could result in the democratization of science.[63] However, this view fails to account for uneven power distribution in data mobilization. Open data can be used and interpreted by anybody, freely, and for any political purpose. Therefore, data produced by so-called nonpartisan citizen scientists can be mobilized by powerful agencies with their own agendas.

This is exactly what happened after Fukushima. In a 2016 document produced by the Fukushima prefectural government, I noticed that the radiation detected by one citizen-science network was listed as comparable to the levels detected in other cities around the world, like Beijing or New York. This gave the impression that radiation exposure in Fukushima had reached normal levels—a tactic that reframed the discussion of risk in terms of simple, naturalistic explanations unrelated to the hazards found in Fukushima.[64] When I pointed out to one citizen scientist that their data were used to minimize radiation risk in official bureaucratic papers (translated into numerous languages and shared worldwide), the individual shrugged it off as the price to pay for producing raw data. While citizen scientists sought alternatives to state measurements, their technoscientific practices of gathering "raw" scientific data were strategically mobilized to endorse state-sanctioned generalizations about the disaster. Separate projects thus harmonized with a common agenda, particularly in crystallizing normative understandings of environmental hazards. In this way, the openness of data "ironically serves to simulate popular legitimacy for policies that are in fact made in a way that is less democratic than ever."[65]

Beyond Japan, nuclear organizations have been inspired by the development of citizen science. During my fieldwork, I witnessed workshops, forums, and conferences surrounding the promise of citizen science in the nuclear domain, with participants from the French Institute of Radiation Protection and Nuclear Safety, the French Nuclear Safety Authority, the Norwegian Radiation Protection Authority, the US Department of Energy, and the Nuclear Energy Agency (among others). The aim of these organizations is not only to ensure nuclear safety but also to promote and restore confidence in nuclear power, especially after Fukushima. IAEA helpfully explains the new role of citizens: "Support by stakeholders is essential for all aspects of post-accident recovery. In particular, engagement of the affected population in the decision making processes is necessary for the success, acceptability and effectiveness of the recovery and for the revitalization of communities. An effective recovery programme requires the trust and the involvement of the affected population. Confidence in the implementation of recovery measures has to be built through processes of dialogue, the provision of consistent, clear and timely information, and support to the affected population."[66]

For IAEA, citizen initiatives like crowdsourcing are ways to "instill confidence in information from official sources."[67] Citizen science subsequently becomes part of a transnational network of risk governance that contributes to emergency communication after nuclear disasters. This is evident in the implementation of citizen-science networks within the National Radioprotection Institute of the Czech Republic, which plans to use civilians as volunteers to improve public confidence in the authorities.[68] France has also been inspired by citizen science in Fukushima, leading the Institut de radioprotection et de sûreté nucléaire to develop a project called "Open Radiation." This project enables citizens to create their own DIY Geiger counters and upload radiation-related data on a centralized platform. As the director of the project, Jean-François Bottollier-Depois, explains, "Open radiation is potentially of interest to actors involved in crisis management. Very soon after an accident, we will be able to provide a lot of data. . . . Having measurements made by the public benefits science, involves citizens and informs them about risks. From a psychological viewpoint, this allows individuals to assess their own risk in real time, with the possibility of 'controlling' their lives, as the feedback from Fukushima shows."[69]

The fact that the nuclear lobby is recognizing the potential of citizen science is worrisome, as this cooption contributes to the normalization of ongoing pollution and the acceptance of future nuclear incidents. Indeed, French nuclear actors plan to freely distribute Geiger counters near nuclear power plant sites, with the aim of reassuring citizens in the case of radiation release.[70] These plans all fall within the pre-3.11 ICRP publication 111, which stressed the importance of recognizing citizens as stakeholders in the management of nuclear disasters.[71] As a consequence, many citizen-science networks are now benefiting from the support of the nuclear lobby. This includes funds provided by Mitsui & Co., Ltd., the Environmental Fund (a manufacturer of power plants), paid travel by ICRP to prestigious foreign conferences, and even a bottle of whisky given by IAEA. As Philip Mirowski argues in his trenchant critique of citizen science, "The irony is that some of the individuals who *do* take part appear to be motivated by a burning distrust of the government or else a rebel anarchism set against large corporations—sentiments that are common among cadres of biohackers. Yet it's those very governments and corporations that are injecting the money and ginning up the momentum behind the movement. Something doesn't stack up."[72]

Scholars employed in nuclear-related centers argue that citizen science "challenges conventional approaches to nuclear safety management, opting instead for inclusive governance, defined as the opening of knowledge and knowledge making to all members of society."[73] An examination of the broader power centers within citizen science nullifies this argument. Citizen science remains a form of micro-scale resistance rather than a clear-cut challenge to the status quo of corporate interests. Following Ferguson and Gupta, it makes sense to "think of the new organizations that have sprung up in recent years not as challengers pressing up against the state from below but as horizontal contemporaries of the organs of the state—sometimes rivals; sometimes servants; sometimes watchdogs; sometimes parasites; but in every case operating on the same level, and in the same global space."[74]

In the end, cooptation happens when governments or corporate lobbies see value in how citizen science saves them time, money, or means, while replicating the gospel of nuclear safety. The blind celebration of citizen agencies by scholars or dubious actors only legitimizes further polluting practices. In a way, it is no different from the strategies of the tobacco lobby in the mid-twentieth century, which tried to market smoking as a form of group bonding, a personal choice, or an act of freedom (represented by the Marlboro Man, who would eventually die from smoking-related diseases). While citizen science can be applauded as a grassroots act of creativity, it is the direct result of "structural violence," which refers to how violence is "integrated in the political, economic, social, and cultural structure, and shows up as inequity in power relationships, social injustice, and in daily life as instances of inequity, disparity, and discrimination."[75] This implies that polluting industries are installed in peripheral, poor, and depopulated regions, coupled with the repeated claims of governments that toxic disasters can never happen, as well as an overreliance on technological fixes that rarely relieve social vulnerabilities. When all else fails, it is always up to the "small" people to pick up the pieces as best they can.

Playing with Tamagotchi

To varying degrees, the initial practices of citizen-science networks clashed with the official management of the Fukushima nuclear disaster. Yet this conflict did not obstruct broader forms of collaboration with the same actors that, ironically, attracted these groups' frustrations in the first place. This relationship is what I have called conflictual collaboration. While citizen science is a form of politics that can legitimize views alternative to the state's, it also reinforces a certain state- or industry-sanctioned governance of this disaster. Citizen science and official science are thus not antithetical.

Beyond Fukushima, the concept of conflictual collaboration can be used to describe how issues of resistance and collaboration are not always necessarily opposed and can happen simultaneously. In other words, civic practices of resistance should not be theorized as de facto opposing governmental tactics or other forms of dominance. Some aspects of civic actions can intersect with governmental tactics at specific levels (e.g., promoting similar understandings of postdisaster recoveries), while other parts can be highly critical of the state governance of contamination (e.g., lack of data, openness, or transparency).

Cooptation is equally a part of the concept of conflictual collaboration, in that the state or corporate entities appropriate some elements of citizen science for purposes different from what was initially intended by citizens. However, cooptation is not always happening against the will of citizen scientists in a kind of disciplinary way. Broader factors, like similar visions of recovery, also enable collaboration with the state or corporate lobbies. In general, conflictual collaboration—being removed from the dual poles of Foucault's governmentality or Li's practices of politics—demonstrates that while some citizen scientists engage in political contestation, their work risks becoming part of the techniques of neoliberal governmentality designed to govern the conduct of populations amid a contaminated environment.

This concept sheds light on two different kinds of citizen science after Fukushima. First, some citizen scientists like Natsuo Amano used their work to highlight the dangers of living in contaminated areas. This kind of citizen science sustained tropes of permanent evacuation, which clashed with the politics of revitalization. Unsurprisingly, the state did not encourage this form of citizen science and even tried to repress it. Their civic endeavor failed to gain momentum at the legal level. In some instances, the Japanese court acknowledged the possibility of radiation risks to the health of citizens, but rejected their demand for official evacuation, arguing in line with a neoliberal ideology that doing so was a question of individual choice and self-responsibility.

Secondly, citizen science can also be used to revitalize the socioeconomic life of Fukushima as well as to promote repatriation. This path indirectly aligns with the state's politics of revitalization, while slowly becoming part of an "emerging system of transnational governmentality" around nuclear energy.[76]

Both kinds of citizen science happen at the same time, but one is favored and encouraged by the government—when the practices and narratives of citizen science coincide with the state politics of revitalization (e.g., raising awareness about Fukushima, lowering anxiety, encouraging repatriation, promoting food consumption) or when citizen science fills in the gaps of state responses by providing free work under the form of monitoring or open data (that can then be interpreted according to the state's standards).

This chapter reveals the importance of further theorizing the texture of neoliberalism in Japanese society rather than considering neoliberal ideology as a kind of "monolithic category of hegemony."[77] Indeed, cultural tropes and social pressures associated with collectivism (*shūdanshugi*) have heavily influenced how neoliberalism is enacted in Japanese society. On the one hand, according to the tenets of neoliberalism, citizens are increasingly encouraged to become self-responsible in the management of radiation risks. On the other hand, they are paradoxically condemned for their selfishness if they use the results of their work to criticize the governance of this disaster or to claim things that go against the perceived communal interests dictated by the state. Mothers who use citizen science to show contamination are labeled as traitors, egoistic beings, and unpatriotic individuals.[78] Yet these mothers are acting *exactly* according to the neoliberal doctrine: they take care of themselves while trying to ensure their own safety. This is the irony of merging neoliberal ideologies with long-held tropes of collectivism that historically promoted group harmony and respect for authority. Both ideologies promote citizen initiatives while condemning those citizens who stray too far from the group.[79]

In the end, anthropologists are well placed to study the sociocultural factors in which citizen science reinforces the power of nation-states and corporate polluters, leading to further social injustices and a greater lack of accountability. But in doing so, anthropology should be careful not to depict scientific practices as "purer" or more democratic simply because citizens mobilize them. The systematic production of more data does not necessarily produce more consensual knowledge; it also creates conflict, noise, and uncertainty, especially within post-truth societies saturated by information and scientific controversies. This bears on the question of the different roles that nonstate actors play in the governance of environmental issues. For Fukushima, it is doubtful that citizen science will successfully place responsibility back onto public-private institutions. Collaboration between state and nonstate actors further raises a set of complicated ethical questions, as citizen scientists merge their local knowledge with the state's and corporate resources. To what degree does citizens' participation put them at risk of adverse health effects? Who will take care of citizen scientists who end up becoming sick? What are the rights of those refusing to participate in such projects? And how can citizen science collaborate with different experts without reinforcing neoliberal models of governance that burden citizens with the responsibilities of environmental protection? These questions will drive important political debates, but the overall picture of Fukushima remains bleak. Throughout my fieldwork, I have seen children wearing dosimeters pinned to their jackets, as one would do with a piece of jewelry. Small monitoring devices were a game for these children, a kind of modern-day *tamagotchi* that taught one about life, but at a more insidious level. Burned into my memory is the image of children smiling with pure delight and playing with monitoring devices as if they were precious toys. In the end, what will be the legacy of citizen science?

Epilogue

This book has attempted to provide a critical study of how precarity is transformed into a politics of revitalization, by stressing the concept of radioactive governance, a process that literally transmutes a story of uncertainty into one of perceived recovery. My aim with this concept was to open a space for theorizing the complexity of governance beyond traditional political institutions, while examining the contradictory dynamics of governance practices. Threading together the intricate web of state actors, civil societies, and NGOs, I have put forward subdimensions of radioactive governance. In summation, these include the coproduction of expertise and politics; the promotion of "good" citizenship within civil society; technological fixes that impart symbolism of revitalization; the strategic mobilization of nostalgia; the foreclosure of political deliberation through a hierarchization of uncertainties; selective teaching practices that perform a normalization of certain hazards; and neoliberal delegations of risks onto the shoulders of citizens. I believe that these tactics of governance can be applied to other situations involving nuclear technology or radioactive contamination beyond Japan. I further encourage anthropologists to examine how these practices can be repurposed in different cultural contexts.

Arriving at the conclusion of the book allows me to question the transformative power of catastrophes. The debate around whether or not major crises bring sociocultural changes has long been raging among disaster scholars. Anthropologist Susanna Hoffman has reflected on this question through a dialectical framing, arguing that "the answer, to my mind, is no, but also decidedly yes."[1] It is worth considering this answer in the context of Fukushima, as it illuminates the changes that have occurred since 2011—and those that have failed to materialize.

At the local level, Fukushima was a disaster that brought tremendous cultural changes, as this book has testified. For many citizens, former ways of life are irretrievable. Agricultural practices have become experiments. Wild animals are radioactive trackers. Gathering information about radiation levels is normalized, like checking the weather. Trust in the government is at the point of no return. Lands farmed for generations are but a memory. And worries about the potential effects of long-term chronic exposure continue to this day. Nevertheless, during my fieldwork I also encountered numerous Japanese citizens who were surprised to see a foreigner studying Fukushima. Their standard response was, "Oh! Isn't that already over?" Their eyebrows raised in surprise was the clearest indication of the effectiveness of the politics of revitalization, which has for all intents and purposes "buried" any potential concerns that most citizens might have had. Life in the major metropolitan centers of Japan goes on as usual.

On a broader anthropological scale, Fukushima also highlights a nonnegligible shift in the governance of nuclear disasters. As opposed to former nuclear disasters, the governance of this catastrophe is no longer cloaked in Cold War secrecy, tight state controls, or mere authoritative top-down measures. What the Fukushima nuclear disaster exemplifies is the impact of network-based governance in the management of catastrophes. However, this form of disaster governance, where citizen scientists, NGOs, and international expert organizations play a role as important as those of the state, is not necessarily more democratic. While there are multiple actors in the governance of this disaster, a dominant, central story remains: a politics of revitalization that promotes certain understandings of recovery. As a result, there is the unfortunate continuation of the same values that led to a nuclear disaster in the first place: an overreliance on technological optimism, the pretension of human mastery over the force of nature, and the hierarchical arrogance of scientific bodies.

This points to a deeper concern, namely, whether or not this disaster has *permanently* impacted Japanese and global society. The politics of revitalization intentionally avoids addressing the broader structural factors that create major disasters. Indeed, there has been no drastic rethinking of our relationship with energy production, nor with our capitalist-induced ways of life, which keep demanding more consumption on the premise of infinite resources. As the disaster approaches its "crystal" fifteen-year anniversary, what are the enduring structural changes left by Fukushima? The lack of change is sobering. A "new" nuclear regulator composed of the same individuals who were part of the former safety agencies.[2] A robust civil society where citizen scientists work for the nuclear lobby. Advances in the R&D of radiological science. I am perhaps pessimistic, but I struggle to identify proactive global changes brought about by this disaster. In many ways, life after Fukushima still seems to reflect an attitude of "business as usual."

In his book *Never Let a Serious Crisis Go to Waste*, Philip Mirowski examines a striking paradox around the 2007–2008 global financial crisis.[3] He argues that while the financial crisis should have revealed the sheer inefficiencies of neoliberal ideology, it ultimately did the opposite: neoliberal economic ideology not only survived the crisis but came out stronger than ever. As he observes, "Nothing substantial has been altered in the infrastructure of the global financial system from its state before the crisis."[4] I see a striking parallel with Fukushima as a disaster that should have brought tremendous changes but failed to lead to paradigmatic societal shifts.

This leads me to wonder whether Fukushima might perhaps very well represent the end of nuclear disasters as we know them. By saying that Fukushima represents the end of nuclear disasters, I do not imply that further accidents will not happen. Quite the contrary; with numerous aging nuclear infrastructures worldwide and increased warfare near nuclear power plant sites, one can confidently predict that more disasters will occur. The Ukraine-Russia War is a clear example, as Russia repeatedly tried to capture the Zaporizhzhia Nuclear Power Plant, bringing the war to the doorstep of a nuclear reactor. Rather, what I mean by the end of nuclear disaster is the end of a former imaginary in which nuclear catastrophes represented drastic events—as shifts from a somehow prior normal state.

Ann Bergman argues that disasters are "potential vehicles for social change," since they can "impinge on how societies are developed and changed in certain directions—both away from something and toward something."[5] The current governance of Fukushima represents the failure of a bolder imagination toward social change. The global narrative around this disaster was not strong enough to warrant changes to the status quo. Globally speaking, Fukushima was not a threshold, not a game changer, not a crisis powerful enough to cause radical rethinking of current ways of life. The changes that happened are cosmetic, and the governance of this disaster still has both feet firmly planted in archaic legacies of what Kim Fortun calls "late industrialism, a historical period characterized by degraded infrastructure, exhausted paradigms, and the incessant chatter of new media."[6] Even the more promising models of governance, like those of citizen science, have either failed to bring a different global trope or have been coopted by neoliberal ideologies that strengthen existing conditions of pollution. No one has moved away from the structure that created this disaster, either in Japan or elsewhere.[7] As the lone wolf that decided to phase out from nuclear power, Germany has been globally critiqued for making a choice that is economically unsound.

The sheer irony is that Fukushima was precisely *the* nuclear disaster that was never supposed to happen. Rising out of the radioactive ashes of World War II, Japan was the poster child for the Atoms for Peace Program. Far from Soviet managerial culture, Japan embodied the values of the liberal world order that sustained an unparalleled nuclear safety culture. It was an apex technological predator at the top of the nuclear food chain. A shining temple to the gods of science and technology. And yet it was subject to a disaster that was deemed unimaginable (*sōteigai*)— and paradoxically a disaster that changed nothing about global faith in technological fetishism. Today, in a kind of post-Nostradamus fashion, experts have realized that the disaster was preventable. Hidden vulnerabilities have been identified and mapped. We simply did not see them in time. Moreover (the narrative continues), it is no surprise that this disaster happened in Japan. After all, aren't the Japanese prone to group thinking? This surely explains their misfortune! God willing, we have now learned from this disaster. Safety measures have been improved. Giant seawalls are being built. Regulatory agencies have been reorganized. Much like Chernobyl, Fukushima has been treated as a "cultural" exception, this time due not to Soviet communism but to Japanese groupism. But now all is well—trust us. We really got it right this time! All you need to do is to relax. Have a plutonium-laced soda, courtesy of Mr. Pluto. What wasn't supposed to happen did happen and we are still here after all—aren't we? So why worry?

Disasters were long thought to be unusual and drastic events that punctuated the history of humankind with their unsettling forces. Fukushima reveals that some disasters might no longer have the societal power that we have endowed them with. Fukushima does not fit within Thomas Kuhn's understanding of paradigmatic shifts.[8]

Still, within the continuation of a certain status quo, we nonetheless find a set of novel imaginaries that increasingly normalize the aftermaths of nuclear disasters as mere accidents that do not deserve to be labeled as major catastrophes. While this process of normalization had already happened in Chernobyl following the end of the Cold War, Fukushima has further solidified specific tropes that downplay the international perception of nuclear disasters.

Throughout this book this process is apparent within five specific narratives. First, we find a hierarchization of hazardous environments, where, for instance, global warming is legitimized by proponents of nuclear power as a more important threat than residual radioactivity. The strategic prioritizing of global warming as a forthcoming apocalypse unfortunately depicts nuclear disasters as events that are localized and bounded to the past. Secondly, we find cultural framing that prevents nuclear disasters from attaining the status of a global threat. That is, nuclear "disasters" are *Soviet* or *Japanese* accidents, but they are never transcultural catastrophes of a global nature. Within this imaginary, nuclear power is not a technology associated with a global threat, but one that is local in nature, if mobilized by a "bad" safety culture. Third, while euphemisms and greenwashing have always existed in the nuclear domain, Fukushima has led to additional semantics erasing any negative connotations of nuclear disasters. Words like "waste," "pollution," and "victims" are eschewed in favor of softer terms like "recycled materials," "removed soils," or "stakeholders," among many others. When there are no more words with which to talk about pollution and victimhood, how can one even speak of a nuclear disaster? Fourth, the promotion of novel subjectivities influenced by neoliberal economic ideologies of empowerment often complexify or nullify issues of justice and accountability, while normalizing life in long-lasting contamination. In such a world, as more and more people are globally exposed to the aftermath of nuclear disasters, empowered citizens now monitor radiation as an end unto itself, while blaming themselves for their increased exposure. Lastly, the endless emphasis on the techno-managerial lessons learned from the accident transforms nuclear disasters into a series of proactive experiences. From something that used to be perceived as world-changing disasters, nuclear accidents become opportunities to strengthen and improve nuclear safety. This celebrating portrayal of the lessons learned during the accident, lessons that mostly served the nuclear industry, further conceals the ongoing harm experienced by nuclear victims by only promoting a positive and homogeneous vision of recovery. These imaginaries shape global responses as to what is considered an ongoing disaster or, in the case of Fukushima, as a mere accident that happened in a distant past, in a country supposedly far away where the Other lives.

The disappearance of this imaginary around nuclear disasters is at risk of being further complicated by the advent of the Anthropocene, which Gabrielle Hecht described as the "apotheosis of waste."[9] In the Anthropocene, the proposed geological era marked by the permanence of human-induced environmental effects, nuclear disasters might no longer be historical tipping points but mere irregularities—speed bumps as we ride the roads of everlasting contamination. After all, for all the harm that Fukushima brought, it is still a blip in the world of ubiquitous pollution: from mercury in sea life, endocrine disruptors in household furniture, and pesticides in breast milk to heavy metals in clothing, microplastic in our bodies, and per- and polyfluoroalkyl substances ("forever chemicals") in our foods. Indeed, there is a never-ending list of other toxicants. How can more contamination become a game changer when we are already living in a toxic world? Can there even be a concept of disaster within the Anthropocene?

This issue of ubiquitous contamination, whether nuclear or not, brings us back to what Hoffman calls a "core concept" of anthropological thought: that of adaptation, which refers to coping with environmental stresses and constraints.[10] Fukushima raises more questions than answers in that regard. How do we adapt to ever-present contamination that will not go away for multiple lifespans? What does it mean to live a meaningful life in the age of the Anthropocene? Where do we go if we cannot recover former baselines of pollution? Do we keep tracking contaminants for the sake of monitoring? Do we keep increasing thresholds of allowable pollution? Do we keep prioritizing the same values that brought us here in the first place?

In the field of disaster studies, adaptation unfortunately often refers to how "people accommodate to the threats surrounding them and readjust in the aftermath of calamity."[11] This definition of "adaptation" implies the ability to bounce back to former ways of life, which will no longer be possible in the Anthropocene. As a species inhabiting the planet, we will have to think long and hard about what adaptation means in the Anthropocene. As a discipline that studies all facets of human history and life, anthropology will have a key role to play in this task. However, a true anthropology of the Anthropocene can only happen with the full cooperation of all anthropological subdisciplines, which at the moment are painfully struggling to collaborate. In addition to the theoretical advances made by sociocultural anthropologists, an anthropology of the Anthropocene would greatly contribute to dialogue with archaeologists, for whom the scraps and detritus of past civilizations are precious artifacts providing a window into human history. The irrevocable presence of pollution in the human body—or the fact that human beings are the only animals influencing their environment through their wastes—also disturbs the question of human evolution, an issue that biological anthropologists are best suited to study. The millennial temporality of nuclear waste, which exceeds the lifespan of contemporary languages, leads to unresolved problems regarding how to communicate environmental risks to future generations. This is a problem best suited for linguistic anthropologists.

The question of adaptation to the Anthropocene remains, in essence, a cultural one. A culture of learning to live with omnipresent pollutants, a culture that does not simply normalize pollution for the sake of the status quo. This is a culture that has yet to be theorized and has yet to be written. The experience of Fukushima gives us pointers on how to shape such a culture as we learn how to navigate the uncharted, polluted seas of our age. The manifold stories of this disaster show how new communities might express agency and creativity, even in toxic conditions. They also show how dubious actors and ideologies can coopt and exploit that agency and creativity. In the postdisaster landscape of Fukushima, we can begin to see the outlines of novel forms of community, resistance, agency, and innovation that might shape our own future—a future that will hopefully be better, in which the economic prosperity of the few is not pitted against the environmental well-being of all. In the end, these stories allow us to think about the kinds of toxic solidarity we can nurture, as opposed to those historically imposed on the wretched.

Amid everything that I saw in Fukushima, there is an image permanently lodged in my brain's cortex. It is a little boy standing in front of his temporary housing barracks. He wears pink pants and a blue shirt. He cannot be more than two years old. He barely walks and relies strongly on both hands to stand near a flight of stairs. A child of the disaster, born into temporary housing. I have snapped a picture of this moment. It lies somewhere in the archives of my field notes. When I feel a sudden state of despair, I take this picture out and look at it. It is a gloomy scene, but for some reason also fills me with hope. There is something about this little boy who cannot yet walk but who nonetheless proudly stands, looking forward with his eyes wide open. A little "stakeholder" of the future—though hopefully not in the neoliberal sense. We can learn much from this other Little Boy as we struggle to stand ourselves, not yet knowing how to walk on the scorched earth of the Anthropocene.

ACKNOWLEDGMENTS

This book would not have been possible without the support of my family. I would like to thank my parents, Michel Polleri and Marie Lavoie, as well as my partner, Cindy Despeignes, for their constant encouragement. Fieldwork for this research was generously funded by the Japan Foundation and the Canadian Social Sciences and Humanities Research Council. The Ontario Graduate Scholarship also provided much-needed financial supports. In Japan, Prof. Atsushi Miura of Saitama University helped me to navigate the meander of an ongoing disaster.

My time as MacArthur Nuclear Security Fellow at the Center for International Security and Cooperation (CISAC), Stanford University, fundamentally shaped the direction of this book. I am especially grateful to Gabrielle Hecht for her supervision, as well as to Siegfried S. Hecker, Kyoko Sato, and Paul N. Edwards for their mentorship. Other professors, staff members, and fellows from CISAC that I would like to thank are Kristin Ven Bruusgaard, Kevin Chen, Hyun-Binn Cho, Fiona Cunningham, François Diaz-Maurin, Rodney C. Ewing, Sidra Hamidi, David Holloway, Yogesh Joshi, Colin H. Kahl, Alla Kassianova, Erik Lin-Greenberg, Marisa MacAskill, Asfandyar Mir, Tim Mungy, Chantell Murphy, Michal Onderco, Steven Pifer, Scott D. Sagan, Harold Trinkunas, Julien de Troullioud de Lanversin, Yeajin Yoon, and Sherry Zaks. My tenure at the Biomedical Ethics Unit of McGill University as a postdoctoral researcher further influenced the book's discussion about ethics and health. I am especially grateful to Nicholas B. King for his supervision during that time. In my current role as an assistant professor in the Department of Anthropology at Université Laval, I benefited from the support and friendship of my colleagues. Conversations and feedback on my work with friends, colleagues, editors, and other scholars have been invaluable for the intellectual life of the book. These include Cécile Asanuma-Brice, Bernard Bernier, Vincent Brillant-Giroux,

Dan Drolette, Yannick Dufresne, Olivier Evrard, Christine Fassert, Valérie Gastebled, Donna M. Goldstein, Hugh Gusterson, Jacob Darwin Hamblin, Reiko Hasegawa, Vincent Ialenti, Robert "Bo" Jacobs, Kohta Juraku, Andreas Kuehn, Sandrine Lambert, Adam Lyons, Allison Macfarlane, Tim Oakes, Emil Pacha Valencia, Benoît Pelopidas, Sergio Sismondo, Magdalena E. Stawkowski, Shinetsu Sugawara, as well as the many members of the MITATE Lab, an international research program on Fukushima issues. Olson Pook and Emily Wright did a wonderful job of fine tuning the manuscript in their role as copyeditors. Two anonymous reviewers also supplied constructive remarks that have been much appreciated. Lastly, my appreciations are directed toward NYU Press staff, with thanks to Jennifer Hammer, Brianna Jean, and Alexia Traganas.

NOTES

INTRODUCTION

1. Shinji Nakahara and Masao Ichikawa, "Mortality in the 2011 Tsunami in Japan." *Journal of Epidemiology* 23,1 (2013): 70–73. doi:10.2188/jea.JE20120114.
2. IAEA, "IAEA Briefing on Fukushima Nuclear Accident." April 12, 2011. www.iaea.org.
3. World Nuclear Association, "Fukushima Daiichi Accident." May 2020. www.world-nuclear.org.
4. Susanna M. Hoffman and Anthony Oliver-Smith, "Introduction to the Second Edition of *The Angry Earth*." In *The Angry Earth: Disaster in Anthropological Perspective*, eds. Anthony Oliver-Smith and Susanna M. Hoffman (Routledge, 2019), 2.
5. Japan Cabinet Office, *Hōshasen risuku ni kansuru kiso-teki jōhō* [Basic Information on Radiation Risk]. 2016. Pamphlet, 17 (author's translation).
6. Shunichi Yamashita, Shinichi Suzuki, Satoru Suzuki, Hiroki Shimura, and Vladimir Saenko, "Lessons from Fukushima: Latest Findings of Thyroid Cancer After the Fukushima Nuclear Power Plant Accident." *Thyroid* 28,1 (2018): 11–22. doi:10.1089/thy.2017.0283.
7. Michel Foucault, *Society Must Be Defended: Lectures at the Collège de France, 1975–76* (Picador, 1997), 241.
8. Jacques Rancière, *Le partage du sensible: esthétique et politique* (La fabrique éditions, 2000).
9. Jacques Rancière, *The Politics of Aesthetics: The Distribution of the Sensible* (Bloomsbury, 2013), 35.
10. Rancière, *The Politics of Aesthetics*, 89; see also Jacques Rancière, *Aux bords du politique* (Gallimard, 1988), 240.
11. Davide Panagia, "'Partage du Sensible': The Distribution of the Sensible." In *Jacques Rancière: Key Concepts*, ed. Jean-Philippe Deranty (Acumen, 2010), 96.
12. See Rancière, *Le partage du sensible*, 13–14; Rancière, *The Politics of Aesthetics*, 89.
13. Jean-Philippe Deranty, "Introduction: A Journey in Equality." In *Jacques Rancière: Key Concepts*, ed. Jean-Philippe Deranty (Acumen, 2010), 11.
14. Rancière, *Aux bords du politique*, 240; see also Erik Swyngedouw, "The Antinomies of the Postpolitical City: In Search of a Democratic Politics of Environmental Production." *International Journal of Urban and Regional Research* 33,3 (2009): 606. doi: 10.1111/j.1468-2427.2009.00859.x.

15 Aya Hirata Kimura, *Radiation Brain Moms and Citizen Scientists: The Gender Politics of Food Contamination After Fukushima* (Duke University Press, 2016), 24.
16 See Olga Kuchinskaya, *The Politics of Invisibility: Public Knowledge About Radiation Health Effects After Chernobyl* (MIT Press, 2014).
17 Adryana Petryna, *Life Exposed: Biological Citizens After Chernobyl* (Princeton University Press, 2013).
18 Mark Bevir, *Governance: A Very Short Introduction* (Oxford University Press, 2012), 1.
19 Erik Swyngedouw, "Governance Innovation and the Citizen: The Janus Face of Governance-Beyond-the-State." *Urban Studies* 42,11 (2005): 1991–2006. doi:10.1080/00420980500279869; Tanya Murray Li, *The Will to Improve: Governmentality, Development, and the Practice of Politics* (Duke University Press, 2007); Julia Eckert, Andrea Behrends, and Andreas Dafinger, "Governance—and the State: An Anthropological Approach." *Ethnoscripts* 14,1 (2012): 14–34. https://boris.unibe.ch.
20 Swyngedouw, "Governance Innovation and the Citizen," 1992.
21 Li, *The Will to Improve*, 228; see also Robin Leblanc, *Bicycle Citizens: The Political World of the Japanese Housewife* (University of California Press, 1999).
22 Timothy Mitchell, *Rule of Experts: Egypt, Techno-politics, and Modernity* (University of California Press, 2002); see also Penny Harvey and Hannah Knox, *Roads: An Anthropology of Infrastructure and Expertise* (Cornell University Press, 2015).
23 James Ferguson and Akhil Gupta, "Spatializing States: Toward an Ethnography of Neoliberal Governmentality." *American Ethnologist* 29,4 (2002): 981–1002. doi:10.1525/ae.2002.29.4.981.
24 Eckert et al., "Governance," 14–15.
25 Michael Hathaway, "Wild Commodities and Environmental Governance: Transforming Lives and Markets in China and Japan." *Conservation and Society* 12,4 (2014): 398. doi:10.4103/0972-4923.155583.
26 Hathaway, "Wild Commodities," 398.
27 Tom Gill, David H. Slater, and Brigitte Steger, eds., *Japan Copes with Calamity* (Peter Lang, 2013).
28 David H. Slater, "Urgent Ethnography." In *Japan Copes with Calamity: Ethnographies of the Earthquake, Tsunami, and Nuclear Disasters of March 2011*, eds. David H. Slater, Brigitte Steger, and Tom Gill (Peter Lang, 2013), 25–49.
29 Anne Allison, *Precarious Japan* (Duke University Press, 2013).
30 Richard J. Samuels, *3.11: Disaster and Change in Japan* (Cornell University Press, 2013).
31 Samuels, *3.11*, 200.
32 Hugh Gusterson, *Nuclear Rites: A Weapons Laboratory at the End of the Cold War* (University of California Press, 1998); Joseph Masco, *The Nuclear Borderlands: The Manhattan Project in Post–Cold War New Mexico* (Princeton University Press, 2006); Barbara Rose Johnston, ed., *Half-Lives and Half-Truths: Confronting the Radioactive Legacies of the Cold War* (School for Advanced Research

Press, 2007); Kate Brown, *Plutopia: Nuclear Families, Atomic Cities, and the Great Soviet and American Plutonium Disasters* (Oxford University Press, 2013); Donna M. Goldstein, "Toxic Uncertainties of a Nuclear Era: Anthropology, History, Memoir." *American Ethnologist* 41,3 (2014): 579–84. doi:10.1111/amet.12087; Joseph Masco, *The Theater of Operations: National Security Affect from the Cold War to the War on Terror* (Duke University Press, 2014); Sonja D. Schmid, *Producing Power: The Pre-Chernobyl History of the Soviet Nuclear Industry* (MIT Press, 2015); Kate Brown, *Manual for Survival: A Chernobyl Guide to the Future* (Norton, 2019); Joseph Masco, *The Future of Fallout, and Other Episodes in Radioactive World-Making* (Duke University Press, 2021); Serhii Plokhy, *Atoms and Ashes: A Global History of Nuclear Disasters* (Norton, 2022); Robert A. Jacobs, *Nuclear Bodies: The Global Hibakusha* (Yale University Press, 2022).
33 Petryna, *Life Exposed*.
34 Petryna, *Life Exposed*, xvii.
35 Petryna, *Life Exposed*, 106.
36 See also Sherry B. Ortner, "Resistance and the Problem of Ethnographic Refusal." *Comparative Studies in Society and History* 37,1 (1995): 174. www.jstor.org.
37 Anthony Oliver-Smith and Roberta E. Goldman. "Planning Goals and Urban Realities: Post-Disaster Reconstruction in a Third World City." *City and Society* 2,2 (1988): 105–26; Brian Wynne, "Misunderstood Misunderstanding: Social Identities and Public Uptake of Science." *Public Understanding of Science* 1,3 (1992): 281–304. doi:10.1088/0963-6625/1/3/004; Anthony Oliver-Smith and Susanna M. Hoffman, eds., *The Angry Earth: Disaster in Anthropological Perspective* (Routledge, 1999); Susanna M. Hoffman and Anthony Oliver-Smith, eds., *Catastrophe and Culture: The Anthropology of Disaster* (School of American Research Press, 2002); Naomi Klein, *The Shock Doctrine: The Rise of Disaster Capitalism* (Metropolitan Books, 2007); Nandini Gunewardena and Mark Schuller, eds., *Capitalizing on Catastrophe: Neoliberal Strategies in Disaster Reconstruction* (Altamira Press, 2008); Vincanne Adams, Taslim Van Hattum, and Diana English, "Chronic Disaster Syndrome: Displacement, Disaster Capitalism, and the Eviction of the Poor from New Orleans." *American Ethnologist* 36,4 (2009): 615–36. doi:10.1111/j.1548-1425.2009.01199.x; Gregory Button, *Disaster Culture: Knowledge and Uncertainty in the Wake of Human and Environmental Catastrophe* (Left Coast Press, 2010).
38 David Bond, "Governing Disaster: The Political Life of Environment During BP Oil Spill." *Cultural Anthropology* 28,4 (2013): 709. doi:10.1111/cuan.12033.
39 Christopher L. Dyer, "The Phoenix Effect in Post-Disaster Recovery: An Analysis of the Economic Development Administration's Culture of Response After Hurricane Andrew." In *The Angry Earth: Disaster in Anthropological Perspective*, eds. Anthony Oliver-Smith and Susanna M. Hoffman (Routledge, 1999), 279.
40 Michel Foucault, *Power/Knowledge: Selected Interviews and Other Writings, 1972–1977*, ed. Colin Gordon (Pantheon Books, 1980), 82.
41 Foucault, *Power/Knowledge*, 83.

42 George E. Marcus, "Contemporary Problems of Ethnography in the Modern World System." In *Writing Culture: The Poetics and Politics of Ethnography*, eds. James Clifford and George E. Marcus (University of California Press, 1986), 168.
43 Bevir, *Governance*, 78; see also Eckert et al., "Governance," 23.
44 Andrew S. Mathews, *Instituting Nature: Authority, Expertise, and Power in Mexican Forests* (MIT Press, 2011), 10.
45 Elizabeth A. Povinelli, *Economies of Abandonment: Social Belonging and Endurance in Late Liberalism* (Duke University Press, 2011), 91.
46 Lila Abu-Lughod, "The Romance of Resistance: Tracing Transformations of Power Through Bedouin Women." *American Ethnologist* 17,1 (1990): 41–55. www.jstor.org/stable/645251.
47 For a good critique of these problems see Li, *The Will to Improve*; Ortner, "Resistance and the Problem of Ethnographic Refusal."
48 Li, *The Will to Improve*, 157.
49 On the latter point see Javier Auyero and Débora Alejandra Swistun, *Flammable: Environmental Suffering in an Argentine Shantytown* (Oxford University Press, 2009).
50 See also Eckert et al., "Governance," 16.
51 Ferguson and Gupta, "Spatializing States."
52 Ferguson and Gupta, "Spatializing States," 990.
53 See Anthony Oliver-Smith, "Anthropology Research on Hazards and Disasters." *Annual Review of Anthropology* 25 (1996): 312. www.jstor.org; Susanna M. Hoffman, "After Atlas Shrugs: Cultural Change or Persistence After a Disaster." In *The Angry Earth: Disaster in Anthropological Perspective*, eds. Anthony Oliver-Smith and Susanna M. Hoffman (Routledge, 1999), 302–25; Anthony Oliver-Smith, "Anthropology in Disaster Research and Management." *Annals of Anthropological Practice* 20,1 (2001): 111–12; Button, *Disaster Culture*; Samuels, *3.11*; Roberto E. Barrios, "What Does Catastrophe Reveal for Whom? The Anthropology of Crises and Disasters at the Onset of the Anthropocene." *Annual Review of Anthropology* 6 (2017): 151–66. doi:10.1146/annurev-anthro-102116-041635.
54 Barrios, "What Does Catastrophe Reveal?," 153.
55 Anthony Oliver-Smith, "'What Is a Disaster?': Anthropological Perspectives on a Persistent Question." In *The Angry Earth: Disaster in Anthropological Perspective*, eds. Anthony Oliver-Smith and Susanna M. Hoffman (Routledge, 1999), 23.
56 Samuels, *3.11*, xiii.
57 Samuels, *3.11*, 184.
58 Anthony Oliver-Smith and Susanna M. Hoffman, "Introduction: Why Anthropologists Should Study Disasters." In *Catastrophe and Culture: The Anthropology of Disaster*, eds. Susanna M. Hoffman and Anthony Oliver-Smith (School of American Research Press, 2002), 3.
59 Oliver-Smith, "'What Is a Disaster?,'" 23.
60 See Allison, *Precarious Japan*.

61 Hoffman, "After Atlas Shrugs," 311; See also Allison, *Precarious Japan*, 185; Adams et al., "Chronic Disaster Syndrome."
62 Bronislaw Malinowski, *Argonauts of the Western Pacific: An Account of Native Enterprise and Adventure in the Archipelagoes of Melanesian New Guinea* (Routledge, 2002); Clifford Geertz, *The Interpretation of Cultures* (Basic Books, 1973).
63 George E. Marcus, "Ethnography in/of the World System: The Emergence of Multi-sited Ethnography." *Annual Review of Anthropology* 24 (1995): 95–117. www.jstor.org/stable/2155931; Mark-Anthony Falzon, "Multi-sited Ethnography: Theory, Praxis, and Locality in Contemporary Research." In *Multi-sited Ethnography: Theory, Praxis, and Locality in Contemporary Research*, ed. Mark-Anthony Falzon (Ashgate, 2016), 1–2.
64 Kim Fortun, "Scaling and Visualizing Multi-sited Ethnography." In *Multi-sited Ethnography: Theory, Praxis, and Locality in Contemporary Research*, ed. Mark-Anthony Falzon (Ashgate, 2016), 82.
65 Mitchell, *Rule of Experts*, 118; see also Donna Haraway, *Primate Visions: Gender, Race, and Nature in the World of Modern Science* (Routledge, 1990); Donna Haraway, *Simians, Cyborgs, and Women: The Reinvention of Nature* (Routledge, 1991).
66 Isabelle Stengers, *Cosmopolitiques VII* (Découverte, 2007), 9 (author's translation).
67 See Alison Rooke, "Queer in the Field: On Emotions, Temporality, and Performativity in Ethnography." *Journal of Lesbian Studies* 13 (2009): 150. doi:10.1080/10894160802695338; Arturo Escobar, *Territories of Difference: Place, Movements, Life, Redes* (Duke University Press, 2008); Julie Cruikshank, *Do Glaciers Listen? Local Knowledge, Colonial Encounters, and Social Imagination* (UBC Press, 2006).
68 For a similar critique see Didier Fassin, *When Bodies Remember: Experiences and Politics of AIDS in South Africa* (University of California Press, 2007), 201.
69 Michelle Murphy, "Alterlife and Decolonial Chemical Relations." *Cultural Anthropology* 32,4 (2017): 496. doi:10.14506/ca32.4.02.
70 See Noah Theriault and Simi Kang, "Toxic Research: Political Ecologies and the Matter of Damage." *Environment and Society* 12,1 (2021): 5–24. doi:10.3167/ares.2021.120102; Ryo Morimoto, *Nuclear Ghost: Atomic Livelihoods in Fukushima's Gray Zone* (University of California Press, 2023).
71 Ryo Morimoto, "Ethnographic Lettering: 'Pursed Lips: A Call to Suspend Damage in the Age of Decommissioning.'" *Critical Asian Studies*. Commentary Board. March 22, 2021. doi:10.52698/ASPR7364.
72 Eve Tuck, "Suspending Damage: A Letter to Communities." *Harvard Educational Review* 79,3 (2009): 409. doi:10.17763/haer.79.3.n0016675661t3n15.
73 Morimoto, "Ethnographic Lettering."
74 Morimoto, "Ethnographic Lettering."
75 Petryna, *Life Exposed*.
76 Yoko Ikeda, "The Construction of Risk and the Resilience of Fukushima in the Aftermath of the Nuclear Power Plant Accident." In *Japan Copes with Calamity:*

Ethnographies of the Earthquake, Tsunami, and Nuclear Disasters of March 2011, eds. David H. Slater, Brigitte Steger, and Tom Gill (Peter Lang, 2013), 170.

77 For a similar critique of cultural relativism in nuclear studies see David H. Price, "Pre-apocalyptic Ethnography of American Nuclear Borderlands." *Dialectical Anthropology* 35 (2011): 51–57. www.jstor.org.
78 Morimoto, "Ethnographic Lettering."
79 Murphy, "Alterlife and Decolonial Chemical Relations," 499.
80 David Bond, "Contamination in Theory and Protest." *American Ethnologist* 48,4 (2021): 400. doi:10.1111/amet.13035.
81 See Thibaud Boncourt, Marielle Debos, Mathias Delori, Benoît Pelopidas, and Christophe Wasinski, "Que faire des interventions militaires dans le champ académique?" *Revue d'histoire* 145 (2020/1): 135–50. doi:10.3917/vin.145.0135.
82 Paul Rabinow, "Representations Are Social Facts: Modernity and Post-Modernity in Anthropology." In *Writing Culture: The Poetics and Politics of Ethnography*, eds. James Clifford and George E. Marcus (University of California Press, 1986), 259.

CHAPTER 1. NUCLEAR MONSTERS AND NUCLEAR SAVIORS

1 Jacobs, *Nuclear Bodies*, 28.
2 Kazumi Matsui, "The City of Hiroshima: Peace Declaration." *Chugoku Shimbun*, August 6, 2016.
3 Lisa Yoneyama, *Hiroshima Traces: Time, Space, and the Dialectics of Memory* (University of California Press, 1999); Jacobs, *Nuclear Bodies*.
4 See Philippe Pelletier, "De la guerre totale (1941) à la guerre de Fukushima (2011)." *Outre-terre* 1,35–36 (2013): 414–15 (author's translation). doi:10.3917/oute.035.0399.
5 Yoneyama, *Hiroshima Traces*, 13.
6 See Gabrielle Hecht, *Being Nuclear: Africans and the Global Uranium Trade* (MIT Press, 2012), 13–14; Gusterson, *Nuclear Rites*, 2.
7 Michelle Murphy, *Sick Building Syndrome and the Problem of Uncertainty: Environmental Politics, Technoscience, and Women Workers* (Duke University Press, 2006).
8 Murphy, *Sick Building Syndrome*, 113.
9 For further explanations about radiation see: Timothy J. Jorgensen, *Strange Glow: The Story of Radiation* (Princeton University Press, 2016); Richard Wolfson and Ferenc Dalnoki-Veress, *Nuclear Choices for the Twenty-First Century: A Citizen's Guide* (MIT Press, 2021), part 1.
10 United States Environmental Protection Agency, "RadTown Radioactive Atom Activity 4: Atomic Stability." N.d., accessed August 24, 2023. www.epa.gov; Centers for Disease Control and Prevention, "Contamination vs Exposure." U.S. Department of Health and Human Services. N.d., accessed November 29, 2015. http://emergency.cdc.gov.
11 Robert P. Gale and Eric Lax, *Radiation: What It Is, What You Need to Know* (Knopf, 2013), 17.

12 Martin Boland, "Explainer: The Difference Between Radiation and Radioactivity." *The Conversation*, December 8, 2013. https://theconversation.com.
13 Sebastiano Venturi, "Cesium in Biology, Pancreatic Cancer, and Controversy in High and Low Radiation Exposure Damage: Scientific, Environmental, Geopolitical, and Economic Aspects." *International Journal of Environmental Research and Public Health* 18,17 (2021): 1. doi:10.3390/ijerph18178934.
14 United States Environmental Protection Agency, "Radionuclides Basics: Iodine." N.d., accessed November 29, 2015. https://www.epa.gov.
15 United States Environmental Protection Agency, "Radionuclides Basics."
16 Gale and Lax, *Radiation*, 19; Robert Jacobs, "The Radiation That Makes People Invisible: A Global Hibakusha Perspective." *Asia-Pacific Journal* 12(31),1 (2014): 1. https://apjjf.org; Tessa Morris-Suzuki, "Touching the Grass: Science, Uncertainty, and Everyday Life from Chernobyl to Fukushima." *Science, Technology & Society* 19,3 (2014): 336. doi:10.1177/0971721814548115; Kate Brown, "Blinkered Science: Why We Know So Little About Chernobyl's Health Effects." *Culture, Theory, and Critique* 58,4 (2017): 423. doi:10.1080/14735784.2017.1358099; Cynthia Folkers, "Disproportionate Impacts of Radiation Exposure on Women, Children, and Pregnancy: Taking Back Our Narrative." *Journal of the History of Biology* 54,1 (2021): 33. doi:10.1007/s10739-021-09630-z.
17 The National Diet of Japan, *The Official Report of the Fukushima Nuclear Accident Independent Investigation Commission* (National Diet of Japan, 2012), section 4.4.1; Hisako Sakiyama, *Haha to ko no tame no hibaku chishiki: genpatsu jiko kara shokuhin osen made* [Exposure Knowledge for Mother and Child: From Nuclear Accident to Food Contamination] (Shinsuisha, 2011).
18 United States Nuclear Regulatory Commission, "Somatic Effects of Radiation." Updated March 9, 2021. www.nrc.gov.
19 National Research Council (US) Committee on the Biological Effects of Ionizing Radiation (BEIR V), *Health Effects of Exposure to Low Levels of Ionizing Radiation: Beir V* (National Academies Press, 1990), chapter 2, "Genetic Effects of Radiation."
20 See Susan Lindee, *Suffering Made Real: American Science and the Survivors at Hiroshima* (University of Chicago Press, 1994).
21 John D. Boice Jr., "Radiation Epidemiology: A Perspective on Fukushima." *Journal of Radiological Protection* 32 (2012): N33. doi:10.1088/0952–4746/32/1/N33.
22 Boice, "Radiation Epidemiology," N33.
23 Boice, "Radiation Epidemiology," N33; World Health Organization, "Ionizing Radiation and Health Effects." 2023. www.who.int.
24 Canadian Nuclear Safety Commission, "Radiation Health Effects." September 12, 2019. https://nuclearsafety.gc.ca.
25 European Commission, "What Are the Health Effects of Exposure to Ionizing Radiation?" 2012. https://ec.europa.eu.
26 Sven Ove Hansson, "Nuclear Energy and the Ethics of Radiation Protection." In *The Ethics of Nuclear Energy: Risk, Justice, and Democracy in the Post-Fukushima Era*, eds. Taebi Behnam and Sabine Roeser (Cambridge University Press, 2015), 19.

27 Sharon Stephens, "Bounding Uncertainty: The Post-Chernobyl Culture of Radiation Protection Experts." In *Catastrophe & Culture: The Anthropology of Disaster*, eds. Susanna M. Hoffman and Anthony Oliver-Smith (School of American Research Press, 2002), 99.
28 United States Environmental Protection Agency, "Radiation Health Effects." N.d., accessed February 1, 2017. www.epa.gov.
29 Centers for Disease Control and Prevention, "Measuring Radiation." 2020. www.cdc.gov.
30 WHO, "Ionizing Radiation and Health Effects."
31 WHO, "Ionizing Radiation and Health Effects."
32 Centers for Disease Control and Prevention, "Contamination vs Exposure."
33 Radiation Emergency Medical Management, US Department of Health and Human Services, "Differences Between Contamination and Exposure." 2025. www.remm.hhs.gov.
34 Centers for Disease Control and Prevention, "Contamination vs Exposure."
35 Pelletier, "De la guerre totale," 415 (author's translation); John W. Dower, "The Bombed: Hiroshimas and Nagasakis in Japanese Memory." In *Hiroshima in History and Memory*, ed. Michael J. Hogan (Cambridge University Press, 1996), 116–17.
36 Hecht, *Being Nuclear*, 24.
37 Jacob Darwin Hamblin, *Poison in the Well: Radioactive Waste in the Oceans at the Dawn of the Nuclear Age* (Rutgers University Press, 2008), 52.
38 Shun'ya Yoshimi, "Radioactive Rain and the American Umbrella." *Journal of Asian Studies* 71,2 (2012): 322. doi:10.1017/S0021911812000046.
39 Hamblin, *Poison in the Well*, 52.
40 Pelletier, "De la guerre totale," 418 (author's translation).
41 Ferenc M. Szasz and Issei Takechi, "Atomic Heroes and Atomic Monsters: American and Japanese Cartoonists Confront the Onset of the Nuclear Age, 1945–80." *The Historian* 69,4 (2007): 730. doi:10.1111/j.1540–6563.2007.00196.x.
42 Robert Jacobs, "The Bravo Test and the Death and Life of the Global Ecosystem in the Early Anthropocene." *Asia-Pacific Journal* 13,29,1 (2015). https://apjjf.org.
43 Tomoe Otsuki, "The Politics of Reconstruction and Reconciliation in U.S.-Japan Relations: Dismantling the Atomic Bomb Ruins of Nagasaki's Urakami Cathedral." *Asia-Pacific Journal* 13,32,2 (2015). https://apjjf.org.
44 See Pelletier, "De la guerre totale," 416 (author's translation).
45 Emma Chanlett-Avery and Mary Beth Nikitin, "Japan's Nuclear Future: Policy Debate, Prospects, and U.S. Interests." *Congressional Research Service*, February 19, 2009. www.crs.gov; Muto Ichiyo, "The Buildup of a Nuclear Armament Capability and the Postwar Statehood of Japan: Fukushima and the Genealogy of Nuclear Bombs and Power Plants." *Inter-Asia Cultural Studies* 14,2 (2013): 171–212. doi:10.1080/14649373.2013.769744.
46 Morris Low, *Visualizing Nuclear Power in Japan: A Trip to the Reactor* (Palgrave Macmillan, 2020).

47 Unryu Suganuma, "Tepco and Nuclear Energy Politics: An Analysis of the Japanese Pentagon." In *Japan After 3/11: Global Perspectives on the Earthquake, Tsunami, and Fukushima Meltdown*, eds. Pradyumna P. Karan and Unryu Suganuma (University Press of Kentucky, 2016), 204.
48 Jeff Kingston, "After 3.11: Imposing Nuclear Energy on a Skeptical Japanese Public." *Asia-Pacific Journal* 11,23,4 (2013). https://apjjf.org.
49 Jeff Kingston, "Japan's Nuclear Village." *Asia-Pacific Journal* 10,37,1 (2012). https://apjjf.org.
50 See Kingston, "Japan's Nuclear Village," 2; Chalmers Johnson, *MITI and the Japanese Miracle: The Growth of Industrial Policy, 1925–1975* (Stanford University Press, 1982).
51 Eiji Oguma, "Japan's Nuclear Power and Anti-Nuclear Movement from a Socio-Historical Perspective." *Working Paper* (2012): 2. Paper translated by Beth Cary.
52 Vlado Vivoda and Geordan Graetz, "Nuclear Policy and Regulation in Japan After Fukushima: Navigating the Crisis." *Journal of Contemporary Asia* 45,3 (2015): 499. doi:10.1080/00472336.2014.981283.
53 See Richard A. Colignon and Chikako Usui, *Amakudari: The Hidden Fabric of Japan's Economy* (Cornell University Press, 2003); Akira Nakamura and Masao Kikuchi, "What We Know, and What We Have Not Yet Learned: Triple Disasters and the Fukushima Nuclear Fiasco in Japan." *Public Administration Review* 71,6 (2011): 896. doi:10.1111/j.1540–6210.2011.02437.x; Vivoda and Graetz, "Nuclear Policy and Regulation in Japan," 499.
54 See Nobumasa Akiyama, "Political Leadership in Nuclear Emergency: Institutional and Structural Constraints." In *Learning from a Disaster: Improving Nuclear Safety and Security After Fukushima*, eds. Scott D. Sagan and Edward D. Blandford (Stanford Security Studies, 2016), 102; Yuko Kawato, "Sécurité nucléaire et avenir de l'énergie: Le débat japonais." *Outre-Terre* 1,35–36 (2013): 472. doi:10.3917/oute.035.0471.
55 Martin Dusinberre and Daniel P. Aldrich, "Hatoko Comes Home: Civil Society and Nuclear Power in Japan." *Journal of Asian Studies* 70,3 (2011): 692. doi:10.1017/S0021911811000866.
56 See Dusinberre and Aldrich, "Hatoko Comes Home"; Allison. *Precarious Japan*, 186; Hiroshi Kainuma, *Fukushimaron: genshiryoku mura wa naze umareta no ka* [Essay on Fukushima: Why Nuclear Villages Were Born] (Seidosha, 2011).
57 Allison, *Precarious Japan*, 186.
58 See MEXT and METI, *Shōgakusei no tame no enerugī fukudokuhon wakuwaku genshiryoku rando* [Supplementary Reader on Energy for Elementary School Students: The Exciting Nuclear Power Land] (MEXT; METI; Japan Foundation for Nuclear Culture Promotion, Science and Culture Department, February 2010). Pamphlet, 25.
59 MEXT and METI, *Chūgakusei no tame no enerugī fukudokuhon. Charenji! Genshiryoku wārudo (kyōshiyō)* [Energy Supplementary Reader for Junior High School Students: Challenge! Nuclear World (teacher edition)] (MEXT; METI;

Japan Foundation for Nuclear Culture Promotion, Science and Culture Department, November 2010).
60 MEXT, *Wakaru! Purusāmaru uran shigen o yūkō katsuyō suru shikumi* [I Understand! Plutonium Mechanism for Effective Use of Uranium Resources] (Agency for Natural Resources and Energy Production, 2010). Pamphlet, 18.
61 This website was retired and can only be accessed through a web history portal: https://warp.da.ndl.go.jp/info:ndljp/pid/1238741/www.enecho.meti.go.jp/genshi-az/index.html.
62 Kazuhiko Hachiya, *Onaka ga itaku natta genpatsu kun* [Nuclear Boy Has a Stomach Ache]. 2011. https://www.youtube.com/watch?v=5sakN2hSVxA.
63 The term "*obake*" also refers to phantoms and implicitly points towards the past memory of Hiroshima and Nagasaki.
64 Kingston, "Japan's Nuclear Village," 1.
65 Suganuma, "Tepco and Nuclear Energy Politics," 224–25.
66 Suganuma, "Tepco and Nuclear Energy Politics," 224.
67 Szasz and Takechi, "Atomic Heroes and Atomic Monsters," 740.
68 Mathieu Gaulène, *Le nucléaire en Asie: Fukushima et après?* (Éditions Philippe Picquier, 2016), 21–22; Low, *Visualizing Nuclear Power in Japan*, 79.
69 See Suganuma, "Tepco and Nuclear Energy Politics," 220; see also Ryū Honma, *Genpatsukōkoku* [Nuclear Advertisement] (Aki Shobō, 2013); Oguma, "Japan's Nuclear Power," 2.
70 Danilyn Rutherford, "Affect Theory and the Empirical." *Annual Review of Anthropology* 45 (2016): 285–300. doi:10.1146/annurev-anthro-102215-095843.
71 Masco, *The Theater of Operations*, 9.
72 Masco, *The Nuclear Borderlands*, 294.
73 Masco, *The Nuclear Borderlands*, 300.
74 Masco, *The Nuclear Borderlands*, 301.
75 Lauren Berlant, *Cruel Optimism* (Duke University Press, 2011).
76 See also Masco, *The Theater of Operations*.
77 Akiyama, "Political Leadership in Nuclear Emergency," 96.
78 Donna M. Goldstein, "Already Innocent: Radioactive Bribes, White-Collar Corruption, and Nuclear Expertise in Brazil." *Culture, Theory and Critique* 59,4 (2018): 359. doi:10.1080/14735784.2018.1514642.
79 Goldstein, "Already Innocent," 367.
80 Mitchell, *Rule of Experts*, 300.
81 Mitchell, *Rule of Experts*, 300.
82 Brett L. Walker, *Toxic Archipelago: A History of Industrial Disease in Japan* (University of Washington Press, 2010), 4.
83 Walker, *Toxic Archipelago*; Kaji Masanori, "Itai-itai Disease: Lessons for the Way to Environmental Regeneration." In *Lessons from Fukushima: Japanese Case Studies of Science, Technology, and Society*, ed. Yuko Fujigaki (Springer, 2015), 141–65.
84 Mitchell, *Rule of Experts*, 43.

85 Donna M. Goldstein and Magdalena E. Stawkowski, "James V. Neel and Yuri E. Dubrova: Cold War Debates and the Genetic Effects of Low-Dose Radiation." *Journal of the History of Biology* 48,1 (2015): 70. doi:10.1007/s10739-014-9385-0.
86 Herbert Abrams, "Cancer Risk from Exposure to Low Levels of Ionizing Radiation." In *Crisis Without End: The Medical and Ecological Consequences of the Fukushima Nuclear Catastrophe*, ed. Helen Caldicott (New Press, 2014), 208–9.
87 ICRP, "The 2007 Recommendations of the International Commission on Radiological Protection. ICRP Publication 103." *Annals of the ICRP* 37,2–4 (2007): 51. www.icrp.org.
88 Goldstein and Stawkowski, "James V. Neel and Yuri E. Dubrova," 70.
89 William F. Morgan and William J. Bair, "Issues in Low Dose Radiation Biology: The Controversy Continues; A Perspective." *Radiation Research* 179,5 (2013): 501. doi:10.1667/RR3306.1.
90 Abrams, "Cancer Risk from Exposure to Low Levels of Ionizing Radiation," 207.
91 Soraya Boudia, "Global Regulation: Controlling and Accepting Radioactivity Risks." *History and Technology* 23,4 (2007): 391. doi:10.1080/07341510701527443.
92 Boudia, "Global Regulation," 392.
93 Boudia, "Global Regulation," 390.
94 Hecht, *Being Nuclear*, 185.
95 Hecht, *Being Nuclear*, 185.
96 United States Nuclear Regulatory Commission, "ALARA." 2021. www.nrc.gov.
97 Hansson, "Nuclear Energy and the Ethics of Radiation Protection," 28.
98 See Shannon Cram, "Living in Dose: Nuclear Work and the Politics of Permissible Exposure." *Public Culture* 28,3 (2016): 519–39. doi:10.1215/08992363-3511526.
99 Hansson, "Nuclear Energy and the Ethics of Radiation Protection," 22.
100 Stephens, "Bounding Uncertainty," 94; Boudia, "Global Regulation," 402.
101 See Cram, "Living in Dose."
102 See Hugh M. Gloster, "Hiroshima in Retrospect." *Phylon* 17,3 (1956): 271–78; Susan Lindee, "Survivors and Scientists: Hiroshima, Fukushima, and the Radiation Effects Research Foundation, 1975–2014." *Social Studies of Science* 46,2 (2016): 184–209. doi:10.1177/0306312716632933.
103 Lindee, "Survivors and Scientists," 185.
104 Goldstein and Stawkowski, "James V. Neel and Yuri E. Dubrova," 72.
105 United States Nuclear Regulatory Commission, "Backgrounder on Biological Effects of Radiation." 2015. www.nrc.gov.
106 Nori Nakamura, "Genetic Effects of Radiation in Atomic-Bomb Survivors and Their Children: Past, Present, and Future." *Journal of Radiation Research* 47,suppl B (2006): B67–B73. doi:10.1269/jrr.47.b67; Jorgensen. *Strange Glow*, 207.
107 Lindee, "Survivors and Scientists"; Jacobs. *Nuclear Bodies*, 21–42.
108 Alice M. Stewart and George W. Kneale, "A-bomb Survivors: Factors That May Lead to a Re-assessment of the Radiation Hazard." *International Journal of Epidemiology* 29,14 (2000): 708–14. doi:10.1093/ije/29.4.708; see also Gayle Green, *The*

Woman Who Knew Too Much: Alice Stewart and the Secrets of Radiation (University of Michigan Press, 1999).
109 Jacobs, "The Radiation That Makes People Invisible," 10.
110 Lindee, *Suffering Made Real*, 28.
111 See Jacobs, *Nuclear Bodies*.
112 Majia Holmer Nadesan, "Nuclear Governmentality: Governing Nuclear Security and Radiation Risk in Post-Fukushima Japan." *Security Dialogue* 50,6 (2019): 523. doi:10.1177/0967010619868442; Jacobs, *Nuclear Bodies*, 42.
113 Masco, *The Theater of Operations*.
114 Johnston, *Half-Lives and Half-Truths*; James C. Rice, *Downwind of the Atomic State: Atmospheric Testing and the Rise of the Risk Society* (New York University Press, 2023).
115 Brown, *Plutopia*.
116 See Jeremy Pearce, "John W. Gofman, 88, Scientist and Advocate for Nuclear Safety, Dies." *The New York Times*, August 26, 2007. www.nytimes.com; Edward Calabrese, "The Gofman-Tamplin Cancer Risk Controversy and Its Impact on the Creation of Beir I and the Acceptance of LNT." *La Medicina Del Lavoro* 14,1 (2023). doi:10.23749/mdl.v114i1.14006.
117 John William Gofman, "Gofman on the Health Effects of Radiation: 'There is No Safe Threshold.'" *University of California San Francisco, Synapse* 38,16 (1994). https://ratical.org.
118 Goldstein, "Toxic Uncertainties of a Nuclear Era," 583.
119 Samuel J. Walker, *Three Mile Island: A Nuclear Crisis in Historical Perspective* (University of California Press, 2004).
120 Plokhy, *Atoms and Ashes*, 137–77.
121 Brown, *Manual for Survival*.
122 Brown, "Blinkered Science," 417.
123 Brown, "Blinkered Science," 417.
124 Magdalena E. Stawkowski, "'I Am a Radioactive Mutant': Emergent Biological Subjectivities at Kazakhstan's Semipalatinsk Nuclear Test Site." *American Ethnologist* 43,1 (2016): 151. doi:10.1111/amet.12269; see also Goldstein and Stawkowski, "James V. Neel and Yuri E. Dubrova."
125 See Brown, *Manual for Survival*.
126 The Chernobyl Forum 2003–2005, *Chernobyl's Legacy: Health, Environmental, and Socio-Economic Impacts and Recommendations to the Governments of Belarus, the Russian Federation, and Ukraine*, 2nd rev. ed. N.d., accessed January 28, 2025. http://hps.org.
127 Magdalena Stawkowski, "Radiophobia Had to Be Reinvented." *Culture, Theory, and Critique* 58,4 (2017): 360. doi:10.1080/14735784.2017.1356740.
128 Stawkowski, "Radiophobia Had to Be Reinvented," 357.
129 Valerie Arnhold, "Normalisation of Nuclear Accidents After the Cold War." *Cold War History* 21,3 (2021): 261–81. doi:10.1080/14682745.2020.1806239.
130 Arnhold, "Normalisation of Nuclear Accidents After the Cold War," 262.

131 IAEA, "International Nuclear and Radiological Event Scale (INES)." N.d. www.iaea.org.
132 See Schmid, *Producing Power*.
133 Arnhold, "Normalisation of Nuclear Accidents After the Cold War," 279–80.
134 Sezin Topçu, "Chernobyl Empowerment? Exporting 'Participatory Governance' to Contaminated Territories." In *Toxicants, Health, and Regulation Since 1945*, eds. Boudia Soraya and Nathalie Jas (Pickering and Chatto, 2013), 135–58.
135 See Soraya Boudia, "Les problèmes de santé publique de longue durée: Les effets des faibles doses de radioactivité." In *La définition des problèmes de santé publiques*, eds. Claude Gilbert and Emmanuel Henry (Éditions de la découverte, 2009), 49; Seizin Topçu, *La France nucléaire: L'art de gouverner une technologie contestée* (Seuil, 2013), chapter 7; Tanja Perko, "How to Communicate About Radiological Risks? A European Perspective." *Fukushima Global Communication Programme Working Paper Series* 19 (2015): 1–13. https://collections.unu.edu.
136 Topçu, "Chernobyl Empowerment?," 146.

CHAPTER 2. THE THEATER OF EXPERTISE

1 Symposium organized at the Soma Civic Center in Soma city, Fukushima, May 7–8, 2016. In Japanese: *"Kodomo to shinsai fukkō" kokusai shinpojiumu 2016—Sōma chihō no 5-nen no ayumi*.
2 Symposium organized at the Mitaka City Social Education Center, February 20, 2016. In Japanese: *Fukushima 6 nen me no genjitsu ni mukiau*.
3 The two conferences were *Dai 112 kai genshiryoku anzen mondai zemi* [112th Nuclear Safety Issues Seminar], February 10, 2016, Kyoto University Research Reactor Institute; *Le nucléaire en sursis. Du local à l'international: Bilan et déductions Quelles politiques énergétiques pour demain?*, March 22, 2016, Maison Franco-Japonaise.
4 Fukushima Prefecture, "Fukushimaken hōshanō sokutei mappu" [Fukushima Prefecture Radioactivity Measurement Map]. N.d., accessed February 12, 2017. www.pref.fukushima.lg.jp.
5 Remarks collected during *Dai 112 kai genshiryoku anzen mondai zemi* and *Le nucléaire en sursis*.
6 Speech given during *Le nucléaire en sursis*.
7 Anna Tsing, *Friction: An Ethnography of Global Connection* (Princeton University Press, 2005), 81.
8 Sheila Jasanoff, ed., *States of Knowledge: The Co-production of Science and Social Order* (Routledge, 2004).
9 Sheila Jasanoff, "The Idiom of Co-production." In *States of Knowledge: The Co-production of Science and Social Order*, ed. Sheila Jasanoff (Routledge, 2004), 3.
10 Sheila Jasanoff, "Afterword." In *States of Knowledge: The Co-production of Science and Social Order*, ed. Sheila Jasanoff (Routledge, 2004), 274.
11 E. Summerson Carr, "Enactments of Expertise." *Annual Review of Anthropology* 39 (2010): 18. doi:10.1146/annurev.anthro.012809.104948; see also Joan H. Fujimura,

"Authorizing Knowledge in Science and Anthropology." *American Anthropologist* 100,2 (1998): 347–60. doi:10.1525/aa.1998.100.2.347; Dominic Boyer, "The Corporeality of Expertise." *Ethnos* 70,2 (2005): 243–66. doi:10.1080/00141840500141345; Harvey and Knox, *Roads*.

12 Carr, "Enactments of Expertise," 17.
13 The National Diet of Japan, *The Official Report of the Fukushima Nuclear Accident*.
14 IAEA, *The Fukushima Daiichi Accident: Report by the Director General*. 2015. Pamphlet, 87. www.pub.iaea.org.
15 Table 2.1 is based on the following materials: Cabinet Office, *Designating and Rearranging the Areas of Evacuation*. July 23, 2012. www.meti.go.jp; Christine Fassert and Reiko Hasegawa, Shinrai Research Project: The 3/11 Accident and Its Social Consequences. Rapport IRSN/2019/00178. 2019. Report, section 2.2. https://en.irsn.fr; IAEA, *The Fukushima Daiichi Accident*, 88; Fukushima on the Globe, "Evacuation Orders and Restricted Areas." N.d., accessed June 13, 2020. http://fukushimaontheglobe.com.
16 World Nuclear Association, "Nuclear Radiation and Health Effects." 2015. www.world-nuclear.org.
17 IAEA, *The Fukushima Daiichi Accident*, 89.
18 Satoko Oka Norimatsu, "Worldwide Responses to the 20 Milliseivert Controversy." *Asia-Pacific Journal: Japan Focus* 10,54,66 (2012). https://apjjf.org.
19 ICRP, "ICRP Publication 111: Application of the Commission's Recommendations to the Protection of People Living in Long-term Contaminated Areas After a Nuclear Accident or a Radiation Emergency." *Annals of the ICRP* 39,3 (2009): 15. www.icrp.org; see also Japan Cabinet Office, *Basic Information on Radiation Risk*. 2016. Pamphlet, 17. www.reconstruction.go.jp.
20 As cited in Toshihiro Higuchi, "Radiation Protection by Numbers: Another 'Man-Made' Disaster." In *Learning from a Disaster: Improving Nuclear Safety and Security After Fukushima*, eds. Scott D. Sagan and Edward D. Blandford (Stanford Security Studies, 2016), 110.
21 ICRP, "ICRP Publication 111," 29.
22 ICRP, "ICRP Publication 111," 30.
23 Naoto Kan, "No Nuclear Power Is the Best Nuclear Power." In *Crisis Without End: The Medical and Ecological Consequences of the Fukushima Nuclear Catastrophe*, ed. Helen Caldicott (The New Press, 2014), 18–19.
24 See Barrios, "What Does Catastrophe Reveal?"
25 ICRP, "Fukushima Nuclear Power Plant Accident." ICRP ref. 4847-5603-4313 (March 21, 2011), 1. www.icrp.org.
26 Hiraoki Koide, "Living in a Contaminated World." In *Crisis Without End: The Medical and Ecological Consequences of the Fukushima Nuclear Catastrophe*, ed. Helen Caldicott (The New Press, 2014), 23.
27 Kyle Cleveland, "Mobilizing Nuclear Bias: The Fukushima Nuclear Crisis and the Politics of Uncertainty." *Asia-Pacific Journal* 12,7,4 (2014). https://apjjf.org.

28 Shin-etsu Sugawara and Kohta Juraku, "Post-Fukushima Controversy on SPEEDI System: Contested Imaginary of Real-Time Simulation Technology for Emergency Radiation Protection." In *The Sociotechnical Constitution of Resilience*, ed. Sulfikar Amir (Palgrave Macmillan, 2018), 207.
29 Kingston, "After 3.11," 6.
30 Sugawara and Juraku, "Post-Fukushima Controversy on SPEEDI System," 208.
31 See Cécile Asanuma-Brice, "Beyond Reality; or, An Illusory Ideal: Pro-Nuclear Japan's Management of Migratory Flows in a Nuclear Catastrophe." *Asia-Pacific Journal* 12,47,1 (2014). https://apjjf.org; Citizen-Scientist International Symposium on Radiation Protection, "The 6th Citizen-Scientists International Symposium on Radiation Protection." 2017. www.iwanami.co.jp.
32 CBC News, "Japanese Government Adviser Quits." *CBC News*, April 30, 2011. www.cbc.ca.
33 CBC News, "Japanese Government Adviser Quits."
34 Masashi Shirabe, Christine Fassert, and Reiko Hasegawa, "From Risk Communication to Participatory Radiation Risk Assessment." *Fukushima Global Communication Programme Working Paper Series* 21 (2015): 3. https://collections.unu.edu; David H. Slater, Rika Morioka, and Haruka Danzuka, "Micro-politics of Radiation: Young Mothers Looking for a Voice in Post–3.11 Fukushima." *Critical Asian Studies* 46,3 (2014): 486. doi:10.1080/14672715.2014.935138.
35 Spiegel, "Studying the Fukushima Aftermath: 'People Are Suffering from Radiophobia.'" *Spiegel*, August 19, 2011. www.spiegel.de.
36 Fassert and Hasegawa, Shinrai Research Project, 116–19.
37 Fassert and Hasegawa, Shinrai Research Project, 118.
38 Majia Holmer Nadesan, *Fukushima and the Privatization of Risk* (Palgrave, 2013), 46.
39 Shunichi Yamashita and Shinichi Suzuki, "Risk of Thyroid Cancer After the Fukushima Nuclear Power Plant Accident." *Respiratory Investigation* 51,3 (2013): 128. doi:10.1016/j.resinv.2013.05.007.
40 Japan Cabinet Office, *Hōshasen risuku ni kansuru kiso-teki jōhō*, 11.
41 IAEA, *The Fukushima Daiichi Accident*, 13.
42 UNSCEAR, Report of the United Nations Scientific Committee on the Effects of Atomic Radiation. Sixtieth session, May 27–31, 2013. Report, 11–12. www.unscear.org.
43 WHO, Health Risk Assessment from the Nuclear Accident After the 2011 Great East Japan Earthquake and Tsunami Based on a Preliminary Dose Estimation. 2013. Report, 8. http://apps.who.int.
44 UNSCEAR, Report of the United Nations Scientific Committee on the Effects of Atomic Radiation, 12.
45 Masafumi Abe, "Fukushima Health Management Survey: To Monitor, Ensure, and Promote the Long-Term Health of Fukushima Residents. Health Management Survey." Fukushima Medical University. 2012.

46 Piers Williamson, "Demystifying the Official Discourse on Childhood Thyroid Cancer in Fukushima." *Asia-Pacific Journal* 12,49,2 (2014). https://apjjf.org.
47 Shinichi Suzuki et al., "Comprehensive Survey Results of Childhood Thyroid Ultrasound Examinations in Fukushima in the First Four Years After the Fukushima Daiichi Nuclear Power Plant Accident." *Thyroid* 26,6 (2016): 843–51. doi:10.1089/thy.2015.0564.
48 Japan Cabinet Office, *Hōshasen risuku ni kansuru kiso-teki jōhō*.
49 Japan Cabinet Office, *Hōshasen risuku ni kansuru kiso-teki jōhō*, 2.
50 The National Diet of Japan, *The Official Report of the Fukushima Nuclear Accident*, Introduction, 15.
51 For a summary of these claims see Morris-Suzuki, "Touching the Grass."
52 Patrick McLaughlin, Bleddyn Jones, and Michael Maher, "An Update on Radioactive Release and Exposures After the Fukushima Dai-ichi Nuclear Disaster." *British Journal of Radiology* 85,1017 (2012): 1224. doi:10.1259/bjr/27017231.
53 Steven Wing, "Epidemiologic Studies of Radiation Releases from Nuclear Facilities." In *Crisis Without End: The Medical and Ecological Consequences of the Fukushima Nuclear Catastrophe*, ed. Helen Caldicott (The New Press, 2014), 194.
54 See Katsuma Yagasaki, "Internal Exposure Concealed: The True State of the Fukushima Nuclear Power Plant Accident." *Asia-Pacific Journal* 14,10,3 (2016). https://apjjf.org.
55 Didier Champion et al., "The IRSN's Earliest Assessments of the Fukushima Accident's Consequences for the Terrestrial Environment in Japan." *Radioprotection* 48,1 (2013): 36. doi:10.1051/radiopro/2012052.
56 Commission de Recherche et d'Information Indépendantes sur la Radioactivité, "Fukushima Daiichi, la catastrophe est toujours en cours" (Association CRIIRAD Laboratoire, Mars 2016).
57 Wladimir Wertelecki, "Congenital Malformations in Rivne, Ukraine." In *Crisis Without End: The Medical and Ecological Consequences of the Fukushima Nuclear Catastrophe*, ed. Helen Caldicott (The New Press, 2014), 130; see also Folkers, "Disproportionate Impacts of Radiation Exposure."
58 See Morris-Suzuki, "Touching the Grass"; Commission de Recherche et d'Information Indépendantes sur la Radioactivité, "Fukushima Daiichi, la catastrophe est toujours en cours."
59 The National Diet of Japan, *The Official Report of the Fukushima Nuclear Accident*, section 5.2.3.
60 IAEA. "The 'Atom for Peace' Agency." N.d., accessed April 29, 2021. www.iaea.org.
61 Alex Rosen, "Critical Analysis of the WHO's Health Risk Assessment of the Fukushima Nuclear Catastrophe." German Section of the International Physicians for the Prevention of Nuclear War. 2013. www.ippnw.de.
62 IAEA, "IAEA, Fukushima Prefecture Sign Cooperation Memorandum." December 15, 2012. www.iaea.org.
63 Boudia, "Global Regulation," 402.

64 Justin McCurry, "Naoto Kan Resigns as Japan's Prime Minister." *The Guardian*, August 26, 2011. www.theguardian.com.
65 See Samuels, *3.11*, 182; William J. Siembieda and Haruo Hayashi, "Japan's Megadisaster Challenges: Crisis Management in the Modern Era." In *Japan: The Precarious Future*, eds. Anne Allison and Frank Baldwin (New York University Press, 2015), 148.
66 METI, *For Accelerating the Reconstruction of Fukushima from the Nuclear Disaster: Major Points*. December 20, 2013. Pamphlet, 1. www.meti.go.jp.
67 METI, *For Accelerating the Reconstruction of Fukushima from the Nuclear Disaster*, 1.
68 Sébastien Lechevalier and Brieuc Monfort, "Abenomics: Has It Worked? Will It Ultimately Fail?," *Japan Forum* 30,2 (2017): 277–302. doi:10.1080/09555803.2017.1394352.
69 IAEA, *The Fukushima Daiichi Accident*, 18.
70 Justin McCurry, "Tokyo 2020 Olympics: Hugs, Tears, and Shouts of 'Banzai' Greet News of Victory." *The Guardian*, September 8, 2013. www.theguardian.com.
71 Takumi Nemoto, "For Accelerating the Reconstruction from the Great East Japan Earthquake." Reconstruction Agency. February 2014. www.reconstruction.go.jp.
72 Reconstruction Agency, "About Us." 2016. www.reconstruction.go.jp.
73 Reconstruction Agency, "The Road to Recovery: Recovery and Reconstruction from the Great East Japan Earthquake." Reconstruction Agency, Promotional video. Running Time, 13:59 minutes. April 22, 2015. http://nettv.gov-online.go.jp.
74 Tomiko Yamaguchi, "Scientification and Social Control: Defining Radiation Contamination in Food and Farms." *Science, Technology & Society* 21,1 (2016): 71–72. doi:10.1177/097172181562.
75 Yamaguchi, "Scientification and Social Control," 71.
76 Swyngedouw, "The Antinomies of the Postpolitical City," 613.
77 Stawkowski, "Radiophobia Had to Be Reinvented."
78 *Higashinihon daishinsai fukushima genpatsu jiko kara 5-nen kokusai shinpojiumu* [International Symposium: Five Years Since the Great East Japan Earthquake, Tsunami, and Nuclear Crisis], March 8, 2016, Fukushima Medical University auditorium.
79 See Peter Dear, "Mysteries of State, Mysteries of Nature: Authority, Knowledge, and Expertise in the Seventeenth Century." In *States of Knowledge: The Co-production of Science and Social Order*, ed. Sheila Jasanoff (Routledge, 2004), 206.
80 Brian Wynne, "Public Participation in Science and Technology: Performing and Obscuring a Political-Conceptual Category Mistake." *East Asian Science, Technology and Society* 1 (2007): 107 (original emphasis). doi:10.1007/s12280-007-9004-7.
81 Gregory Button, "The Negation of Disaster: The Media Response to Oil Spills in Great Britain." In *The Angry Earth: Disaster in Anthropological Perspective*, eds. Anthony Oliver-Smith and Susanna M. Hoffman (Routledge, 1999), 130.
82 See Marita Sturken, "The Aesthetics of Absence: Rebuilding Ground Zero." *American Ethnologist* 31,3 (2004): 311–25. doi:10.1525/ae.2004.31.3.311.
83 Stephens, "Bounding Uncertainty," 92.

84 Laura Nader and Hugh Gusterson, "Nuclear Legacies: Arrogance, Secrecy, Ignorance, Lies, Silence, Suffering, Action." In *Half-Lives and Half-Truths: Confronting the Radioactive Legacies of the Cold War*, ed. Barbara Rose Johnston (School for Advanced Research Press, 2007), 301.
85 Kimura, *Radiation Brain Moms and Citizen Scientists*, 29.
86 Kimura, *Radiation Brain Moms and Citizen Scientists*, 38.
87 See Mikihito Tanaka, "Agenda Building Intervention of Socio-Scientific Issues: A Science Media Centre of Japan Perspective." In *Lessons from Fukushima: Japanese Case Studies of Science, Technology, and Society*, ed. Yuko Fujigaki (Springer, 2015), 49–51.
88 Shin-ichi Kurokawa and Akemi Shima, "A Glass Badge Study That Failed and Betrayed Residents: A Study with Seven Violations of Ethical Guidelines Can Be No Ground for Government Policies." *KAGAKU* 89,2 (2019): e0017; see also Greenpeace, *On the Frontline of the Fukushima Nuclear Accident: Workers and Children Radiation Risks and Human Rights Violations*. March 2019. Pamphlet, 48.
89 Asahi Shimbun, "Radiation Doses Underestimated in Study of City in Fukushima." *The Asahi Shimbun*, January 9, 2019. www.asahi.com.
90 Kurokawa and Shima, "A Glass Badge Study That Failed and Betrayed Residents," e0021.
91 See Morimoto, *Nuclear Ghost*.
92 Takeo Doi, *The Anatomy of Dependence* (Kodansha International, 2002).
93 Yoshikuni Igarashi, *Bodies of Memory: Narratives of War in Postwar Japanese Culture, 1945–1970* (Princeton University Press, 2012), 73.
94 Harumi Befu, "Concepts of Japan, Japanese Culture, and the Japanese." In *The Cambridge Companion to Modern Japanese Culture*, ed. Yoshio Sugimoto (Cambridge University Press, 2009), 27; see also Harumi Befu, *Hegemony of Homogeneity: An Anthropological Analysis of Nihonjinron* (Trans Pacific Press, 2001).
95 The National Diet of Japan, *The Official Report of The Fukushima Nuclear Accident Independent Investigation Commission—Executive Summary* (The National Diet of Japan, 2012), 9.
96 Naoko Shimazu, "The Fukushima Report Hides Behind the Cultural Curtain." *The Guardian*, July 6, 2012. www.theguardian.com.
97 Igarashi, *Bodies of Memory*, 74.
98 Dorinne K. Kondo, *Crafting Selves: Power, Gender, and Discourses of Identity in a Japanese Workplace* (University of Chicago Press, 1990).
99 Kondo, *Crafting Selves*, 300.
100 Igarashi, *Bodies of Memory*, 74–75.
101 Igarashi, *Bodies of Memory*, 74.

CHAPTER 3. THE RISE OF CITIZEN SCIENCE
1 Rick Bonney, "Citizen Science: A Lab Tradition." *Living Bird* 15,4 (1996): 7–15.
2 Caren B. Cooper, Janis Dickinson, Tina Phillips, and Rick Bonney, "Citizen Science as a Tool for Conservation in Residential Ecosystems." *Ecology and Society* 12,2 (2007): 11. doi:10.5751/ES-02197-120211.

3   Rick Bonney, Tina B. Philips, Heidi L. Ballard, and Jody W. Enck, "Can Citizen Science Enhance Public Understanding of Science?" *Public Understanding of Science* 25,1 (2016): 2–16. doi:10.1177/0963662515607; Anne Bowser, Alex Long, Metis Meloche, Elizabeth Newbury, and Meg King, "Filling Data Gaps: A Citizen Science Solution." Science & Technology Innovation Program, Wilson Center. April 2020. www.wilsoncenter.org.
4   Gwen Ottinger, "Buckets of Resistance: Standards and the Effectiveness of Citizen Science." *Science, Technology, and Human Values* 35,2 (2010): 244–70. doi:10.1177/01622439093371.
5   Sara Ann Wylie, Kirk Jalbert, Shannon Dosemagen, and Matt Ratto, "Institutions for Civic Technoscience: How Critical Making Is Transforming Environmental Research." *The Information Society* 30 (2014): 116–26. doi:10.1080/01972243.2014.875783.
6   Alan Irwin, *Citizen Science: A Study of People, Expertise, and Sustainable Development* (Routledge, 1995), xi.
7   Ikeda, "The Construction of Risk and the Resilience of Fukushima," 154–55.
8   Vincent Ialenti, *Deep Time Reckoning: How Future Thinking Can Help Earth Now* (MIT Press, 2020), 6.
9   Kimura, *Radiation Brain Moms and Citizen Scientists*, 116.
10 Kimura, *Radiation Brain Moms and Citizen Scientists*, 116.
11 Irwin, *Citizen Science*, 108.
12 Nicolas Sternsdorff-Cisterna, *Food Safety After Fukushima: Scientific Citizenship and the Politics of Risk* (University of Hawai'i Press, 2018).
13 Sternsdorff-Cisterna, *Food Safety After Fukushima*, 3.
14 Kimura, *Radiation Brain Moms and Citizen Scientists*.
15 Kimura, *Radiation Brain Moms and Citizen Scientists*, 4.
16 Dorinne K. Kondo, *Crafting Selves: Power, Gender, and Discourses of Identity in a Japanese Workplace* (University of Chicago Press, 1990), 259.
17 Kimura, *Radiation Brain Moms and Citizen Scientists*, 25.
18 Shun'ichi Yamashita, *Fukushima terusa shitsugi ōtō* [Fukushima Terusa Q&A]. 2011. https://www.youtube.com/watch?v=M4oOX4TXh8c.
19 RFC Radio Fukushima, "Kōenkai naiyō: hōshasen to watashitachi no kenkō to no kankei" [Lecture Content: Relationship Between Radiation and Our Health]. *RFC Radio Fukushima*, March 25, 2011. www.rfc.co.jp.
20 Similar ailments have been reported in anthropological studies. See Sarah D. Phillips, "Fukushima Is Not Chernobyl? Don't Be So Sure." *Somatosphere*, March 11, 2013. http://somatosphere.net.
21 Ayaka Löschke, "A Victims' Movement Against the Termination of Housing Support for Voluntary Evacuees." *Japan Forum* 33,2 (2021): 189. doi:10.1080/09555803.2018.1552309.
22 The National Diet of Japan, *The Official Report of the Fukushima Nuclear Accident*, chapter 4, 22.
23 Fassert and Hasegawa, Shinrai Research Project, 18.

24 Löschke, "A Victims' Movement," 206.
25 Löschke, "A Victims' Movement," 191.
26 Rika Morioka, "Mother Courage: Women as Activists Between a Passive Populace and a Paralyzed Government." In *Japan Copes with Calamity: Ethnographies of the Earthquake, Tsunami, and Nuclear Disasters of March 2011*, eds. David H. Slater, Brigitte Steger, and Tom Gill (Peter Lang, 2013), 195.
27 Kondo, *Crafting Selves*, 44.
28 Slater et al., "Micro-politics of Radiation," 485.
29 Cécile Asanuma-Brice, *Fukushima, dix ans après. Sociologie d'un désastre* (Éditions de la Maison des sciences de l'homme, 2021), 137.
30 See Kimura, *Radiation Brain Moms and Citizen Scientists*, 146.
31 Donna M. Goldstein, "Experimentalité: Pharmaceutical Insights into Anthropology's Epistemologically Fractured Self." In *Medicine and the Politics of Knowledge*, ed. Susan Levine (HSRC, 2012), 121.
32 Seiji Yasumura et al., "Study Protocol for the Fukushima Health Management Survey." *Journal of Epidemiology* 22,5 (2012): 375. doi:10.2188/jea.je20120105.
33 See The National Diet of Japan, *The Official Report of the Fukushima Nuclear Accident*, chapter 4, 95–96.
34 Williamson, "Demystifying the Official Discourse on Childhood Thyroid Cancer in Fukushima," 2.
35 Murphy, *Sick Building Syndrome*, 9.
36 Kim Fortun, *Advocacy After Bhopal: Environmentalism, Disaster, New Global Orders* (University of Chicago Press, 2001), 354.
37 Fortun, *Advocacy After Bhopal*, 354.
38 UNSCEAR, Report of the United Nations Scientific Committee on the Effects of Atomic Radiation, 11–12.
39 Ellis Krauss, Kuniaki Nemoto, Robert J. Pekkanen, and Aiji Tanaka, "Party Politics, Elections, and (Mis-)trust in Japan." *Japan Forum* 29,1 (2017): 22. doi:10.1080/09555803.2016.1227352.
40 Nicholas Shapiro, "Attuning to the Chemosphere: Domestic Formaldehyde, Bodily Reasoning, and the Chemical Sublime." *Cultural Anthropology* 30,3 (2015): 374. doi:10.14506/ca30.3.02.
41 Rika Morioka, "Gender Difference in Risk Perception Following the Fukushima Nuclear Plant Disaster." *Fukushima Global Communication Programme Working Paper Series* 12 (2015): 2. https://collections.unu.edu.
42 Thomas Feldhoff, "Visual Representations of Radiation Risk and the Question of Public (Mis-)Trust in Post-Fukushima Japan." *Societies* 8,2 (2018): 10. doi:10.3390/soc8020032.
43 Feldhoff, "Visual Representations of Radiation Risk," 10.
44 Akiko Hemmi and Ian Graham, "Hacker Science versus Closed Science: Building Environmental Monitoring Infrastructure." *Information, Communication & Society* 17,7 (2014): 833. doi:10.1080/1369118X.2013.848918.
45 For the cleaning of monitoring posts see: Morris-Suzuki, "Touching the Grass."

46 IAEA, *The Fukushima Daiichi Accident*, 89.
47 Noboru Takamura, *Getting to Know the Current Situation of Fukushima*. Tourism Exchange Center of Fukushima Prefecture. N.d. Pamphlet, 4.
48 Consumer Affairs Agency, *Current Situation of Foods in Japan: Basic Information on Radioactive Materials in the Standard Limits of Japanese Foods and Ways of Measuring the Radiation*. Government of Japan. September 2013. Pamphlet, 4.
49 Sternsdorff-Cisterna, *Food Safety After Fukushima*; Kimura, *Radiation Brain Moms and Citizen Scientists*.
50 For a similar point see The National Diet of Japan, *The Official Report of the Fukushima Nuclear Accident*, chapter 4, 93.
51 Nicolas Sternsdorff-Cisterna, "Food After Fukushima: Risk and Scientific Citizenship in Japan." *American Anthropologist* 117,3 (2015): 457. doi:10.1111/aman.12294.
52 Panagia, "'Partage du Sensible,'" 96.
53 Panagia, "'Partage du Sensible,'" 96.
54 *Japanese Dictionary Takoboto*, version 1.6.6.
55 Daniel J. Blackburn et al., "Occurrence of Thyroid Papillary Carcinoma in Young Patients: A Chernobyl Connection?" *Journal of Pediatric Endocrinology and Metabolism* 14,5 (2001): 503–6. doi:10.1515/jpem.2001.14.5.503; Luc A. Michel and Julian E. Donckier, "Thyroid Cancer 15 Years After Chernobyl." *The Lancet* 359,9321 (2002): 1947. doi:10.1016/S0140-6736(02)08754-8.
56 I use the term "politics of victimization" to differentiate the network's understanding of postdisaster recovery from the mainstream "politics of revitalization," which is more closely associated with state policies.
57 Jonathan A. Cole, "The Right to Demand: Citizen Activism and Environmental Politics in Japan." *Journal of Environment & Development* 3,2 (1994): 78. doi:10.1177/1070496594003002.
58 Akira Kurihara, *Shōgen minamatabyō* [Testimony of Minamata Disease] (Iwanami Shoten, 2000); Akihiro Ogawa, "The New Prominence of the Civil Sector in Japan." In *Routledge Handbook of Japanese Culture and Society*, eds. Victoria Lyon Bestor, Theodore C. Bestor, and Akiko Yamagata (Routledge, 2011), 194.
59 Leblanc, *Bicycle Citizens*; Kimura, *Radiation Brain Moms and Citizen Scientists*, 117.
60 Scott Schnell, "The Rural Imaginary: Landscape, Village, Tradition." In *A Companion to the Anthropology of Japan*, ed. Jennifer Robertson (Blackwell Publishing, 2008), 215.
61 See Leblanc, *Bicycle Citizens*, 63; Kimura, *Radiation Brain Moms and Citizen Scientists*, 117.
62 Kimura, *Radiation Brain Moms and Citizen Scientists*, 24.
63 Stefanie Graeter, "To Revive an Abundant Life: Catholic Science and Neoextractivist Politics in Peru's Mantaro Valley." *Cultural Anthropology* 32,1 (2017): 119. doi:10.14506/ca32.1.09.
64 Graeter, "To Revive an Abundant Life," 121.
65 See Tsing, *Friction*, chapter 4.
66 Mathews, *Instituting Nature*, 23.

67 Löschke, "A Victims' Movement," 190.
68 Löschke, "A Victims' Movement," 190.
69 Löschke, "A Victims' Movement," 206.
70 Asahi Shinbun, "Fukkō-shō 'jiko sekinin' hatsugen, yatō ga hihan yotō kanbu mo kugen" [The Ruling Party and Opposition Criticized the Reconstruction Minister's "Self-Responsibility" Remark]. *Asahi Shinbun*, April 5, 2017. www.asahi.com.
71 Ellen G. Garvey, "'facts and FACTS': Abolitionists' Database Innovations." In *"Raw Data" Is an Oxymoron*, ed. Lisa Gitelman (MIT Press, 2013), 91.
72 Garvey, "'facts and FACTS,'" 91.
73 Hiroshima Peace Memorial Museum, "Let's Look at the Special Exhibit." Hiroshima Peace Site. 2007. www.pcf.city.hiroshima.jp.
74 Kyoko Sato, "What the Bomb Has Done: Victim Relief, Knowledge, and Politics." In *Living in a Nuclear World*, eds. Bernadette Bensaude-Vincent, Soraya Boudia, and Kyoko Sato (Routledge, 2022), 27.
75 Löschke, "A Victims' Movement," 195.
76 Sato, "What the Bomb Has Done," 27.
77 See in particular Kondo, *Crafting Selves*.
78 Morioka, "Mother Courage," 198.
79 Kimura, *Radiation Brain Moms and Citizen Scientists*, 26.
80 Abu-Lughod, "The Romance of Resistance," 47.
81 Löschke, "A Victims' Movement," 193 (author's emphasis).
82 According to the Takoboto Japanese dictionary (version 1.9.8), there are multiple meanings to the word "*seishin*": "mind, spirit, soul, heart, ethos, attitude, mentality, will, intention, spirit (of a matter), essence, fundamental significance." What the individual in question tried to convey was that the ethos of Japanese society, or the attitude of Japanese citizens, had changed for the worse after the Fukushima nuclear disaster.
83 Karen Brodkin, "Remember When Writing Was Fun? Why Academics Should Go on a Low Syllable, Active Voice Diet." In *Anthropology off the Shelf: Anthropologists on Writing*, eds. Alisse Waterston and Maria D. Vesperi (Blackwell, 2009), 33 (original emphasis).
84 Ortner, "Resistance and the Problem of Ethnographic Refusal," 191.

CHAPTER 4. EVERYTHING IS UNDER CONTROL

1 Scott Frickel and M. Bess Vincent, "Hurricane Katrina, Contamination, and the Unintended Organization of Ignorance." *Technology in Society* 29,2 (2007): 183. doi:10.1016/j.techsoc.2007.01.007.
2 Frickel and Bess Vincent, "Hurricane Katrina," 184.
3 Mary Douglas, *Purity and Danger: An Analysis of Concepts of Pollution and Taboo* (Routledge Classics, 2002), 3.
4 Douglas, *Purity and Danger*, 44.
5 See Peter C. van Wyck, *Signs of Danger: Waste, Trauma, and Nuclear Threat* (University of Minnesota Press, 2005); Joshua Reno, "Waste and Waste Manage-

ment." *Annual Review of Anthropology* 44 (2015): 558. doi:10.1146/annurev-anthro-102214-014146; Murphy, "Alterlife and Decolonial Chemical Relations"; Vincent Ialenti, "Drum Breach: Operational Temporalities, Error Politics, and WIPP's Kitty Litter Nuclear Waste Accident." *Social Studies of Science* 51,3 (2021): 364–91. doi:10.1177/0306312720986609; Bond, "Contamination in Theory and Protest."

6   Max Liboiron, Manuel Tironi, and Nerea Calvillo, "Toxic Politics: Acting in a Permanently Polluted World." *Social Studies of Science* 48,3 (2018): 332. doi:10.1177/0306312718783087.
7   Sternsdorff-Cisterna, *Food Safety After Fukushima*, 101.
8   Champion et al., "The IRSN's Earliest Assessments of the Fukushima Accident's Consequences," 11; Sternsdorff-Cisterna, *Food Safety After Fukushima*, 101.
9   Champion et al., "The IRSN's Earliest Assessments of the Fukushima Accident's Consequences," 30; Nuclear Emergency Response Headquarters, "Progress of the 'Roadmap for Immediate Actions for the Assistance of Residents Affected by the Nuclear Incident.'" November 17, 2011. www.meti.go.jp.
10 Plokhy, *Atoms and Ashes*, 269.
11 CEC, *Fukushimaken kankyō sōzō sentā—kankyō hōshasen sentā* [Fukushima Prefecture Center for Environmental Creation—Environmental Radiation Monitoring Center]. 4th edition. April 2017. Pamphlet, 1.
12 CEC, *Kankyō sōzō sentā—Fukushima no kankyō kaifuku sōzō ni mukete* [Center for Environmental Creation: Aiming for Environmental Recovery and Creation in Fukushima]. N.d. Pamphlet, 6.
13 CEC, *Kankyō sōzō sentā*, 6.
14 CEC, *Fukushimaken kankyō sōzō sentā—kankyō hōshasen sentā* [Fukushima Prefecture Center for Environmental Creation—Environmental Radiation Monitoring Center]. 3rd edition. April 2016. Pamphlet, 1.
15 *Dairokkai hōshasen keisoku fōramu Fukushima*. [Sixth "Radiation Measurement Forum Fukushima"], July 5, 2016, Kyoto University, Tokyo office. Organizer: Japan Society for the Promotion of Science # 186 Committee; *Hōshanō josen no tame no kokusai shinpojiumu* [International Symposium on Decontamination of Radioactive Materials], July 8, 2016, Fukushima Prefecture Cultural Center. Organizer: The Society for Remediation of Radioactive Contamination in Environment. Sponsored by: MOE.
16 Joseph Masco, "Nuclear Technoaesthetics: Sensory Politics from Trinity to the Virtual Bomb in Los Alamos." *American Ethnologist* 31,3 (2004): 350. doi:10.1525/ae.2004.31.3.349.
17 "Monitor (n.)." *Online Etymology Dictionary*. N.d., accessed February 4, 2025. www.etymonline.com.
18 Li, *The Will to Improve*, 126.
19 Bruno Latour, *Politics of Nature: How to Bring the Sciences into Democracy* (Harvard University Press, 2004), 24, 22 (original emphasis).
20 Latour, *Politics of Nature*, 22.

21 Cabinet Office, *Designating and Rearranging the Areas of Evacuation*; METI, *Practical Operations for Designating Areas to Which Evacuation Orders Have Been Issued as Newly Designated Areas*. 2012. www.meti.go.jp; Fukushima on the Globe, "Evacuation Orders and Restricted Areas."
22 Reconstruction Agency, "Genshiryoku saigai kara no fukkō saisei" [Recovery and Revitalization from the Nuclear Disaster]. N.d., accessed October 5, 2023. www.reconstruction.go.jp.
23 See Sezin Topçu, "Catastrophes nucléaires et 'normalisation' des zones contaminées: Enjeux politiques, économiques, sanitaire, démocratiques et éthiques." *Les Notes de la FEP* 8 (Mai 2016): 1–12.
24 For a similar argument see Fassert and Hasegawa, Shinrai Research Project, 108.
25 MOE, *Act on Special Measures Concerning the Handling of Environment Pollution by Radioactive Materials Discharged by the NPS Accident Associated with the Tohoku District—Off the Pacific Ocean Earthquake That Occurred on March 11, 2011.* November 11, 2011. http://josen.env.go.jp.
26 MOE, "Measures for Decontamination of Radioactive Materials Discharged by TEPCO'S Fukushima Daiichi NPS Accident. Off-site Decontamination Measures." N.d., accessed February 22, 2016. http://josen.env.go.jp.
27 MOE, *Progress on Off-site Cleanup and Interim Storage in Japan*. January 2016. Pamphlet, 5.
28 MOE, "Special Decontamination Areas and Intensive Contamination Survey Areas." 2022. www.env.go.jp.
29 While the state often refers to radioactive contamination as a problem restricted to Fukushima, the creation of Intensive Contamination Survey Areas is an indirect acknowledgment of wider radioactive contamination throughout Japan. It is especially interesting to note that Tokyo does not fall within the jurisdiction of such areas, though it faced contamination. Symbolically speaking, this demonstrates that the capital of Japan cannot be considered "contaminated."
30 Fukushima Prefectural Government, *Steps for Revitalization in Fukushima. Revitalization and Comprehensive Planning Division, Planning and Coordination Department*. 2016. Pamphlet, 14.
31 MOE, *What Does "Recycling of Removed Soil" Mean?* October 2022. Pamphlet, 1. http://josen.env.go.jp.
32 MOE, *Progress on Off-site Cleanup*, 13.
33 Cited from Fassert and Hasegawa, Shinrai Research Project, 108.
34 Fassert and Hasegawa, Shinrai Research Project, 108.
35 MOE, *Shirabete nattoku hōshasen* [Investigating Radiation]. Fukushima Environmental Recovery Office. 2014. Pamphlet, 8.
36 Japan Guide, "Fukushima Prefecture." N.d., accessed October 1, 2022. www.japan-guide.com.
37 MOE, *Progress on Off-site Cleanup*, 9.

38 Fukushima Booklet Publication Committee, *10 Lessons from Fukushima: Reducing Risk and Protecting Communities from Nuclear Disasters*. 2015. Pamphlet, 9.
39 Champion et al., "The IRSN's Earliest Assessments of the Fukushima Accident's Consequences," 30.
40 Alexey V. Yablokov, "What the World Health Organization, International Atomic Energy Agency, and International Commission on Radiological Protection Have Falsified." In *Crisis Without End: The Medical and Ecological Consequences of the Fukushima Nuclear Catastrophe*, ed. Helen Caldicott (The New Press, 2014), 108; see also Jian Zheng et al., "Isotopic Evidence of Plutonium Release into the Environment from the Fukushima DNPP Accident." *Scientific Reports* 2,304 (2012): 1–8. doi:10.1038/srep00304.
41 Ryohei Ikehara et al., "Novel Method of Quantifying Radioactive Cesium-Rich Microparticles (CsMPs) in the Environment from the Fukushima Daiichi Nuclear Power Plant." *Environmental Science & Technology* 52,11 (2018): 6390–98. doi:10.1021/acs.est.7b06693.
42 See Physics World, "Fukushima May Have Scattered Plutonium Widely." *Physics World*, July 20, 2020. www.physicsworld.com; see also Science Daily, "New Evidence of Nuclear Fuel Releases Found at Fukushima," *Science Daily*, February 28, 2018. www.sciencedaily.com.
43 Pierre Le Hir and Philippe Mesmer, "L'accident de Fukushima a dispersé des 'billes' de césium radioactif jusqu'à Tokyo." *Le Monde*, July 6, 2016. www.lemonde.fr (author's translation).
44 Murphy, *Sick Building Syndrome*.
45 Frickel and Bess Vincent, "Hurricane Katrina," 184.
46 Sugita Hall, Saitama, Warabi. June 2016.
47 See BioTrend, "Autoradiography Standards." N.d., accessed October 6, 2023. www.biotrend.com.
48 Satoshi Mori, *Hōshasen-zō—hōshanō o kashika suru* [Radiographic Image: Visualizing Radioactivity]. 2016. Pamphlet.
49 Autoradiograph. N.d., accessed November 4, 2022. www.autoradiograph.org/e.
50 Given at Bunkō-ku akademī meidai, March 13, 2016.
51 Kagaya Masamichi and Satoshi Mori, *Hōshasen-zō hōshanō o kashika suru* [Radiographic Images: Visualizing Radioactivity] (Kōseisha, 2015).
52 Marilyn Ivy, *Discourses of the Vanishing: Modernity, Phantasm, Japan* (University of Chicago Press, 1995), 165.
53 *3/11 shinpojiumu fukushima o wasurenai ~ Fukushima daiichi genpatsujiko kara 5-nen, cherunobuiri genpatsujiko kara 30-nen* [3/11 Symposium, Let's Not Forget Fukushima—5 Years Since the Fukushima Dai'ichi Nuclear Accident, 30 Years Since Chernobyl], March 11, 2015, House of Councillors, Tokyo.
54 For the limit of decontamination see also The National Diet of Japan, *The Official Report of the Fukushima Nuclear Accident*, section 4.5.2.

55 *Kaku to hibaku wo nakusu sekai shakai forum 2016—Zenjitsu fōramu kaisai* [From No Nukes World Social Forum 2016: Full Day Forum], March 27, 2016, Korean YMCA, Tokyo; see also his memoir: Minoru Ikeda, *Fukushima genpatsu sagyō-in no ki* [Memories of a Fukushima Nuclear Power Plant Worker] (Hachigatsu Shokan, 2016).

56 Olivier Evrard, Patrick Laceby, and Atsushi Nakao, "Effectiveness of Landscape Decontamination Following the Fukushima Nuclear Accident: A Review." *Soil* 5,2 (2019): 333–50. doi:10.5194/soil-5-333-2019.

57 From *Hōshanō josen no tame no kokusai shinpojiumu*.

58 Evrard et al., "Effectiveness of Landscape Decontamination," 333.

59 MOE, *Inoshishi kara taisetsu na ie wo mamoru: Hisaichi no inoshishi taisaku* [Let's Protect Our Home from Wild Boars: Wild Boars Measures in Disaster Areas]. Wildlife Division. 2015. Pamphlet.

60 Nancy Rosenberger, "Japanese Organic Farmers: Strategies of Uncertainty After the Fukushima Disaster." *Ethnos* 81,1 (2016): 12. doi:10.1080/00141844.2014.900101; see also Tom Gill, "This Spoiled Soil: Place, People, and Community in an Irradiated Village in Fukushima Prefecture." In *Japan Copes with Calamity: Ethnographies of the Earthquake, Tsunami, and Nuclear Disasters of March 2011*, eds. David H. Slater, Brigitte Steger, and Tom Gill (Peter Lang, 2013), 201–33.

61 Cécile Asanuma-Brice, Olivier Evrard, and Thomas Chalaux, "Why Did So Few Refugees Return to the Fukushima Fallout–Impacted Region After Remediation? An Interdisciplinary Case Study from Iitate Village, Japan." *International Journal of Disaster Risk Reduction* 85,1 (2023): 103498. doi:10.1016/j.ijdrr.2022.103498.

62 Jonah Fontela, "Tokyo Olympic Torch Relay Begins Four-Month Journey." April 22, 2021. https://olympics.com.

63 MOE, *What Does "Recycling of Removed Soil" Mean?*, 6.

64 Kengo Kikuyama, "Contaminated Soil Piles Up in Vast Fukushima Cleanup Project." *NHK*, March 18, 2022. www3.nhk.or.jp.

65 MOE, *What Does "Recycling of Removed Soil" Mean?*, 5.

66 Tokyo Shinbun, "Osen tsuchi no 'sairiyō' ha susumu no ka?" [Will the "Reuse" of Contaminated Soil Progress?]. *Tokyo Shinbun*, July 19, 2021. www.tokyo-np.co.jp.

67 Shin Watanabe, "Disposing of Fukushima's Contaminated Soil." *NHK World*, March 10, 2019. www3.nhk.or.jp.

68 MOE, *What Does "Recycling of Removed Soil" Mean?*, 21.

69 MOE, *The Usage of Removed Soil from Fukushima Prefecture in MOE Office*. 2020. Pamphlet, 1.

70 Douglas, *Purity and Danger*, 44.

CHAPTER 5. COMMODIFIABLE PHANTASM

1 Jennifer Robertson, "Furusato Japan: The Culture and Politics of Nostalgia." *International Journal of Politics, Culture, and Society* 1,4 (1988): 494. www.jstor.org.

2 Gill, "This Spoiled Soil," 202.

3   Cabinet Office of Japan, "Five Years Down the Road to Reconstruction." *Highlighting Japan* 96 (2016): 19.
4   METI, *Fukushima de, hajimatte iru koto* [What Is Happening in Fukushima]. *METI Journal*, February/March 2015, 5.
5   Kathleen Stewart, "Nostalgia: A Polemic." *Cultural Anthropology* 3,3 (1988): 227.
6   See Robertson, "Furusato Japan," 494; Dusinberre and Aldrich, "Hatoko Comes Home," 696; Gill, "This Spoiled Soil," 201.
7   Schnell, "The Rural Imaginary," 213.
8   Millie Creighton, "Consuming Rural Japan: The Marketing of Tradition and Nostalgia in the Japanese Travel Industry." *Ethnology* 36,3 (1997): 239. doi:10.2307/3773988; see also Robertson, "Furusato Japan," 494.
9   See Gill, "This Spoiled Soil," 201–2; Ivy, *Discourses of the Vanishing*.
10 I would like to thank an anonymous reviewer of *Ethnos* for underscoring this point.
11 Yoshiaki Nohara, "Rural 'Furusato Nozei' Beer, Beef Thank-Yous Costing Urban Japan Much-Needed Revenues." *The Japan Times*, January 13, 2017. www.japantimes.co.jp.
12 Dusinberre and Aldrich, "Hatoko Comes Home," 701.
13 Tim Choy, *Ecologies of Comparison: An Ethnography of Endangerment in Hong Kong* (Duke University Press, 2011), 48.
14 Choy, *Ecologies of Comparison*, 49.
15 Creighton, "Consuming Rural Japan," 239.
16 Creighton, "Consuming Rural Japan," 242.
17 Ivy, *Discourses of the Vanishing*, 26.
18 Robertson, "Furusato Japan," 496.
19 Dusinberre and Aldrich, "Hatoko Comes Home," 701–2.
20 Karl Marx, *Capital*. Volume 1, *A Critique of Political Economy* (Penguin Classics, 1992).
21 Benoît Heilbrunn, *La consommation et ses sociologies* (Armand Colin, 2020), 109 (author's translation).
22 Ivy, *Discourses of the Vanishing*, 22.
23 Masco, *The Nuclear Borderlands*, 15.
24 Ivy, *Discourses of the Vanishing*.
25 Higashinihon daishinsai 5-shūnen fukkō fōramu, aratana sutēji fukkō sōsei e [Great East Japan Earthquake Fifth Anniversary Reconstruction Forum: Toward a New Stage of the Reconstruction/Creation], June 6, 2016, Iino Hall and Conference Center, Tokyo.
26 For a full Japanese transcript see: Reconstruction Agency. Higashinihon daishinsai 5-shūnen fukkō fōramu [Great East Japan Earthquake Fifth Anniversary Reconstruction Forum]. June 2016. www.reconstruction.go.jp.
27 Reconstruction Agency, *Eliminating Negative Reputation Impact: Reconstruction from Nuclear Disaster and the History of Safety and Revitalization of Fukushima*. 2016. Pamphlet, 4.

28 Nemoto, "For Accelerating the Reconstruction from the Great East Japan Earthquake," 16.
29 Reconstruction Agency, *The Tohoku Coastal Areas Were No Longer What They Used to Be*. N.d., accessed April 18, 2016. Pamphlet, 7. www.reconstruction.go.jp.
30 NPO hōjin chiiki gakushū purattofōmu kenkyūkai, *Furusato o manabu kodomo-tachi/furusato o tsutaeru kōrei-sha no deban-dzukuri* [Children Learning Their Hometown/Creating a Turn for the Elderly to Convey Their Hometown]. 2013. www.reconstruction.go.jp.
31 Reconstruction Agency, "Atarashī Tōhoku"—sakubun kontesuto—sakuhin bunshū ["New Tōhoku"—Composition Contest—Collection of Works]. 2016. www.reconstruction.go.jp.
32 Reconstruction Agency, *"Kokoro no fukkō" jigyō no jisshi ni tsuite* [About the Implementation of "Reconstruction of Heart" Business]. 2015. www.reconstruction.go.jp.
33 Reconstruction Agency, *Dentō no "shimimochi" o mamori, jisedai e* [Protecting the Traditional "Frozen-Mochi" and Passing It to the Next Generation]. 2019. www.reconstruction.go.jp.
34 Reconstruction Agency, *Atarashii tōhoku: sendō moderu jireishū vol. 2* [New Tōhoku Model Case Book vol. 2]. Reconstruction Agency, Comprehensive Policy Group. February 2016.
35 Reconstruction Agency, *Min'na de jitsugen! Omoshiro aidia* [Realized By All: Interesting Ideas!]. March 2019. Pamphlet, 16. www.reconstruction.go.jp.
36 Reconstruction Agency, *Min'na de jitsugen!*, 22.
37 Lindsey A. Freeman, *Longing for the Bomb: Oak Ridge and Atomic Nostalgia* (University of North Carolina Press, 2015), 41.
38 Robertson, "Furusato Japan," 494.
39 See Reconstruction Agency, *Sutātoappu kigyō* [Start-Up Business]. 2016. www.reconstruction.go.jp.
40 Reconstruction Agency, *Min'na de jitsugen!*, 15.
41 Reconstruction Agency, *Current Status of Reconstruction and Challenges*. March 2016. Pamphlet, 2. www.reconstruction.go.jp.
42 Benedict Anderson, *Imagined Communities: Reflections on the Origin and Spread of Nationalism* (Verso Books, 2006).
43 Robertson, "Furusato Japan," 496.
44 Fukushima Innovation Coast Promotion Organization, "Fukushima Innovation Coast Framework." N.d., accessed April 11, 2022. www.fipo.or.jp.
45 METI, *Fukushima de, hajimatte iru koto*, 12.
46 Robertson, "Furusato Japan," 500.
47 For more on *madei* see Gill, "This Spoiled Soil," 209.
48 Madei Garden Village, "Michinoeki Madeikan English Guide." N.d., accessed April 13, 2022. http://madeikan.com.
49 Japan Times, "Gutted Fukushima Shrine's Famed Wolf Paintings Reproduced." *Japan Times*, November 8, 2016. www.japantimes.co.jp.

50 Ivy, *Discourses of the Vanishing*, 65.
51 MOE, "Measures for Decontamination of Radioactive Materials."
52 Fukushima Booklet Publication Committee, *10 Lessons from Fukushima*, 40.
53 MOE, "Measures for Decontamination of Radioactive Materials."
54 See Jacques E. C. Hymans, "After Fukushima: Veto Players and Japanese Nuclear Policy." In *Japan: The Precarious Future*, eds. Anne Allison and Frank Baldwin (New York University Press, 2015), 110–38.
55 Greenpeace, *On the Frontline of the Fukushima Nuclear Accident*, 7.
56 Fukushima Booklet Publication Committee, *10 Lessons from Fukushima*, 40.
57 METI, "METI Selected a Successful Applicant for the Subsidy Project for the Contaminated Water Issue (Large-Scale Demonstration Project of Multi-Nuclide Removal Equipment with Superior Performance)." 2016. www.meti.go.jp.
58 Erik Swyngedouw, "Apocalypse Forever? Post-political Populism and the Spectre of Climate Change." *Theory, Culture & Society* 27,2–3 (2010): 220. doi:10.1177/0263276409358728.
59 Klein, *The Shock Doctrine*.
60 Masco, *The Nuclear Borderlands*, 22.
61 Masco, *The Nuclear Borderlands*, 22.
62 Alf Hornborg, "Objects Don't Have Desires: Toward an Anthropology of Technology Beyond Anthropomorphism." *American Anthropologist* 123,4 (2021): 761. doi:10.1111/aman.13628.
63 See Fassert and Hasegawa, Shinrai Research Project, 28; Morimoto, *Nuclear Ghost*, 85.
64 Fassert and Hasegawa, Shinrai Research Project, 28.
65 Allison, *Precarious Japan*, 14.
66 See Dusinberre and Aldrich, "Hatoko Comes Home," 696; Kainuma, *Fukushimaron*.
67 Robertson, "Furusato Japan," 495.
68 Berlant, *Cruel Optimism*, 180.
69 Gill, "This Spoiled Soil," 202.
70 Freeman, *Longing for the Bomb*, 39.
71 Fortun, *Advocacy After Bhopal*, 10.
72 Allison, *Precarious Japan*, 174.
73 Ivy, *Discourses of the Vanishing*, 104.
74 Ivy, *Discourses of the Vanishing*, 23.
75 Petryna, *Life Exposed*, 73.
76 For more on this difference see Sternsdorff-Cisterna, "Food After Fukushima," 457.
77 Marx, *Capital*, vol. 1.
78 Petryna, *Life Exposed*.
79 See Ivy, *Discourses of the Vanishing*; Creighton, "Consuming Rural Japan."
80 Freeman, *Longing for the Bomb*, 41.
81 Freeman, *Longing for the Bomb*, 41.

82 Machiko Kusahara, "The Panorama in Meiji Japan: Horizontal and Vertical Perspectives." *Early Popular Visual Culture* 18,4 (2020): 400–421. doi:10.1080/17460654.2021.2016212.
83 Kusahara, "The Panorama in Meiji Japan."
84 Kuchinskaya, *The Politics of Invisibility*, 81.
85 I would like to thank an anonymous reviewer of the journal *Ethnos* for underscoring this important point.
86 Ivy, *Discourses of the Vanishing*.
87 I would like to thank an anonymous reviewer of the journal *Ethnos* for underscoring this important point.
88 Ivy, *Discourses of the Vanishing*, 103.
89 See William Cronon, ed., *Uncommon Ground: Rethinking the Human Place in Nature* (Norton, 1996).

CHAPTER 6. POSTPOLITICAL UNCERTAINTIES

This chapter first appeared as: Maxime Polleri, "Post-political Uncertainties: Governing Nuclear Controversies in Post-Fukushima Japan." *Social Studies of Science* 50,4 (2020): 567–88. doi:10.1177/0306312719889405. It was revised for this manuscript.

1 The quotations and explanations that follow are derived from two lecture series: Kōreberu hōshaseihaikibutsu no saishū shobun zenkoku shinpojiumu [ima aratamete kangaeyō chisō shobun] kagakuteki yūbōchi no teiji ni mukete [National Symposium on the Final Disposal Site of High-Level Radioactive Waste: Rethinking the Geological Disposal Now; Toward the Presentation of Scientific Promising Area], May 9, 2016, Otemachi Sankei Plaza Hall, Tokyo. Sponsor: METI and NUMO; Zenkoku shinpojiumu [ima aratamete kangaeyō chisō shobun] kagaku-teki tokusei mappu no teiji ni mukete [National Symposium: Rethinking the Geological Disposal Now; Toward the Presentation of the Scientific Characteristics Map], June 17, 2017, JA Building, Hiroshima. Sponsor: METI and NUMO.
2 Kingston, "After 3.11," 7.
3 See METI, "Supporting the Reconstruction of Fukushima." *METI Journal* Special Report (February/March 2014). www.meti.go.jp; METI, "What Is Progressing in Fukushima." *METI Journal* Feature 1 (March 2015). www.meti.go.jp.
4 See Swyngedouw, "The Antinomies of the Postpolitical City," 601–20.
5 Swyngedouw, "The Antinomies of the Postpolitical City," 601.
6 Swyngedouw, "The Antinomies of the Postpolitical City," 609; see also Swyngedouw, "Apocalypse Forever?"
7 Button, *Disaster Culture*, 16.
8 See Button, *Disaster Culture*; David Michaels, *Doubt Is Their Product: How Industry's Assault on Science Threatens Your Health* (Oxford University Press, 2008); Robert N. Proctor, "Agnotology: A Missing Term to Describe the Cultural Production of Ignorance (and Its Study)." In *Agnotology: The Making and*

Unmaking of Ignorance, eds. Robert N. Proctor and Londa Schiebinger (Stanford University Press, 2008), 1–36.

9 Andrew S. Mathews, "Scandals, Audits, and Fictions: Linking Climate Change to Mexican Forests." *Social Studies of Science* 44,1 (2014): 84. doi:10.1177/0306312713490330.

10 Sarah J. Whatmore, "Mapping Knowledge Controversies: Science, Democracy, and the Redistribution of Expertise." *Progress in Human Geography* 33,5 (2009): 588. doi:10.1177/0309132509339841.

11 Robert N. Proctor, *Cancer Wars: How Politics Shapes What We Know and Don't Know About Cancer* (Basic Book, 1995), 8.

12 Andrew DeWit, "Japan's Energy Policy Impasse." *Asia-Pacific Journal* 12,14,1 (2014). https://apjjf.org; Kawato, "Sécurité nucléaire et avenir de l'énergie."

13 Kiyoshi Kurokawa, *Kisei no toriko: Gurūpushinku ga nihon o horobosu* [Regulatory Capture: 'Groupthinking' Will Destroy Japan] (Kōdansha, 2016); Nakamura and Kikuchi, "What We Know, and What We Have Not Yet Learned."

14 Hymans, "After Fukushima."

15 See Kimura, *Radiation Brain Moms and Citizen Scientists*; Sternsdorff-Cisterna. *Food Safety after Fukushima*.

16 Sheila Jasanoff and Sang-Hyun Kim, "Containing the Atom: Sociotechnical Imaginaries and Nuclear Power in the United States and South Korea." *Minerva* 47 (2009): 119. doi:10.1007/s11024-009-9124-4.

17 Hideyuki Hirakawa and Masashi Shirabe, "Rhetorical Marginalization of Science and Democracy: Politics in Risk Discourse on Radioactive Risks in Japan." In *Lessons from Fukushima: Japanese Case Studies of Science, Technology, and Society*, ed. Yuko Fujigaki (Springer, 2015), 61; Asanuma-Brice. *Fukushima, dix ans après*, 119.

18 Yoko Fujigaki, "The Processes Through Which Nuclear Power Plants Are Embedded in Political, Economic, and Social Contexts in Japan." In *Lessons from Fukushima: Japanese Case Studies of Science, Technology, and Society*, ed. Yoko Fujigaki (Springer, 2015), 7–25; Suganuma, "Tepco and Nuclear Energy Politics."

19 Jasanoff and Kim, "Containing the Atom," 120.

20 Jasanoff and Kim, "Containing the Atom," 119.

21 Jasanoff and Kim, "Containing the Atom," 123.

22 Jasanoff and Kim, "Containing the Atom," 122.

23 As Yuko Kawato summarizes, "NISA, which regulated nuclear energy, was part of METI, which promotes the nuclear energy industry. NSC, which is responsible for consulting on nuclear security and verifying the action of NISA, depended on the cabinet office, itself subservient to the ministries promoting nuclear energy." Kawato, "Sécurité nucléaire et avenir de l'énergie," 472 (author's translation).

24 Nakamura and Kikuchi, "What We Know, and What We Have Not Yet Learned," 896.

25 David Batty, "Japan Shuts Down Last Working Nuclear Reactor." *The Guardian*, May 5, 2012. www.theguardian.com.

26 Kingston, "Japan's Nuclear Village," 9.
27 Hymans, "After Fukushima," 115.
28 Naoyuki Mikami, "Public Participation in Decision-Making on Energy Policy: The Case of the 'National Discussion' After the Fukushima Accident." In *Lessons from Fukushima: Japanese Case Studies of Science, Technology, and Society*, ed. Yuko Fujigaki (Springer, 2015), 87–122.
29 Mikami, "Public Participation in Decision-Making on Energy Policy," 88.
30 Mikami, "Public Participation in Decision-Making on Energy Policy," 115; Vivoda and Graetz, "Nuclear Policy and Regulation in Japan," 501–2.
31 Kingston, "After 3.11," 4.
32 See Fassert and Hasegawa, Shinrai Research Project, 19; Cabinet Office, *Designating and Rearranging the Areas of Evacuation*; METI, "Supporting the Reconstruction of Fukushima." *METI Journal* Special Report (February/March 2014). www.meti.go.jp.
33 METI, Japan's Challenges Towards Recovery. March 2012. www.meti.go.jp.
34 The following quotations and explanations are derived from two symposiums: Shigen no nai nihon, shōrai enerugī no sugata ni kansuru shinpojiumu [Japan Without Resources: A Symposium Toward the Shape of Our Future Energy], March 16, 2016, Fukui Public Hall, Fukui Prefecture. Sponsor: METI, Agency for Natural Resources and Energy; Shigen no nai nihon, shōrai enerugī no sugata ni kansuru shinpojiumu [Japan Without Resources: A Symposium Toward the Shape of Our Future Energy], June 13, 2016, Hyogo Prefectural Civic Center, Kobe. Sponsor: METI, Agency for Natural Resources and Energy.
35 METI, "Leading the Asian Market Through the 'Enevolution' Initiative." *METI Journal* Feature 1 (November 2015): 4. www.meti.go.jp.
36 Hymans, "After Fukushima," 121.
37 See Government of Japan, *Economic Impact of the Great East Japan Earthquake and Current Status of Recovery*. 2011. Pamphlet, 16–17.
38 Philippe Pelletier, *La fascination du Japon: Idées reçues sur l'archipel japonais* (Le Cavalier Bleu, 2018), 114 (author's translation).
39 See METI, "Exploring Japan in 2050." *METI Journal* Feature 1 (July 2015): 5. www.meti.go.jp; METI, "Leading the Asian Market," 5.
40 Kawato, " Sécurité nucléaire et avenir de l'énergie," 478 (author's translation).
41 Vivoda and Geordan, "Nuclear Policy and Regulation in Japan," 494.
42 Bruno Latour, *We Have Never Been Modern* (Harvard University Press, 1993); Swyngedouw, "The Antinomies of the Postpolitical City," 613.
43 See Pelletier, *La fascination du Japon*, 137 (author's translation).
44 METI, *Mission of METI*. N.d., accessed January 15, 2016. Pamphlet, 7. www.meti.go.jp.
45 Low, *Visualizing Nuclear Power in Japan*, 206.
46 See Hiromi Mizuno, *Science for the Empire: Scientific Nationalism in Modern Japan* (Stanford University Press, 2009).
47 DeWit, "Japan's Energy Policy Impasse," 1.

48 Agence France-Presse, "Jeunes professionnels du nucléaire au Japon, un profil à contre-courant." *MSN*, December 21, 2022. www.msn.com.
49 Low, *Visualizing Nuclear Power in Japan*, 25.
50 Swyngedouw, "The Antinomies of the Postpolitical City," 601.
51 Martina Igini, "Gas and Nuclear Turn Green as EU Parliament Approves New Taxonomy." *Earth*, October 13, 2022. https://earth.org.
52 METI, "Japan's 14 Priority Areas for Carbon Neutrality by 2050." December 21, 2020. www.meti.go.jp.
53 Jasanoff and Kim, "Containing the Atom," 120.
54 Sheila Jasanoff and Sang-Hyun Kim, "Sociotechnical Imaginaries and National Energy Policies." *Science as Culture* 22,2 (2013): 195. doi:10.1080/09505431.2013.786990.
55 Jasanoff and Kim, "Containing the Atom," 119.
56 Jasanoff and Kim, "Sociotechnical Imaginaries and National Energy Policies," 193.
57 Mathews, *Instituting Nature*, 4.
58 Mathews, *Instituting Nature*, 4.
59 Mitchell, *Rule of Experts*.
60 Mathews, *Instituting Nature*, 174–75.
61 Mathews, *Instituting Nature*, 23.
62 Jacques Rancière, *Disagreement* (University of Minnesota Press, 1998), 30. Cited in Swyngedouw, "The Antinomies of the Postpolitical City," 607.
63 Anne M. Fisker-Nielsen, "Grassroot Responses to the Tohoku Earthquake of 11 March 2011: Overcoming the Dichotomy Between Victim and Helper." *Anthropology Today* 28,3 (2012): 20. doi:10.1111/j.1467–8322.2012.00873.x.
64 Morioka, "Gender Difference in Risk Perception," 6.
65 Button, *Disaster Culture*, 155.
66 Contrast Harutoshi Funabashi, "Why the Fukushima Nuclear Disaster Is a Man-Made Calamity." *International Journal of Japanese Sociology* 21,1 (2012): 71. doi:10.1111/j.1475–6781.2012.01161.x.
67 Jasanoff, "The Idiom of Co-production," 1–12.
68 Carol Cohn, "Sex and Death in the Rational World of Defense Intellectuals." *Signs* 12,14 (1987): 687–718. www.jstor.org.
69 For a similar argument see Charis Thompson, "Co-producing CITES and the African Elephant." In *States of Knowledge: The Co-production of Science and Social Order*, ed. Sheila Jasanoff (Routledge, 2004), 83.
70 Mainichi Shinbun, "Tōden: josenhi futan ōjizu . . . 13 nenmatsu ikō no keikaku-bun" [TEPCO: No Commitment to Cover Decontamination Costs . . . for Plans After the End of 2013]. *Mainichi Shinbun*, December 28, 2015. http://mainichi.jp.
71 Cabinet Office, *Designating and Rearranging the Areas of Evacuation*.
72 Nuclear power plants were indeed first built for militaristic purpose. See Robert Jacobs, "Born Violent: The Origins of Nuclear Power." *Asian Journal of Peacebuilding* 7,1 (2019): 9–29. doi:10.18588/201905.00a074.
73 Vivoda and Graetz, "Nuclear Policy and Regulation in Japan," 504.

74 Swyngedouw, "The Antinomies of the Postpolitical City," 610.
75 Bülent Diken and Carsten Bagge Laustsen, "7–11, 9/11, and Postpolitics." *Alternatives* 29.1 (2004): 7, cited in Swyngedouw, "The Antinomies of the Postpolitical City," 609.
76 See David Magnus, "Risk Management versus the Precautionary Principle: Agnotology as a Strategy in the Debate over Genetically Engineered Organisms." In *Agnotology: The Making and Unmaking of Ignorance*, eds. Robert N. Proctor and Londa Schiebinger (Stanford University Press, 2008), 250–65; David Michaels, "Manufactured Uncertainty: Contested Science and the Protection of the Public's Health and Environment." In *Agnotology: The Making and Unmaking of Ignorance*, eds. Robert N. Proctor and Londa Schiebinger (Stanford University Press, 2008), 90–107.
77 Button, *Disaster Culture*, 14.
78 Stephens, "Bounding Uncertainty"; Brown, *Manual for Survival*.
79 Petryna, *Life Exposed*, 39 (original emphasis).
80 Kuchinskaya, *The Politics of Invisibility*. See also Topçu, "Catastrophes nucléaires et 'normalisation' des zones contaminées"; Arnhol, "Normalisation of Nuclear Accidents After the Cold War."
81 Swyngedou, "The Antinomies of the Postpolitical City," 601–20; Rancière, *The Politics of Aesthetics*.
82 Marilyn Strathern, "Future Kinship and the Study of Culture." *Futures* 27,4 (1995): 428. doi:10.1016/0016-3287(95)00014-N.
83 See Alan Irwin, "Constructing the Scientific Citizen: Science and Democracy in the Biosciences." *Public Understanding of Science* 10 (2001): 1–18. doi:10.3109/a036852; Melissa Leach, Ian Scoones, and Brian Wynne, eds., *Science and Citizens: Globalization and the Challenge of Engagement* (Zed Books, 2005); David Demerrit, "The Promises of Participation in Science and Political Ecology." In *The Routledge Handbook of Political Ecology*, eds. Tom Perreault, Gavin Bridge, and James McCarthy (Routledge, 2015), 224–34; Sebastian Ureta, "A Very Public Mess: Problematizing the 'Participative Turn' in Energy Policy in Chile." *Energy Research & Social Science* 29 (2017): 127–34. doi:10.1016/j.erss.2017.04.009.
84 Sergio Sismondo, *An Introduction to Science and Technology Studies* (Blackwell, 2010), 183.
85 Thompson, "Co-producing CITES and the African Elephant," 83.

CHAPTER 7. RADIOACTIVE PERFORMANCES
This chapter first appeared as: Maxime Polleri, "Radioactive Performances: Teaching About Radiation After the Fukushima Nuclear Disaster." *Anthropological Quarterly* 94,1 (2021): 93–123. doi:10.1353/anq.2021.0015. It was revised for this manuscript.
1 Ulrich Beck, *Risk Society: Towards a New Modernity* (Sage Publications, 1992), 22; Stawkowski. "'I Am a Radioactive Mutant,'" 148.
2 CEC, *Kankyō sōzō sentā: fukushima no kankyō kaifuku sōzō ni mukete* [Center for Environmental Creation: Aiming for Environmental Recovery and Creation in Fukushima]. Center for Environmental Creation. 2019. Pamphlet.

3 Eyal Ben-Ari and Sabine Frühstück, "The Celebration of Violence: A Live-Fire Demonstration Carried Out by Japan's Contemporary Military." *American Ethnologist* 30,4 (2003): 541. doi:10.1525/ae.2003.30.4.540.
4 Ben-Ari and Frühstück, "The Celebration of Violence," 551.
5 Ben-Ari and Frühstück, "The Celebration of Violence," 550.
6 Judith Butler, *Bodies That Matter: On the Discursive Limits of Sex* (Routledge, 1993), 188.
7 See Donna M. Goldstein, "Invisible Harm: Science, Subjectivity, and the Things We Cannot See." *Culture, Theory and Critique* 58,4 (2017): 321–29. doi:10.1080/14735784.2017.1365310.
8 Petryna, *Life Exposed*.
9 Kuchinskaya, *The Politics of Invisibility*.
10 Hecht, *Being Nuclear*, 14.
11 See the previous chapters, as well as Hirakawa and Shirabe, "Rhetorical Marginalization of Science and Democracy."
12 Irwin, *Citizen Science*.
13 Jeff Kingston, "Renewing and Reframing Hiroshima." *Asia-Pacific Journal* 17,15,6 (2019): 5. https://apjjf.org.
14 Nippon TV News 24 Japan, "Virtual Reality Revives Wartime Hiroshima." *YouTube*. August 14, 2020. https://www.youtube.com/watch?v=-qL4TCZxRo0.
15 Hecht, *Being Nuclear*, 6.
16 Pelletier, *La fascination du Japon*, 268 (author's translation).
17 Kuchinskaya, *The Politics of Invisibility*, 67.
18 See Pelletier, *La fascination du Japon*, 270–71 (author's translation).
19 Hecht, *Being Nuclear*, 10.
20 Low, *Visualizing Nuclear Power in Japan*, 212.
21 As Hecht argues, "For all the efforts at making nuclear things exceptional, there were opposing attempts to render them banal." Hecht, *Being Nuclear*, 8.
22 Hachiya, *Onaka ga itaku natta genpatsu kun*.
23 Wynne, "Misunderstood Misunderstanding."
24 Fassert and Hasegawa, Shinrai Research Project, 71.
25 Alexis Dudden, "The Ongoing Disaster." *Journal of Asian Studies* 71,2 (2012): 354. doi:10.1017/S002191181200006X.
26 Kim Fortun, "From Bhopal to the Informating of Environmentalism: Risk Communication in Historical Perspective." *Osiris* 2,19 (2004): 284. doi:10.1086/649407.
27 Beck, *Risk Society*, 4.
28 Melissa Leach, Ian Scoones, and Brian Wynne, "Introduction: Science, Citizenship, and Globalization." In *Science and Citizens: Globalization and the Challenge of Engagement*, eds. Melissa Leach, Ian Scoones, and Brian Wynne (Zed Books, 2005), 5.
29 Hecht, *Being Nuclear*, 10.
30 CEC, *Kankyō sōzō sentā: fukushima no kankyō kaifuku sōzō ni mukete*, 2–8.
31 MOE, *Shirabete nattoku hōshasen*, 20.

32 CEC, *Fukushimaken kankyō sōzō sentā kōryūtō no gaiyō* [Overview of the Fukushima Prefecture Environmental Creation Center Exchange Building]. N.d. Pamphlet, 7.
33 Takamura, *Getting to Know the Current Situation of Fukushima*, 3.
34 Hansson, "Nuclear Energy and the Ethics of Radiation Protection," 31.
35 Steven Starr, "The Contamination of Japan with Radioactive Cesium." In *Crisis Without End: The Medical and Ecological Consequences of the Fukushima Nuclear Catastrophe*, ed. Helen Caldicott (The New Press, 2014), 45.
36 Cram, "Living in Dose," 525.
37 Venturi, "Cesium in Biology"; International Physicians for the Prevention of Nuclear War, "The Fukushima Nuclear Disaster." *Medicine & Global Survival* Special Edition (June 2011): 2–6. www.fukushima-disaster.de.
38 International Physicians for the Prevention of Nuclear War, "The Fukushima Nuclear Disaster," 6.
39 International Physicians for the Prevention of Nuclear War, "The Fukushima Nuclear Disaster," 6.
40 Gabrielle Hecht, "The Bananization of Nuclear Things." *Somatosphere*, November 18, 2013. http://somatosphere.net.
41 Kuchinskaya, *The Politics of Invisibility*, 64.
42 Ben-Ari and Frühstück, "The Celebration of Violence," 550.
43 Inuhiko Yomota, *Kawaii ron* [Theory on Cuteness] (Chikuma Shinsho, 2006).
44 Adrian David Cheok, "Kawaii: Cute Interactive Media." In *Imagery in the 21st Century*, eds. Oliver Grau and Thomas Veigl (MIT Press, 2011), 252.
45 CEC, *Fukushimaken kankyō sōzō sentā kōryūtō no gaiyō*, 7.
46 Shunsuke Nozawa, "Characterization." *Semiotic Review* 3 (2013). https://semioticreview.com.
47 See Sakiyama, *Haha to ko no tame no hibaku chishiki*; UNSCEAR, *Biological Mechanisms of Radiation Actions at Low Doses: A White Paper to Guide the Scientific Committee's Future Programme of Work* (United Nations, 2012), chapter 4.
48 MOE, *Shirabete nattoku hōshasen*, 17–18.
49 MOE, *Shirabete nattoku hōshasen*, 33.
50 MOE, *Shirabete nattoku hōshasen*, 33.
51 See Iwaki Tarachine, "The Results of Food Radiation Measurement in April and May: 100 Items." 2014. www.tarachineiwaki.org.
52 Nozawa, "Characterization."
53 Carr, "Enactments of Expertise," 19.
54 CEC, *Fukushimaken kankyō sōzō sentā kōryūtō no gaiyō*, 8.
55 Latour, *We Have Never Been Modern*.
56 See Gabrielle Hecht, "Nuclear Janitors: Contract Workers at the Fukushima Reactors and Beyond." *Asia-Pacific Journal* 11,1,2 (2013). https://apjjf.org; Marie Ghis Malfilatre, "L'impossible confinement du travail nucléaire. Expérience professionnelle et familiale de salariés sous-traitants exposés à la radioactivité." *Travail et emploi* 147 (2016):101–24. doi:10.4000/travailemploi.7202.

57 Laura Miller, "Cute Masquerade and the Pimping of Japan." *International Journal of Japanese Sociology* 20,1 (2011): 18. doi:10.1111/j.1475-6781.2011.01145.x.
58 Sabine Frühstück, *Uneasy Warriors: Gender, Memory, and Popular Culture in the Japanese Army* (University of California Press, 2007), 136.
59 Hecht, *Being Nuclear*, 338 (original emphasis).
60 Mizuno, *Science for the Empire*, 143-61.
61 NIRS headquarters are located in Chiba prefecture, not far from Tokyo. Chiba was also affected by the nuclear disaster as some areas were found to have radiation hot spots.
62 Ben-Ari and Frühstück, "The Celebration of Violence," 550.
63 International Physicians for the Prevention of Nuclear War, "The Fukushima Nuclear Disaster," 62 (original emphasis).
64 Julie Gordon, "Nuclear Renaissance Could Fizzle After Japan Quake." *Reuters*, March 13, 2011. www.reuters.com.
65 Atsushi Komori, "'Nuclear Village' Website Closed Down After Host of Complaints." *The Asahi Shimbun*, April 15, 2019. www.asahi.com.
66 Frühstück, *Uneasy Warriors*, 144.
67 Hamblin, *Poison in the Well*, 192.
68 Goldstein, "Invisible Harm," 325.
69 Goldstein, "Invisible Harm," 325.
70 Government of Japan, "Fukushima Today." 2017. www.japan.go.jp.
71 Government of Japan, "Fukushima Today."
72 Japan Atomic Energy Agency, *Fukushima kenkyū kaihatsu bumon—Fukushima no fukkō ni mukete* [Sector of Fukushima, Research and Development: Towards the Restoration of Fukushima]. 2016. Pamphlet, 9.
73 Mizuno, *Science for the Empire*, 171.
74 Government of Japan, *Report on the 5th Science and Technology Basic Plan*. Council for Science, Technology, and Innovation Cabinet Office. December 18, 2015. Pamphlet, 6.
75 Butler, *Bodies That Matter*, 95.
76 Petryna, *Life Exposed*.
77 Robert Jacobs, "Atomic Kids: Duck and Cover and Atomic Alert Teach American Children How to Survive Atomic Attack." *Film and History* 40,1 (2010): 25-44. doi:10.1353/flm.0.0142.
78 Masco, *The Theater of Operations*, 43.
79 Masco, *The Nuclear Borderlands*, 28.
80 Oliver-Smith, "Anthropology Research on Hazards and Disasters," 319; Joshua Reno, "Beyond Risk: Emplacement and the Production of Environmental Evidence." *American Ethnologist* 38,3 (2011): 517. doi:10.1111/j.1548-1425.2011.01320.x.
81 Shirabe et al., "From Risk Communication to Participatory Radiation Risk Assessment," 3.
82 Even among the experts at NIRS, tensions were present. I met one high-ranking scientist who voiced a preference for the evacuation of children from irradiated

areas rather than the construction of child-focused educational centers, but her warnings were sidelined from official channels of risk communication.
83 Fukushima Innovation Coast Framework, "About Us–The Great East Japan Earthquake and Nuclear Disaster Memorial Museum." 2020. www.fipo.or.jp.
84 These expressions are taken directly from the Japanese website of the Great East Japan Earthquake and Nuclear Disaster Memorial Museum. www.fipo.or.jp.
85 Ryan Sayre, "The Un-Thought of Preparedness: Concealments of Disaster Preparedness in Tokyo's Everyday." *Anthropology and Humanism* 36,2 (2011): 222. doi:10.1111/j.1548-1409.2011.01093.x.
86 Asahi Shimbun, "Don't Criticize Government or TEPCO, Guides in Fukushima Told." *Asahi Shimbun*, September 23, 2020. www.asahi.com.
87 Beck, *Risk Society*, 76 (original emphasis).

CHAPTER 8. CONFLICTUAL COLLABORATION

This chapter first appeared as Maxime Polleri, "Conflictual Collaboration: Citizen Science and the Governance of Radioactive Contamination After the Fukushima Nuclear Disaster." *American Ethnologist* 46,2 (2019): 214–26. doi:10.1111/amet.12763. It was revised for this manuscript.

1 Daniel Aldrich, "Rethinking Civil Society: State Relations in Japan After the Fukushima Accident." *Polity* 45,2 (2013): 264. doi:10.1057/pol.2013.2.
2 See Rosenberger, "Japanese Organic Farmers"; Sternsdorff-Cisterna, "Food After Fukushima," 456; Kimura, *Radiation Brain Moms and Citizen Scientists*.
3 Wylie et al., "Institutions for Civic Technoscience"; Susanne Hecker, Muki Haklay, Anne Bowser, Zen Makuch, Johannes Vogel, and Aletta Bonn, "Innovation in Open Science, Society, and Policy: Setting the Agenda for Citizen Science." In *Citizen Science: Innovation in Open Science, Society, and Policy*, eds. Susanne Hecker et al. (UCL Press, 2018), 1–23.
4 Li, *The Will to Improve*, 12.
5 Irwin, *Citizen Science*, 115.
6 Irwin, *Citizen Science*, 129–30.
7 Sheila Jasanoff and Marybeth Long Martello, "Conclusion: Knowledge and Governance." In *Earthly Politics: Local and Global in Environmental Governance*, eds. Sheila Jasanoff and Marybeth Long Martello (MIT Press, 2004), 348.
8 David Harvey, *A Brief History of Neoliberalism* (Oxford University Press, 2007).
9 See Miyako Inoue, "Language and Gender in an Age of Neoliberalism." *Gender & Language* 1,1 (2007): 79–91. doi:10.1558/genl.2007.1.1.79; Sherry B. Ortner, "Dark Anthropology and Its Others: Theory Since the Eighties." *Hau: Journal of Ethnographic Theory* 6,1 (2016): 52. doi:10.14318/hau6.1.004; Ferguson and Gupta, "Spatializing States," 989.
10 Michel Foucault, "Governmentality." In *The Foucault Effect: Studies in Governmentality*, eds. Graham Burchell, Colin Gordon, and Peter Miller, translated by Pasquale Pasquino (University of Chicago Press, 1991), 87–104.
11 Inoue, "Language and Gender in an Age of Neoliberalism," 85.

12 Barrios, "What Does Catastrophe Reveal?," 160.
13 Michel Foucault, *The Birth of Biopolitics: Lectures at the Collège de France, 1978–79*, ed. Michel Senellart, translated by Graham Burchell (Palgrave Macmillan, 2008), 226.
14 See Swyngedouw, "Governance Innovation and the Citizen," 1993; see also Rebecca Lave, "Neoliberalism and the Production of Environmental Knowledge." *Environment and Society* 3,1 (2012): 19–38. doi:10.3167/ares.2012.030103; Katrin Vohland, Maike Weisspflug, and Lisa Pettibone, "Citizen Science and the Neoliberal Transformation of Science: An Ambivalent Relationship." *Citizen Science: Theory and Practice* 4,1 (2019): 1. doi:10.5334/cstp.186.
15 Philip Mirowski, "Against Citizen Science." *Aeon*, November 20, 2017. https://aeon.co.
16 Abu-Lughod, "The Romance of Resistance," 42.
17 Fortun, "Scaling and Visualizing Multi-sited Ethnography," 75.
18 Abu-Lughod, "The Romance of Resistance," 47; see also Kondo, *Crafting Selves*, 221.
19 Tsing, *Friction*, 246; Hathaway, "Wild Commodities."
20 Kathleen H. Pine and Max Liboiron, "The Politics of Measurement and Action." *Proceedings of the 33rd Annual ACM Conference on Human Factors in Computing Systems* (2015): 1. doi:10.1145/2702123.2702298.
21 Max Liboiron, "Disaster Data, Data Activism: Grassroots Responses to Representations of Superstorm Sandy." In *Extreme Weather and Global Media*, eds. Julia Leyda and Diane Negra (Routledge, 2015), 159.
22 Kirk Jalbert and Abby J. Kinchy, "Sense and Influence: Environmental Monitoring Tools and the Power of Citizen Science." *Journal of Environmental Policy & Planning* 18,3 (2016): 384. doi:10.1080/1523908X.2015.1100985.
23 See Jacobs, *Nuclear Bodies*.
24 Helen Caldicott, "Introduction." In *Crisis Without End: The Medical and Ecological Consequences of the Fukushima Nuclear Catastrophe*, ed. Helen Caldicott (The New Press, 2014), 6.
25 See Shannon Cram, "Becoming Jane: The Making and Unmaking of Hanford's Nuclear Body." *Environment and Planning D: Society and Space* 33,5 (2015): 796–812. doi:10.1177/0263775815599317.
26 Jalbert and Kinchy, "Sense and Influence," 392.
27 Feldhoff, "Visual Representations of Radiation Risk," 14.
28 Christine Fassert and Tatiana Kasperski, "Risques nucléaires: à quand la fin du monopole des experts internationaux?" *The Conversation*, April 23, 2021. https://theconversation.com.
29 Hirakawa and Shirabe, "Rhetorical Marginalization of Science and Democracy," 60.
30 Regarding the production of ignorance see Brown, *Manual for Survival*.
31 Olga Kuchinskaya, "Citizen Science and the Politics of Environmental Data." *Science, Technology, & Human Values* 44,5 (2019): 877. doi:10.1177/0162243919858669.

32 Ottinger, "Buckets of Resistance."
33 Petryna, *Life Exposed*.
34 Tsing, *Friction*, 250–51.
35 Thierry Ribault and Nadine Ribault, *Les sanctuaires de l'abîme: Chronique du désastre de Fukushima* (éditions de l'Encyclopédie des Nuisances, 2012); Topçu, *La France nucléaire*, 226; Boudia Soraya, "Trivialising Life in Long-Term Contaminated Areas: The Nuclear Political Laboratory." In *Living in a Nuclear World*, eds. Bernadette Bensaude-Vincent, Soraya Boudia, and Kyoko Sato (Routledge, 2022), 185–202.
36 Topçu, "Chernobyl Empowerment?," 137.
37 Aya Kimura, "Fukushima ETHOS: Post-disaster Risk Communication, Affect, and Shifting Risks." *Science as Culture* 27,1 (2017): 98–117. doi:10.1080/09505431.2017.1325458.
38 Wynne, "Misunderstood Misunderstanding."
39 Petryna, *Life Exposed*.
40 Stawkowski, "'I Am a Radioactive Mutant.'"
41 See Daniel Aldrich, *Site Fights: Divisive Facilities and Civil Society in Japan and the West* (Cornell University Press, 2008); Kainuma, *Fukushimaron*; Allison, *Precarious Japan*, 186.
42 Yusuke Yamashita, "How Does the Restoration of Tohoku Society Begin? Center and Periphery in the Great East Japan Earthquake." *International Journal of Japanese Sociology* 21,1 (2012): 9. doi:10.1111/j.1475-6781.2012.01172.x.
43 See Tsutomu Hashimoto, "Discourses on Neoliberalism in Japan." *Eurasia Border Review* 5,2 (2014): 99–119. http://hdl.handle.net/2115/57859.
44 See Hashimoto, "Discourses on Neoliberalism in Japan," 108; Inoue, "Language and Gender in an Age of Neoliberalism," 84.
45 Allison, *Precarious Japan*, 28.
46 See Hemmi and Graham, "Hacker Science versus Closed Science."
47 See Tsing, *Friction*.
48 Gilles Hériard-Dubreuil and Stéphane Baudé, "Local Populations Facing Long-Term Consequences of Nuclear Accidents: Lessons Learned from Chernobyl and Fukushima." *Fukushima Global Communication Programme Working Paper Series* 17 (2015): 3. https://collections.unu.edu.
49 All the following examples are derived from direct observation, as well as from Sakaue's documents and pamphlets.
50 Cram, "Living in Dose," 522.
51 Nihon Bunseki Sentā, *Heisei 20 nendo jigyō hōkokusho* [Japan Chemical Analysis Center 2008 business report]. 2008. www.jcac.or.jp.
52 Tatsuhiko Kodama, "Radiation Effects on Health: Protect the Children of Fukushima." *Asia-Pacific Journal* 9,32,4 (2011). https://apjjf.org; Yagasaki, "Internal Exposure Concealed."
53 See Boudia, "Les problèmes de santé publique de longue durée," 49; Perko, "How to Communicate About Radiological Risks?"; François Rollinger, Jacques Lochard, and Thierry Schneider, "Lessons Learnt by IRSN About

the Involvement of Experts Towards the Population in Contaminated Areas in Fukushima Prefecture." *Annals of the ICRP* 45,2_suppl (2016): 99–104. doi:10.1177/0146645316666497.
54 See Gwen Ottinger, "Constructing Empowerment Through Interpretations of Environmental Surveillance Data." *Surveillance & Society* 8,2 (2010): 231–33. doi:10.24908/ss.v8i2.3487; Liboiron et al., "Toxic Politics."
55 Phil Brown et al., "A Lab of Our Own: Environmental Causation of Breast Cancer and Challenges to the Dominant Epidemiological Paradigm." *Science, Technology, & Human Values* 31,5 (2006): 501. doi:10.1177/0162243906289610.
56 Lave, "Neoliberalism and the Production of Environmental Knowledge," 31.
57 Rollinger et al., "Lessons Learnt by IRSN."
58 Shirabe et al., "From Risk Communication to Participatory Radiation Risk Assessment," 21.
59 See Hiroshi Ishizuka and Yasuo Tomatsu, "Locals Opposed to Removal of Most Dosimeters in Fukushima." *The Asahi Shimbun*, July 9, 2018. www.asahi.com.
60 See "Radiation Monitors in Fukushima to Be Scrapped After Malfunctioning to the Tune of ¥500 Million a Year." *The Japan Times*, May 21, 2018. www.japantimes.co.jp.
61 MOE, *Dai 6-kai kenmin kōza 'hōshasen kyōshitsu'* [The 6th Prefectural Lecture: "Radiation Classroom"]. 2012. http://josen.env.go.jp.
62 Caren B. Cooper, Lisa M. Rasmussen, and Elizabeth D. Jones, "Perspective: The Power (Dynamics) of Open Data in Citizen Science." *Frontiers in Climate* 3 (2021): 2. doi:10.3389/fclim.2021.637037.
63 Hemmi and Graham, "Hacker Science Versus Closed Science."
64 Hirakawa and Shirabe, "Rhetorical Marginalization of Science and Democracy."
65 Ferguson and Gupta, "Spatializing States," 993.
66 IAEA, *The Fukushima Daiichi Accident*, 18.
67 IAEA International Experts Meeting, *Radiation Protection After the Fukushima Daiichi Accident: Promoting Confidence and Understanding*. 2014. White Paper, 31. www-pub.iaea.org.
68 Jan Helebrant and Petr Kuča, *New Approach to Radiation Monitoring: Citizen Based Radiation Measurement*. National Radiation Protection Institute. N.d., accessed March 25, 2023. https://inis.iaea.org.
69 Institut de radioprotection et de sûreté nucléaire, "Les citoyens mesurent eux-mêmes la radioactivité." 2016. www.irsn.fr.
70 Revue Générale Nucléaire, "Un compteur Geiger pour le grand public." Société française d'énergie nucléaire, February 29, 2016. www.sfen.org; Pierre Mangin, "Nuages radioactifs: un kit Open source pour surveiller l'environnement." *Silicon*, November 14, 2017. www.silicon.fr.
71 Makoto Miyazaki, "ICRP 111 to Fukushima no genjitsu rinshō to shite no kenkai" [ICRP 111 and the Reality of Fukushima: A Clinician's View]. *Fukushima Global Communication Programme Working Paper Series* 20 (2015): 1–7. https://collections.unu.edu.

72 Mirowski, "Against Citizen Science" (original emphasis).
73 Michiel van Oudheusden, Joke Kenens, Go Yoshizawa, and Nozomi Mizushima, "Workshop Report: Learning from Citizen Science After Fukushima." May 2019. SCK•CEN Brussels, 3.
74 Ferguson and Gupta, "Spatializing States," 994.
75 Takuya Tsujiuchi, "Post-traumatic Stress Due to Structural Violence After the Fukushima Disaster." *Japan Forum* 33,2 (2021): 175. doi:10.1080/09555803.2018.1552308.
76 Ferguson and Gupta, "Spatializing States," 990.
77 Kondo, *Crafting Selves*, 225.
78 Kimura, *Radiation Brain Moms and Citizen Scientists*.
79 For a similar problem in Singapore see Chua Hui Ching Emily, "Survival by Technopreneurialism: Innovation, Imaginaries, and the New Narrative of Nationhood in Singapore." *Science, Technology and Society* 24,3 (2019): 527–44. doi:10.1177/0971721819873202.

EPILOGUE

1 Hoffman, "After Atlas Shrugs," 319.
2 Kingston, "After 3.11," 4.
3 Philip Mirowski, *Never Let a Serious Crisis Go to Waste: How Neoliberalism Survived the Financial Meltdown* (Verso Books, 2014).
4 Mirowski, *Never Let a Serious Crisis Go to Waste*, 14.
5 Ann Bergman, "Future Matter Matters: Disasters as a (Potential) Vehicle for Social Change; It's About Time." In *Disaster upon Disaster: Exploring the Gap Between Knowledge, Policy, and Practice*, eds. Susanna M. Hoffman and Roberto E. Barrios (Berghahn Books, 2022), 319.
6 Kim Fortun, "Ethnography in Late Industrialism." *Cultural Anthropology* 27,3 (2012): 460. doi:10.1111/j.1548–1360.2012.01153.x.
7 For instance, Goldstein underscores how "Brazil has pursued construction of a third nuclear power plant in spite of the Fukushima disaster, even while its citizens share apocalyptic visions of what a catastrophic nuclear event would look like." Donna M. Goldstein, "Fukushima in Brazil: Undone Science, Technophilia, Epistemic Murk." *Culture, Theory and Critique* 58,4 (2017): 391. doi:10.1080/14735784.2017.1357480.
8 Thomas S. Kuhn, *The Structure of Scientific Revolutions* (University of Chicago Press, 2012).
9 Gabrielle Hecht, "Interscalar Vehicles for an African Anthropocene: On Waste, Temporality, and Violence." *Cultural Anthropology* 33,1 (2018): 111. doi:10.14506/ca33.1.05.
10 Susanna M. Hoffman and Anthony Oliver-Smith, "Introduction to the Second Edition of *The Angry Earth*." In *The Angry Earth: Disaster in Anthropological Perspective*, eds. Anthony Oliver-Smith and Susanna M. Hoffman (Routledge, 2019), 4.
11 Hoffman and Smith, "Introduction to the Second Edition of the Angry Earth," 4.

INDEX

Page numbers in *italics* indicate Tables and Photos

ABCC. *See* Atomic Bomb Casualty Commission
Abe, Shinzo: Abenomics, 67–68; "*fukkō*" plan under, 67–69, 107; nuclear power polices under, 177–78; Reconstruction Agency formed under, 68, 107
Abu-Lughod, Lila, 113
Act No. 48 (Japan) (2012), 80
Act on Special Measures Concerning the Handling of Radioactive Pollution, Japan, 124
acute radiation sickness, 99
adaptation, in Anthropocene epoch, 260–61
agriculture, farming and: citizen science network and, 221; decontamination of, 139–40; radiation tracking and, *238*, 255–56
ALARA philosophy. *See* "as low as reasonably achievable" philosophy
All-Campus Joint Struggle League, 188
Allison, Anne, 10–11, 158, 240
Amano, Natsuo: as citizen scientist, 92–95, 100, 102, 107–12, 252; Geiger counters and, 89; radiation contamination fears, 91; radiation exposure risks for, 90–91; Reiter syndrome, 91; relocation to Tokyo, 88; as voluntary evacuee, 88–89, 218
animals, wild flora and: bioaccumulation of radiation in, 138–39; contamination of, 138–39

Anthropocene epoch: adaptation in, 260–61; anthropology of, 260–61; Chernobyl nuclear power plant disaster and, 2; Fukushima Dai'ichi power plant meltdown and, 2; nuclear disasters as symbols of, 2, 260; radioactive governance in, 30; Three Mile Island nuclear disaster and, 2
anthropomorphic radionuclides, 207
antinuclear movement: Antinuclear Tent, 190, *191*; Ministry of Economy, Trade and Industry and, 188–89; politics of victimization and, 106–7
Antinuclear Tent, 190, *191*
anxiety rates, after Fukushima meltdown, 70
apoliticism, in Japan, politics of victimization and, 102–3
Araki, Emiko, 97–98
Arnhold, Valerie, 53
"as low as reasonably achievable" philosophy (ALARA philosophy), 49–50, 243
Astro Boy, 44–45
atmospheric radiation, 124
Atomic Bomb Casualty Commission (ABCC), 50
atomic divorce, 90, 149–50
Atomic Energy Commission, in US, 51–52
Atoms for Peace Program, 37–38, 258
Atsumi, Tora, 221–22, 237

307

Barefoot Gen (hadashi no gen) (manga comic book), 31
Barrios, Roberto, 224
Basedow's disease, 108
Beck, Ulrich, 219
Belarus, 54; Chernobyl Law in, 111; radioactive performances in, 196–97
Ben-Ari, Eyal, 196
Bergman, Ann, 257
Bess, Vincent, 133
Bevir, Mark, 9, 14
bioaccumulation, in animals, 138–39
biological citizens, 167, 235
biopower, 5
body-centric damage narratives, 23
Bond, David, 25
Botollier-Depois, Jean-François, 249
Brown, Kate, 51
Button, Gregory, 175

Caldicott, Helen, 230
Canadian Nuclear Safety Commission, 35
cancers. *See* thyroid cancers
capitalism. *See* disaster capitalism
carbon monoxide (CO_2), 155; radioactive waste risks compared to, 15
Carr, Summerson, 58
CEC. *See* Center for Environmental Creation
censorship, about nuclear power, 42–43
Center for Environmental Creation (CEC), 119; radioactive performances and, 195, 201–2, 206, 209, 220
cesium, 34–35, 92, 99, 132, 203
Chernobyl Law, 111
Chernobyl nuclear power plant disaster: as Anthropocene symbol, 2; Cold War context for, 12; decontamination strategies for, 135; Ethos and, 239; Fukushima Dai'ichi power plant meltdown compared to, 2; government secrecy over, 11–12, 52–53; IAEA classification of, 2, 53; radiation monitoring and testing at, 118–19; residual radioactivity after, 56
children: as citizen scientists, 93–94; during Emergency Era, 11; evacuation from Fukushima, 105, *105*; explanation of nuclear disasters to, 199; in *furusato*, 165–67; International Symposium on Disaster Management and Recovery for Children and Communities, 55, 78; politics of victimization and, 110–12; radiation-induced illnesses in, 4–5, 92; *suikawari* game, 165–66, *166*; thyroid cancer rates among, 5, 55
children's literature, educational materials and: Astro Boy, 44–45; on nuclear power, 41–42
Children's Peace Monument, 31
Choy, Tim, 145
chronic low-dose exposure, 99
chronic radiation syndrome, 53
Chugoku Shimbun, 32
citizen movements, by victims, 15
citizens, citizenship and: biological, 167, 235; discrimination against Fukushima citizens, 70–71; good citizenship, 255; *hibakusha*, 70–73, 107–10; passive, 219; scientific citizenship, 99
citizen science, citizen scientists and: Amano and, 92–95, 100, 102, 107–12, 252; Araki and, 97–98; children as, 93–94; civic distrust in government as influence on, 84; in civil society, 257; consumption of radiation-related knowledge, 99; Cornell Lab of Ornithology, 84; critical analysis of government information, 99; data collection and, 86, 229–33, 236, 248–49; deconstruction of, 85; deflation of expertise and, 85; on environmental dangers, 84; ethnographical approach to, 86; farmers and, 221; feminist politics and, 113; food monitoring/safety and, 97–98, 105; food security and, 97–98;

after Fukushima meltdown disaster, 85–87; gatherings and meetings for, 98–100; Geiger counters for, 94–96, 96; governance forms influenced by, 84; government-patronized scholars, 85; as grassroots movement, 86; historical development of, 84; *ibasho* and, 100–102; ideological bias and, 106; institutional support of, 249; Japanese nuclear industry support of, 248; Kobayashi and, 100–102; mapping of radiation zones, 96; masculinity roles and, 94; neoliberalization of, 223–25, 252–54; NGOs and, 94; nonprofit organizations created by, 97–98; open data, 248–49; origins of, 84; political pressure for, 100–101; politics of revitalization and, 114–15, 252; politics of victimization and, 102–13; protection of life and, 112–15; radiation governance and, 85; radiation risks and, 195; radiation testing by, 95–96, 96; scientific citizenship and, 99; social pressure for, 100–101; study groups for, 98–100; Sv hunters and, 94–96; in US, 84; women as, 94, 113; workshops for, 98–100

Citizens' Nuclear Information Center, 18, 43

civic participation, in radiation tracking and monitoring: citizen science and, 223–25, 227–28, 232–33; Cold War context for, 231–32; collaboration in, 223; collaboration with agencies and organizations, 247–51; conceptual approach to, 222–23; conflictual collaboration and, 225–26, 251–52; consumption of data, 235–36; of contaminated mushrooms, 244, 244; of contamination levels, 234–36; data collection, 229–33, 236, 248–49; with DIY monitoring devices, 226–29; with dosimeters, 244–45; by farmers, 238, 255–56; with Geiger counters, 226–30; hormesis hypothesis and, 231–32; institutional cooptation of, 247–52; Japanese cultural pressures as influence on, 236; neoliberal governance and, 223–25; practical radiological protection culture and, 242–46; radiophobia and, 231; raw data interpretation, 226–33; recovery strategies, 237–39; resistance and, 223; by returning evacuees, 238; in rural areas, 240–41; of soil samples, 233; state abandonment and, 240–42; TEPCO and, 245–47

civil society: citizen scientists in, 257; governance and, 15

CO2. *See* carbon monoxide

Cohn, Carol, 186

Cold War: Atoms for Peace program and, 37–38, 258; Chernobyl nuclear disaster during, 12; civic participation in radiation tracking and, 231–32; nuclear weapons arms race during, 51–52

Cole, Jonathan, 102

collective memory, of nuclear disasters, 115

commodifiable phantasm: definition of, 144; *furusato* and, 144, 146

conflictual collaboration, 225–26, 251–52

contaminated soil, cleanup supplies for, 3

contamination, contaminated spaces and: in artistic works, 133; as external effect, 36; of fruits and vegetables, 123; after Fukushima Dai'ichi meltdown, 64; of *furusato*, 143–44; governance of, 30; Intensive Contamination Survey Areas, 124–25; internal, 76; of *Lucky Dragon Five*, 38; politics of revitalization and, 141; quality of life influenced by, 99–100; rationalization of, 175–76; residual, 134–35; SPEEDI program for, 62; whole-body counters for, 214–15; of wild animals, 138–39

Cool Biz policy, 179

Cool Japan ideology, 210

Cornell Lab of Ornithology, 84
Cram, Shannon, 230, 243
Creighton, Millie, 146
cultural determinism, 81
culture. *See* Japanese culture
cute/cuteness. *See kawaii*

damage biology, 76–78
data collection, by citizen scientists, 86, 229–33, 236, 248–49
decontamination, of nuclear disaster areas, *138*; under Act on Special Measures Concerning the Handling of Radioactive Pollution, 124; agriculture and farming and, 139–40; at Chernobyl, 135; definition of, 117; discard studies and, 117–18; ecosystem imbalance and, 138–39; forest management and, 138; of *furusato*, 153–56; in Iitate village, 136–37; Intensive Contamination Survey Areas and, 124–25; International Symposium on Decontamination of Radioactive Material, 121; limits of, 135–40; Ministry of the Environment and, 124–26, 128, 136–37, 141–42; monitoring and testing and, 117; politics of revitalization and, 127; pollution and, 117–18; potted plants as symbol of, 142; of radioactive waste, 118; of radionuclides, 118; remediation measures, 141; in rural areas, 138; Special Decontamination Areas, 125–26; as symbolic of state power, 140–42; in Tomioka, 135–36; through waste disposal, 136
Decontamination Info Plaza (DIP), 126–27, 136, 200–202, *208, 209, 210,* 213
depression rates, after Fukushima meltdown, 70
DIP. *See* Decontamination Info Plaza
disaster capitalism, 155
disaster recovery and governance strategies: under Act no. 48, 80; "*fukkō*" plan, 67–69, 107; International Symposium on Disaster Management and Recovery for Children and Communities, 55, 78; Japanese culture as influence on, 79–83; NGOs and, 256; Reconstruction Agency and, 68, 107; through relocation, 5. *See also specific topics*
disaster studies, 13, 260–61; Japanese culture and, 79–83
discard studies, 117–18
Discourses of the Vanishing (Ivy), 170
discrimination, in Japan: cultural practices and, 82; against Fukushima citizens, 70–71; *hibakusha,* 70–71
distribution of the sensible, 7
DNA damage: damage biology and, 76–78; mutations as, 36; from radiation exposure, 35–36, 75
Dobashi, Masayuki, 21
Doi, Takeo, 79–80
dosimeters, 119, 244–45
Douglas, Mary, 117

earthquakes, Fukushima Dai'ichi power meltdown after, 2; Great East Japan Earthquake and Nuclear Disaster Memorial Museum, 218–19
East Asia: postwar context for, 37. *See also specific countries*
Easter Island, Japan compared to, 178–79
ecotourism, 149
Eisenhower, Dwight, Atoms for Peace Program and, 37–38, 258
Emergency Era *(kinkyū jidai),* in Japan, 12, 14–17; children during, 11; disaster studies and, 13; social precarity during, 10–11; urgent ethnography and, 10
energy security policies, 179, 181–83
environment, environmental issues and: Ministry of Economy, Trade and Industry policies, 181–83; radiation bioaccumulation in animals, 138–39; residual radioactivity as influence on, 56

Environmental Radiation Monitoring Center, 116, 119, 121
ethnocentrism, politics of victimization and, 113
ethnographic approaches, ethnography and: to citizen science, 86; Emergency Era and, 10; to radioactive performances, 197
ethnographic fieldwork: authoritative narratives about, 20; multi-site, 17; politics of, 20–25; postvictimization approach in, 23–25; in radioactive spaces, 17–19; relativism in, 24; "suspending damage" in, 23
Ethos, 239–43
European Union (EU), 183
evacuations, evacuation procedures/zones and, *125*; under Chernobyl Law, 111; of children from Fukushima, *105*, *105*; civic participation by returning evacuees, 238; financial support for evacuees, 112–13; for Fukushima Dai'ichi meltdown, 59–61, *60–61*; from *furusato*, 164–71; relocations risks with, 4; self-responsibility for, 89; Uno and, 4–5; voluntary, 4–5
exclusion zones, 123–24; Tomioka as, 143
expertise: citizen science and, 85; definition of, 57–58; deflation of, 85; of *hibakusha*, 72–73; about nuclear disasters, 57–59; othering of, 74–75; politics of expertise, 83, 176; regimes of, 57–59; as set of practices, 58–59. *See also* politics of expertise

farming. *See* agriculture
Fassert, Christine, 127
Feldhoff, Thomas, 94–95, 231
feminism, feminist theory and, citizen science and, 113
Ferguson, James, 9, 15
FHMS. *See* Fukushima Health Management Survey

films and television, nuclear power in, 44–45
Financial Crisis of 2007–2008, 257
First Nations peoples, radiation exposure for, 51
food monitoring. *See* food safety
Food Radiation Screening System, 233
food safety, food security and: citizen science and, 97–98, 105; radionuclides and, 97
forest management, decontamination of nuclear disasters and, 138
Fortun, Kim, 17, 92, 162–63, 258
Foucault, Michel, 5
Freeman, Lindsey, 150
Frickel, Scott, 133
Frühstück, Sabine, 196, 213–14
fūhyō higai (harmful rumors), 75–79, 151; radioactive performances and, 200
Fujio, Rin, 76–77, 82, 92
"*fukkō*" plan (revival, reconstruction, and restoration), 67, 69; Reconstruction Agency and, 68, 107
Fukushima citizens. *See hibakusha*
Fukushima Dai'ichi power plant, meltdown at: as Anthropocene symbol, 2; anxiety rates after, 70; Chernobyl nuclear disaster compared to, 2; citizen science after, 85–87, 92–112; contamination zones after, *64*; depression rates after, 70; discrimination against Fukushima citizens, 70–71; after earthquake, 2; evacuation zones for, 59–61, *60–61*; fifteen-year anniversary of, 256–57; fifth-year anniversary of, 69–74; "*fukkō*" plan after, 67–69, 107; government transparency approach, 12; health effects of, 63, 65–66; historical context of, 1, 13; IAEA classification of, 2; investigation commission for, 65–66; lack of public trust in governance approaches to, 62–63; mental health effects of, 63, 70;

312 | INDEX

Fukushima Dai'ichi power plant (*cont.*) nostalgia after, 144–47; politics of revitalization and, 3, 13; PTSD rates after, 70; residual radioactivity after, 56; social bonds as result of, 1–2; social issues after, 63; TEPCO and, 154, 157–58, 162; Three Mile Island nuclear disaster compared to, 2; transnational governmentality and, 16; after tsunami, 2

Fukushima Health Management Survey (FHMS), 65, 71–72

Fukushima Prefecture, Japan: civic practices in, 89; discrimination against citizens from, 70–71; fragmentation of community in, 2; Fukushima Pride campaign, 148; Kasumigaseki district, 187–88; radiation monitoring in, *120*; reputational damage to, 71; residual radioactivity in, 183. *See also hibakusha*

Fukushima Pride campaign, 148

furusato (native land/old village): atomic divorce, 149–50; children in, 165–67; commodifiable phantasm and, 144, 146; contamination of, 143–44, 171; cultural narratives for, 171; decontamination of, 153–56; definition of, 143; as delimited physical space, 170; ecotourism and, 149; evacuation of, 164–69; evacuee experience and, 170–71; hometown tax and, 145; as Liberal Democratic Party election platform, 144; memory and, 163–64; for Nakagawa, 3–4; new, 165–67; political mobilization and, 145; as political touchstone, 169–71; as public policy, 144–45; Reconstruction Agency and, 149, 151–53; regeneration of, 149; restoration of, 149, 151–53; returning residents, 160–62; rice cakes tradition, 156; *suikawari* game, 165–66, *166*; Westernization of Japan and, 146, 150

gamma rays, 131
Garvey, Ellen, 109
Geiger counters, 226–30; for citizen scientists, 94–96, *96*; NGOs and, 19
Genbaku Dome, 31
gender, in Japanese culture, 90; masculinity and, 94
Germany: economic criticisms of, 258; nuclear energy phaseout in, 181–82
Gill, Tom, 10, 144–45, 161
global warming, 180–81
Goldstein, Donna, 46, 52
governance practices, governments and: citizen science as influence on, 84; civil society and, 15; NGOs and, 15; nuances of, 14; participatory, 54; politics of revitalization and, 7; practice of politics and, 224–25; radioactive, 8–10; transnational, 16. *See also* disaster recovery and governance strategies; secrecy
Graeter, Stefanie, 106
Grambow, Bernd, 132
Great East Japan Earthquake and Nuclear Disaster Memorial Museum, 218–19
Greenpeace, 154
groupism, Japanese, 258
Gupta, Akhil, 9, 15

Hachiya, Kazuhiko, 199
hadashi no gen. *See Barefoot Gen*
Hansson, Sven Ove, 49
harmful rumors. *See fūhyō higai*
Hasegawa, Ken'ichi, 135
Hasegawa, Reiko, 127
Hatayama, Yukio, 44–46
Hathaway, Michael, 10
Hayano, Ryugo, 55, 78
heart issues, radiation-induced, 92
Hecht, Gabrielle, 33, 197
Heilbrunn, Benoît, 146
hereditary effects, from radiation exposure, 35

INDEX | 313

hibakusha (Fukushima citizens): discrimination against, 70–71; as experts on disaster, 72–73; Medical Care Law of 1957 and, 109; mobilization of, 72–73; politics of victimization and, 107–10
High Energy Accelerator Research Organization, 78
high-level radioactive waste (HLW), 172
Hirono village, 161–62
Hiroshima, Japan: antinuclear demonstrations in, 33; atomic bomb drops in, 31; Children's Peace Monument in, 31; *Chugoku Shimbun* newspaper, 32; Genbaku Dome in, 31; public medical insurance in, 108
Hiroshima Peace Memorial Museum, 18, 198, 217; annual remembrances, 32; exhibits in, 31; Obama at, 32
HLW. *See* high-level radioactive waste
Hoffman, Susanna, 16, 255
hometown tax, 145
hormesis hypothesis, 231–32

IAEA. *See* International Atomic Energy Agency
Ialenti, Vincent, 85
ibasho (place where one belongs), 100–102, 153. *See also furusato*
ICRP. *See* International Commission on Radiological Protection
Igarashi, Yoshikuni, 81
Iitate village (Japan): decontamination of, 136–37; radiation monitoring and testing in, 129–30, *131*, 135; Reconstruction Agency in, 153
Ikeda, Minoru, 135
Ikeda, Yoko, 24
illnesses, radiation-induced: acute radiation sickness, 99; Basedow's disease, 108; in children, 4–5, 92; chronic low-dose exposure, 99; heart issues, 92; thyroid cancer, 5, 55, 108
Imamura, Masahiro, 107

Imanaka, Tetsuji, 56–57
imperceptibility. *See* regimes of imperceptibility
Inaba, Tatsuya, 79–80, 82
Indonesia, political involvement in, 106
inhabitants of a place. *See jūmin*
Innovation Coast Framework, 152
Inoue, Miyako, 224
insurance. *See* medical insurance
Intensive Contamination Survey Areas, 124–25
International Atomic Energy Agency (IAEA): Atoms for Peace program and, 37–38; Chernobyl nuclear disaster classification by, 2, 53; citizen initiatives, 249; Fukushima Dai'ichi nuclear meltdown classification by, 2; International Nuclear and Radiological Event, 53; radiation-induced health effects and, 63, 65; Three Mile Island nuclear disaster classification by, 2; World Health Organization and, 66
International Commission on Radiological Protection (ICRP), 48, 59–61
International Nuclear and Radiological Event, 53
International Symposium on Decontamination of Radioactive Material, 121
International Symposium on Disaster Management and Recovery for Children and Communities, 55, 78
ionizing radiation, 34–35
Irwin, Alan, 86, 224
Ivy, Marilyn, 135, 145, 153–54, 170–71

JAEA. *See* Japan Atomic Energy Agency
Japan: Act No. 48, 80; Act on Special Measures Concerning the Handling of Radioactive Pollution, 124; administrative governance structures in, 14; All-Campus Joint Struggle League, 188; Atoms for Peace Program and, 258; bubble economy in, 16;

Japan (*cont.*)
bureaucracy in, 14; Center for Environmental Creation, 119, 195, 201–2, 206, 209, 220; culture as impact on disaster governance, 79–83; Easter Island comparisons, 178–79; Emergency Era for, 10–17; energy security policies in, 179, 181–83; government policy of secrecy in, 32; groupism in, 258; Japan Atomic Energy Agency, 121, 213, 215; *kabuki* theater in, 82–83; Liberal Democratic Party in, 38, 144; map of, 6; Medical Care Law of 1957, 109; Meiji Era, 169; Ministry of Economy, Trade and Industry in, 41, 172–94; Ministry of Education, Culture, Sports, Science, and Technology in, 41, 62, 104, 119; Ministry of the Environment, 124–26, 128, 136–37, 141–42, 206; Ministry of International Trade and Industry in, 40–41, 173; National Institute of Radiological Sciences, 200–201, 211, 213–14, *214*; National Security Council of Japan, 62; Nuclear and Industrial Safety Agency in, 62; nuclear exceptionalism in, 198, 211; nuclear power in, 37–39, *39*, 44–45; Nuclear Regulation Agency, 247; Nuclear Safety Commission, 177; postwar context for, 37; propaganda for nuclear power in, 38–39; Reconstruction Agency in, 68, 107, 147–56; restricted political participation in, 102; Self-Defense Forces in, 196, 205, 210; technological infrastructure in, 89; TEPCO in, 154, 157–58, 162, 245–47; Triple Disaster in, 67–68; US military occupation of, 32; Westernization of, 146, 150; women in, 90. *See also* Japanese culture; *specific cities; specific islands; specific prefectures; specific topics*
Japan Atomic Energy Agency (JAEA), 121, 213, 215

Japan Council Against Atomic and Hydrogen Bombs, 32
Japanese culture, disaster governance influenced by, 79; Cool Japan ideology, 210; cultural determinism and, 81; discriminatory practices and, 82; groupism and, 258; negative impacts of, 80; *Nihonjinron* and, 81–83; politics of expertise and, 83; politics of revitalization, 83; social system norms in, 80; state-sanctioned gender expectations and, 90
Japan's Challenge Towards Recovery report, 178
Japan Times, 153
Jasanoff, Sheila, 58, 176
jūmin (inhabitants of a place), 22

kabuki theater, 82–83
Kagaya, Masamichi, 133–35
Kajima Corporation, 155–56
Kajiwara, Akane, 111–12
Kan, Naoto, 61–62, 177
Kaneko, Haruko, 75–77, 82
Kasumigaseki district, 187–88
Kato, Keisuke, 153
Katsuma, Kazuyo, 181
Kawabata, Tetsuo, 188, 190
Kawaguchi-Mahn, Emi, 181–82
kawaii (cute/cuteness), 208–10
Kawashima, Naomi, 233–37
Kimura, Aya, 87, 104
Kingston, Jeff, 42
kinkyū jidai. *See* Emergency Era
knowledge deficit, 199
Kobayashi, Mari, 100–102
Koide, Hiroaki, 56
Kondo, Dorinne, 82, 87
Kosako, Toshiso, 62–63, 241
Kuchinskaya, Olga, 232
Kuhn, Thomas, 259
Kurokawa, Shin'ichi, 78
Kurozawa, Ken'ichi, 116, 120–21
Kusahara, Machiko, 169

late industrialism, 258
Latour, Bruno, 209
Lave, Rebecca, 246
LDP. *See* Liberal Democratic Party
Li, Tania, 9, 123, 224–25
Liberal Democratic Party (LDP), in Japan, 38; *furusato* as election platform for, 144
Liboiron, Max, 228
Life Exposed (Petryna), 12–13
Life Span Study (LSS), 50–51, 66
Lindee, Susan, 50
linear nonthreshold (LNT), for radiological protection, 48–49
"Little Boy" (atomic bomb), 31
LNT. *See* linear nonthreshold
Lochard, Jacques, 239
Löschke, Ayaka, 89, 111, 113
Low, Morris, 39, 199
LSS. *See* Life Span Study
Lucky Dragon Five, contamination of, 38, 47

MacArthur, Douglas, 37
Marcus, George, 14
Marshall Islands, 51
Marx, Karl, 155
Masco, Joseph, 44–45, 122, 155
masculinity, citizen scientists and, 94
Mathews, Andrew, 14, 106, 184
media, nuclear power in: *Barefoot Gen*, 31; corporate support in, 42–43; films and television, 44–45; newspapers, 32, 153
Medical Care Law of 1957, Japan, 109
medical insurance: for Hiroshima survivors, 108; under Medical Care Law of 1957, 109; for Nagasaki survivors, 108
Meiji Era, in Japan, 169
memory, *furusato* and, 163–64. *See also* collective memory
mental health: anxiety rates, 70; depression rates, 70; after Fukushima Dai'ichi meltdown, 63, 70; posttraumatic stress disorder, 70, 74
METI. *See* Ministry of Economy, Trade and Industry
MEXT. *See* Ministry of Education, Culture, Sports, Science, and Technology
Michinoeki Madeikan, 152–53
microsieverts, 114
Mikami, Naoyuki, 177
Miller, Laura, 210
Minamata Convention, 102
Ministry of Economy, Trade and Industry (METI), 41; anti-nuclear movement and, 188–89; Antinuclear Tent and, 190, *191*; Cool Biz policy, 179; economic efficiency policies, 181–83; electric power generation policies, 183–87; energy security policies, 179, 181–83; environmental policies, 181–83; global warming rhetoric and, 180–81; Japan's Challenge Towards Recovery report, 178; Mizunami Underground Research Facility, 172, *174*; nuclear energy promoted by, 177; "nuclear green energy" agenda, 183; nuclear imaginaries and, 181–83; nuclear power and, 173–87; Nuclear Safety Commission and, 177; nuclear safety myths, 193–94; nuclear uncertainty arguments and, 173–77, 186–91; politics of expertise, 176; postpolitical uncertainties and, 192–93; radiation risk assessment, 192; safety policies, 181–83; Small Modular Reactors and, 183; technostrategic language for, 186; vertical administration structure in, 187
Ministry of Education, Culture, Sports, Science, and Technology (MEXT), 41, 62, 104, 119
Ministry of the Environment (MOE), 124–26, 128, 136–37, 141–42; radioactive performances and, 206

Ministry of International Trade and Industry (MITI), 40–41, 173
Mirowski, Philip, 225, 250, 257
Mita, Kumiko, 108
Mitchell, Timothy, 9, 20, 47, 184
MITI. *See* Ministry of International Trade and Industry
Mizunami Underground Research Facility, 172, *174*
Mizuno, Hiromi, 211, 216
mochi tradition, 158–59
MOE. *See* Ministry of the Environment
monitoring. *See* food safety; radiation monitoring and testing
Mori, Satoshi, 133–34
Morimoto, Ryo, 23, 25
Morioka, Rika, 90, 112
multi-site ethnographic fieldwork, 17
multi-site ethnography, 17
Murphy, Michelle, 23, 33, 92, 133
mutual assured destruction, nuclear power and, 47
myths about nuclear safety, 39–48; Ministry of Economy, Trade and Industry and, 193–94; radioactive performances and, 219; safety culture, 259. *See also* nuclear safety

Nagai, Junpei, 43
Nagasaki, Japan, 47; medical insurance in, 108
Nakagawa, Jun'ichiro, *furusato* for, 3–4
National Institute of Radiological Sciences (NIRS), 200–201, 211, 213–14, *214*
National Refugee Association, 4
native land. *See furusato*
neoliberal governance, neoliberalism and, 253; of citizen science, 223–25; civic participation in radiation tracking and, 223–25; Ethos and, 239; scope of, 224
Never Let a Serious Crisis Go to Waste (Mirowski), 257

new *furusato*, 165–67
newspapers, nuclear power in: *Chugoku Shimbun*, 32; *Japan Times*, 153
"New Tōhoku" campaign, 148
NGOs. *See* nongovernmental organizations
Nidecker, Andreas, 212–13
Nihonjinron (theories on Japaneseness), 81–83
NIRS. *See* National Institute of Radiological Sciences
NISA. *See* Nuclear and Industrial Safety Agency
Nishimura, Junsō, 185–96
Noda, Yoshihiko, 177
nongovernmental organizations (NGOs): citizen scientists and, 94; disaster governance and, 256; Ethos, 239–43; Geiger counters and, 19; state functions and, 15
nonprofit organizations (NPOs), by citizen scientists, 97–98
nostalgia: critical, 168–69; after Fukushima meltdown disaster, 144–47; marketing of, 144–47. *See also* commodifiable phantasm
Nozawa, Shunsuke, 206
NPOs. *See* nonprofit organizations
Nuclear and Industrial Safety Agency (NISA), in Japan, 62
nuclear banality, 198–200, 211
nuclear disasters: Anthropocene epoch and, 2, 260; chronic radiation syndrome, 53; collective memory of, 115; explanations to children about, 199; hierarchization of, 259; International Nuclear and Radiological Event classification of, 53; International Symposium on Disaster Management and Recovery for Children and Communities, 55, 78; methodological approach to, 259–62; normalization of, 259; posttraumatic stress disorder

after, 74; recoding narratives on, 73–74; regimes of expertise about, 57–59; safety culture and, 259; urgency of, 59–63, 65–69. *See also* Chernobyl nuclear power plant disaster; disaster recovery and governance strategies; Fukushima Dai'ichi power plant; Three Mile Island nuclear power plant disaster; *specific topics*
nuclear era, 44
nuclear exceptionalism, 198, 211
"nuclear green energy" agenda, 183
nuclearity, as concept, 197
nuclear power: during Abe administration, 177–78; antinuclear movements, 33, 38; Canadian Nuclear Safety Commission, 35; censorship about, 42–43; in children's literature, 41–42; civilian, 33; controversies about, 173–77; educational agenda, 41–42; energy lobbies for, 40–41, 43; energy security policies and, 179, 181–83; fetishization of, 182–83; in films, 44–45; global context for, 32–33; illusions about control of, 47–48; in Japan, 37–39, 39, 44–45; licensing for, 40; in media, 42–43; Ministry of Economy, Trade and Industry and, 173–87; mutual assured destruction concept with, 47; political uncertainties about, 173–77; post-political approach to, 174–75; propaganda for, 38–39; safety myths about, 39–48; Small Modular Reactors, 183; in Ukraine, 257; as unlimited energy source, 45–46; in US popular culture, 44–45. *See also specific topics*
Nuclear Regulation Agency, 247
nuclear safety: affective structures, 44–46; illusion about control of nuclear power, 47–48; internationalization of, 53–54; licensing as element of, 40; Ministry of Economy, Trade and Industry policies, 181–83; Ministry of International Trade and Industry, 40–41; myths about, 39–48; regulatory capture and, 40–41; scientific ostracism and, 42; state regulation factors in, 40–41; US guidelines industry, 51–52. *See also* nuclear disasters
Nuclear Safety Commission, 177
nuclear technoaesthetics, 122
nuclear village, 40; scientific ostracism and, 42
Nuclear Waste Management Organization (NUMO), 172, 205
nuclear weapons, nuclear testing and: Atomic Bomb Casualty Commission and, 50; Atoms for Peace Program and, 37–38, 258; during Cold War, 51–52; Japan Council Against Atomic and Hydrogen Bombs, 32; by Soviet Union, 37
NUMO. *See* Nuclear Waste Management Organization

Obama, Barack, 32
old village. *See furusato*
Oliver-Smith, Anthony, 16
Ono, Eiko, 108–10
open data, for citizen scientists, 248
Ortner, Sherry, 114

Panagia, Davide, 101
participatory governance, as risk management approach, 54
passive citizenship, 219
Pelletier, Philippe, 198
perceptibility. *See* regime of perceptibility
Perry, Matthew C. (Commodore), 16
Peru, 106
Petryna, Adriana, 12–13, 24, 167, 192
place where one belongs. *See ibasho*
plutonium, 35, 203–4
politics of expertise: Japanese culture and, 83; Ministry of Economy, Trade and Industry and, 176

318 | INDEX

politics of revitalization: citizen scientists and, 114–15, 252; contamination and, 141; decontamination of nuclear disaster areas and, 127; distribution of the sensible and, 7; Fukushima Dai'ichi meltdown and, 3, 13; governance practices and, 7; Japanese culture and, 83; by political regime, 7–8; radiation monitoring and, 127; radiophobia and, 7; scope of, 7

politics of victimization: antinuclear movement and, 106–7; apoliticism and, 102–3; children and, 110–12; citizen science/scientists and, 102–13; definition of, 285n56; ethnocentrism and, 113; *hibakusha*, 107–10; public opinions on politics, 102–3

pollution, decontamination and, 117–18; under Act on Special Measures Concerning the Handling of Radioactive Pollution, 124

posttraumatic stress disorder (PTSD), 70; after nuclear disasters, 74

postvictimization approach, in ethnographic fieldwork, 23–25

Povinelli, Elizabeth, 15

practical radiological protection culture (PRPC), 242, 244–46; ALARA principle and, 243

practice of politics, 224–25

Precarious Japan (Allison), 10–11

Proctor, Robert, 175

propaganda, for nuclear power, 38–39

PTSD. *See* posttraumatic stress disorder

public trust, in disaster governance: after Fukushima power plant meltdown, 62–63; in radiation/radioactive governance, 62–63; after 3.11 disaster, 93

Purity and Danger (Douglas), 117

quality of life, radioactive contamination as influence on, 99–100

radiation, radioactivity and: bioaccumulation of, 138–39; cesium and, 34–35, 92, 99, 132, 203; definition of, 9, 34; deterministic effects of, 35; environmental impact of, 56; fear of, 7; international perspectives on, 48–54; International Symposium on Decontamination of Radioactive Material, 121; ionizing, 34–35; linear nonthreshold for, 48–49; low doses of, 48; measurement of exposure to, 36; monitoring of, 21–22; National Institute of Radiological Sciences, 200–201, 211, 213–14, *214*; as natural element, 201–4; nonionizing, 34; plutonium and, 35, 203–4; radionuclides, 34–35; residual, 56, 123; safety perspectives on, 48–54; science of, 7; Sievert value, 36; somatic effects of, 35; strontium and, 76, 203, 206–7; transmutation and, 9; X-rays, 34, 36. *See also* contaminated soil; contamination; radiophobia

radiation hazards, 18–19; global context for, 32–33; sources of, 36–37

radiation-induced illnesses. *See* illnesses

Radiation Measurement Forum Fukushima, 121–22

radiation monitoring and testing, 21–22; of atmospheric radiation, 124; Center for Environmental Creation and, 119; for cesium, 132; for Chernobyl, 118–19; by citizen scientists, 95–96, *96*; color-coded zoning restrictions and, 129; conceptual approach to, 117–18; decontamination practices and, 117; definition of, 117; with dosimeters, 119; Environmental Radiation Monitoring Center, 116, 119, 121; in exclusion zones, 123–24; fixed posts, 131–32; in Fukushima City, *120*; for gamma rays, 131; in Iitate village, 129–30, *131*, 135; by Japan Atomic Energy Agency, 121; limits of, 128–35; mapping of, 118–24; by MEXT,

119; Nuclear Regulation Agency, 247; outside of lab contexts, 128–40; politics of revitalization and, 127; Radiation Measurement Forum Fukushima, 121–22; for radionuclides, 131–32; regimes of imperceptibility and, 133; research and development for, 121; of residual radioactivity, 123; as symbolic of state power, 140–42; in Tomioka, 130–32; by US Department of Energy, 119; in villages, 129–30; weather patterns for, 118–24. *See also* civic participation

radiation/radioactive governance: in Anthropocene, 30; citizen scientists and, 85; lack of public trust in, 62–63; methodological approach to, 26–30; scope of, 8–10; state policies on radiation thresholds, 76–77; state power compared to, 9; Swyngedouw on, 9; transmutation and, 9

radiation risks, radiation exposure and: ALARA principle for, 49–50; calculation of, 49–51; chronic low-dose exposure, 99; chronic radiation syndrome, 53; citizen scientists and, 195; Cold War secrecy as influence on, 66; communication strategies for, 197–200; DNA damage from, 35–36, 75; dual uncertainty of, 92; emergency exposure situations, 60; exceptionality of, 198–200; existing exposure situations, 60; for First Nations peoples, 51; *fūhyō higai* and, 75–79; Fukushima Health Management Survey and, 65, 71–72; global context for, 32–33; hereditary effects as result of, 35; hypervisibility of, 198; ICRP recommendations for, 59–61; International Commission on Radiological Protection, 48; Life Span Study for, 50–51, 66; long-term effects of, 65; Ministry of Economy, Trade and Industry assessment of, 192; participatory governance management approaches, 54; planned exposure situations, 60; radiation-controlled areas, 104–5; studies on, 77–78; symposia on, 77–78; for Tanizaki, 3; WHO assessments of, 65. *See also* illnesses; radioactive performances

radiation zones: color-coded zoning restrictions, 129; exclusion zones, 123–24, 143; mapping of, 96; repatriation schedules for, 124; Special Decontamination Areas, 125–26; zones of exclusion, 123–24

radioactive performances: in Belarus, 196–97; case studies, 200; Center for Environmental Creation and, 195, 201–2, 206, 209, 220; communication strategies, 197–200; Cool Japan ideology and, 210; Decontamination Info Plaza, 126–27, 136, 200–202, *208,* 209, *210,* 213; ethnographic approaches to, 197; food sources and, 204; *fūhyō higai* and, 200; hazards of, 216–20; *kawaii* and, 208–10; Ministry of the Environment and, 206; National Institute of Radiological Sciences and, 200–201, 211, 213–14, *214;* nuclear banality and, 198–200, 211; nuclear exceptionalism, 198, 211; nuclearity concept and, 197; nuclear safety myth and, 219; passive citizenship and, 219; performativity theories and, 196; presentation of, 195–96; reframing nuclear waste as cute, 205–11; resilience discourses and, 219; scientific and technology and, 211–16; scientific patriotism and, 211; in Ukraine, 196

radioactive spaces: ethnographic fieldwork in, 17–19; *furusato* as, 170. *See also* contamination; radiation hazards; radiation risks

radioactive waste: carbon monoxide risks compared to, 15; Fukushima returnees disregard of, 3. *See also* contaminated soil; waste disposal

radionuclides: anthropomorphic, 207; cesium, 34–35, 92, 99, 132, 203; decontamination of, 118; food safety and, 97; monitoring and testing of, 131–32; plutonium, 35, 203–4; radioactivity as result of, 34–35; strontium, 76, 203, 206–7
radiophobia, 7, 231
Rancière, Jacques, 7
Reconstruction Agency (Japan), 68, 107, 154–55; Fukushima Pride campaign, 148; hope tropes, 147; in Iitate village, 153; Innovation Coast Framework, 152; *Michinoeki Madeikan* and, 152–53; "New Tōhoku" campaign, 148; repatriation strategies, 147–48; resilience strategies, 147, 150–53; restoration of *furusato* culture, 149, 151–53; technological innovations and, 147; temporary housing policies, 156–59; tourism strategies by, 149–51
regime of perceptibility, 33
regimes of imperceptibility, 33; radiation monitoring and testing and, 133
relativism, 24
relocation: disaster recovery through, 5; evacuation risks and, 4; to Tokyo, 88
repatriation schedules, for radiation zones, 124
repatriation strategies, 147–48
residual radioactivity, 123; in Chernobyl, 56; in Fukushima, 183; in Japan, 56
resilience strategies, 147, 150–53; radioactive performances and, 219
revival, reconstruction, and restoration plan. See "*fukkō*" plan
rice cakes, as tradition, 156. See also mochi tradition
Robertson, Jennifer, 143, 150, 159
rural areas, villages and: civic participation in radiation tracking in, 240–41; decontamination of, 138; radiation monitoring and testing in, 129–30

Russia: Chernobyl Law in, 111; invasion of Ukraine, 257. See also Soviet Union

safety culture, 259
Sakaue, Kimiko, 239, 245
Samuels, Richard J., 11
Sasaki, Sadako, 31
Sato, Kyoko, 109
Schnell, Scott, 102
science, definition of, 86
science and technology studies (STS), 33
scientific citizenship, 99
scientific patriotism, 211
secrecy, as governmental policy: for Chernobyl nuclear disaster, 11–12, 52–53; in Japan, 32; in Soviet Union, 11–12
Self-Defense Forces, in Japan, 196, 205, 210
self-responsibility, for evacuees, 89
Shimazu, Naoko, 81
Shōriki, Matsutarō, 43
Sievert value (Sv), for radiation effects, 36; citizen scientists and, 94–96; microsieverts, 114
Slater, David, 10
social issues, after Fukushima Dai'ichi meltdown, 63
social movements: All-Campus Joint Struggle League, 188; antinuclear movement, 106–7, 188–90, *191*; citizen science as, 86
social precarity, 158; during Emergency Era, 10–11
Soviet Union: culture of secrecy in, 12; early nuclear tests by, 37; Ukraine independence from, 12–13. See also Chernobyl nuclear power plant disaster; Cold War
Special Decontamination Areas, 125–26
SPEEDI program, 62
state power: centralization of, 14; decontamination as symbolic of, 140–42; radiation monitoring and testing as symbolic of, 140–42; radioactive

governance compared to, 9. *See also specific agencies; specific topics*
Steger, Brigitte, 10
Stenger, Isabelle, 20
Stephens, Sharon, 74
Stewart, Alice, 50
strontium, 76, 203, 206–7
STS. *See* science and technology studies
suikawari game, 165–66, *166*
Sv. *See* Sievert value
Swyngedouw, Erik, 9, 68–69, 155, 174–75, 190, 225

Tadanobu, Daisuke, 68
Takagi, Tsuyoshi, 147–48
Takagi, Yōsuke, 172
Takeda, Masuji, 110
Tanizaki, Atsuo, 1, 3, 128–30
Taxonomy Delegated Act, EU (2023), 183
technostrategic language, 186
TEPCO. *See* Tokyo Electric Power Company
testing. *See* nuclear weapons; radiation monitoring and testing
Tezuka, Osamu, 44–45
theories on Japaneseness. *See Nihonjinron*
Thomas, Gerry, 55
3.11 disaster, in Japan, 11; Great East Japan Earthquake and Nuclear Disaster Memorial Museum, 218–19; public mistrust after, 93. *See also* earthquakes; Fukushima Dai'ichi power plant; tsunamis
Three Mile Island nuclear power plant disaster: as Anthropocene symbol, 2; Fukushima nuclear disaster compared to, 2; IAEA classification of, 2
thyroid cancers, 74, 101–2, 108; in children, 5, 55; incidence rates for, 104; screening effects of, 55
Tokyo, Japan: Citizens' Nuclear Information Center, 18; evacuation of, 61; House of Councilors, 4

Tokyo Electric Power Company (TEPCO): civic participation in radiation tracking and, 245–47; Fukushima meltdown disaster and, 154, 157–58, 162
Tomioka, Japan: decontamination of, 135–36; within exclusion zone, 143; radiation monitoring and testing in, 130–32; waste disposal, 155–56. *See also furusato*
Topçu, Seizin, 54, 239
tourism: ecotourism, 149; Reconstruction Agency and, 149–51
transmutation, in radiation process, 9
transnational governmentality, 16
Triple Disaster, in Japan, 67–68, 147. *See also* earthquakes; Fukushima Dai'ichi power plant; tsunamis
Tsing, Anna, 57–58, 106, 237
tsunamis, Fukushima Dai'ichi power plant meltdown as result of, 2
Tuck, Eve, 23

Uchibori, Masao, 148
UK. *See* United Kingdom
Ukraine: biological citizens in, 235; Chernobyl Law in, 111; independence from Soviet Union, 12–13; radioactive performances in, 196; Russian invasion of, 257; Zaporizhzhia Nuclear Power Plant in, 257
UN. *See* United Nations
United Kingdom (UK), radiation exposure levels in, 49
United Nations (UN), Scientific Committee on the Effects of Atomic Radiation, 65
United States (US): Atomic Bomb Casualty Commission in, 50; Atomic Energy Commission, 51–52; Atoms for Peace Program, 37–38, 258; citizen scientists in, 84; Department of Energy in, 119; Japan occupied by, 32; nuclear safety guidelines in, 51–52; radiation exposure levels in, 49; Three Mile Island disaster in, 2. *See also* Cold War

Uno, Akiko, voluntary evacuation by, 4–5
UNSCEAR. *See* United Nations
US. *See* United States

victims, victimhood and: citizen movements and, 15; committed, 113; as passive state, 24; postvictimization approach, 23–24; tropes of, 23; Western concept of, 113
villages, village life and: abandonment of, 2; Hirono village, 161–62; nuclear, 40, 42; radiation monitoring and testing in, 129–30. *See also furusato;* Iitate village; rural areas
voluntary evacuations, 4–5, 88–89, 218

waste disposal, after nuclear disasters: decontamination through, 136; high-level radioactive waste, 172; Nuclear Waste Management Organization and, 172, 205; reframing nuclear waste as cute, 205–11; in Tomioka, 155–56

Whatmore, Sarah J., 175
WHO. *See* World Health Organization
whole-body counters, for contamination, 214–15
women: atomic divorce and, 90; as citizen scientists, 94, 113; in Japan, 90. *See also* gender
World Health Organization (WHO): International Atomic Energy Agency and, 66; on radiation risks, 65

X-rays, 34, 36

Yablokov, Alexey, 132
Yamaguchi, Setsuko, 157–59, *160*
Yamaguchi, Tomiko, 68
Yamamoto, Ryūzō, 180
Yamashita, Shun'ichi, 57, 63, 85, 88
Yoshino, Kyōji, 179

Zaporizhzhia Nuclear Power Plant, 257
zones. *See* radiation zones

ABOUT THE AUTHOR

MAXIME POLLERI is Assistant Professor in the Department of Anthropology at Université Laval and a member of the Graduate School of International Studies. As an anthropologist of science and technology, he studies the governance of disasters and waste with a focus on nuclear topics.